D. M. SHAPIRO

31 July 2004

SIMON

SIMON

A political biography of
Sir John Simon

DAVID DUTTON

AURUM PRESS

First published 1992 by Aurum Press Ltd,
10 Museum Street, London WC1A 1JS
Copyright © 1992 by David Dutton

A catalogue record for this book is available
from the British Library

ISBN 1 85410 204 4

10 9 8 7 6 5 4 3 2 1
1996 1995 1994 1993 1992

Photoset in Linotron Times by Northern Phototypesetting Co. Ltd., Bolton
Printed in Great Britain by Hartnolls Ltd.

CONTENTS

IN MEMORY OF MY FATHER

ACKNOWLEDGEMENTS

The author acknowledges the gracious permission of Her Majesty The Queen to use material which has been previously published and is subject to copyright.

Transcripts of Crown-copyright material appear by permission of the Controller of H.M. Stationery Office.

All quotations from the letters and writings of Sir John Simon are by permission of the Second Viscount Simon.

For permission to quote from unpublished material in their possession or of which they own the copyright, the author willingly thanks the following: the Rt. Hon. Julian Amery, M.P.; the Viscount Astor; the Earl Baldwin of Bewdley; Sir Colville Barclay; the Lord Birdwood; the Bodleian Library, Oxford; the Lady Boothby; the British Library of Political and Economic Science; Churchill Archives Centre, Cambridge; the Clerk of the Records of the House of Lords; Mrs. A. Eggar; the Viscount Esher; Mr. George Lane Fox; Mr. John Grigg; the Earl of Halifax; the Lord Harlech; the India Office Library and Records; the Lord Kennet; Professor Anne Lambton; the Liverpool Record Office, Liverpool Libraries and Arts Department; the Lady Lloyd; Mr. H. R. P. Lloyd; Sir John McEwen; the Master, Fellows and Scholars of Churchill College in the University of Cambridge; the Master and Fellows, University College, Oxford; Major-General the Viscount Monckton of Brenchley; Mr. Alexander Murray; Mrs. Paul Paget; the Public Record Office; the Marquess of Salisbury; Professor Edward Segal; Sir William Shakespeare; Mr. Charles Strachey; the Syndics of Cambridge University Library; the Viscount Tenby; the Trustees on behalf of the Trevelyan family; the University of Birmingham; the Warden and Fellows of New College Oxford; the Lord Wigram.

For permission to print extracts from published material the author offers his thanks to the following: the Countess of Avon; B. T. Batsford Ltd.; the Birmingham Post and Mail Ltd.; Bradford and District Newspapers; Jonathan Cape Ltd.; Frank Cass and Co. Ltd.; Century Hutchinson Ltd.; the Rt. Hon. Paul Channon, M.P.; William Collins Sons and Co. Ltd.; the Earl of Crawford; Ewan Macnaughton Associates; Express Newspapers plc; Eyre and Spottiswoode Publishers; the Rt. Hon. Michael Foot, M.P.; Victor Gollancz Ltd.; Grafton Books; Guardian Newspapers Ltd.; the Rt. Hon. the Lord Hailsham; Harper and Row, Publishers, Inc.; Sir Rupert Hart-Davis; Mr. John Harvey; William Heinemann Ltd.; Professor R. F. V. Heuston; David Higham Associates Ltd.; Sir Charles Hobhouse; Hodder and Stoughton; the Institute of Contemporary British History; Mr. Robert Rhodes James, M.P.; the Rt. Hon. the Lord Jenkins of Hillhead; the Trustees of the Liddell Hart Centre for Military Archives; the Liverpool Daily Post and Echo Ltd.; Professor John McEwen; Macmillan Publishers Ltd.; Macmillan Publishing Company; the late Mr. Malcolm Muggeridge; Frederick Muller Ltd.; John Murray (Publishers) Ltd.; the National Library of Wales; Mr. Nigel Nicolson; the Observer Ltd.; Oxford University Press; Mr. J. W. Pownall-Gray; Mr. Nicholas Roskill; Dr. A. L. Rowse; the John Rylands University Library of Manchester; the Spectator Ltd.; the Spenborough Guardian Group; Sweet and Maxwell Ltd.; the late Mr. A. J. P. Taylor; Professor Christopher Thorne; Times Newspapers Ltd.; Unwin Hyman Ltd.; the Virago Press; Weidenfeld and Nicolson Ltd.; Western Mail and Echo Ltd.; Professor Trevor Wilson; the Yorkshire Post.

Every effort has been made to trace the owners of copyright material. If the author has inadvertently infringed the copyright of any individual, he trusts that his apology will be accepted.

PREFACE

'I think someone like Sir John Simon would be hard to summon the enthusiasm to write about, even though he was an important figure who held a lot of senior offices, of whom a modern biography probably ought to be written.' So wrote the distinguished political biographer, John Campbell, a couple of years ago. I have had less difficulty in summoning up enthusiasm than Dr. Campbell anticipated. But it is pleasant to name some of those who have helped to sustain that enthusiasm during the preparation of this biography.

Simon's only son, the second Viscount Simon, encouraged me to tread where other prospective biographers have feared to go, and has been helpful and supportive throughout. My publisher, Piers Burnett, has been the model of efficiency in getting this book through the press after delays for which he bears no responsibility.

Those who knew Simon or worked with him are now a dwindling band. But I learned much from conversations with Lord Home of the Hirsel and Lord Sherfield. For answering my letters about Simon I am grateful to the late Sir Richard Acland, the late Lord Boothby, Mr. R. A. Cole-Hamilton, the late Sir John Colville, Lord Denning, the late Mr. H. Montgomery Hyde, Viscount Muirshiel, Lord Shawcross, Lord Strauss and the late Lord Trend.

I have spent many hours in many libraries and archives preparing this book, but it would not be invidious to single out for special thanks the staff of the Modern Manuscripts Room at the Bodleian Library, Oxford, where the bulk of Simon's papers are housed.

My indebtedness to other scholars will be obvious to anyone who glances at the references within this book. But particular thanks are owed to the following: Professor E. B. Segal, whose thesis on Simon deserves to be known by a wider audience; Mr. Andrew Lownie, who allowed me to read his interesting and informative Cambridge dissertation. It was a pleasure when he also became my most efficient literary agent; Dr. Philip Williamson who provided me with a host of useful references from his own exhaustive researches on the origins of the National Goverment of 1931; and my colleagues Philip Bell and Patrick Buckland who found time among their own crowded schedules to read the work in typescript and offer helpful suggestions for improvement.

Typing has been expertly and cheerfully carried out by Mrs. Angela MacEwen, Mrs. Betty Plummer, Mrs. Peggy Rider, Mrs. Julie Smiles and Mrs. Pam Thompson. Christine Giuliani showed that checking proofs could actually be fun.

I am happy to acknowledge financial support from the University of Liverpool Research Fund.

With help on this scale the author hopes that the finished work has some merit. For its shortcomings he accepts sole responsibility.

David Dutton
Liverpool, October 1991

INTRODUCTION

The historian who must, in the future, seek to evaluate the life and career of John, Viscount Simon will be faced with a difficult puzzle . . . Why at the end of a life filled with such extraordinary success and activity does one feel a certain sense of inadequacy and frustration?[1]

On 3 September 1939, six hours after the British declaration of war against Hitler's Germany, Neville Chamberlain called the first meeting of his new War Cabinet. Of its nine members two 'represented an older generation'[2] and had the unique experience of having been present at an equally momentous gathering a quarter of a century earlier. Meeting on 4 August 1914, the British cabinet, headed by Herbert Asquith, had taken the fateful decision which determined Britain's entry into the First World War. One of these two men was Winston Churchill, recalled by Chamberlain at the outbreak of hostilities to the office of First Lord of the Admiralty, the same position he had held in 1914. The other was John Allsebrook Simon, then Chancellor of the Exchequer, ranking second in the government behind only the Prime Minister. Twenty-five years earlier he had been Asquith's Attorney-General with, unusually, a seat in the cabinet.

If John Simon had done nothing else in his political career, which lasted almost as long as Churchill's own – and the two men were almost exact contemporaries with just twenty-one months between them in age – it should have been enough to command the historian's attention. Yet this book has no need to begin with the apology, now common in the writing of twentieth-century British history, justifying another book on this theme or a further volume on that. Rather it requires an explanation of why there has not before been a significant biography of a man whose career at the top encompassed four decades of British political history. John Simon was never Prime Minister. Indeed he was never close to becoming Prime Minister. Yet beneath the premiership his collection of the great offices of state is as distinguished as anyone's in the twentieth century. The combination of Home Office, Foreign Office, Exchequer and Woolsack remains unique. Upon whatever topic the political historian of the years 1906 to 1945 fixes his attention, the person of John Simon is likely to impinge, often to a considerable extent. There is scarcely a monograph in this area from which Simon's name is completely absent. In many his role is clearly critical.

Yet, more than three decades after his death, no one has felt compelled to devote a full-length study to Simon's career as a whole. A solitary biography by C. E. Bechhofer Roberts ('Ephesian') was published in 1938 while Simon was still actively involved in high political life.[3] An earlier volume had been promised in 1932 from the pen of R. Hopkin Morris but failed to see the light of day. Though Roberts' book emphasises the legal rather than the political side of Simon's life, it is not without value, especially as Simon himself appears to have provided much of the material upon which parts of it were based. But Roberts' lack of access to archives, both public and private, his inevitable absence of perspective, together with the appearance over the last half century of a mass of scholarly research touching upon his subject, from which the prospective biographer must rightly draw, compel the need for a new assessment of Simon's career.

All politicians are understandably concerned about the verdict which history will impose upon them. In Simon's case this concern was intense. In the last months of his life he was still, more than twenty years on, busy defending himself against the attacks which surrounded perhaps the most criticised episode of his career – his handling of the Manchurian crisis and particularly his speech to the Special Assembly of the League of Nations in December 1932. The appearance in 1952 of Reginald Bassett's account of the Manchurian affair and in particular its stout defence of Simon's role therein was a source of considerable satisfaction to him.[4] It worried Simon to think of what the historian might make of him. 'I am afraid', he wrote when contemplating a volume of memoirs, 'I have a fastidious feeling about the thing being undertaken by someone else.'[5] Yet Simon's autobiography, published in 1952, adds very little to our knowledge and understanding, offering few insights into its author's character.[6] With studied intent the writer of *Retrospect* remains an enigma.

A study of Simon's career based solely on the politician's own papers would produce a very different picture of the man from that which readily emerges from the writings of his contemporaries. Simon was by no stretch of the imagination a popular figure. 'Some people', thought A. L. Rowse, 'made quite a thing of disliking him'.[7] Many who worked with him in cabinet or met him in parliament or public life disliked him intensely. Of this truth a few illustrations must suffice. Duff Cooper confessed that he hated Simon,[8] while Harold Nicolson called him a 'foul man' and likened him to a 'toad and a worm'.[9] For Brendan Bracken the appropriate comparison was with Uriah Heep.[10] Sir Ronald Lindsay compared Simon to an adder;[11] for Anthony Eden he was merely 'snaky'.[12] As far as Beatrice Webb was concerned, he was among the most unpleasant personalities she had met.[13]

Yet Simon's private papers reveal an infinitely kindly, considerate and thoughtful man and there are few traces of the animus which other sources so readily convey. It seems likely that Simon destroyed much documentation himself.[14] What survives has clearly been left to convey the best possible impression of its subject. Even Simon's occasional diary, though valuable and sometimes revealing, betrays a self-consciousness which suggests that Simon was writing with posterity in mind.[15] He himself admitted that it was 'disgustingly egotistical'.[16]

If Simon alienated so many of his contemporaries, it is perhaps not surprising that even in death he has had the same impact upon historians. Successful biographers usually, though not always, need to feel a sense of sympathy and rapport with their subjects.[17] In Simon's case this attraction has presumably been absent. As one potential chronicler of his career put it:

Long years of work on a figure with whom one does not feel at least *some* personal rapport is too daunting a prospect for me, and perhaps for others.[18]

Yet there was another John Simon than the cold, insincere and almost dehumanised sychophant who emerges from so many contemporary descriptions. Rowse exaggerates when he asserts that 'nobody loved him'.[19] Witnesses as varied as C. B. Fry, Leo Amery and Sir John Colville expressed their liking for him. An attractive and sympathetic character did emerge on those rare occasions when Simon let down his guard to reveal the man behind the usually impenetrable mask. Many were alienated from Simon by his apparent lack of human frailty. 'If Sir John Simon is to become interesting,' wrote one critic:

he must show us that he can fail, he must be discovered in some splendid indiscretion, he must burst through the panoply of restraint with some flame of passion.[20]

But for the more perceptive observer human frailty was present in fair measure. A Liberal colleague of many years standing summed up the problem. 'Every night John Simon kneels by his bedside and prays "Oh Lord make me a good fellow".'[21] Perhaps this prayer was never fully answered.

Be that as it may, for historians to ignore those whom they do not like or admire is a luxury which history itself cannot afford. John Simon was a prominent participant in British political and legal history. He was involved in significant events and made his mark upon them. The absence of a modern life of him is a glaring lacuna in twentieth-century British political biography which this author is pleased to attempt to fill.[22]

Notes

1 *Law Quarterly Review*, April 1954.
2 W. S. Churchill, *The Gathering Storm* (London, 1948) p. 328.
3 C. E. Bechhofer Roberts, *Sir John Simon* (London, 1938).
4 R. Bassett, *Democracy and Foreign Policy* (London, 1952); Simon to Bassett 17 Jan. 1953, 'Your book gives me new hope that history may do justice to British policy in those difficult times,' Simon Papers (Hereinafter S P) 101 fo. 128.
5 Simon to J. Hutchinson 19 Dec. 1944, S P 95 fo. 51.
6 Viscount Simon, *Retrospect* (London, 1952).
7 A. L. Rowse, *All Souls and Appeasement* (London, 1961) p. 16.
8 Duff Cooper to Clarissa Eden 21 Aug. 1952, cited J. Charmley, *Duff Cooper*

(London, 1986) p. 236; cf. Cooper to Simon n.d. [1952], 'I have read "Retrospect" during my holiday and it has added a great deal to my enjoyment.' S P 100 fo. 197.

9 N. Nicolson (ed.), *Harold Nicolson: Diaries and Letters 1939–45* (London, 1967) pp. 333, 405–7.

10 B. Bracken to Lord Beaverbrook 16 March 1939, cited C. E. Lysaght, *Brendan Bracken* (London, 1979) p. 160.

11 J. Vincent (ed.), *The Crawford Papers* (Manchester, 1984) p. 585.

12 R. R. James, *Anthony Eden* (London, 1986) p. 295.

13 Beatrice Webb diary 9 June 1940.

14 For evidence that Simon weeded his private papers see Simon to Bernard Darwin 31 Dec. 1940, S P 87 fo. 46 and Simon to W. P. Watt 29 Jan. 1943, S P 92 fo. 132.

15 'The tone is too obviously disingenuous and retouched; there is too much explanatory material and historical background provided, as if to enrich the account of the expected biographer, and occasionally there is evidence of conscious emendation.' E. B. Segal, 'Sir John Simon and British Foreign Policy: the Diplomacy of Disarmament in the Early 1930s,' University of California Ph.D. thesis, 1969, pp. 7–9.

16 As note 5.

17 An interesting recent exception is provided by David Carlton, *Anthony Eden* (London, 1981).

18 Edward Segal to the author 30 Aug. 1985.

19 As note 7.

20 A. G. Gardiner, *Pillars of Society* (London, 1916) p. 274.

21 Sir D. Foot, *British Political Crises* (London, 1976) p. 123.

22 What follows is essentially a political life. Simon's importance as a lawyer is assessed by R. F. V. Heuston, *Lives of the Lord Chancellors 1940–1970* (Oxford, 1987). Some of the courtroom dramas in which Simon was involved are described in Roberts, *Simon* and H. Montgomery Hyde, *United in Crime* (London, 1955).

CHAPTER ONE

ASCENDING THE LADDER

There was a huge party of children – and *one* interesting man. Simon, the KC, of whom you have heard . . . I should think the future holds something big for him.[1]

Unlike so many of his political contemporaries, John Simon was not born into a life of affluence and luxury. He entered the world on 28 February 1873 at 16 Yarburgh Street in Moss Side, Manchester, the only son of the Revd. Edwin and Mrs. Fanny Simon. Yarburgh Street was one of Manchester's hundreds of long roads of terraced houses with bay windows and twelve-foot front gardens, the visible expression of the city's sprawling growth following the Industrial Revolution. Edwin Simon, like three of his five brothers, was a Congregational minister, pastor of Zion Chapel in the Hulme district of the city. His wife, Fanny, who hailed from north Worcestershire, was said to be descended from Margaret, Countess of Salisbury, the daughter of the Duke of Clarence, brother of Edward IV. It was perhaps the sole mark of distinction in the simple, but modestly cultured, family circle in which John Simon grew up, acquiring in his earliest years a love of learning which would never leave him. Years later, when he had achieved national and international fame, Simon enquired of a cabinet colleague:

Is not reading and study also a necessary element in a balanced life?[2]

It was an attitude which Simon imbibed from his parents and particularly his mother, to whom he was devoted. As he later wrote:

Certainly my parents made the first ten years of my life, passed in a poky, uninteresting house in a Manchester suburb, a paradise of enchantment and delight for me.[3]

Mrs Simon, too, recalled the simple but profound pleasures of her son's childhood:

Our enjoyments were mostly those we made for ourselves and the pleasure we got from trying to make each other happy, so that my son grew up to love the simple and beautiful things of life.[4]

A particular delight was to visit the Lancashire County Cricket Club at Old Trafford. Forty years on, Simon took pride in his Wisden-like recollections of the flannelled heroes of his boyhood. Annual family holidays to the Pembrokeshire coast, whence the Simon family originated, were yet another highlight. Here, as they walked through the countryside, mother and son planned, endearingly if unrealistically, to build a house for their old age in a protected fold of the hills and to call the house 'At the Back of the North Wind'. Yet perhaps Simon's early life was too self-contained, restricted to the loving but strict and almost puritanical circle of his own family.

I was, as I realise now, a lonely boy with too few intimates . . . I was diffident and uneasy, too prone to blush and too ready to be overwhelmed.[5]

Simon was educated first by his mother and then at kindergarten in Manchester. At the age of ten the family moved to Bath where Edwin Simon became President of the Somerset Congregational Union. The young boy now moved to King Edward's School in Broad Street, but four years later won a £60 a year scholarship to Fettes College in Edinburgh. Without this financial support the educational opportunities which now opened up for Simon would probably never have materialised. Like most self-made men Simon never forgot the debt which he owed to his school and university. His first sight of the formidable edifice of Fettes left a lasting mark upon him:

The impression made on me then by the ridged roofs and frail spire standing out against the northern sky, with the row of lights running along the upper storeys and the dark mass of central porch with turreted wings below . . . has never left me.[6]

Here, in five crucial years of youth and adolescence, Simon's character, mind and attitudes developed.

Edinburgh air, combined with Fettes traditions, makes the ordinary boy as hard as nails for the rest of his life.

'I think', he surmised half a century later, 'my own fitness is largely due to surviving the Edinburgh spring five years running and changing into flannels every day of my life there whatever the weather.'[7]

Simon came to venerate the memory of Dr. Potts, the school's headmaster, and he had a particular affection and respect for John Yeo, his housemaster. He kept in touch with the school throughout his life and in the 1930s recalled that few things had ever given him a more comforting thrill than the knowledge that he had won Yeo's esteem, as when

he sent for me at the beginning of my last year and handed me, without a word, Matthew Arnold's poems with an inscription recording the fact that I was the first from his house to be Head of the School.[8]

It was at Fettes that Simon's outstanding academic and intellectual ability first became apparent. It was also here that he determined to pursue a career in the law despite his mother's hope that he would become a doctor. There were the first signs too of an interest in politics, while Simon rose steadily to become Head Boy of the school. In his first term he won a prize for French and over the following five years picked up numerous others, especially for English, Divinity and Drawing. To the school's Literary Society, which had replaced the defunct Debating Society, Simon delivered an eloquent paper on Wordsworth. He won several Governors' Prizes for English essay and poetry, and more than once recited at Founder's Day concerts. Academic distinction was matched by considerable sporting achievements. For three years he was a member of the fives team and captain in his last year. Second in the mile, he made occasional appearances for the rugby fifteen. Only of his cricket did *The Fettesian* of 1892 leave a less than flattering description:

A feeble bat at the beginning of term, but improved towards the end on faster wickets. As a wicket-keeper an entire failure.[9]

Such were Simon's prodigious academic talents that Fettes noted less his achievement in securing an open scholarship to Wadham College, Oxford in 1891 than his failure to gain such a triumph at Balliol. This was in fact no loss for Simon arrived at Wadham at the most distinguished period in its history. Among those whose college careers coincided or overlapped with his own were F. E. Smith, who like Simon would one day rise to the Lord Chancellorship, C. B. Fry, whose athletic talents tended to outshine his own very considerable intellectual gifts, and F. W. Hirst, the future journalist and destined like Simon to make his own mark in Liberal politics. At the time of his arrival at Wadham in 1892 Simon was a fresh-faced youth with curly brown hair and blue eyes. He became a genial and popular member of the college with a reputation for unselfishly devoting himself to college interests. One contemporary noted 'a curious iron-like certainty in his dealing with any pursuit, coupled with an imperturbable suavity'.[10]

Simon led the sort of well-balanced student existence which has been the envy of many an undergraduate before and since. His existing record of academic achievement was maintained. After obtaining Second Classes in Mathematical and Classical Moderations, Simon secured a First in Greats in 1896 and won the Barstow Law Scholarship. Colleagues noted those intellectual qualities which were to become his hallmark:

Perhaps the two most characteristic are and were lucidity in exposition and subtlety in analysis . . . He would expound to me some legal refinement with such clarity and earnestness that, impressed with its importance, I would try to repeat the point to the next friend I happened to meet. But in my hands the thing became vague and blurred until the distinction, which he had made so plain, faded away.[11]

On the sporting field Simon was a member of a famous rugby team which also included F. E. Smith and Fry. It was a team which enjoyed considerable success in university sport and though there must have been many others of greater athletic prowess, few more cerebral fifteens can have taken to the field. But it was in the Oxford Union that Simon made his most conspicuous mark. Here he overcame much of his youthful shyness and became an effective speaker, though he never achieved the style and panache of a natural orator. After two terms as Junior Treasurer Simon was elected President of the Union in 1896.

It was through the Union that Simon and Smith began a close relationship – friendship conveys a feeling of warmth which was never present between them – which was to last until Smith's early death in 1930. The characters of the two men were too dissimilar ever to allow the one fully to accept the other on equal terms. Smith found Simon pompous and unnecessarily discreet. 'He felt that there was some humbug somewhere and he took a shot at it.'[12] One heated argument between the two men in Smith's rooms ended at midnight 'with Simon tipping F. E. out of his chair and F. E. squirting soda water at Simon'.[13] In academic matters Simon was unquestionably the finer scholar, but it was in their speeches at the Union that the contrast between them was most marked:

Simon used always to stick to the essence of his argument: he could and did hit hard enough in debate, but he was always earnest, lucid, persuasive, forcible. F. E. on the other hand, though he always knew his case, cultivated a theatrically pugnacious style, making liberal use of ridicule and contempt; he excelled in the 'cheap score' as Simon used to say.[14]

Though there seems to be no truth in the legend that the two men decided by the toss of a coin which of them would join the Conservative party and which the Liberals – their political affiliations were fixed before they even met – Simon and Smith did agree that neither in his future legal career should take silk before the other. It was a pact which was maintained. The two men took silk on the same day in February 1908, though Simon upset his rival by making his application without consulting Smith in advance.[15]

It was while he was still an undergraduate that Simon had his first experience of national politics. His nonconformist upbringing ensured that he would support the cause of Liberalism. Campaigning in South Oxfordshire on behalf of the Liberal candidate, Herbert Samuel, Simon had his baptism on the hustings.

I remember standing on a cart, with my back to a brick wall . . . and orating to three men and a dog; I am afraid without much success.[16]

At the end of 1896 Hirst persuaded Simon and four other young Liberals to join him in producing a volume of essays on Liberalism. Simon's contribution on 'Liberals and Labour' was a remarkably mature effort for a young man in his early twenties. A passage which he wrote on the problems of sectionalism within the post-Gladstonian party bears quotation:

What is, above all, needed is a more comprehensive grasp of the basis of Liberal policy, both in order to justify the details of its development, and in order to establish the interconnection of its several parts. The increasing complexity of civic life and the consequently increasing subdivision of political interests has left many Liberals ignorant and careless of the broader aspects of their faith. It is easy for each of us to see how his own political hobby is a rigid application of Liberal theory, even if that theory be but vaguely comprehended; but it is difficult to appreciate the justice and importance of applications on which others lay chief stress.[17]

But before Simon himself made a more active contribution to Liberal politics, there were further academic hurdles to surmount. After securing his First, Simon determined to try for a fellowship at All Souls and began furiously to study the law. While preparing for the examination, Simon shared lodgings with L. S. Amery who had as his goal the other available fellowship in history. Both men were successful and for Simon it meant the beginning of an association with the college which lasted until his death and which became increasingly important to him. Towards the end of his life he wrote:

Looking back, I feel that, apart from domestic happiness, nothing in my life has meant so much to me as the comradeship, now extending over more than half a century, of the fraternity of All Souls, where I am now the Senior Fellow.[18]

Coming down from Oxford at the end of 1898, Simon passed his final examination and was called to the bar at the Inner Temple. He became a pupil of A. J. Ram and then of Sir Reginald Acland, later Judge Advocate of the Fleet. The law was an uncertain profession for a man of no private means and Simon had already spent a brief period after graduation in Manchester, working under C. P. Scott as a leader writer on the *Manchester Guardian*. In his early years at the bar he continued to write occasional pieces for the paper and at the beginning of the Boer War joined with five other young Liberals to run the weekly *Speaker*, a forerunner of *The Nation*. In it Simon confirmed his radical credentials by striking a distinctly pro-Boer stance. Coaching pupils for the bar examinations provided further supplementary income. But Simon's abilities in chambers rapidly made a good impression and after his six months' tuition with Acland he was invited to stay on and to devil for his chief. Simon joined the Western Circuit, made his first appearance at the Bristol Quarter Session in April 1899 and earned just £27 in his first year. Rapidly, however, he moved into the highest class of civil practice in London. 'I should think,' said F. E. Smith in February 1901, 'you have done better than anyone without influence has ever done at the London bar before.'[19]

From the beginning Simon sought to establish a reputation as an advocate whose skills could be trusted in the most diverse areas. In his early years he developed an interest in such varied directions as railway cases and international law. He made a point of appearing once a year in the divorce court. His recipe for success was, he once said, 'a good clerk and a good digestion',[20] but in reality his achievements resulted from a combination of ability and sheer hard work. He took infinite pains over the preparation of his cases. A contemporary recalled that he regularly worked through the night two or three times a week.[21] Yet in court Simon seemed to perform with effortless ease. His strength lay in his ability to analyse and clarify the most complicated of issues. His method was not to sway a jury with overpowering oratory but to persuade it with logic and reason. He had a special skill of arguing in a way which led those who heard him inevitably and remorselessly to the conclusion which followed from his premises. His courtroom triumphs were the result of intellectual superiority. In his methods of cross-examination Simon followed the style of Sir Edward Carson in his belief that the first question asked is of the greatest importance, aiming to go to the heart of the matter which the barrister seeks to establish.[22]

Later in his career there were those who found Simon a difficult master to work for. It is thus worth noting the testimony of those who shared his early days at the bar. One recalled:

Busy as he was, he found time to tutor us all. Each of us was sent every day one of his briefs to tackle. As soon as he was ready to deal with it he sent for the pupil who had made a note on it, and if the latter had attempted to draft some necessary 'pleading', he actually corrected the pupil's work as if he were a schoolmaster and used for the final draft as much as he could of it.[23]

Yet there were other characteristics already evident which many found less attractive. One was a studied courtesy which failed to carry the smack of sincerity. In court he tended to be elaborately, even unnecessarily, polite.[24] A second trait was Simon's meticulous and obsessive attention to detail. A legal contemporary later recalled a singular incident.

On reaching the Underground at the Temple Station, we pupils promptly boarded the nearest coach. Simon hurried forward to the front of the train. When we arrived at Westminster Bridge he was already at the top of the stairs waiting for us. 'If you fellows were hustlers,' he said, 'you would have known that the front carriages always stop nearest the exit at Westminster.'[25]

These early years in the law were marred by a tragic and decisive event in Simon's life. In 1899 he married Ethel Mary Venables, a student whom he had met at Oxford and whose uncle was the historian, J. R. Green. Two daughters were born in 1900 and 1901, but a few days after the birth of a son in September 1902, Mrs. Simon died. The idea that Simon could not afford the medicines which his wife needed seems unlikely,[26] since the Simons were already affluent enough to employ domestic staff. But there is a suggestion that Simon may have placed excessive faith in homoeopathic remedies.[27] If the young widower was indeed left with some sense of guilt over his wife's death, it may help one to understand not his grief, which is entirely explicable, but the intensity and lasting depth of his desolation. For the next fifteen years Simon sought to combine the demands of his ever-advancing career with the role of dutiful father. Existing tendencies in his character now became exaggeratedly marked. Simon's natural shyness intensified and he buried himself in his work with reinforced and obsessive commitment. But instead of a slow recovery from a low point of despair, contemporaries noted a permanent change in Simon's personality. As one attempted to rationalise it:

Simon discovered, no doubt, little by little . . . that the sympathy of friends was but a poor substitute for the sympathy of a devoted wife. As the years passed he seemed to grow gradually colder; he appeared to be no longer in need of sympathy, but only of admiration, and this, not because he was unduly vain, but because it helped him to do his work to his own satisfaction.[28]

It seems probable, to judge from the accounts of those who knew him as a young man that, without this early tragedy in his life, the world might have come to have a more favourable impression of John Simon.

It was soon after Simon's bereavement that his legal career took a first major step forward. In 1903 the Solicitor-General, Sir Edward Carson, found himself called upon to act on behalf of the British Government in relation to a complicated case concerning the boundary between Canada and the American territory of Alaska. The excellence of Simon's work had already been brought to Carson's attention and, aware of the recent tragedy in the young barrister's career, the Solicitor-General wrote to Simon to advise him that the only possible remedy for his grief lay in the pre-occupation of intense work. Accordingly, Carson invited Simon to join him in the preparation of the case. In the event, the case went to arbitration and the main contention on the Canadian side failed, but Simon attracted much enthusiastic attention on account of his performance. Just thirty years of age, Simon had assuredly arrived in the first of his chosen careers.

Yet, despite his undoubted talents in this field, the law could never offer Simon complete satisfaction or fulfilment. Though written near the end of his long political life, Simon's comment in his memoirs chimes naturally with an attitude from which he never deviated:

I have never rated the practice of the law as falling within the higher ranges of human achievement, or thought that the legalistic view is the last word in wisdom . . . Advocacy, as practised at the English Bar, is just a way of earning one's living – a very exacting way, calling for the strictest observance of the rules of honour and of faithfulness to duty. . . . But it is argument within blinkers.[29]

This was written in the 1950s, but almost half a century earlier Simon had reacted angrily when a colleague suggested that there were higher callings – such as literature – than that of political life.[30] Accordingly, with his success at the bar assured and with his income growing handsomely, Simon began to turn his eyes to the prospect of a parliamentary career.

He had been invited to stand at the general election of 1900, but was dissuaded from doing so. It was a wise decision, since the next few years gave him the chance to make some money at the bar before launching into a political career. Finally, Simon was adopted as the prospective Liberal candidate for the Walthamstow division of Essex in April 1905. Several constituencies had shown an interest in the young Liberal who was already an active member of the Eighty Club, then the leading propagandist organisation for younger party members, but the crucial factor seems to have been the support and backing of Herbert Gladstone, the Liberal Chief Whip. Gladstone clearly undertook to meet the cost of the campaign, 'without which I could not hope to face the expenses of candidature.'[31] Simon offered to withdraw from Walthamstow if Gladstone preferred to endorse another Liberal, Noel Buxton, but was not tempted by the offer of standing for West St Pancras. In the event, Gladstone gave his support for Simon in Walthamstow.[32]

Walthamstow had one of the largest electorates of any constituency in the country and normally returned a Unionist. Simon, though, did not have much time to nurse this 'great populous track'.[33] Balfour's Unionist government had been in a state of mounting disarray ever since Joseph Chamberlain's celebrated pronouncement in Birmingham in May 1903 on the need to introduce tariff reform, and a general election was widely regarded as imminent. In the event Balfour finally resigned in December 1905, allowing Sir Henry Campbell-Bannerman, with less difficulty than had been anticipated, to form a minority Liberal administration. It was therefore Campbell-Bannerman who sought and secured a dissolution of parliament and an election in January 1906. Simon's campaign was typical of Liberal candidates at this time. His appeals were in support of free trade and in opposition to the scandal of Chinese labour in South Africa. He announced himself to be a committed Home Ruler while accepting that a Liberal government would not attempt to introduce this measure without a further appeal to the electorate. Benefiting from the anti-Unionist tide which swept across all but a few areas of the country, Simon was elected with a majority of 4,000 in a straight fight with his Unionist opponent.

The 1906 result seemed at the time to mark a high-water mark in the fortunes of the Liberal party. Four hundred Liberal MPs were returned. On the opposition benches there sat a mere 157 Unionists. Even allowing for Labour members and Irish Nationalists, whose tendency anyway was to support the new government, Campbell-Bannerman had a massive overall majority in the House of Commons. Only in retrospect has 1906 come to be viewed as a deceptive *annus mirabilis* in the party's history. Simon thus took his seat on the back benches when Liberalism boasted an array of talented luminaries such as has seldom been assembled at one time. In particular, the front bench of Campbell-Bannerman, and later of Asquith, must rank among the most distinguished of the twentieth century. It therefore speaks well of Simon's qualities that he was soon able to rise from the ruck of newly elected hopefuls as a man marked out for early promotion. F. E. Smith, elected as a Unionist at the same election, had an altogether easier task to establish his standing among the depleted ranks of the official opposition. Beatrice Webb was among those who soon spotted Simon's prodigious talents. Dining in February with a group of young Liberals, all of whom would make their mark in the party, including Herbert Samuel, Reginald McKenna, C. F. Masterman and H. W. Massingham, she singled out Simon as 'by far the most brilliant'. Not one to lavish praise lightly, Mrs. Webb observed 'a conventional mind but excellent working intellect, a charming person, agreeable voice and manner'.[34] How Simon reacted to his first taste of parliamentary life is unclear. To Beatrice Webb he seemed still to be obsessed by his widowerhood and claimed to be bored by Westminster after only three days. 'Rufus Isaacs has shown me a quiet corner to which I retire and work at my briefs.'[36]

On the crowded government benches in the House of Commons it could not have been easy for Simon to make his mark. The new member for Walthamstow trod carefully. His first step was to put down a question to the President of the Local Government Board in May about a hospital in his constituency. At the end of July he raised with the Foreign Secretary the matter of a traffic accident involving one of his constituents and a Portuguese diplomat. But it was not until August that Simon made his maiden speech. The occasion was well chosen. Simon spoke during the committee stage of the Trade Disputes Bill, introduced by the government in answer to an electoral pledge to nullify the effects of the famous Taff Vale judgment of 1901. This had established the legal liability of a trade union for damages caused by industrial action. By this speech Simon showed that the persuasive logic of his argument, which had already made such an impression in the courts, could be transferred with profit to the House of Commons. Simon gave a lucid review of the present position, impressing upon the House the necessity for a change in the law as it then stood.[36] Sensibly Simon did not make the mistake of addressing the Commons too frequently or of endeavouring to secure notoriety. Whenever he spoke it was on a subject which he understood and his speeches usually had the effect of bringing fresh insight to those who listened to him. It was a mark of his skill that Simon's early parliamentary performances were noted not only by his own side but also by the opposition. The Unionist leader, Arthur Balfour, a man who probably appreciated intellect above all other human qualities, was among those who paid tribute, while in July 1907 George Wyndham recorded that a speech which Simon made opposing Preference was 'nearly perfect; indeed, perfect, but for a faint touch of the "superior person".'[37]

Like the Liberal government itself Simon seemed to be heading for great things. The King's confidant, Lord Esher, singled him out as 'a very attractive and clever man.'[38] At the same time Simon's legal career continued to prosper. In 1908, and still only thirty-five years of age, Simon took silk, an essential step if he were to move into the top echelon of the legal profession. In February 1909 he was appointed Standing Counsel to the University of Oxford and that September accepted a seat on the Royal Commission on the Selection of JPs. Even before his elevation to the government front bench, Prime Minister Asquith was making 'confidential use' of Simon's legal brain,[39] and it was clear that when next a law officer needed to be appointed the honourable member who spoke with such quiet confidence from the second bench on the government side would be asked to fill the vacancy.

If there was one cloud on the Liberal horizon during these first years of government it was the readiness of the Unionist-dominated House of Lords to use its powers to block or frustrate the reforming zeal of the administration. The Lords' decision in November 1909 to reject Lloyd George's budget defied long-standing precedent and inaugurated a constitutional crisis which had not been fully resolved by the outbreak of European War in 1914 and in whose later stages Simon himself played a not insignificant role. The immediate consequence was to force Asquith to call a general election for January 1910. In Walthamstow Simon's campaign focused on the iniquities of the Lords' decision, but he also reminded his electors of his commitment to free trade and opposition to food taxes. Nationally the Unionist party staged a marked recovery, virtually wiping out the government's massive majority of 1906, though still leaving it in office through the support of Labour and Irish members. This pattern was followed in Walthamstow where, after a 'long and laborious' contest, Simon's majority dropped to just over 2,000 in a straight fight with his Unionist opponent. Simon regarded his victory, secured with trade union and Labour support, as a mandate for a bold policy to curb the powers of the upper chamber and he lost no time in putting this view before the Prime Minister.[40] He proposed a procedure whereby taxes could continue to be collected without the passage of the budget. Indeed he urged Asquith to announce that no further steps would be taken to carry the Finance Bill until after a Lords Limitation of Powers Bill had been enacted. Asquith chose a rather more cautious line of approach but was obviously impressed with his young supporter. When in October 1910 the appointment of Sir William Robson as a Law Lord necessitated a minor government reshuffle, Asquith offered Simon the post of Solicitor-General. At thirty-seven he was the youngest holder of this office since the 1830s.

The Solicitor-General is essentially the junior law officer of the Crown. In the circumstances it was not surprising that Simon reacted with something short of unbridled enthusiasm to this first entry into government service. He would, he told Asquith, have been inclined to remain a private member if he did not believe that political opportunity sometimes beckoned even a Solicitor-General. 'It is the political rather than the legal side of things which attracts me.'[41] To a friend and fellow MP Simon was even more blunt:

I am glad to be on the Front Bench – I am not so sure if I care about being a Law Officer. I don't know much Law, but all I do know is rather arid.[42]

It was also characteristic of the radical within Simon that he objected, perhaps only for the sake of form, to the award of the customary knighthood associated with his office. 'It is not a small thing to a young man to have a disfiguring operation performed upon him against his will, the mark of which he will carry through life.' He feared also that among a working-class electorate a knighthood might be interpreted as sycophancy.[43] Though, at Asquith's insistence, Simon had to accept his title, on his other concern that he might, by virtue of his office, find himself effectively precluded from political activity, his fears were unfounded. Seldom if ever in the history of the twentieth century have politics and the law been so inextricably inter-twined as they were immediately before the First World War. The combina-tion of the constitutional crisis which led to the Parliament Act of 1911, and the government's political necessity after the general elections of 1910 to introduce a third Home Rule Bill for Ireland – its timetable dictated with eerie precision by the terms of the Parliament Act – ensured that this was so. The Osborne judgment of December 1909, stipulating that trade unions could not use their funds for political purposes, and the government's attempt in 1912 to introduce a wide-ranging franchise and registration bill added further constitutional and legal dimensions to the contemporary political debate. Indeed, it was the Osborne judgment which saw Simon invited to a meeting of the cabinet for the first time.[44] Inevitably, therefore, the law officers found themselves playing a more overtly political role than was normal, a fact emphasised by the elevation of Rufus Isaacs, the Attorney-General, to cabinet rank in 1912. As Solicitor-General Simon was far more than the 'kind of office boy for the Government' that he had feared.[45] It was not long before Asquith began to ask him to wind up important debates for the government. The first occasion came in February 1911 when Simon closed a two-day debate on Imperial Preference with special reference to the Canadian-American Reciprocity negotiations. He was less satisfied with his performance than were others:

I am told I did well. . . . But I was too provocative and scolded the other side instead of addressing our own followers.[46]

When in February 1912 F. E. Smith made his first speech from the opposi-tion front bench in moving the official amendment to the King's Speech, the government put up his old adversary Simon to oppose him.[47]

Simon experienced the curious and not altogether welcome distinction of having to fight three election campaigns in Walthamstow in the course of 1910. His elevation to the government in October, ten months after the first general election of that year, necessitated a further appeal to his constituents under the law which then required the new holders of offices of profit under the crown to submit themselves for re-election. In a straight fight with the Unionists Simon increased his majority on a reduced overall poll. Yet his by-election victory may well have encouraged Asquith to fight with some confidence a further general election in December following the breakdown of the Constitutional Conference called to settle the question of the powers of the House of Lords by consent.[48] This time the election was fought specifically to provide the government with a mandate to curb the Lords' authority and, in another straight fight with a Unionist, Simon managed to push up his majority to almost 4,000.

As Solicitor-General Simon also had important work to do, not in parliament or on the hustings, but in the courts. At the beginning of 1911 he and the Attorney-General had the unusual task of acting for the newly enthroned King, George V, in a libel case. The defendant, one Edward Mylius, had published an article in a republican leaflet in Paris which claimed that the monarch had contracted a marriage in Malta in 1890 and therefore that his marriage to the Queen three years later was bigamous. It was not particularly difficult for Simon to show that the story itself was unfounded, but the constitutional position of the King in his own court of law might have posed some problems. It was Simon who advised the King that his actual appearance in court to give testimony would be unconstitutional, but as Simon recorded at the time:

We were lucky to bring the Mylius case to so satisfactory an end. If M., instead of justifying, had pleaded guilty and explained that he was only repeating what thousands of reputable people had said for years without being prosecuted for it, we could never have established the falsity of the lie so effectually.[49]

To mark his gratitude the King appointed both Simon and Isaacs Knight Commander of the Royal Victorian Order, an award in the personal gift of the sovereign. Two years later when Simon became a Privy Councillor the King showed what a good impression Simon had made upon him. Receiving a letter of thanks from the Solicitor-General, George V noted, 'A charming letter from a very nice man.'[50]

Simon's relations with Rufus Isaacs, the Attorney-General and his immediate superior, were warm and cordial, establishing a friendship which lasted until Isaacs' death in 1935. When in 1912 the Attorney-General's career was threatened by his injudicious holding of shares in the American Marconi Company, Simon was quick to offer advice.

Rufus called me to his room and disclosed to me confidentially that the actual investment was in American Marconis. I wrote to him the same night to implore him to come down to the House the next day to state this further fact, and by this candour remove all ground for suspicion, however unfounded. "I am not alone in this matter" was his reply.[51]

Though the American company was independent of the British Marconi Company, from which the Postmaster-General, Herbert Samuel, had recently accepted an important tender to construct a chain of wireless stations, Isaacs' behaviour was undoubtedly a serious error of judgment. As Simon later concluded, it was odd that one who was so wise in advising others should not have seen that the correct course was to explain his position fully and candidly to the House of Commons.[52] This indiscretion had not yet become an issue of public and parliamentary debate when, much to his disappointment, Isaacs was passed over for the succession to Lord Loreburn on the Woolsack. The promotion from Attorney-General to Lord

Chancellor was one which had come to be regard«
occasion Simon went so far as to write a memorandu.
stressing that there was no legal bar on a Jew becomir.

Another extra-parliamentary crisis to attract the
attention came with the sinking of the White Star liner,
maiden voyage across the Atlantic in April 1912. In th«
which followed this disaster, Simon appeared with Isaacs ι
Board of Trade as the government department responsible fo   .., υι
merchant vessels. Simon's searching questioning of witnesses helped produce the improved safety regulations recommended by the court of enquiry.

In removing the veto power of the House of Lords, the Parliament Act of
1911 opened up tempting new possibilities for the government and two
important legislative measures occupied much of Simon's attention during
that year. One was Lloyd George's scheme for National Insurance. That
part of the government bill which dealt with unemployment insurance was
entrusted to the President of the Board of Trade, Sydney Buxton, with
Simon to assist him. Working with civil servants including William
Beveridge, Simon played a significant role in formulating the government's
proposals and piloting them through the House of Commons. Behind the
scenes Simon was also busy drawing up plans for a comprehensive franchise
and registration bill. This time his chief was Pease, the President of the
Board of Education. Precise proposals were presented to the cabinet in
December 1911 and aimed to introduce a one-man-one-vote scheme for an
anticipated 9½ million male voters based on a six months' residential qualification. Speed was of the essence if the bill was going to pass into law in
time for a new parliamentary register to be prepared for use at the next
general election, anticipated in 1915.[54] This bill, however, was lost when in
January 1913 the Speaker ruled that the inclusion of female suffrage amendments at the Committee stage would so change its nature as to necessitate its
withdrawal. Faced with the Speaker's decision, the government decided not
to try to proceed with the measure.

Considering that his post did not carry with it cabinet rank, Simon was
nonetheless emerging as a key member of the administration. It was a sign of
his stature within the Liberal party that he decided that at the next general
election he should leave his increasingly secure stronghold at Walthamstow
and contest the politically sensitive constituency of North-West Manchester.
Though his willingness to offer himself as a standard bearer of free trade and
of the party's fortunes won considerable praise, there was also concern that
Simon should be guaranteed an alternative parliamentary base should his
bold coup fail to be rewarded.[55] Alarmed reactions in the Unionist party to
the prospect of Simon's candidature in Manchester were a sign of the respect
which he now commanded.[56]

In October 1912 Lord Morley noted that among ministers invited to
Balmoral Simon 'enjoyed the greatest favour, everyone speaking well of

other things – 'not a political asset'.[59] Sir Almeric Fitzroy, Clerk of the Privy Council, who had heard much in Simon's praise, was disappointed by personal acquaintance. 'His abilities are no doubt as great as people say, but he was devoid of the magnetism I had expected.'[60] And if Simon did not yet have enemies among his political colleagues, there were certainly those who could not be listed as friends. One such was David Lloyd George, Chancellor of the Exchquer since Asquith's elevation to the premiership, who noted,'Simon is a clever fellow, clear-headed but pedantic. He wants everything very precise.'[61]

These points are worth noting. They stand as markers for the future. But it would be wrong to imply that there were many clouds on Simon's personal political horizon at this time. After three years as Solicitor-General promotion came in October 1913 when Isaacs was removed from the government to become Lord Chief Justice. Asquith offered the vacant post of senior law officer in terms designed to appeal to the new incumbent:

I trust you will see your way to succeed the A. G. (without prejudice to a *political* future) with a seat in the Cabinet.[62]

In following Isaacs into the cabinet Simon no doubt appreciated his immersion into the central policy-making body of government. Yet the combination of the two roles – law officer and cabinet minister – was an unusual one, a confusion of functions which made it difficult for the Attorney-General to preserve the necessary degree of legal impartiality on issues where he was also involved at a political level.[63] The arrangement was one which Simon later recognised to be unwise:

If the Attorney-General is a party to the earlier deliberations of the Cabinet out of which the need for technical guidance has arisen, it may be difficult for him to approach the problem ultimately presented to him as a lawyer with an entirely open mind.[64]

By the time that Simon entered the cabinet, the Liberal government was engrossed in what proved to be the most difficult phase of its legislative programme. Under the slow but inevitable provisions of the Parliament Act, two highly contentious measures were making their way towards the statute book. The Attorney-General was one of the ministers specially charged with responsibility for the Government of Ireland Bill and the Welsh Disestablishment Bill. To both Simon was firmly committed on personal grounds, but it was the former which preoccupied the attention of the government. Set against Asquith's irreversible commitment to Home Rule was the equally adamant refusal of Protestant Ulster, abetted by an increasingly obdurate and threatening parliamentary opposition, to accept the authority of a prospective Dublin-based parliament. Simon quickly found himself involved in the difficult question of the supply of arms to potential rebels in Ulster. At meetings of the cabinet on 24 and 25 November, Simon advised that since the lapsing of the Coercion Acts in 1906 no special statutory power existed in Ireland to prohibit the importation and use of arms. But he was confident that the customs regulations gave the government power to prevent the export or import of arms from or into the United Kingdom.[65] On 1 December, on the basis of Simon's advice and under the impact of evidence that two private armies were being organised in Ireland, the cabinet decided to issue the necessary Royal Proclamations, and considerable success was thereafter achieved in controlling the importation of further arms into the country. Simon's advice was also sought on whether it would be possible to prosecute the leaders of the Ulster Loyalists. Simon argued that arrest and prosecution for such offences as treason, felony and illegal drilling were quite possible, though the government judged that the dangers of civil unrest and the difficulty of securing a conviction from any Irish jury made it counter-productive to act on the Attorney-General's advice.[66]

At many times in modern British history there has been an element of playacting in the adversarial confrontation of government and opposition in national politics. In 1913 and 1914 the passion and animosity were only too real. The threat of civil disorder, even civil war, in Ireland was taken quite seriously. In such circumstances the last thing that the Liberal government needed was a rift in its own ranks. Yet as 1913 came to a close Asquith faced a major dispute involving some of his most senior colleagues. It was a conflict in which Simon played an important part.

Tension had long been inherent in the cabinet over foreign and defence policy between its radical and Liberal Imperialist wings. It was perhaps only Edward Grey's almost exclusive control over the country's external relations which prevented more serious and regular difficulties. But the costs of defence expenditure had inevitable implications for the government's social reforming zeal as the Dreadnought building programme had illustrated as early as 1908. Matters almost inevitably came to a head when Winston Churchill succeeded Reginald McKenna as First Lord of the Admiralty in October 1911, for although Churchill had opposed the original Dreadnought programme he now 'embraced the cause of naval might as eagerly as he had retrenchment.'[67] The First Lord clearly proposed to secure peace by preparing for war. Added to this was a growing personal opposition to Churchill from cabinet colleagues who objected to his overbearing manner and too ready willingness to intervene in cabinet discussions, no matter how removed the subject was from the First Lord's departmental concerns.

Though Churchill's estimates for 1913–14 got through the cabinet without difficulty, when at the end of 1913 he proposed a further increase of £3 millions, trouble erupted. Each of the cabinet radicals saw the probability of a cherished scheme of social improvement fading away and it was Simon who became their champion. On 11 December he warned Seely, the War Minister, that the estimates were scandalous and called for a clear statement of the level of German expenditure to show that Britain had been increasing her naval power at a rate which the spending of her potential enemy did not justify. Seely was careful to warn Churchill of the storm that was brewing and urged the First Lord to present his case so as to show that German naval expenditure did indeed justify his own proposals.[68] Lloyd George interpreted Simon's attitude as representing a determination to drive Churchill out of the cabinet,[69] and certainly Simon seemed ready to contemplate a parting of the ways. To Asquith he scribbled, 'the loss of W. C., though regrettable, is *not* by any means a splitting of party.' Yet, as Simon continued, the prospects in the event of a major cabinet crisis were daunting:

1 Dissolution now, if we were beaten, means that Parliament Act is utterly destroyed; House of Lords reconstructed on Tory lines which only a revolution can alter; Home Rule and Welsh Disestablishment lost.

2 The probability of losing Gen Election is great – *not* because Country is against Home Rule or in favour of Admiralty Extravagance – but because our *keenest* supporters will think we have given up causes to which we are pledged.[70]

Simon favoured an increased naval strength of just two more capital ships and allowing Churchill to resign. It was not thought that any other member of the cabinet would go with him, while Simon and Lloyd George were suspicious that Churchill was in any case only waiting for a favourable opportunity to return to the Unionist party and that his resignation over an Irish issue might be more damaging to the party.[71] It was one of the few occasions in their long careers when Lloyd George and Simon could claim – however briefly – to be genuine political allies:

Tonight I am with Sir John Simon who is entirely with me and if necessary will go with me.[72]

Even so, Lloyd George was more inclined to compromise than was Simon, hoping that Churchill would be able to offer savings in other directions than battleship construction.

By 18 January Simon was suggesting that Churchill's actual expenditure for 1914–15 might rise to £56 millions, and Lloyd George, McKenna and Samuel agreed with him that Churchill must be forced to resign.[73] But the possibility of a promise to reduce the estimates for 1915–16, while leaving those for 1914–15 intact, saw Lloyd George begin to waver. He was ready to accept estimates for 1914 of £54 millions and chided Simon, 'a kind of Robespierre', for his apparent vendetta against Churchill.[74] Simon, 'alert, incisive', remained suspicious of all pledges coming from Churchill. He insisted that putting a spendthrift in charge of a great spending department inevitably meant extravagant expenditure and that if there were any reality in the proposed reductions there was no point in postponing them for a year.[75]

On 21 January Simon, together with Lloyd George, Samuel and Beauchamp confronted the Prime Minister. They insisted that the party would never accept the proposed increases unless, 'as a guarantee against such future events', Churchill retired from the Admiralty and preferably from the cabinet altogether. ' "Oh", said the PM, "this is a personal question?" "No," replied Simon somewhat unconvincingly, "a question of temperament." '[76] Asquith spoke of a 'conclave of malcontents' and was clearly worried about the outcome:

Ll.G. was there, but Simon, Samuel and of all people Beauchamp are far the most aggressive and most anti-Winston. I doubt increasingly whether the thing can be patched up.[77]

Simon now began to distance himself from Lloyd George, who failed throughout the crisis to pursue a consistent line. After further talks with the Chancellor on the afternoon of 25 January he wrote to make it plain that he would not acquiesce in Churchill's figure of £54 millions, especially as the original agitation had been directed against a supposed figure of £50 millions. 'The upshot of the crusade for economy is, so far, an increase of £4 millions: a conclusion at once tragical and laughable.'[78] At the cabinet on 27 January Lloyd George appeared to have come to a deal with Churchill and the attack on the Admiralty was led by Simon, McKenna and Hobhouse. 'Churchill defended himself with what Simon afterwards described as wonderful fecundity of mind, and with the vigorous though ineffectual support of Haldane to whom no one seemed to attach much importance.'[79]

It was significant that Lloyd George was absent from a dinner attended on 28 January by Simon, Runciman, Beauchamp, McKenna and Hobhouse, where all were of one mind to let Asquith know that they were ready to resign rather than accept Churchill's extravagant estimates. This was despite the fact that at the cabinet earlier that day Asquith had appealed to 'the whole pack not to split at such a time on such a point'.[80] On the following day the group deputed Simon and Beauchamp to present a long letter signed by them all to the Prime Minister. Asquith thanked them for having put their case and assured them that he would give their views full consideration.[81] Written in Simon's hand, the letter attempted to place the row over the naval estimates in the context of the government's legislative preoccupations. 'The question remains whether the figures now put forward by the First Lord, and the plan now tentatively suggested by the Chancellor of the Exchequer for dealing with them, are best calculated to make more certain the happy issue of the legislative programme to which you and we stand committed.' The total figure in question was 'unprecedented', the increase 'unexampled' at a time of apparent international calm and might well lead to a renewed naval race with the Germans, thereby undermining the retrenchment proposed for 1915–16. The domestic political consequences were equally serious. Labour would be alienated, backbench radicals were likely to dissent and Ulster Unionists were only too ready to embarrass the government. The loss of by-elections on the issue might fatally compromise the prospects for Home Rule, while increased taxation could strain the capacity of a free trade economy.[82]

A cabinet revolt on the scale which seemed to be presaged if Churchill's line prevailed appeared on the surface to pose a potentially mortal threat to Asquith's government. Yet there is some evidence that the Prime Minister was less concerned than might have been expected. In the first instance the majority of the dissidents were of the second rank in the cabinet pecking order. From the Chief Whip, moreover, Asquith heard that Simon, whom he nicknamed 'the Impeccable', was the 'real and *only* stubborn Irreconcilable'.[83] Lloyd George even doubted whether, in the last resort, Simon would make Churchill's estimates a resignation issue.[84] At all events, by the middle of February the crisis had passed and no resignations had been tendered. On 11 February the cabinet agreed to total estimates of more than £51½ millions, while Churchill promised to effect substantial reductions the following year. The outcome left the First Lord in good heart. It must be assumed that Simon was not.[85] For the Attorney-General the episode had involved a curious mixture of principle and personal prejudice against Churchill. On neither count had he been satisfied.

With the affairs of the Admiralty resolved, the cabinet was able to turn its attention to the final act in the Irish drama. The fear of civil conflict in Ulster dominated the government's thoughts until the very outbreak of European war that August. In March Simon was appointed to a cabinet committee to consider the military situation in Ulster and particularly the possibility of Ulster Volunteers attempting to seize police and military barracks and depots of arms and ammunition.[86] Tension came to a head in the late spring with the so-called Curragh Mutiny, which highlighted the cabinet's unwillingness to confront the issue of coercion head on. Simon found himself among a minority of ministers who wanted to stand firmly by their Irish Nationalist allies, deploring signs of weakness which could only give the upper hand to Edward Carson and his Ulstermen. 'If we *said* we were going on and *got our own people to believe us*, C[arson] would regard a Provisional government as a false step.'[87] It was a stance which Simon was still maintaining at the end of July following the breakdown of the last-minute attempt at compromise at the Buckingham Palace Conference.[88] Increasingly, however, the majority of the cabinet was moving towards a solution which allowed for the exclusion of Protestant Ulster from the provisions of the Home Rule Bill. Simon proposed an ingenious variation to this central problem:

make *no* provision in the Bill for Protestant Ulster *save for a limited period* such as six years. When the 6 years came to an end, there would be no statutory provision, so far as the Government of Ireland Bill 1914 is concerned, for the government of Protestant Ulster at all. It would neither fall automatically within Home Rule Ireland, nor would it, by virtue of the present Bill, enjoy statutory exclusion beyond the 6 years. Consequently Parliament would be obliged to undertake in, say, 1920 the duty of providing for the future government of Protestant Ulster.[89]

As Edwardian England and its Liberal administration tottered unknowingly and innocently towards catastrophe, there could be no doubt that John Simon had become a key figure in the government. His services were in widespread demand.

I am *distracted* with Canteen prosecutions, Revenue Bills, Home Rule suggestions, Colonial Office opinions, and every form of misdirected clamour![90]

At a political level Simon appeared to be well favoured by the Prime Minister. If at this time Asquith had fallen victim to the proverbial omnibus, there were those who believed that Simon might have been his chosen successor. Certainly the Attorney-General was by temperament and ability a politician far more in the Asquithian mould than was Lloyd George. Additionally, Simon figured prominently in the Prime Minister's social life at this time. Yet, as Asquith's biographer remarks, Simon was 'not so much a friend as a very frequently encountered acquaintance'.[91] Though appreciative of Simon's qualities, the premier found him 'precise and uninspiring',[92] and relished his daughter's description of the Attorney-General's 'synthetic geniality'. There was a side to Asquith's character which preferred more adventurous personalities.[93] Be that as it may, in the early summer of 1914, Irish difficulties notwithstanding, the prospects lying before Simon, still a very young man in political terms, were glittering indeed. A contemporary assessment, written without the corrupting imposition of hindsight, helps to capture the astonishing achievement of this self-made man and the expectations entertained for him:

[Fairies] crowded round the cradle of John Allsebrook Simon and showered their gifts upon him. And, best of all, there was no uninvited fairy to turn all the blessings to bitterness – unless, indeed, unqualified success is a malignant elf in disguise . . . Whatever he wanted he has got. Whatever he wants, one feels he will get . . . [Simon] is in the rare position of having either of the two great offices in the State within his ultimate reach . . . He has more rivals in his own stable for the Premiership than Mr. [F. E.] Smith has. For the Lord Chancellorship he has none.[94]

What was true of Simon was true also of the party of which he was a leading light. It is too easy for historians of Liberalism, mindful of the havoc wreaked by four years of total war, to antedate the party's decline. In 1914 the Liberal government had emerged victoriously from three successive general elections. The challenge of Labour seemed for the time being to have been contained. Conservatism was as yet showing few signs of becoming the natural governing party of twentieth-century Britain. No one could have known that independent Liberalism had less than a year of government left before it.

But then came the War.

Notes

1 M. Brett (ed.), *Journals and Letters of Reginald Viscount Esher* vol. ii (London, 1934) pp. 429–30.
2 Simon to S. Hoare 23 March 1938, Templewood MSS XVIII: 4.
3 Undated note by Simon, SP 6 fo. 50.
4 *Sunday Times* 1 Nov. 1936.
5 *Retrospect* pp. 21–2.
6 *Fifty Years of Fettes: Memories of Old Fettesians 1870–1920* (Edinburgh, 1931) p. 123.
7 Simon to J. Brierley 13 Jan. 1943, SP 92 fo. 94.
8 *Memories of Old Fettesians* p. 124.
9 Information from *The Fettesian*, supplied by Mr. R. A. Cole-Hamilton, Keeper of the Register, Fettes College.
10 C. B. Fry, *Life worth Living* (London, 1939) p. 87.
11 Article by C. B. Fry, *Cleckheaton Guardian* 18 July 1930.
12 M. Bowra, *Memories 1898–1939* (London, 1966) pp. 140–1.
13 E. C. Bentley, *Those Days* (London, 1940) p. 81.
14 Ibid, p. 77.
15 J. Campbell, *F. E. Smith: First Earl of Birkenhead* (London, 1983) p. 176; Lord Birkenhead, *F. E.: The Life of F. E. Smith, First Earl of Birkenhead* (London, 1959) p. 97.
16 Simon to H. Samuel 5 March 1944, Samuel MSS A/155 (xi) 62; Viscount Samuel, *Memoirs* (London, 1945) p. 22.
17 J. Simon and others, *Essays in Liberalism* (London, 1897) p. 104.
18 *Retrospect* p. 40.
19 F. E. Smith to Simon 25 Feb. 1901, SP 47 fos. 54–5.
20 H. Montgomery Hyde, *Norman Birkett* (London, 1964) p. 92.
21 J. Scobell Armstrong, *Yesterday* (London, 1955) p. 68.
22 H. Montgomery Hyde, *United in Crime* (London, 1955) p. 58.
23 Scobell Armstrong, *Yesterday* p. 118.
24 R. Heuston, *Lives of the Lord Chancellors 1940–70* (Oxford, 1987) p. 40; H Slesser, *Judgment Reserved* (London, 1942) p. 73.
25 Scobell Armstrong, *Yesterday* p. 118.
26 J. Colville, *The Fringes of Power* (London, 1985) p. 766.
27 Simon to C. P. Trevelyan 20 Feb. 1902, Trevelyan MSS Ex 102.
28 Scobell Armstrong, *Yesterday* pp. 119–20.
29 *Retrospect* p. 61.
30 As note 28.
31 Simon to H. Gladstone 7 April 1905, Gladstone MSS Add MS 46062 fo. 191;

Gladstone later sent Simon a cheque for £380, Simon to Gladstone 15 Feb. 1906, ibid 46064 fo. 21.

32 Simon to Gladstone 30 March 1905 and 3 April 1905, ibid 46062 fos. 179–80, 187–8.

33 Simon to C. P. Trevelyan 5 May 1905, Trevelyan MSS 15.

34 B. Webb diary 22 Feb. 1906. Compare her later diary comment (9 June 1940) that Simon ranked with Hugh Dalton as the least pleasant characters she had met in politics.

35 B. Webb diary 22 Feb. 1906.

36 House of Commons Debates, 4th Series, vol. 162, cols. 1738–40. The Conservative, William Bridgeman, who did not hear Simon's maiden speech, was told that among the new Liberal intake Simon was 'the best of them all'. P. Williamson (ed.), *The Modernisation of Conservative Politics* (London, 1988) p. 33.

37 *Retrospect* p. 74; J. Mackail and G. Wyndham, *Life and Letters of George Wyndham* (London, n.d.) ii, 577. Wyndham incorrectly referred to this speech as Simon's 'maiden'. In the collection of his speeches, published in 1930 under the title *Comments and Criticisms*, Simon's speech on the third reading of the Trade Disputes Bill in November 1906 is described as his 'maiden'.

38 Brett, *Esher* ii, 429–30. Churchill, already a cabinet minister, noted that Simon was 'a young King's Counsel of distinguished ability'. Churchill to King Edward VII 30 March 1910, R. S. Churchill, *Winston S. Churchill* vol. 2 (London, 1967) p. 430.

39 Simon to Asquith 5 Feb. 1910, Asquith MSS 12 fos. 111–13.

40 Ibid.

41 Ibid 27 Sept. 1910, Asquith MSS 12 fos. 185–6.

42 Simon to W. Runciman 8 Oct. 1910, Runciman MSS 35.

43 Simon to Vaughan Nash 7 Oct. 1910, SP 48 fos. 47–8.

44 Simon diary 22 Feb. 1911, SP 2 fo. 5.

45 Bechhofer Roberts, *Simon* p. 80.

46 Simon diary 9 Feb. 1911, SP 2 fo. 5.

47 J. Campbell, *F. E. Smith* p. 320.

48 *Retrospect* p. 82; see also the cartoon in the *Westminster Gazette* of 5 Nov. 1910. As Home Secretary in June 1915 Simon introduced a bill to remove the need for newly appointed ministers to seek re-election during the War.

49 Simon diary 3 Feb. 1911, SP 2 fo. 4.

50 K. Rose, *George V* (London, 1983) p. 85.

51 Simon diary 31 Dec. 1935, SP 7 fo. 44.

·52 *Retrospect* p. 91.

53 Ibid pp. 88–9. Haldane's claims to the Woolsack – a position he had desired at the formation of the Liberal government back in 1905 – were, however, strong. A year later Isaacs became Lord Chief Justice, thereby leaving the senior law office vacant for Simon.

54 M. Pugh, *Electoral Reform in War and Peace 1906–18* (London, 1978) pp. 36–7.

55 C. P. Scott to Simon 1 Aug. 1913, SP 49 fos. 144–5.

56 P. F. Clarke, *Lancashire and the New Liberalism* (Cambridge, 1971) p. 308.

57 Sir A. Fitzroy, *Memoirs vol. 2* (London, n.d.) pp. 493–4.

58 Lord Riddell, *More Pages from My Diary* (London, 1934) p. 117.

59 Ibid.

60 Fitzroy, *Memoirs* ii, 505.

61 J. McEwen (ed.), *The Riddell Diaries 1908–23* (London, 1986) p. 68.

62 Asquith to Simon 15 Oct. 1913, SP 49 fo. 173.

63 Simon was the first Attorney-General to go straight into the cabinet immediately upon his appointment.

64 *Retrospect* p. 90.

65 E. David (ed.) ,*Inside Asquith's Cabinet* (London, 1977) p. 152; P. Jalland, *The Liberals and Ireland* (Brighton, 1980) p. 210.

66 Jalland p. 213.

67 T. Morgan, *Churchill: Young Man in a Hurry 1874–1915* (New York, 1982) p. 315.

68 R. S. Churchill and M. Gilbert, *Winston S. Churchill* ii, companion pt 3 (London, 1969) pp. 1824–5.

69 Riddell, *More Pages* p. 190.

70 Undated pencil note from Simon to Asquith, Asquith MSS 25 fos. 148–9.

71 T. Wilson (ed.), *The Political Diaries of C. P. Scott 1911–1928* (London, 1970) p. 73.

72 K. O. Morgan (ed.), *Lloyd George: Family Letters 1885–1936* (Cardiff, 1973) p. 166.

73 T. Wilson (ed.), *Scott Diaries* p. 75.

74 M. Fry, *Lloyd George and Foreign Policy 1890–1916* (Montreal, 1977) p. 176; see also McEwen, *Riddell Diaries* p. 78. 'Masterman described the attitude of Simon and Samuel as being indecent, their one desire being to hound Winston out of the Cabinet. He said, "This is evident from their manner. They cannot conceal it." '

75 Wilson (ed.), *Scott Diaries* p. 77.

76 David (ed.), *Asquith's Cabinet* pp. 155–6.

77 Asquith to his wife 21 Jan. 1914, cited J. Spender and C. Asquith, *Life of Herbert Henry Asquith* (London, 1932) ii, 76.

78 Simon to Lloyd George 26 Jan. 1914, Lloyd George MSS C/8/3/6.

79 David (ed.), *Asquith's Cabinet* p. 158.

80 A. Marder, *From the Dreadnought to Scapa Flow* vol. 1 (London, 1961) pp. 324–5.

81 David (ed.), *Asquith's Cabinet* p. 160.

82 Simon, Beauchamp, Hobhouse, McKenna and Runciman to Asquith 29 Jan. 1914, Asquith MSS 25 fos. 170–7; Jalland, *Liberals and Ireland* pp. 188–9.

83 M. and E. Brock (eds.), *H. H. Asquith: Letters to Venetia Stanley* (Oxford, 1982) p. 43 (emphasis added).

84 Wilson (ed.), *Scott Diaries* p. 78.

85 It is interesting to note that Austen Chamberlain deemed a speech which Simon made to the House of Commons that evening 'a failure'. Sir A. Chamberlain, *Politics from Inside* (London, 1936) p. 612.

86 Asquith to George V 13 March 1914, R. S. Churchill, *Winston S. Churchill* ii, 488.

87 Note by Simon 25 May 1914, Lloyd George MSS C/12/2.

88 David (ed.), *Asquith's Cabinet* p. 176.

89 Simon memorandum n.d. Asquith MSS 39 fos. 172–5; David (ed.), *Asquith's Cabinet* p. 170.

90 Simon to Mrs M. K. Trevelyan 16 May 1914, Trevelyan MSS Ex 108.

91 R. Jenkins, *Asquith* (London, 1964) p. 270.
92 Brocks (eds.), *Asquith Letters* p. 186.
93 M. Bowra, *Memories* p. 205.
94 A. G. Gardiner, *Pillars of Society* (London, 1916) pp. 269–74.

CHAPTER TWO

RELUCTANT WARRIOR

When Sir John Simon comes to write his autobiography he will have one advantage over the whole lot of us when he comes to the story of the War, when the more he compresses the better it will be for him. The smaller the chapter, the fewer the details about what he did as a politician in the War, the better it will be for his fame.[1]

Simon's biographer, able to survey his life as a whole, cannot help being struck by the clearly marked turning points of his career. Two emerge within the four-year compass of the First World War. The most obvious was Simon's resignation from the government in January 1916. The first was the coming of the War itself. This was a traumatic moment for all holding responsibility in British politics. Though perhaps no one anticipated the level of destruction and misery which would follow, some seemed to be conscious that an era in European history was drawing to a close. But for Simon it appears with hindsight to mark the first slip in his seemingly effortless ascent of the British political ladder. For many Simon's standing was permanently compromised by the line which he took towards British participation in the continental war.

So deeply engrossed was the Liberal government in the parochial affairs of Ireland and so accustomed had the cabinet become to Sir Edward Grey's monopoly of foreign affairs that the European crisis of July 1914 was comparatively far advanced before Asquith and his colleagues gave serious consideration to the question of British involvement in a Franco-German War. Simon may even have been the last minister to recognise that the Irish crisis paled into insignificance when set against the developments in Europe, arguing that Britain could not despatch a force to France because all troops would be needed to meet a possible civil conflict in Ulster.[2] Despite Grey's ascendancy there had always been more potential within the Asquith cabinet for a major breach on a question of foreign policy than on any other issue. It is clear that for much of the crisis of 1914 Asquith could not rely on a numerical majority of his cabinet colleagues to support a firm declaration of support for France. Yet this is not to say that a large and committed anti-war group of fixed and resolved purpose ever existed. Rather there were as many as ten or twelve waverers who felt varying degrees of disquiet at the prospect of intervention.[3] These men lacked genuine agreement among themselves and produced no clear leader. Lloyd George, who might by temperament and past history have been expected to head a radical protest, was among the first to be won over to the Asquith-Grey camp. Simon, though no doubt the ablest and most articulate of the others, still in 1914, despite his growing stature, lacked the seniority to lead such a revolt. Yet among the waverers Simon showed a greater degree of hesitation than most of his colleagues.

When in late July the cabinet finally came to discuss the question of Belgian neutrality and British obligations under the treaty of guarantee of 1839 – precisely the sort of legal issue where the Attorney-General might be expected to make a significant contribution – it was noticeable that Simon 'contributed scarcely anything'.[4] On 31 July and 1 August Simon in conjunction with the veteran Gladstonian, John Morley, tried to secure a declaration that Britain would in no circumstances intervene. Morley stressed that their views were shared by the great industrial centres of the North of England and by the banking and commercial authorities in London,[5] but Grey made it clear that the adoption of this proposal would entail his resignation. Asquith would have followed him and without these two ministers it was unlikely that the government could have continued. 'We came', noted Asquith of the meeting of 1 August, 'every now and again near to the parting of the ways.' At this stage, however, he already doubted whether Simon would go as far as resignation.[6] In the event the cabinet decided against any immediate despatch of the British Expeditionary Force to the continent.

With hindsight it is clear that the crucial decisions concerning Britain's position were taken on Sunday, 2 August. The cabinet met at 11 a.m. and again in the evening. Significantly, when Simon and a group of other ministers consulted prior to the first meeting of that day, they were agreed that while they were not prepared to enter the War as the situation then stood, an event such as the wholesale invasion of Belgium might cause them to reconsider.[7] When the cabinet met, John Burns, President of the Board of Trade, announced his resignation in response to the cabinet's assurance that Britain would protect the French coast and shipping from attacks by the German fleet. Though no other minister yet showed his hand, Morley still considered that Simon, Lloyd George and he were 'all three for resignation' and the Prime Minister was also convinced that a split was imminent.[8] After lunch Simon remained determined to 'resist at all costs the bellicose inferences from the entente' and wondered whether he had been wrong not to announce his resignation along with Burns.[9] When the cabinet reassembled in the evening Simon passed a note to Burns, who had been asked to attend despite his determination to resign. In it he urged him to delay his resignation until the following day, as 'I am disposed to think 7 or 8 of us may be with you'.[10] That evening Simon dined with George Riddell, Charles Masterman, the Labour leader Ramsay MacDonald and Lloyd George at Riddell's home in Queen Anne's Gate. His mood was grave; MacDonald described him as 'broken'.[11] Gloomily he talked of precedents, arguing that Britain had always been wrong to intervene on the continent. 'Why should we support a country like Russia?'[12] Eventually Simon produced a letter of resignation which was sent to Asquith that evening.

The statement which Grey made to Cambon this afternoon, and which he does not propose to reveal to Germany until the announcement is made in the House of Commons tomorrow, will, I think, be regarded as tantamount to a declaration that we take part in this quarrel with France and against Germany. I think we should not take part, and so I must resign my post.

Simon expressed his willingness to delay announcing his resignation until after the Foreign Secretary had spoken to the Commons 'for if we are involved in war . . . the last thing I wish is to accentuate divisions.' On his own departure, however, he seemed determined: 'in any case please find a new Attorney-General'.[13]

Thus when the cabinet met at 11.15 a.m. on the following morning, Asquith's problems were mounting. There was considerable uncertainty about the number of ministers who might resign, though Simon, Morley and Beauchamp seemed more likely to go than remain. Simon spoke after Morley. His statement to his cabinet colleagues was brief and emotional. 'Quivering lip and tears in his eyes', he appeared as determined as Morley to resign.[14] Lloyd George, whose views were clearly changing, made a strong appeal to Simon and other doubters not to go, or at least to delay their departure. Germany had now demanded unimpeded passage through Belgium.[15] Eventually all except Burns agreed to stay until Grey had made his statement to the Commons and the Commons had indicated its view.[16]

During the afternoon, however, Asquith placed considerable pressure on Simon to remain at his post. There is no record of precisely what the two men discussed, but by the evening it was clear that both Simon and Beauchamp were going to stay. An exchange of letters confirmed the position. Asquith wrote:

I have thought much over what you said this afternoon. I fully realise your point of view. And I am most anxious that, whatever I ask you to do, should not in any way compromise your future. In that respect, I think that I can fully safeguard you. After full reflection (in which I have in every respect had regard to your strong convictions), I am clearly of the opinion that, at such a moment as this, you have something that nearly approaches to a public duty, for the time being at any rate, to remain.[17]

To this Simon replied:

I feel in view of the assurance in your letter that I must respond to the appeal which it contains, and I am doing so with good will; though with a heavy heart.[18]

The important question is clearly Simon's motivation during these difficult hours. This is important not only in explaining why Simon remained in the government, but also because the interpretations which were made then and later began to colour that unfavourable portrait of him which has so blighted his historical reputation. It was perhaps the first illustration of the difficulties Simon had throughout his career in convincing people that his actions at important times were dictated by creditable motives. Hobhouse, the Postmaster General, felt that in agreeing to wait until after Grey had spoken in the Commons, Simon's conduct was 'almost despicable, because he pretended to a very special and personal abhorrence of killing in any shape'.[19] Discussing the episode some years later, Charles Masterman went even further. In his view Simon had waited to see which way the wind was blowing, noted the reaction of the Commons to Grey's speech and decided not to resign. 'Fancy shilly-shallying on a matter of right and wrong like that,' commented C. P. Scott contemptuously.[20] With an equal absence of charity historians have read into the exchange of letters between the Attorney-General and the Prime Minister a hint of future personal advancement sufficient to keep Simon at his post.[21] Yet it is equally possible to interpret Simon's actions in a way that does more credit to him.

Simon's was a complex mind. His motivation at this, as at other critical moments of his career, is not open to simplistic analysis. There is enough contemporary evidence to show that the decision whether or not to resign caused Simon great agonising and anguish. On 4 August Scott found him 'worn and tired'. At lunch Scott was 'more than ever impressed with his utter prostration'. Morally and physically Simon was like 'a man half-dead'. He did not know what to suggest or what to do.[22] It seems unlikely that Simon's actions were dictated by a cold and clinical analysis of his own self-interest. It is probably wrong to think that in the mounting tension of early August any single factor determined Simon on the line he eventually took. All his instincts and inclinations as an upholder of the radical traditions of pre-war Liberalism would have been against British participation, but there were powerful forces pressing him in the opposite direction. One was a sense of loyalty to his colleagues and to the Liberal party. As the crisis developed it became clear that Britain would intervene: the only question left was the political complexion of the British government that did so. On the day after his decision to remain had been taken Simon told Christopher Addison that an important consideration with him had been that any substantial number of resignations would have led to a Coalition government, 'which would assuredly be the grave of Liberalism'.[23] Had Simon gone, his potential for influence would have been limited. C. P. Scott confirmed his suspicion that opposition to the government line on the model of the Boer War would have been untenable. 'The stakes were too great.'[24] Germany's behaviour must surely also have played its part in Simon's calculations. After the meeting of the cabinet on the morning of 4 August Simon told Scott that he had been entirely deceived about Germany, recognising now that the war party there dictated policy and had deliberately played for and provoked the conflict.[25] Rather than just trimming in the wake of the parliamentary reaction to Grey's House of Commons speech on 3 August, it seems probable that Simon himself was moved by this performance, as he himself later claimed.[26]

None of this necessarily means that Simon ultimately embraced the idea of British intervention with enthusiasm. The issue of Belgian neutrality no doubt made it easier for him to swallow the government line, though it was probably not an unequivocal point of principle for him. Asquith's reference to safe-guarding Simon's future may just as well refer to the possibility of his withdrawal from the government at a later date, as to a veiled hint of ministerial advancement. A month into the War Simon was still insisting that he had acted to prevent the appearance of political disruption in the face of a grave national danger. This did not mean that he had withdrawn his objection to the basic policy. Riddell found him 'still very anti-war, peace at any price.'[27] He remained, thought C. P. Scott, 'an unattached member of the Cabinet and sits very lightly.'[28]

At all events Simon remained in a cabinet from which only Burns and Morley withdrew, this pair creating scarcely a ripple in the government's equanimity. Yet permanent damage had been done to Simon's reputation, at least in some minds. There were those who saw an unwillingness to face difficulties or assume responsibility for critical decisions. Where Simon had agonised over issues which were not clear-cut and without qualification, others sensed only equivocation. It was a reputation which would haunt the rest of his career.

The war crisis had clearly shaken Simon and left him ill at ease. He was, heard Asquith, in a very disgruntled mood, 'in trouble about his soul' and talking moodily of going to the front.[29] Throughout the autumn he never fully settled back into his work.[30] There were those who attributed Simon's problems to the continuing constitutional anomaly of the senior law officer holding a seat at the cabinet table, but in truth the difficulty was more fundamental. For some time Simon was unsure whether he had done the right thing in withdrawing his resignation. Nonetheless the Prime Minister still found him among the more useful of his colleagues in the early cabinet discussions on war policy,[31] possibly because he was prepared to question Kitchener's right to a monopoly of military information.[32] In October Simon had the chance to see the military situation for himself when visiting France with Lloyd George and Lord Reading. His inclusion in the party may have reflected the Chancellor's wish to convince someone known to be close to the Prime Minister of the need for more effective military action.[33]

By the spring Simon seemed to have recovered his composure. Asquith found the time to amuse his sweetheart, Venetia Stanley, by drawing up a ranking list of his cabinet colleagues in which he placed Simon joint seventh after Crewe, Grey, McKenna, Lloyd George, Churchill and Kitchener.[34] He was, the Prime Minister thought, becoming more useful as the War went on, particularly in the detailed work of cabinet committees.[35] 'I consider that his curve is moving steadily upward, now that he is convalescent from the malaise of last autumn.'[36] Hobhouse found him a very hard-working colleague and sensed a boundless ambition, with whose aims Simon would let nothing interfere.[37] That ambition clearly felt restrained in the office of Attorney-General and in mid-March 1915 Simon opened his heart to the Prime Minister on the frustrations of his position. Acknowledging that Asquith had done him a great favour in preventing his resignation – and political suicide – in August, Simon confessed to hating the law and being wedded to politics. 'He evidently chafes and frets in his present cage.' For the first time Asquith hinted at possible eventual promotion to the Home Office.[38] For the time being, however, Simon remained confined to the legal aspects of the War and the drafting of necessary legislation. His office did not carry a seat on the War Council which Asquith formed in November in the vain hope of speeding up the decision-making processes of government. His innate liberalism made him reluctant to recommend the suppression of seditious publications. 'I think myself,' he wrote of one piece by Horatio Bottomley, 'that we must let the access [sic] of misdirected zeal work itself out as it will do in a very few days.'[39] But the prosecution of alleged German spies came easier to him. One of the most interesting cases was that of Anton Kuepferle, who claimed to be an American citizen of Swiss birth, but whom Simon rightly believed to be a German officer. Kuepferle was tried in May 1915 but committed suicide during an adjournment in Simon's cross-examination.

History may conclude that Simon showed considerable foresight in predicting in August 1914 that the formation of a coalition government would entail the 'grave of Liberalism'. Nonetheless, when that development took place the following May, Simon was, at least in the short term, one of the gainers from the accompanying reconstruction of the cabinet. Historians have picked over every available piece of evidence without reaching a definitive conclusion on the pressures which moved Asquith to take the opposition parties into his administration. Simon did not play a role of any great significance in determining these events, but his experience does cast light upon the overall situation. Though Fitzroy predicted that Simon would be one of the casualties of the exercise,[40] he was in fact one of the few participants able to turn down one great office of state and await the offer of another.

Central to the reorganisation of the government and effectively a precondition of Unionist participation within it was the removal of Lord Haldane from the Woolsack. Haldane's pre-war attitude towards Germany had allowed Unionists to impugn his wartime patriotism. It was perhaps a sign that Asquith did not hold all the cards during this crisis that he had to accede to opposition pressure on this point, though Haldane had in any case by now lost Asquith's favour. Yet the fact that his senior office was offered to Simon strengthens the argument of those who have seen Asquith rather than his

Unionist opponents as the real architect of the reorganised government. Simon, like Haldane, had been attacked in the Conservative press, yet Asquith could think in terms of elevating him rather than dropping him from the government. Indeed it is interesting to note that those on the Liberal side who prospered in the reconstructed cabinet were essentially those of whom Asquith had spoken highly in his earlier musings to Venetia Stanley.

Simon would have been the youngest Lord Chancellor in history at forty-two. Lawyers found it difficult to imagine that anyone would decline the blue ribbon of their profession. Lord Justice Darling thought him 'the maddest lawyer in London' when he heard that Simon had done so.[41] But, after several days of reflection, turn it down he did. Simon discussed his position with Lloyd George on the night of 17 May and determined that he would not on any account go to the House of Lords. He was, however, anxious to give up the Attorney-Generalship and move into an area more intimately linked with the war effort. The discussion focused on three possible options – the Local Government Board, the Board of Trade and the Chief Secretaryship for Ireland. Of the three only the Board of Trade appealed to Simon. At least it offered him 'the hope of shuffling off this lawyer's coil which I have endured for so long'.[42] Simon's reasons for declining the Lord Chancellorship are entirely understandable. His dissatisfaction with the governmental legal offices was well known. Though the honour of elevation to the Woolsack in comparative youth would have been great, it would have left considerable question marks over Simon's political future. The office of Lord Chancellor has tended to mark the pinnacle of the holder's career and ex-Lord Chancellors have not usually moved on to other political posts, though Birkenhead and Hailsham were to be exceptions in the twenties and thirties. More assuredly, though, elevation to the peerage would probably have ruled out Simon's hopes of getting to the top in British politics. At this stage of his career he clearly believed that he had a sporting chance of succeeding Asquith in the Liberal leadership.

In view of the attitude he had shown at the outbreak of hostilities, it was not surprising that Simon viewed the prospect of coalition with considerable misgivings. Co-habitation with the proponents of a very different political philosophy held no attraction for him. Many who, like Simon, had voiced their misgivings in August 1914 now left the government and radicals feared that Simon and those who remained would be 'helpless before a solid force of Tories'.[43] Liberal MPs met to consider the situation on 19 May and Simon told a colleague that it would be no bad thing for the meeting to 'blow up steam' and let the Prime Minister know he could not count on the blind adherence of his party.[44] He felt bitterly about the sacking of Haldane while expressing relief that it was not he who had to replace him.[45] But at a personal level Simon's hopes were fulfilled. On 25 May Asquith offered him the Home Office, a more senior department than any he had discussed with Lloyd George and one which he accepted with enthusiasm.[46] 'I am glad,' he told the Lord Chief Justice, 'to be among the breakers.'[47]

Simon held office as Home Secretary for only seven months, but it was a period of critical importance for Britain's conduct of the War. By early 1915 it was apparent that, if victory were to be achieved, the country would have difficulty in maintaining its traditional stance of limited liability towards continental power struggles. Furthermore, during the course of the year the expectations fondly entertained by some that there might exist an easier route to success than that offered by the Western Front crashed in the ruins of the Dardanelles campaign. It was the hope of many of the protagonists of coalition that the infusion of Conservatism might dispel once and for all the *laissez-faire* doctrines of the government and Asquith's illusion that the War could be waged on the basis of 'business as usual'. Such hopes were largely disappointed. On the one hand, as has been argued above, it was Asquith and the Asquithian ethos which continued to dominate the councils of government after May 1915. On the other, the Prime Minister still failed to streamline a cumbersome decision-making machinery which was not ideal for peacetime government, let alone the demands of total war. Not surprisingly Simon found himself the object of some of the criticisms of those who still felt that not everything had been done to ensure ultimate victory. He was perceived to be closely linked with Asquith on both personal and political grounds, while his position as Home Secretary left him particularly vulnerable. He was not the man to stamp ruthlessly upon the voices of dissent nor extinguish totally the rights of individual liberty for the sake of the national good.

By the summer of 1915 the critics of the new government were already calling for further changes. 'I agree,' wrote F. S. Oliver to Leo Amery, Simon's old contemporary at All Souls, 'that Squiff and Squiffery (Simon, Birrell and *hoc genus omnium*) must go.' 'Liberalism,' he went on, 'in the worst sense of that vile word . . . is dead, *dead, dead.*'[48] The last was a sentiment which Simon, with rather different emotions, probably shared. The Imperialist Lord Milner, a prime mover in the drive to create a more effective war directorate, expressed himself in very similar terms in August. What was needed, he believed, was 'the consistent display of qualities which are the absolute antithesis of what we know of Asquith, McKenna, Simon *et hoc genus omne*.'[49] Likewise Walter Long, an elder statesman of the Conservative party, regarded Simon as 'no better than McKenna'.[50] Yet while the Home Secretary was not sufficiently strident for the protagonists of all-out war, his behaviour also disappointed those who looked to him to protect traditional Liberal values inside an increasingly compulsionist government. Simon, from his earlier career, knew personally some of the leaders of the Union of Democratic Control, a body which had been set up in September 1914 less in outright opposition to the War than as an attempt to steer the national war effort on to more enlightened tracks. Meetings of the Union were occasionally broken up amid violent scenes in the excess of

patriotic zeal which still characterised the nation in 1915. C. P. Trevelyan
had a personal interview with Simon but got little satisfaction about future
protection. It was difficult for men like Trevelyan to appreciate the delicacy
of Simon's position. Whatever his gut instincts, he was a senior government
minister, loyal to the Prime Minister and his policies. Trevelyan's comment
that Simon 'might easily have been on our side of the fence with another
ounce weight of moral courage' showed neither charity nor understanding.[51]
When the police seized a stock of UDC pamphlets in August, Trevelyan
reacted angrily, accusing Simon of not having lifted a finger to suppress the
press attacks upon the Union and its suggestions about the future peace.
Even though Simon was not directly responsible for what had happened –
this had been instigated by the Director of Public Prosecutions acting for the
new Attorney-General, Sir Edward Carson – Trevelyan accurately posed
the dilemma which Simon now faced:

I hope you will take a fair view of where you are going. You remained in the
Government because you thought that it would be well to have some Liberalism left
in high places. Do you imagine that, if you start with this, you are going to be able to
stop? The outcome before long must be that you will have to begin imprisoning men
for their opinions. For you cannot think that in England you are going to silence us,
or anyone else, by police bullying of this kind . . . It is at present incredible to me,
who have hitherto regarded you as an exceptionally clear-sighted Liberal, that you
should become the instrument of reaction.[52]

Simon was in a similarly difficult position regarding the activities of the No
Conscription Fellowship against the government's Derby Scheme, which
many accurately foresaw as the harbinger of compulsion. Pressure was
strong to mount a prosecution, but all Simon's sympathies were with the
voices of dissent. When confronted with a report of the Fellowship's
activities he merely minuted, 'I think it is politic to avoid proceedings if
possible.'[53]

When press attacks came from the right Simon was understandably
readier to take action. In October the Home Secretary arranged for a dossier
to be printed showing the 'poisonous effect' abroad of Northcliffe's *Times*
and *Daily Mail*. Simon was ready to ban their publication, but the cabinet
did not endorse his plan.[54] On 6 November, however, *The Globe* was
suppressed for reporting that Lord Kitchener had been forced to resign from
the government because of the intrigues of his colleagues.[55] Simon spoke on
the matter in the Commons on 30 November, but even so could not avoid the
criticism of opponents within the government and outside. The speech
seems to have been arranged with the Prime Minister behind the back of the
cabinet, or at least the Unionist members of it.[56] Churchill commented that
Simon had made a long attack on Northcliffe 'which would certainly have
been very damaging if it had not been made by a prig and a bore',[57] while
Lord Riddell noted Simon's 'evident anxiety to meet the newspaper editors'.
'He is a sly fellow eaten up with ambition.'[58]

Yet while Simon's erstwhile allies on the left became increasingly disillusioned with his ministerial performance, the Home Secretary was working behind the scenes to uphold traditional Liberal values. On the issue of conscription he was clear. He and Walter Runciman 'concerted measures to confound the conscriptionists', working inside the cabinet and in the parliamentary lobby, and encouraging political agitation.[59] But the pressure of Simon's opponents mounted constantly, causing the Home Secretary to set out his thoughts to Asquith at the end of August 1915. The conscription controversy was being conducted, thought Simon, on terms that were grossly unfair to the opponents of the proposed innovation. The majority of those who were determined to resist it kept silent in the interests of national unity and because 'we are confident that at the right moment you [Asquith] will deal faithfully with the conspirators.' The advocates of National Service on the other hand showed no such restraint. The time had come, according to the Home Secretary, for Asquith to make more clear the weighty arguments against conscription:

A pronouncement from you that, having examined the contentions on either side, you are satisfied that the change could not be made without imperilling national unity to a degree for which no military reorganisation would compensate, would have an immense effect.[60]

Yet leading from the front was no more characteristic of Asquith's wartime premiership that it was of Simon himself. The Prime Minister, moreover, was no longer as wedded to the voluntary principle as Simon imagined. Not surprisingly the dispute within the government rumbled on. Increasingly Simon came to regard Lloyd George as his leading opponent on the conscription issue. Differences within the cabinet were so acute that Simon believed that the country might have to face a general election on the issue.[61] But he expressed his determination to stand by the Prime Minister, confident that Asquith would never betray his trust.[62]

By December it was becoming clear that the battle was not going Simon's way. The figures that came out of the Derby Scheme offered patent justification at least to bring in the conscription of single men and on 3 December Simon sent the Prime Minister his letter of resignation. Not even the persuasive talents of his old colleague Lord Reading could, it seemed, make Simon change his mind. He was, he argued, not thinking of his personal convenience but of the public service: 'Home Office work cannot go on much longer with a locum tenens.'[63] Yet once more Simon hesitated. Asquith set up a small cabinet committee chaired by Walter Long to consider 'what form any amendment to the law in the direction of compulsion should take', and made the Home Secretary a member of it.[64] For the time being the question of resignation was deferred. Simon's contribution to the deliberations of the committee is not recorded, but it seems unlikely that he had anything constructive to offer. Two days after Christmas he wrote again to the Prime Minister. This time his decision was irrevocable.

My firm conviction is that whatever additional numbers may be got by it, compulsion
would produce disunion, and would so make the country weaker instead of stronger;
consequently I could not in any circumstances support it.[65]

Simon attended his last cabinet meeting the following day.

For a while it seemed that the level of support for Simon within the cabinet
might be such as to compel the government to think again. While the Prime
Minister 'dropped on the right [pro-conscription] side', McKenna and
Runciman objected to the decision to introduce conscription and said that
they too would have to consider their positions.[66] Asquith wrote to the three
dissenters later that day in terms designed to appeal as much to their vanity
as to their reason. There were, he stressed, no three colleagues whom on
both personal and public grounds he valued more highly and would more
acutely miss. Stressing that he himself would gladly be released from the
burdens of government but for a sense of duty, Asquith called upon his
ministers to avoid delivering 'a shattering blow to the Government and I
honestly believe to the National Cause'.[67] Worse, however, was to follow.
The next day Edward Grey, the Foreign Secretary, told Asquith that should
McKenna and Runciman leave, he would be obliged to follow them. Though
Grey was not the force within the government that he had been until the
outbreak of hostilities, his resignation might still have had fatal consquences
for Asquith's continued premiership. Desperate efforts were now made to
limit the damage. While Asquith worked on Grey, Maurice Hankey, Secretary to the War Committee and a far more significant figure at the level of
policy making than his bureaucratic status might suggest, sought a possible
basis for compromise. Significantly there were subtle variations in the
thoughts of those who opposed the proposed Military Service Bill. Hankey
found out that even Robertson, the Chief of the Imperial General Staff,
shared the concern of some of the dissidents that the country's economic
resources might be insufficient to support a long war. He suggested that the
proposed legislation should proceed but that the military and economic
authorities should meet to determine just how many divisions the country
could afford to maintain. Hankey's proposals were enough to persuade
Runciman and McKenna to remain at their posts.[68]

For Simon, however, a subtly different point of principle was at stake.
Though not unmoved by the Prime Minister's entreaties he could not be
brought to change his mind. 'You will not doubt,' he told Asquith, 'that in
taking another course I am acting under the compulsion of a conviction
which I cannot disregard.'[69] When the cabinet met on New Year's Day
Simon was not present. His resignation had been announced that morning.
Though differences of opinion remained acute, Grey, McKenna and
Runciman all seemed ready to fight their corner from within. There were no
further withdrawals.

As with his actions at the time of the War's outbreak, the question of Simon's motivation is all-important. The opinions of contemporary observers are significant less because they accurately reflect the workings of Simon's mind than because they reveal the difficulty which lesser intellects had in appreciating his point of view. Even Asquith spoke a little unkindly at this time of Simon 'in his self-righteousness'.[70] Lord Selborne, the President of the Board of Agriculture, could not understand why a man who had drawn up a bill to compel serving professional soldiers to continue in the army should now resign over the prospect of compelling those who had hitherto given no service.[71] On the surface Simon's attitudes did seem to be inconsistent. When told that Raymond Asquith, the Prime Minister's elder son, was about to join up, he had not replied with the expected show of anguish and dismay. 'No, I think it's quite right. The time has now come when one can only feel sorry for those who are unable to go'.[72] Only days before his resignation he had written disparagingly of 'Quakers, conscientious objectors and cranks' in a memorandum presented to the cabinet.[73] One of his last official acts as Home Secretary was to turn down an appeal from the socialist Philip Snowden to remit the sentences on two individuals sentenced to six months' hard labour for publishing a leaflet opposing conscription and the War.[74]

Not surprisingly, many interpreted Simon's withdrawal less as a matter of conviction and honour than as a political miscalculation. Sir Almeric Fitzroy found an explanation which matched the complexity of Simon's motivation only in terms of his own tortuous vocabulary:

his mental disposition, ignoring the broad harmonies of conduct, leads him to dwell on superficial contradictions – an intermittent scrupulosity of conscience finds its complement in the timidity of the over-trained lawyer.[75]

Howard Baker, MP, suggested that Simon wanted to make himself 'conspicuous in the favour of the Liberal Party with an eye for the future'.[76] Lord Esher perhaps held a similar view. '[Simon] will be Prime Minister one of these days, for sure. . . .'[77] F. E. Smith was among those who thought that Simon had banked on not being alone in his resignation, a view shared by Lord Curzon.[78]

Simon probably was disappointed to find that no other cabinet minister followed him on to the back benches over the conscription question,[79] but this is not to question the sincerity of his motivation. The point of principle for him that it was wrong to compel a man to be a soldier was narrow but crucial. Nothing better attested to the centrality of his Liberal convictions. Secondary calculations confirmed him in his view. Simon believed that the political turmoil which would result from the abandonment of the voluntary principle would destroy national unity and not justify the increase in numbers for the Front. In this respect he miscalculated badly. The trend of public opinion was moving strongly towards conscription. The country wanted to win the War and was ready to accept the necessary sacrifices. But if there was any popular opposition to conscription its suppression would, of course, become the responsibility of the Home Secretary, a task for which Simon had no stomach. There is also evidence that Simon anticipated that the Military Service Bill was ultimately intended for the purpose of industrial coercion.[80] But in resigning at this time, what Simon could not have anticipated was that his loss of office would extend for more than fifteen years. The stunning progress which had taken Simon so rapidly up the ladder of political advancement to one of the great offices of state, had come to an abrupt halt. He would spend the middle years of political life waiting for a second chance. At least in terms of his own career there is poignant understatement in Simon's remark written many years later: 'I have long since realised that my opposition was a mistake.'[81]

Contemporary comments also reveal the extent to which Simon's standing had fallen since the outbreak of the War. His departure was 'no loss', thought Winston Churchill.[82] The pity was that he had not been followed by others who had 'not got their hearts in the war'.[83] F. E. Smith's reaction was predictable despite his already long association with Simon. 'Sliman' [sic] was pegging out 'a claim in the garbage' and had 'done himself in'.[84] But most revealing was the comment of Sir Almeric Fitzroy, Clerk to the Privy Council:

With all his brilliant gifts he is no great loss to the Government; neither as Attorney-General nor Secretary of State has he fulfilled the hopes of his friends. He would have done better for his fame if he had not listened to the voice of ambition, and followed the example of Lord Morley and John Burns.[85]

Like the party which he represented and the political philosophy which he espoused Simon had been the victim of the War itself. Its demands ran counter to his inner beliefs about the legitimate relationship between the state and the individual. Its effective waging called for a ruthlessness which, for all his ambition, was not within him.

Yet the impact of war could never be erased. If Simon's brand of nineteenth-century Liberalism was to cope with the sort of society whose advent the War had hastened, he too would need to change. His old friend Leo Amery confronted Simon with the dilemma which now faced him. His letter to Simon, written a week after the latter's resignation, merits extensive quotation:

You and the political principles and traditions you most cherish have come up against the facts of a new world which is incompatible with them. Whatever their intrinsic truth they have no real relation to the facts of today – or of many years past. The peculiar conserving effects of our party system have kept them politically alive for more than a generation after their time. But the last ten years have been, not the herald of some great advance but the last backwash of a tide that has run out and may not come back for generations.

Amery was clear on how Simon should now react.

Don't be tempted by your feelings to throw yourself hence-forward into a campaign of opposition and waste the rest of your life in vain opposition to all the inevitable changes that the new order of things will bring with it during the war and after the war . . . Sit down and think the world out for yourself anew. Become for a few years a dispassionate student of the Empire's and the world's affairs – or of the affairs of a single factory or backstreet. Then come back again, five years hence or ten years hence, with a new view and a new message. You will still be young, you will still have the prestige of all you achieved before the war, and above all you will be in the position of being able to get something real done instead of merely striving for the rest of your days to fight against the whole main stream of the Nation's life and thought.[86]

It would be some time before Simon responded to Amery's advice, but there was something in what he said.

Central to Simon's problems at the beginning of 1916 was his political isolation. It was, as Margot Asquith pointed out, ironic that just when Conservatives such as Selborne, Curzon and Austen Chamberlain were threatening resignation because the Prime Minister would not go far enough, Simon should leave the government because he had gone too far.[87] It was not that Simon was alone in his opposition to conscription. Indeed those who agreed with him were sometimes referred to as the 'Simon group'. Yet the majority of anti-conscriptionists were to the left of Simon in general political terms and had not hitherto been his natural allies. By the summer Simon was acting in conjunction with the members of the Independent Labour Party, a political and parliamentary association which could not have been envisaged before 1914. Colonel Repington, military correspondent of *The Times* thought of Simon's new colleagues as 'the riff-raff of the Left' and it is clear that Simon too felt uncomfortable in his new surroundings, regarding many of his supporters as 'cranks'.[88] For the time being, however, the ex-minister determined to make the best of a bad job. If he could use his unquestioned debating talents to rally to his cause some of the many moderate Liberals who at heart detested conscription, his position might be greatly strengthened. Disquiet in the House of Commons could not but encourage opposition in the country, perhaps rendering the new law inoperable. But the government was not slow to cut the ground from under Simon's feet. Two days after his resignation a revised draft of the Military Service Bill was issued containing the additional ground of conscientious objection to bearing arms on which exemption might be claimed.[89]

The crucial first test came with Simon's speech on the Military Service Bill on 5 January. By general consent the speech was a failure, badly received by the House as a whole. In a leading article *The Times* commented that the speech was 'long and not convincing . . . and not to the point'.[90] Simon tried to argue that the debate concerned a basic change in national life rather than a redemption of Asquith's pledge of November that married men would not be asked to serve until all single men had enlisted. There was some justice in his criticism of discrepancies in the quoted figures and of defects in the National Register and the recruiting machinery generally. But none of this could escape the fact that the Prime Minister's pledge could not possibly be kept without some measure of compulsion.[91] Simon claimed that the condition that compulsion should only be adopted by general consent had been abandoned. Instead it appeared that compulsion was being introduced without regard to the numbers to be conscripted or the strength of opposition.[92] Asquith, though, insisted that no question of principle was involved, while for the Unionists Arthur Balfour pleaded with Simon not to rock national unity by forcing a division.

On the surface the outcome of the debate was not unsatisfactory for Simon. Richard Holt, one of the dissidents, believed they had at least 'made out a case.'[93] Though 403 members voted for the government, 105 went into the opposing lobby, while more than a hundred others abstained. Significantly, however, out of the 105 outright opponents sixty were Irish Nationalists. The effective opposition thus comprised eleven Labour members and thirty-four Liberals.[94] Several Liberal critics of conscription such as J. W. Wilson and Charles Hobhouse 'failed us at the last moment' and either supported the government or abstained.[95]

The experience of opposing those who had so recently been his colleagues left Simon shaken and anxious to be reassured that he had taken the right step. But as the government rushed the Military Service Bill through its various parliamentary stages, there was little time for Simon to reflect. The forthcoming second reading debate left him fearful of a less sympathetic reaction than had been given to what was effectively his resignation speech on 5 January. To C. P. Scott of the *Manchester Guardian* he seemed 'much too full of these little sensitivenesses which don't consort with the vigour of the fighting man. It was all an intellectual exercise to him and he had none of the joy of battle.' To Scott Simon outlined his strategy. He would go through with his opposition to the end of the Bill's committee stage, then accept the result and end on a conciliatory note, conscious that such an attitude would disappoint his supporters. Simon 'hated his task', felt his effective isolation deeply and 'hoped he was right'.[96]

Downhearted by the way things had turned out Simon considered joining the army, a step which Winston Churchill – now clearly feeling sorry for his former colleague in his misfortunes – encouraged him to take. Churchill, himself at the Front with the Sixth Royal Scots Fusiliers, wrote Simon a note:

telling him he is vy welcome to come here if he likes. I will look after him and teach him soldiering and he wd be a pleasant companion to teach me law . . . A cabinet minister can fight in the trenches; but to be drilled by a sergeant in the barrack yard – invests adversity with a squalid air.[97]

For the time being, however, Simon preferred to soldier on in parliament and in February became chairman of a small organisation of anti-conscriptionists, intended to be some form of permanent opposition.[98] At the end of the month Simon launched a further attack on what had now become the Military Service Act, claiming that it was not being administered fairly. He argued that men exempted on the basis that they were indispensible in civilian occupations were still being persuaded to enlist and that medical certificates were being torn up by recruiting officers.[99] Again, in the Army Estimates debate on 16 March, Simon spoke as the government's principal critic, attacking the workings of conscription, especially with regard to married men who were now being called up.[100]

In the following month rumours circulated that Asquith was ready to stand down. On 19 April Simon joined more than a hundred other Liberal MPs in passing a resolution that Asquith's continued premiership was a national necessity. The first resolution submitted to the meeting would have given the Prime Minister a blank cheque and it was on Simon's suggestion that the wording was modified.[101] Yet Asquith would have been ready to take Simon back into the fold. Augustine Birrell's resignation following the Easter Rising in Dublin left the premier 'in despair for a Chief Secretary' and regretting that Simon was not available.[102] It was, though, a sign of the changed nature of Simon's position after his resignation that others envisaged for him a very different role from renewed ministerial service under Asquith. The anti-imperialist theoretician J. A. Hobson wanted Simon to hold himself in readiness to take the lead if military deadlock compelled negotiations for peace. Then he could take up 'the endeavour to recover or retain the lost or imperilled fortresses of political and civil liberty, i.e. a fight against militarism, conscription, protection and bureaucratic nationalism, for liberty, sound finance and constructive internationalism.'[103] Simon does not appear to have responded to this appeal. Perhaps association with someone of Hobson's left-wing credentials was more than he could stomach. Yet he was concerned at the absence of clearly stated war aims and looked for a pronouncement 'in plain black and white' of the irreducible minimum for which the Allies were ready to go on fighting until the point of exhaustion.[104] For the time being Simon took refuge in renewed legal work, presiding over the judicial inquiry into the shooting of the pacifist Sheehy Skeffington in Portobello Barracks. Yet even this was 'a horrid job'.[105] The second half of the year saw him active in parliament on the Special Register Bill – 'a bill which is going to add a series of absentees to the register and is going to do nothing else'[106] – and as a member of the First Speaker's Conference considering electoral reform, where he was particularly effective in shaping the report produced in January 1917.[107]

Despite the attitude he had adopted in April, the fall of Asquith's Coalition in December, and its replacement by a government headed by Lloyd George, caused Simon no regrets. Thomas Jones saw him 'rubbing his hands almost gleefully.'[108] In the circumstances Christopher Addison's evidence that Simon played a part in thwarting an attempted compromise to the governmental crisis, whereby Asquith would have remained Prime Minister without being a member of the proposed small war directorate, seems entirely plausible.[109] The fact was that Simon welcomed the opportunity to rejoin his former colleagues and escape from the left-wing embrace which had been his political impediment since January. Attributing all evil to 'Northcliffe plus conscription', Simon now called for 'a Liberal opposition – patriotic in the real Asquith sense' to get the country out of its present 'awful hole'.[110] The division in the Liberal ranks in December 1916 was far more fundamental than a personal quarrel between Lloyd George and Asquith. Two very different conceptions of Liberalism existed in the camps of the two men's supporters and Simon had no doubts about which offered him his natural home.

Simon and Liberals who felt as he did had a clear view of what to do next. Assiduous attendance at the Commons and purposeful leadership of his followers would, according to Richard Holt, enable Asquith to recapture the initiative and put a rapid end to 'the L. G. villainy'.[111] But Asquith would not play the role for which Asquithians hoped. In part paralysed by his own patriotism, the former Prime Minister realised that he would not be able to form another war government even if Lloyd George were defeated in parliament. After the change of government he singularly failed to inspire those Liberals who were looking for a forthright defence of their party's principles or to provide effective parliamentary leadership. In the circumstances it was not surprising that Simon soon began to reconsider his position. During the illness of the new Home Secretary, Herbert Samuel, he offered his services to Lloyd George to help in the drafting and preparation of the new Representation of the People Bill.[112] Later in 1917 Simon even agreed to represent the Prime Minister in a libel case against two Liberal newspapers before his conscience got the better of him and convinced him that he should withdraw from the case.[113]

The progress of the War, despite America's entry in April, left Simon increasingly demoralised. A secret session of the Commons in May convinced him that there was still no prospect of imminent victory and that 'we must go on bleeding at every pore until next [year]'.[114] Yet while victory was still elusive, the idea of a compromise peace with Germany remained a non-starter as far as the government was concerned. Dissatisfied with the work he was able to do in parliament – 'Committes on the future of railways and on the control of coal are offered me'[115] – still uneasy about some of the associations which political opposition involved, and keen to show that the line he had taken over conscription was by no means synonymous with anti-war pacifism, Simon took the decision to enlist. As Simon's motives were so often questioned during the course of his long career, it is pertinent to note that at forty-two he was over military age and that it would now have been easy for him to return to the lucrative private legal practice which he had relinquished on becoming Solicitor-General. He offered his services with commendable modesty:

as long as you do not turn me on to a lawyer's job, I will exhibit my only military qualification, viz: a willingness to do what I am told as well as I can.[116]

General Haig, Commander-in-Chief of the British Army in France, formed a favourable impression of his new recruit – 'most charming and very able' – and decided with some prompting from Asquith to employ him as an intelligence officer in the Flying Corps, attached to General Trenchard's staff.[117] Despite an inauspicious first encounter with Trenchard in October 1917 at which Simon felt the rough edge of the general's tongue, a good working relationship soon developed between the two men, even to the extent that Trenchard later spread exaggerated stories of Simon's heroic prowess.[118]

Though political allies regretted his departure,[119] Simon found considerable satisfaction in his new environment, though he never changed his mind about the hideous waste of life which the War entailed. 'Flying (except that beastly spiral descent) is gorgeous.'[120] The Royal Flying Corps was 'one of the most wonderful things of the war',[121] and though 'a complete ignoramus' Simon felt he was again being of some little use.[122] Trenchard found Simon particularly useful when he entrusted to him the task of purchasing supplies and materials for the Air Force from French manufacturers in Paris. Simon felt fitter and his nerves were steadier after his arrival at the front. 'Soldiering suits me very well,' he told his old chief, Lord Reading.[123] Yet there were undoubtedly other and more personal reasons for Simon's increasing peace of mind. In Paris in December he remarried after fifteen years of widowerhood. His bride, Kathleen Manning, was the widow of a Dublin doctor. She had originally been employed by Simon as governess for his children. Later, and no longer in Simon's household, she had invoked his assistance on behalf of her son Brian who had become a prisoner of war in Germany. The renewed relationship quickly blossomed into romance.

It was perhaps renewed domestic happiness which encouraged Simon to give further thought to his political future. He had by now abandoned his earlier intention to seek election in Manchester, but his success in a post-war contest at Walthamstow, which had never been a truly safe seat, was by no means certain and there were attempts to make him consider standing for Pembrokeshire where the traditions of Liberalism seemed more firmly entrenched.[124] At all events Simon's services were once more in considerable demand by the beginning of 1918 as the War began to take a decisive turn. While Lord Beauchamp, a fellow waverer from the cabinet of 1914, urged him to return to parliament to put backbone into Asquith's opposition, the War Office sought Simon's services in a special intelligence post at General Headquarters.[125] But the event which brought together Simon's war service and his role as a politician was a crisis over Trenchard's position at the head of the Royal Flying Corps. Trenchard had experienced a difficult relationship with the government since the appointment of Lord Rothermere, brother of Lord Northcliffe, as Secretary for Air in November 1917. It was perhaps inevitable that two men of such independent and forceful character should clash and Trenchard became progressively convinced that Rothermere was seeking to undermine his position. Trenchard found his political chief intolerably arrogant and obstinate and their relationship deteriorated rapidly after the middle of February 1918. Finally Trenchard submitted his resignation in mid-March, though the formal announcement of this was delayed until the beginning of April.

As both a commissioned officer under Trenchard's command and a member of parliament Simon was in a difficult position, but he made it clear that he would speak in Trenchard's defence when the Commons debated the Air Service Vote.[126] Rothermere, who had earlier questioned the propriety of Simon's position to Lloyd George, protested – but to no avail.[127] As Simon told the House, in a vigorous defence of Trenchard, he 'could not discharge the duty which lies upon me . . . if I sat silent throughout this debate and did not endeavour to indicate to the House what I certainly must observe is very necessary that the House should know.'[128] When Rothermere himself resigned from the government shortly afterwards, Simon was pleased but conscious that this was but poor compensation for the loss of Trenchard:

I assert without hesitation that he is the finest organiser in the fighting services. . . . If you know Trenchard personally, you know that he is a jewel of the first water who sets an example to a great many other people in the matter of straightness and modesty.[129]

Not surprisingly Simon paid dearly in the pages of the Northcliffe press for his loyalty to Trenchard.[130]

In August John Buchan, Minister of Information, sounded Simon out about the possibility of taking on the post of British High Commissioner in Washington. Simon, however, was not enthusiastic, raising problems about his seat in parliament and eventually declined the offer.[131] Churchill, now Minister of Munitions, finding Simon 'well disposed to the Government and . . . quite ready to recognise the facts of the situation,' wanted him to become chairman of a Reconstruction and Demobilisation Committee of the Ministry of Munitions.[132] But Simon chose instead to accept an offer from Addison to head a Wages Awards Committee whose brief was to investigate the problems relating to compulsory wage awards that would be posed by the return of peace. The appointment ended his career in the forces and he returned 'with renewed faith in the future of England if only we tackle the problems of reconstruction in the right way'. Though not self-evidently a matter of compelling importance the work appealed to Simon. He was concerned that the shared experience of war should be used to the benefit of post-war industrial relations.

Each side has got to know more of the other and everybody has in a measure been contributing to a common end out in France. It will be a dreadful disaster if this is followed by violent times and disagreements at home.[133]

The end of the war came with almost as much suddenness as had its advent. After so many disappointed expectations there were those who were ready to believe that hostilities would never cease. Military planners certainly envisaged that the struggle would continue throughout 1919. Simon had been at the front when in March the German forces had launched their last desperate attempt, before the full weight of the American war machine arrived in Europe, to secure that military victory which had hitherto been denied to both sides. Thereafter Germany was constantly on the defensive. By the autumn her position was desperate. Victory finally came not through a massive military triumph but as the result of the slow yet remorseless exhaustion of Germany's capacity to carry on. On 11 November, after more than four years and perhaps nine million fatal casualties, the fighting ceased. Along with everyone else who had survived Simon prepared to pick up the pieces of his pre-war career.

Notes

1 Speech by Lloyd George, reported in *Evening Standard* 10 Nov. 1934.
2 Fry, *Lloyd George and Foreign Policy* p. 206.
3 C. Hazlehurst, *Politicians at War – July 1914 to May 1915* (London, 1971) chapter 5, passim.
4 Viscount Morley, *Memorandum on Resignation, August 1914* (London, 1928) p. 3.
5 Fitzroy, *Memoirs* ii, 338.
6 Brocks (eds.), *Asquith Letters* p. 140.
7 Hazlehurst, *Politicians* p. 66. Those meeting with Simon were Lloyd George, Harcourt, Beauchamp, Pease and Runciman.
8 Morley, *Memorandum* p. 14; Fry, *Lloyd George* p. 197; Samuel, *Memoirs* p. 104.
9 Morley, *Memorandum* p. 16; Diary of J. A. Pease for 2 Aug. 1914, K. Wilson (ed.), 'The Cabinet Diary of J. A. Pease 24 July to 5 Aug. 1914', *Proceedings of the Leeds Philosophical and Literary Society* xix, 3 (1983) p. 47.
10 Simon to Burns 2 Aug. 1914, SP 50 fo. 96. Burns replied, 'It is then too late.'
11 D. Marquand, *Ramsay MacDonald* (London, 1977) p. 164.
12 J. McEwen (ed.), *The Riddell Diaries 1908–1923* (London, 1986) p. 87.
13 Simon to Asquith 2 Aug. 1914, SP 2 fo. 17.

14 Morley, *Memorandum* p. 26.

15 H. Asquith, *Memories and Reflections* (London, 1928) ii, 20.

16 E. David (ed.), *Asquith's Cabinet* p. 180.

17 Asquith to Simon 3 Aug. 1914, SP 2 fo. 17.

18 Simon to Asquith 4 Aug. 1914, ibid fo. 18.

19 David (ed.), *Asquith's Cabinet* p. 180.

20 L. Masterman, *C. F. G. Masterman: A Biography* (London, 1939) p. 330.

21 Hazlehurst, *Politicians* p. 112; A. J. A. Morris, *Radicalism against War* (London, 1972) p. 401.

22 T. Wilson (ed.), *Scott Diaries* pp. 96–7.

23 C. Addison, *Politics from Within* (London, 1924) i, 38; C. Addison, *Four and a half Years* (London, 1934) i, 35.

24 P. Clarke, *New Liberalism* pp. 196–7.

25 T. Wilson (ed.), *Scott Diaries* p. 96.

26 *Retrospect* p. 95.

27 McEwen (ed.), *Riddell Diaries* p. 89.

28 T. Wilson, *Scott Diaries* p. 103.

29 Brocks (eds.), *Asquith Letters* p. 200.

30 Fitzroy, *Memoirs* ii, 586.

31 Brocks (eds.), *Asquith Letters* p. 179.

32 Hazlehurst, *Politicians* p. 148.

33 J. Grigg, *Lloyd George: From Peace to War* (London, 1985) p. 179.

34 Brocks (eds.), *Asquith Letters* p. 452.

35 Margot Asquith diary 7 March 1915, cited M. Gilbert, *Winston S. Churchill* vol. 3 (London, 1971) p. 330.

36 Brocks (eds.), *Asquith Letters* p. 475.

37 David (ed.), *Asquith's Cabinet* pp. 229–30.

38 Brocks (eds.), *Asquith Letters* p. 482.

39 T. Wilson, *The Downfall of the Liberal Party 1914–1935* (London, 1968) p. 171.

40 Fitzroy, *Memoirs* ii, 593.

41 Addison, *Politics from Within* i, 59.

42 Simon to Lloyd George 18 May 1915, Lloyd George MSS C/8/3/8. R. F. V. Heuston, *Lives of the Lord Chancellors 1885–1940* (Oxford, 1964) p. 265, suggests that the addressee of this letter was Sir Stanley Buckmaster, but Simon seems to have written to 'L. G.' rather than 'S[olicitor] G[eneral]'.

43 A. J. A. Morris, *C. P. Trevelyan 1870–1958: Portrait of a Radical* (Belfast, 1977) p. 135.

44 David (ed.), *Asquith's Cabinet* p. 245.

45 Addison, *Four and a half Years* i, 82; Heuston, *Lord Chancellors 1885–1940* p. 224.

46 Asquith to Simon 25 May 1915 and Simon to Asquith 25 May 1915, SP 50 fos. 203 and 205.

47 Simon to Reading 3 June 1915, SP 51 fo. 51.

48 J. Barnes and D. Nicholson (eds.), *The Leo Amery Diaries* vol. 1 (London, 1980) p. 123.

49 P. Lockwood, 'Milner's Entry into the War Cabinet in 1916', *Historical Journal* 7, 1, (1964) p. 120.

50 Sir C. Petrie, *Walter Long and his Times* (London, 1936) pp. 193–4.

51 M. Swartz, *The Union of Democratic Control in British Politics during the First World War* (Oxford, 1971) pp. 109–10.
52 Trevelyan to Simon 22 Aug. 1915, C. P. Trevelyan MSS 76.
53 J. Rae, *Conscience and Politics* (Oxford, 1970) pp. 18–19.
54 Simon to Asquith 30 Oct. 1915, SP 51 fos. 103–4.
55 Simon diary Nov. 1915, SP 2 fo. 27.
56 A. Chamberlain to Simon 1 Dec. 1915, SP 51 fo. 157; C. à C. Repington, *The First World War 1914–1918* vol. 1 (London, 1920) pp. 83–4.
57 Gilbert, *Churchill* iii, 593.
58 McEwen (ed.), *Riddell Diaries* p. 138.
59 Hazlehurst, *Politicians* p. 268.
60 Simon to Asquith 25 Aug. 1915, SP 51 fos. 89–91.
61 T. Wilson, *Scott Diaries* p. 134.
62 David, *Asquith's Cabinet* p. 256.
63 Simon to Asquith 3 Dec. 1915, Asquith MSS 28 fo. 279.
64 Rae, *Conscience* p. 22; R. J. Q. Adams and P. Poirier, *The Conscription Controversy in Great Britain 1900–1918* (London, 1987) p. 133.
65 Simon to Asquith 27 Dec. 1915, SP 52 fos. 22–3.
66 Rae, *Conscience* p. 25; K. O. Morgan (ed.), *Family Letters* p. 181.
67 Asquith to Simon, R. McKenna and W. Runciman 28 Dec. 1915, SP 52 fos. 26–7.
68 Rae, *Conscience* pp. 25–6; Grigg, *From Peace to War* p. 330; D. French, *British Strategy and War Aims 1914–1916* (London, 1986) p. 172.
69 Simon to Asquith 29 Dec. 1915, Asquith MSS 28 fos. 281–2.
70 Jenkins, *Asquith* p. 388.
71 Note by Selborne on his cabinet colleagues, 1916, Selborne MSS 80 fo. 288.
72 C. Asquith, *Diaries 1915–1918* (London, 1968) p. 88.
73 Memorandum for cabinet 24 Dec. 1915, CAB 37/139/53.
74 D. Boulton, *Objection Overruled* (London, 1967) p. 89.
75 Fitzroy, *Memoirs* ii, 616.
76 C. Asquith, *Diaries* p. 117.
77 Brett, *Esher* iv, 1.
78 Campbell, *F. E. Smith* p. 425; Repington, *First World War* i, 107.
79 McEwen (ed.), *Riddell Diaries* p. 144.
80 S. Koss, *Asquith* (London, 1976) p. 203.
81 *Retrospect* p. 107.
82 Gilbert, *Churchill* iii companion pt 2 p. 1355.
83 Ibid, p. 1354.
84 Ibid, p. 1366.
85 Fitzroy, *Memoirs* ii, 616.
86 Amery to Simon 8 Jan. 1916, SP 52 fos. 91–3.
87 D. Bennett, *Margot: A Life of the Countess of Oxford and Asquith* (London, 1984) p. 265.
88 Repington, *First World War* i, 102; T. Wilson, *Scott Diaries* p. 172.
89 Rae, *Conscience* pp. 27–8. The wording was later changed to 'undertaking combatant service'.
90 *The Times* 6 Jan. 1916.
91 Addison, *Politics from Within* i, 244.

92 House of Commons Debates, 5th Series, vol. LXXVII, cols. 962–78.

93 Holt diary 9 Jan. 1916, 920 DUR 1/10.

94 Rae, *Conscience* pp. 36–7; K. Robbins, *The Abolition of War* (Cardiff, 1976) pp. 78–9.

95 Holt diary 9 Jan. 1916, 920 DUR 1/10.

96 T. Wilson, *Scott Diaries* pp. 172–3. In his speech on second reading Simon was careful to stress that his opposition to conscription, based both on principle and pragmatism, implied no lack of patriotism. H. and C. Debs, 5th Series, vol. LXXVII, cols. 1645–58. But on this occasion only 39 members voted against the government.

97 Gilbert, *Churchill* iii companion pt 2 p. 1369.

98 Holt diary 4 Feb. 1916, 920 DUR 1/10.

99 Spender and Asquith, *Asquith* ii, 208; H. of C. Debs, 5th Series, vol. LXXX, cols. 923–35.

100 Gilbert, *Churchill* iii companion pt 2 p. 1456; H. of C. Debs, 5th series, vol. LXXX, cols. 2307–2322.

101 Addison, *Four and a half Years* i, 197.

102 Spender and Asquith, *Asquith* ii, 216.

103 Hobson to Simon 25 May 1916, SP 52 fos. 155–8.

104 Simon to H. W. Massingham 9 Aug. 1916, ibid fo. 170.

105 Simon to Sir Robert Chalmers 1 Aug. 1916, Asquith MSS 43 fo. 274.

106 H. of C. Debs, 5th Series, vols. LXXXV–LXXXVI.

107 M. Pugh, *Electoral Reform* p. 88.

108 K. Middlemas (ed.), *Thomas Jones: Whitehall Diary* (London, 1969) vol. 1 p. 8.

109 Addison, *Four and a half Years* i, 271.

110 Simon to Margot Asquith 6 Dec. 1916, SP 51 fo. 1.

111 Holt diary 18 Dec. 1917, 920 DUR 1/11.

112 Simon to Lloyd George 16 April 1917, Lloyd George MSS F45/7/1.

113 McEwen (ed.), *Riddell Diaries* p. 205.

114 Simon diary 10 May 1917, SP 2 fo. 34.

115 Simon to Brigadier-General J. Charteris 1 Oct. 1917, ibid 53 fo. 90.

116 Simon to Charteris 24 Sept. 1917, ibid fo. 82.

117 R. Blake (ed.), *The Private Papers of Douglas Haig 1914–1919* (London, 1952) p. 260; M. Bentley, *The Liberal Mind 1914–1929* (Cambridge, 1977) p. 50.

118 A. Boyle, *Trenchard* (London, 1962) pp. 258–9; L. Sanderson to Bechhofer Roberts 7 Feb. 1938, SP adds 3 fo. 7.

119 See, for example, Holt diary 29 Oct. 1917, 920 DUR 1/11.

120 Simon to Reading 25 Nov. 1917, Reading MSS Eur F118/101.

121 Simon to Lloyd George 10 Nov. 1917, Lloyd George MSS F 45/7/3.

122 As note 120.

123 Simon to Reading 31 Dec. 1917, Reading MSS Eur F118/101.

124 Lord St Davids to Simon 17 Jan. 1918, SP 54 fos. 71–2.

125 Beauchamp to Simon 27 Jan. 1918, ibid fos. 166–7. See also a similar appeal from Leif Jones, Jones to Simon May 1918, SP 55 fos. 113–14: 'Asquith comes seldom and intervenes very little: McKenna only looks in for odd moments: McK. Wood is there but silent: Runciman has been ill: Samuel . . . is industrious, able, makes clever speeches: but there are seldom heights in his level excellence. We want you there to lead.' G. Macdonough to Trenchard 18

Feb. 1918, SP 55 fo. 20.

126 Simon to Rothermere 23 April 1918, SP 55 fo. 84.
127 Rothermere to Lloyd George 23 April 1918, Lloyd George MSS F 44/5/6.
128 H. of C. Debs, 5th Series, vol. 105, col. 1344.
129 Simon to Joynson Hicks 26 April 1918, SP 55 fos. 98–9.
130 See, for example, the paragraph in the *Weekly Despatch* cited in R. Pound and G. Harmsworth, *Northcliffe* (London, 1959) p. 666.
131 Buchan to Simon 24 Aug. 1918, SP 55 fos. 157–9 and Simon's notes for his reply 29 Aug. 1918, fo. 160.
132 Churchill to Lloyd George 28 Aug. 1918, Lloyd George MSS F 8/2/35.
133 Simon to C. P. Merriam 16 Oct. 1918, SP 55 fos. 204–5.

CHAPTER THREE

LOSING AN EMPIRE

You are still young. Your career will not in the end suffer. On the contrary, I am convinced that your personal position, and the assurance of a great future in public affairs, are strengthened.[1]

When War struck Europe in 1914 John Simon was a prominent and rising member of a government which had been in power for more than eight years. His career seemed to have developed an irresistible momentum of its own. His expectation and that of others must reasonably have been that even higher office and possibly the premiership itself were within his grasp. The immediate succession to Asquith and his office were not out of the question. Four years later most of these hopes lay in ruins. Despite a brief period as Home Secretary, Simon had by 1918 fallen out of the mainstream of frontline politics, his career floundering in the turmoil of Liberal dissension and disunity. The party which was to have been the vehicle of his further advance was in danger of becoming an impediment to his future ambition. Though contemporaries may not have assessed the situation with such clarity, Liberalism perhaps faced terminal decline. Several volumes have been written seeking to explain the downfall of the British Liberal party. The biography of a single individual, however prominent, cannot provide the forum in which the conflicting theories of demise are properly examined. Yet Simon's career after 1918 does serve to focus many of the problems of his party as a whole. For a time he appeared, like Liberalism itself, a curious irrelevancy within the changed political climate of the post-war era, destined, as Leo Amery had warned,[2] to the status of perpetual exclusion. More than a decade was to elapse in 'the cold shades of Opposition'[3] before Simon's fortunes could take off once more.

Lloyd George, anxious to benefit from the mood of patriotic euphoria which understandably gripped the nation in the hour of victory, decided to call a general election with almost indecent haste. Lloyd Georgeite Liberals and Bonar Law's Conservative party maintained their wartime alliance, symbolised now in the issuing of the famous 'Coupon' or letter of endorsement to approved candidates. Independent Liberalism under Asquith faced an impossible task. Simon, despite his earlier decisions, found himself contesting the Walthamstow division once again, or rather the East division of what was now two constituencies. Simon disparaged the Coupon which would, he said, lead to 'dummy members' and called for the election of more independent spirits such as himself. But his campaign captured only one of the two largely incompatible moods of idealism and vindictiveness which infused the British electorate at this time. His election address put forward a Wilsonian aspiration for the future:

The greatest lesson of the war is that there must never be another war. It should be an essential condition of the terms of peace that the civilised states of the world should combine to prevent a fresh outburst.[4]

Not surprisingly the issue of conscription figured prominently in his speeches. He bitterly opposed the Coalition line that the ending of conscription in Britain depended on its abolition elsewhere.

Conscription has got to go. It has got to go now. It has got to go for ever. It has got to go, whatever other countries do.[5]

The ending of conscription was also included in Simon's own version of the Fourteen Points, along with temperance, the restoration of trade union rights, the establishment of a League of Nations, the implementation of an eight-hour day and minimum wage, and the early return of the country's fighting men. But Simon could neither express nor identify with that intense nationalism which pervaded the country at the end of 1918. It was illustrative that the Conservative candidate in East Walthamstow proclaimed to the electorate: 'If you want to back up the men who have won the War, vote for Johnson, the Coalition and Lloyd George.'[6] When polling day came Simon secured only 36 per cent of the vote in a straight fight with his Conservative opponent and lost by more than 4000 votes.

Simon's personal disaster merely mirrored that of Independent Liberalism as a whole. No greater reversal has confronted a British political party in the present century than that experienced by Liberalism between the elections of 1910 and that of 1918. The Asquithian Liberals were reduced to a mere 26 members in the new House – scarcely enough effectively to dispute with Labour for the privilege of designation as the official Opposition. The Liberals had gone from governing to third-party status without pausing at an intermediate stage. Thereafter the party struggled between millstones which threatened to grind it out of existence. In a sense these were the Conservative and Labour parties, but perhaps even more important were an electoral system designed to favour two rather than three parties and a growing credibility gap in the electorate's perception of Liberalism as a potential party of government. Asquith himself was defeated at East Fife and a similar fate befell the whole of his front bench with the solitary exceptions of Donald Maclean and George Lambert. When a journalist asked Simon to comment on this rout, he responded bravely: 'We have been snowed under, but snow melts.' Thirty years later, however, he added an appropriate postscript. 'But while snow melts, it may in the meantime crush the life out of that which it has buried.'[7]

Yet if Simon was downhearted at the time he scarcely showed it in his subsequent behaviour. Earning a living was no problem. He could return to his legal career and watch his income soar. In the 1920s he had an annual income from the bar of £30,000 or £40,000.[8] In addition there was plenty of interesting work to do outside the courts. In September 1919 he accepted an invitation from H. A. L. Fisher, the President of the Board of Education, to sit on a Royal Commission investigating the finances of the ancient universities. But politics continued to occupy most of Simon's energies. In the three years from the beginning of 1919 he made over 120 public speeches. Like most leading Liberals he seems to have believed that the party's best interests would now be served by the emergence of a new leader to replace Asquith.[9] But without a seat in parliament Simon's own claims to the diminished Asquithian inheritance were increasingly overshadowed by those of Donald Maclean.[10] In what was generally a very fluid political situation many Liberals began to reconsider their political futures. Large numbers decided that their destinies lay within other political parties, particularly Labour. Hugh Dalton was among those who wished that Simon's talents, especially as a lawyer, were available to Labour,[11] but Simon at this stage entertained no thoughts of changing his party allegiance. At the same time his relations with Lloyd George were at a low ebb and, regarding the Coalition government with total contempt, he set his face against the reunion of the warring Liberal factions, rejecting the blandishments of those who sought to win him over.[12] Some of his attacks on the Prime Minister and his government were remarkably outspoken considering that the two men had so recently been cabinet colleagues. In the summer of 1921, for example, he spoke of Lloyd George's qualities:

Cleverness, ingenuity, adroitness! There has been nothing like it in human history. But, after all, character is more than cleverness. Sticking to a principle is more than adroitly shifting from one position to another. And, in the view of Liberals, Mr Lloyd George has shown himself a faithless trustee of their traditions and beliefs.[13]

His feelings for Lloyd George were fully reciprocated by the Prime Minister, who perhaps still felt aggrieved at Simon's withdrawal from his libel case in 1917.[14]

Simon's name was associated with several constituencies before his return to parliament at the 1922 general election. If, however, Simon and Liberalism were to make a political comeback they had to show that their message still had relevance for the electorate in the changed political climate of post-war Britain. It has been wisely stressed that there is no clear break in British history pinpointed at December 1916 between an individualist past and a collectivist future. Similarly it is clear that the governments of Campbell–Bannerman and Asquith had grasped the nettle of interventionism long before the coming of European war.[15] But that is not to deny that there did exist a strand of purist Liberalism which seemed not to have changed its political philosophy since the heyday of *laissez faire* in the nineteenth century, and which after December 1916 rallied, *faute de mieux,* behind Asquith – despite the latter's pre-war credentials which placed him firmly on the party's right. Yet with Asquith, whatever his failings, out of parliament, Independent Liberalism hardly cut an impressive figure in the years of the post-war Coalition. The party seemed to be shrouded in gloom, as if completely overpowered by the magnitude of the electoral catastrophe which had befallen it. Asquith did return to parliament following a by-election in Paisley in 1920, but the position scarcely improved thereafter. The Asquithian court became 'an extra-parliamentary conclave of the elder venerated, meeting in spacious drawing-rooms to await the second coming.'[16] As for Simon himself, he showed little sign of appreciating that the divisions of pre-war years were no longer at the centre of the political stage. His major pre-occupations remained Free Trade and 'economy', a crusade to reduce wasteful government expenditure. Old fashioned *laissez faire* would, he believed, open the way for social progress, industrial prosperity, security of employment and a high standard of living.[17] His call was still for Gladstonian Liberalism, though he could not rekindle the passion and vitality of the original.

Lloyd George's hostility towards Simon was very apparent when the latter attempted to return to parliament at the end of 1919. When a vacancy arose in the Spen Valley division of Yorkshire following the death of the sitting Coalition Liberal member, Asquith himself considered standing. In the event, however, Simon was proposed and adopted by the local Liberal association, which was anxious to run an Independent Liberal on this occasion. Up to this time Lloyd George had willingly supported Coalition Unionists against Asquithians, but had stopped short of engineering a direct confrontation between competing Liberals. At Spen Valley he took a different line, even though many prominent government supporters regarded his action in putting forward a Coalition Liberal candidate as needlessly provocative. As the Liberal vote was clearly going to be split, it is evident that the desire to exclude Simon had become more important to Lloyd George than the election of a government supporter. A little earlier the Prime Minister had written to his mistress, Frances Stevenson, of his health:

I want to be in such a condition that even John Simon's return won't upset me. I am rather afraid that is what is going to happen. If it does it will be a disagreeable and disconcerting fact and will take a good deal to get over for it will undoubtedly weaken my influence.[18]

With the campaign under way Lloyd George expressed the hope that Simon would come at the bottom of the poll 'as he deserved'.[19] Robert Sanders, Deputy Chairman of the Conservative party, seeing Lloyd George before visiting the constituency, found him 'mad keen to beat Simon'. 'I don't care who wins if that blighter is last.'[20] The result of the by-election was entirely predictable. The Coalition Liberal siphoned off enough votes from Simon to deliver the seat to the Labour man, Tom Myers. The Spen Valley result came to be seen as a signal moment in Labour's transition from the status of party of protest to that of party of government.

With the road to Westminster still blocked, Simon turned his attention to fresh issues, using the public platform to voice his views. After the comparative respite of the war years the problem of Ireland soon re-emerged with renewed intensity among the concerns of the British government. With the independence movement passing increasingly into the extremist hands of Sinn Fein, the British authorities responded with measures of reprisal and punishment which did no credit to the long history of British involvement in Ireland. Simon, spurred on by his Irish wife, was outraged by the excesses of the notorious Black and Tans, and made a series of speeches up and down the country condemning the government's policy. In November 1920 a Peace with Ireland Council was formed with Lord Henry Bentinck as chairman and Simon among its backers. Such a line was inevitably unpopular with many Coalition supporters and even Asquith's headquarters disapproved of the vehemence of Simon's attacks. But Simon was intent upon 'straight hitting' and 'downright denunciation' of British iniquities in Ireland.[21] In a letter to *The Times* on 25 April 1921 he condemned the government's policy as 'politically disastrous and morally wrong . . . exposing us to the scorn of the world'.

In Liverpool the local Conservative party boss, Archibald Salvidge, made strenuous efforts to prevent Simon from addressing a meeting and, when the Chief Constable, fearful that rioting might result, advised the abandonment of the meeting, Simon withdrew his acceptance of an invitation to speak.[22] Simon himself considered that a speech he made on the issue in the Central Hall was the finest of his career and later paid full tribute to the role played by 'my brave good wife' in the campaign. She 'went down to the Cardigan by-election [of February 1921] and made speeches morning, noon and night, which so touched the hearts of the Welsh men and Welsh women that Lloyd George couldn't keep up his defence of the blackguardism which was being perpetrated.'[23] Lady Simon described the respective roles of husband and wife in terms which did little for Simon's reputation for decisive action:

One day he came home with a bad cold and went to bed. I walked up and down the room, crying. 'How can you lie there', I said, 'while these dreadful things are being done in my country?' Then he got up and started on his campaign and never stopped.[24]

The standing of the Coalition government progressively deteriorated throughout 1921 and 1922 as one by one its policies appeared to turn sour. Even more important than policies, however, was a semi-presidential style of government which, as Simon recognised, the British people would not accept outside the necessities of wartime.[25] Without offering much in the way of constructive alternative, Simon was able to profit from a growing feeling that Lloyd George had somehow flouted the conventional norms of civilised conduct, to which misdeed the very existence of a coalition – the prostitution of political principle – bore witness. Coalition meant 'the complete degradation of politics. It substitutes persons for principle, cleverness for conviction.'[26] The time had come, he told an audience in Yorkshire in February 1922, for a reversion to honesty in politics. Why had the Coalition government lost the confidence of the country?

It was not because there were not able men in the Government or that its leader was not clever. But cleverness was not everything and perhaps something might be said for a policy which, even if it were not quite so nimble, was the same policy today as it was yesterday . . . The fundamental error made by the Government was its lack of consistent devotion to political principle.[27]

The international situation offered the government little comfort. Despite maintaining a high diplomatic profile – usually at the expense of his Foreign Secretary, Lord Curzon – Lloyd George had still failed to effect a final settlement of European affairs. The world's continuing high level of expenditure on arms caused Simon much sorrow[28] and his long-standing misgivings over the Versailles settlement seemed now to be vindicated.[29]

An election was in the air throughout 1922 and Simon was at pains to nurse his constituency in Spen Valley. In a speech in April he gave six reasons for his commitment to Liberalism. It was to Liberalism, he asserted, that the nation owed its political, civil and religious freedoms. Liberalism was the best means for securing practical social reforms. It stood for freedom in industrial affairs. Liberalism involved just taxation and thrifty expenditure. After the ruin and destruction of the War, Liberalism was more than ever needed to re-establish international relations and secure a lasting peace. And finally, Liberalism was 'a practical creed, based on principles and convictions which embrace and serve all citizens who believe in work, sympathy, progress and fair play'.[30] What, however, determined the fate of the Coalition government was not the opposition of Independent Liberalism but the mounting unease of its own Conservative backbenchers, brought to a head over Lloyd George's handling of the Chanak crisis in the autumn. At the celebrated meeting at the Carlton Club on 19 October 1922, Conservative MPs refused to follow the advice of their leader, Austen Chamberlain, and voted to resume their independence at the forthcoming general election. Almost immediately Lloyd George resigned and the Coalition was at an end. The King invited Bonar Law, now elected Conservative leader in Chamberlain's stead, to form the first purely Conservative government for nearly seventeen years. To secure his position Law straight away called an election. Its date was fixed for 15 November.

Simon, who had recently been approached to stand as Liberal candidate in Roxburgh and Selkirk, determined to renew his efforts in Spen Valley. 'I have for a long time past looked forward to winning Spen Valley back for

Liberalism at the General Election, and now that the opportunity is coming I am going to seize it.'[31] His campaign was predictable and somewhat unimaginative. He evidently still believed that Liberalism could reassert itself as a party of government:

the only Liberalism that is worth fighting for is Liberalism pure and simple. If you mix it with Toryism you produce a mixture which may be palatable at first, but which won't keep and ultimately goes bad.[32]

Yet with only 333 candidates for a parliament of over 600 seats, Asquith's Liberals could not realistically expect to control the outcome of the election without the co-operation of the Lloyd Georgeites, who on the whole continued to seek accommodation with the Conservatives. That Lloyd George should still be flirting with Birkenhead and other leading Tories caused Simon no concern. 'Liberal chances ought to be very good indeed,' he surmised to Lord Grey.[33] The main elements of Simon's campaign were the issues which had pre-occupied him since the end of the War. He denounced the extravagance of the Coalition, while at the same time condemning the Labour proposals for a capital levy, on which he wrote an article for the *Daily Mail*. He called for reduced expenditure on armaments, the abandonment of expensive commitments in Mesopotamia and Palestine and for a drastic revision of the Treaty of Versailles. 'We have to get entirely out of our minds the notion that four years ago made such a compelling appeal, that somehow our own progress and happiness are going to be promoted by the wretchedness, misery and subjection of other nations.'[34] His final word to his electors was that the next House of Commons ought to contain out and out Free Traders – 'the sort of Free Trader I am'.[35]

On a poll of nearly eighty-five per cent Simon increased his vote by more than 3000 from the by-election of 1919 and secured a majority of 787 over Myers, the sitting Labour member, in a three-cornered contest. Simon could point to something approaching a Liberal revival in the West Riding of Yorkshire with further victories in Bradford, Huddersfield and Penistone, but over the country as a whole the picture was far from encouraging. Admittedly, more than sixty Liberal MPs were elected but this advance was more than outweighed by several alarming features. The party's best results were in traditionally Liberal rural areas and only one of their forty-three gains was from the Labour party. Furthermore the party now seemed to have no secure regional base and it had done particularly poorly in three-cornered contests. 'People have either gone back to Conservatism or have swung right over to Labour' was Simon's analysis. He sensed 'a very grave danger' that Liberalism might be 'crushed out between the upper and nether millstone', but took comfort that Liberalism remained 'the only real guarantee of vigorous progress' and, rather fondly, that there was a great deal of sympathy for it in the country which had not been expressed at the polls.[36]

The general election of 1922 showed how difficult it would be for the Liberal party to re-emerge as a serious contender for power in the new three party system which had been superimposed upon a political structure designed for only two competitors. The combination of a first past the post electoral system and a preponderance of three-cornered contests in the elections of the 1920s produced a series of highly unrepresentative results in which a slight shift in votes could lead to a marked change in representation. Sometimes this worked to the advantage of the Conservatives; sometimes Labour benefited. But Liberalism was almost invariably a loser. In very rough terms in 1922 the party had secured a fifth of the popular vote but only a tenth of the seats in the new House of Commons. The Conservative election campaign had been focused on the Labour challenge in a way that was designed to polarise the political debate and at the same time squeeze out the Liberal party as a largely irrelevant factor. Yet since 1918 Liberalism had not really succeeded in answering the basic question of where it stood in relation to Labour. The Liberal party's most logical course was to reassert its leadership of the radical left, but many of the party's more advanced thinkers had already begun to seek refuge in the Labour movement. Liberalism's inability to recover this position left a vacuum for Labour and helped seal the party's fate. By the end of the decade Liberalism had largely forfeited its claims to a working-class base. It is interesting to note that at this stage Simon appeared to show more sympathy with Labour than with the Conservatives, with whose fortunes his own later career would be so closely involved. In his Spen Valley campaign he stressed that he had never joined in the abusive clamour against the Labour party and that he agreed with many things in its manifesto. Though 'Socialism would make a man into a machine', he had always found when it came to practical business that the immediate objects which he wanted to pursue were objects which Labour men and women also wanted to pursue. 'He had found it so throughout all his public life.'[37] If such ideas implied a future electoral arrangement with Labour, the rest of the decade would show that no salvation for Liberalism lay in that direction.

It was clearly a time for Liberal leaders to consult as to their future strategy. Immediately after the election Simon went down to Oxford to discuss the situation with Asquith, who had scraped home at Paisley by three hundred votes. The two men decided that Simon should become deputy leader of the party and Simon agreed to give up all professional work that might interfere with his parliamentary duties.[38] On 20 November he dined with William Wedgwood Benn. The way to save the party, they agreed, was to hammer out a Liberal policy on domestic issues. 'We must get out of the way of treating Unemployment, Housing and Health as "Labour" subjects.' A few days later Simon was elected Sessional Chairman of the party by his fellow MPs to take the place of Donald Maclean who had lost his seat at Peebles. Thus, at least in terms of the internal dynamics of the Liberal party, Simon's position had been restored. Asquith was now seventy years of age and only a shadow of his former self. In preparing to abandon much of his legal work Simon clearly anticipated that he rather than the ageing nominal leader would be carrying the bulk of responsibility for parliamentary leadership. But turning the leadership of a parliamentary rump into real political power was altogether another matter. A prerequisite was obviously a reunion of the divided forces of Liberalism if for no other reason than that the party needed Lloyd George's money to sustain its electoral viability. On the other hand a reunion with Lloyd George would not only require many past harsh words to be unsaid. It would throw into question Simon's claims to the succession when Asquith finally withdrew from the party's front line. 'The whole problem of Liberal reunion', reported the *Evening Standard*, 'will soon resolve itself into the single question of Liberal leadership. Asquith, Lloyd George or Simon?'[40]

A short session of the new parliament began on 20 November and ended on 15 December. Simon argued that the new Conservative government was no different from its predecessor. There would still be extravagant defence commitments and excessive expenditure on armaments. Simon found that the deputy leadership took up all his time and complained that 'politics on these lines is a very expensive business'. His first speech was on the constitution of the new Irish Free State – 'a final farewell to Irish affairs' – and he also spoke on the growing problem of unemployment. His most significant contribution to the proceedings of the House was to move a Liberal amendment to the Address on 4 December calling for the repeal of the Safeguarding of Industries Act, which had been passed in 1921. Yet while more than twenty Coalition Liberals went into the lobby with Simon on the issue, he could still assert that 'our Liberals feel themselves to be closer to the Labour party than to the Coalition Liberals, for the latter is [sic] still supporting the Government on most occasions and Lloyd George remains an enigma.'[41] When C. P. Scott discussed the same question with him early in the New Year, the editor of the *Manchester Guardian* was disappointed to find 'no suggestion of a big, energetic, generous Liberal movement which would sweep the whole party together and make artificial divisions and names meaningless'. 'I think Lloyd George is done' was about all Simon had to say on the subject.[42] Even so, in February Simon had rather grudgingly to allow Lloyd George to make minor amendments to a Liberal motion on the French occupation of the Ruhr.[43]

But if Simon would not discuss the question of Liberal reunion, he could not prevent Lloyd George from doing so, nor could he stop spontaneous moves towards fusion in the constituencies. Two by-elections in Anglesey and Ludlow saw Coalition Liberals and Asquithians coming together and efforts towards reunion were beginning in other constituencies. In February Lloyd George made an important speech in Edinburgh on the theme of reunion in which he stressed the need to face the common enemy of Labour

and denied that he sought the leadership of a reunited party. If this represented a dove of peace, Simon wasted no time in shooting it down, though
recognising that this would entail 'a fine old row'. The best way of meeting to
discuss Liberal reunion, he suggested, would be in the opposition lobby on
each and every parliamentary division. That at least would test the good
faith of the Lloyd Georgeites.[44] He developed the theme in a speech to his
constituents:

The idea that what is called Liberal unity will be suddenly achieved by some dramatic
gesture, by secret conclaves and historic handshakes, with, I suppose, flashlight
photographers and special interviewers – that seems to me altogether too romantic
and pictorial . . . [Unity] will come by sincere Liberals, without regard for the past,
working and fighting for the same things and voting in the same lobby.[45]

Yet in reality Lloyd George was not far from the truth when he surmised that
Simon was against unity primarily because it challenged his chance of the
leadership.[46] Lloyd George even believed that Simon deliberately raised
matters such as Mesopotamia in the House of Commons to accentuate
divisions between the two Liberal factions.[47]

Despite the on-going problems of the Liberal party Simon continued to
make his mark in parliament and the country during 1923. His stock rose
steadily despite a rather unseemly public clash with Birkenhead in which the
former Lord Chancellor rebuked Simon for his nonchalant neglect in
absenting himself without explanation from the opening of an appeal case in
which he was leading.[48] On the public platform Simon pursued familiar
themes. The purity of his political creed remained a continuing refrain.
'What was Liberalism,' he asked an audience in Aberystwyth. It was 'an
attitude of mind about public affairs which always preserved a just balance
between the heart and the head'.[49] Foreign affairs were also prominent
among his concerns with calls for the recognition of the Soviet regime in
Russia and for a more enthusiastic espousal of the cause of the League.[50] In
the House of Commons two of Simon's speeches attracted particularly
enthusiastic notice and stood out like 'landmarks in the story of the session'.[51] On 13 March he asked a series of penetrating questions on the
continuing French occupation of the Ruhr. If France's intention was to
detach the Rhineland area from Germany, 'we are witnessing the sowing of
the seeds of the next European war'.[52] In such a situation it concerned him
that the League of Nations had not developed into the guardian of the peace
which the negotiators of 1919 had hoped and that power politics continued
to prevail.[53] Then in July he spoke in a debate on socialism. It was, he said, a
system which attempted to do battle with the most fundamental characteristics of human nature, less a humanising agency than a strait-jacket.[54]
These two speeches, noted the *Observer*, saw Simon emerge as 'a great
House of Commons personality'. He had been 'the outstanding success of
the session'.[55] Similarly the *Daily News* described him as one of the

conspicuous successes of the session, while according to the *Westminster Gazette* he was 'the finest debater in the House of Commons at the present time'.[56]

With Liberal reunion apparently blocked, at least among the leadership at Westminster, Simon's position as heir apparent to the diminished throne of Liberalism seemed strong. He would, assured one supporter, 'soon be in the sort of position Gladstone was when Palmerston's sun was setting'.[57] What Simon could not have anticipated, however, was that Stanley Baldwin, the new Conservative Prime Minister, would succeed where every Liberal had failed, in reuniting the two warring factions. Baldwin had taken over from the ailing Bonar Law in May with the parliamentary majority secured by his predecessor the previous November still intact. In a speech in Plymouth on 25 October, however, Baldwin announced his wish for a fresh mandate to introduce tariffs. He was hampered in taking such a step by a pledge given by Law not to impose them without the nation's express approval. The announcement had the immediate effect of polarising the political debate. Still in the early 1920s no single issue was as likely to cement the disparate strands of Liberalism into a united whole as the defence of Free Trade. Baldwin's confidant, Thomas Jones, later argued that Liberal reunion was an unexpected and miscalculated by-product of the Prime Minister's decision to call an election.[58] But it is just as possible that this development was high among Baldwin's own calculations. The reunification of the Liberal party meant also the final removal of any lingering danger of a renewed Lloyd George coalition, while at the same time opening up the probability of healing the wounds which had existed in the Conservative party since the Carlton Club meeting a year earlier.

At the time that Baldwin took what many contemporaries regarded as a leap in the dark rather than a carefully thought-out piece of political strategy, Lloyd George was in the United States. But shortly after his return a combined committee of Liberals which included Asquith, Simon, Lloyd George and Sir Alfred Mond managed to hammer out a joint election manifesto, agreeing to fight as a united party across the country. It was announced that Liberal candidates would be fielded in such numbers as to make united Liberalism a practical alternative to the present government. For this to take place, of course, Lloyd George's financial support was the *sine qua non*. Not surprisingly the balance of power within the party changed almost overnight with the advantage shifting dramatically towards the former Coalitionists. As Beatrice Webb put it, the Liberals were

reunited under the leadership of Asquith, but really under the leadership of Lloyd George and Winston (Simon having faded into the background), supplied with both oratory and money by the Lloyd George faction . . .[59]

At least the Liberal party was able on the issue of Free Trade to present a coherent image to the electorate for perhaps the first time since the end of the War. Only days earlier Neville Chamberlain had said that to discover the policy of the Asquithian Liberals was like looking in a dark cupboard for a black hat which was not there.[60] Now Simon could launch into a forthright defence of classical nineteenth-century *laissez-faire* liberalism. 'This desperate plunge into Protection', he warned an audience in Glasgow, 'without analysis or argument, on the plea that it would help the unemployed is nothing less than a cruel and thoughtless imposture.'[61] He argued that Baldwin's decision to exempt certain foods from tariffs, because otherwise a rise in the cost of living would result, was a tacit admission that tariffs generally were bound to raise prices. The party made some attempt to steal the clothes so recently and so successfully worn by Bonar Law and Baldwin and to say that both Conservatives and Labour were proposing risky experiments while only the Liberal party could be trusted not to shift its financial policy from month to month.[62] Indeed the Liberals' campaign rested overwhelmingly on a negative defence of Free Trade. Lloyd George was almost alone in making a few more radical and constructive statements.

Simon concentrated his campaign energies in Yorkshire, lending assistance to other hard-pressed Liberal candidates in the area even though his own position in Spen Valley was far from secure. His wife too played an active role, as she was to do for the next decade of Simon's political life until plagued by ill-health in the later 1930s. Hard work came easily to Lady Simon. In her earlier life she had qualified as a midwife and then worked long hours to lessen the sufferings of mothers in the East End of London. Now, as a political campaigner, she held afternoon meetings in the homes of women Liberals, while attending two or three further meetings each evening with her husband at which she usually made a short speech herself, directed at female voters. 'She is always very brief', noted the *Manchester Guardian*, 'but very telling, for she has personality.'[63] Partnership with Lloyd George was not easy for Simon, but the two men appeared on a joint platform in Leeds where Simon asserted that the hatchet had been buried and that it was now time to bury it in the skull of protection.[64] But it was noticeable that Simon did not publish a telegram of support for his election in Spen Valley sent by Lloyd George 'for Liberal Unity only disgusted some of my keenest supporters and would not gain me a single vote'.[65]

In purely statistical terms the general election saw a marked revival in Liberal fortunes. With thirty per cent of the popular vote, 158 members were elected and, with no party having an absolute majority, the Liberals would clearly hold the balance of power in the new parliament. In Spen Valley there was little change from the last contest with Simon's majority going up by just three hundred votes. Not all features of the election, however, brought satisfaction to the Liberal party. The most disappointing factor was the failure to make any significant inroad into the Labour vote. But even more importantly Liberalism now found itself faced with a tactical dilemma – the creation of its own relative success at the polls. The party's long-term future might well depend on the correct decisions now being taken. Simon's initial comment on the election result – that it showed that the country would have nothing to do with protection – was right enough,[66] but what was not clear was the nature of the government which should now emerge. The Liberals faced the unenviable choice of sustaining a Conservative government or installing a minority Labour one in its place. The Conservatives with 258 seats remained by far the largest single party in the House of Commons, but Labour and the Liberals, who had both fought on a Free Trade platform, could between them muster 349 seats. The question was clearly whether Labour as the larger of the two anti-tariff parties should now be given the opportunity to form a government. This fundamental problem found the leadership of the party badly divided. Their indecision reflected the fact that the party, and especially its Asquithian wing, had not since 1918 faced up to what Mr. Cowling has styled the 'impact of Labour' and the implications of this for the continued survival of Liberalism as a potential governing party. It also bore witness to the continuing mutual distrust of the Asquithian and Lloyd Georgeite factions.

When Liberal leaders met soon after the election to decide upon their immediate strategy, Simon strongly supported Asquith in urging that the Liberals should vote with Labour to turn out Baldwin when the new House of Commons assembled and then that, if Labour succeeded in forming a government, the Liberals should combine with the Conservatives to oust that too. Thereafter, with no one prepared to force yet another general election, the Liberals would be in a position to replace Labour.[67] Such a scenario may have been somewhat fanciful, but it had at least the merit of maintaining Liberal individuality in the eyes of the electorate. Lloyd George, however, was hostile and without an agreement being reached the meeting was adjourned. By the time that it reconvened, Asquith had changed his mind (though Simon had not) and was now not prepared to go beyond voting against the existing Baldwin government. The Liberal attitude towards any resultant Labour administration would be non-committal. Lloyd George, who clearly envisaged sustaining a Labour government in power, accepted this as a step in the right direction. The change of plan did not, however, please Simon.[68] His misgivings were well founded since in effect the Liberals were now going to vote Labour into office without really considering what they would do thereafter and without seeking to extract any promises from Labour of legislation beneficial to themselves such as electoral reform. When Asquith addressed the parliamentary party on 18 December he was perhaps right to say that a Labour government could hardly be tried under safer conditions. His further remarks, on the other hand, were tragically misplaced. 'It is we, if we understand our business, who really control the situation.'[69] More prescient were Austen Chamberlain's famous words in the House of Commons a month later:

[Asquith] has taken his choice and he has by that choice constituted his own immortality. He will go down to history as the last Prime Minister of a Liberal Administration. He has sung the swan song of the Liberal Party. When next the country is called upon for a decision, if it wants a Socialist Government it will vote for a Socialist; if it does not want a Socialist government it will vote for a Unionist. It will not vote again for those who denatured its mandate and betrayed its trust.[70]

The new parliament met on 8 January 1924 with Baldwin still in office, effectively challenging the opposition parties to remove him. After a heated debate on the Address, a vote was taken on a Labour amendment on 21 January which brought the government down and effectively installed Labour in its place. The majority of the Liberal party, including Simon, supported Labour in the critical vote, though it is worth noting that ten MPs voted with the government. Simon spoke in the debate with characteristic elegance. 'Sir John Simon is the forensic artist,' commented the *Morning Post*:

His sallies, his pathetic whispers, his dramatic shouts and his argumentative thrusts are all carefully marshalled. They come in the right place and are uttered in the right way.[71]

But it was an occasion when form was not enough. 'While the position of the Conservatives and of the Labour Party is clear and logical, not all the dexterity of Sir John Simon . . . can place that of the Liberals on a solid footing.'[72] Over the next few weeks there was a marked contrast between the stance Simon maintained in public and the feelings he revealed to friends and colleagues. Simon defended the Liberal strategy to his constituents. He did not believe that many Labour supporters were really extreme revolutionaries at all. Labour MPs were not riotous Bolsheviks.[73] This was true, but as Simon certainly recognised, it missed the point. Wedgwood Benn found him 'greatly depressed.' 'He kept prowling about, muttering "I am making no impression".'[74]

The Liberal party's central problem still remained to decide where it stood in relation to Labour. Parliamentary arithmetic was against the Liberals. As there were more Conservative MPs than Labour, it would not be enough for the Liberal party to abstain if Labour was going to survive future parliamentary battles. Liberals could not simply acquiesce in Labour government. They had positively to support it. Simon told an audience in Bradford that the party meant to support the new government as long as it confined itself to issues of international peace and social and industrial reform, where fundamental Liberal interests lay.[75] This did not tell anyone very much and besides it concealed an on-going difference of opinion between Asquith and Lloyd George. The former now reverted to the sort of 'wait and see' posture which had become his trade mark, presumably assuming that Labour would make so disastrous an attempt at the tasks of government that the waiting would not be greatly extended. Lloyd George, on the other hand, clearly envisaged some more positive sort of co-operation between the two parties, at least during the first months of the new government. In fact Liberalism desperately needed to reassert its own identity. This was particularly true in the circumstances of 1924. While the Conservatives quietly buried the idea of tariff reform once more, Labour – and particularly the Prime Minister, Ramsay MacDonald – saw it as their primary task to establish their credentials as a respectable and moderate party of government. In such a situation Liberalism, at least as a party political force, was in danger of losing its *raison d'être*. Those who had voted Liberal to resist the dangers of socialism realised either that the Conservative party represented a more effective bulwark or else that Labour was not as dangerous as they had supposed and could serve as the vehicle for those radical aspirations which had previously attracted them to Liberalism.

The poverty of the Liberal party's last election campaign, based as it had been upon a largely negative defence of a piece of inherited doctrine of dubious relevance to the third decade of the twentieth century, now became apparent. There was a pressing need for the party to lay claim to a set of clearly defined policies, particularly in the social and economic sphere, which would differentiate it from its rivals by the time of the next general election. Such a development was unlikely without genuine party unity and effective leadership at the top. Yet neither factor was present in the course of 1924. The shallowness of the reconciliation effected by Baldwin's pronouncement on tariffs was soon revealed. On major issues the party could still not present a united front. On questions such as Labour's decision to discontinue the Singapore naval base and the Eviction Bill in April the whips could exert little discipline among Liberal MPs. Divided counsels characterised the party at the highest levels. At the end of May the Conservatives led an assault on the government's failure to reduce unemployment. Benn described a meeting in Asquith's room:

A long debate on what we should do on the Unemployment Vote on Thursday. Lloyd George and Simon are both keen on defeating the Government . . . Masterman and I . . . took the reverse line.[76]

Asquith, whose position in the party had been theoretically strengthened by the relatively poor performance at the polls of the ex-Coalitionists, was in ill health and absent from Westminster for much of March. As Benn put it:

Policy at the present moment is very difficult. Mr. A. of course works in the background with Conferences with the Mausoleum. Ll.G. will appear from time to time to force the Party into stunts. Party meetings are difficult to hold, but without them, trouble will ensue. Brilliant nagging at the Government is all very well but seems to me to lead nowhere.[77]

In such a situation Simon was perhaps the man to take charge, but his attitude at the time was scarcely conducive to effective action. Colleagues found him at his most exasperating in these months of Labour government.[78] Though he said that he formed 'the amalgam between H. H. A. and L. G.' and that he was 'having a busy time',[79] others were less impressed with his performance. He was 'very dispirited' at losing the chairmanship of the party, a position which was allowed to lapse,[80] and, with the Liberal front bench 'speaking with two voices', Simon was 'seldom there'.[81] Simon could still make an effective parliamentary speech and was probably at his best when warning of the dangers of a future war.[82] Yet still in May something was 'making John Simon terribly gloomy'. Benn was unconvinced that the problem lay, as rumour suggested, in difficulties over his daughter's wedding to a Roman Catholic. 'He hung about the Debate, with a bundle of notes, speaking to no-one and not intervening.'[83] That month a perceptive article appeared in the *Evening Standard* which merits extensive quotation:

Sir John Simon compromised an inestimably lucrative practice at the Bar to enter into the fight for Mr. Asquith's reversion. He became assiduous in his attendances in the House of Commons and spoke upon every available occasion. He used every artifice and wile to ingratiate himself . . . He was deferential to the rank and file and it was not long before Sir Donald Maclean was forgotten and Sir John became unquestionably marked out as his leader's successor. All was thus serene when the clouds suddenly gathered. There was talk of Liberal unity. Sir John . . . opposed it tooth and nail. They hurled insults at Mr. Lloyd George . . . they threatened to resign if the 'Welshman' were ever readmitted within the fold. Why? Partly – let us do them the credit – upon principle, partly because they know that the list of seniority must be revised. An unexpected General Election upset their plans and unity was forced upon them. Then arose the question which has yet to be answered. Would Sir John Simon have to give way to Mr. Lloyd George? He had fought, he had sacrificed so tremendously to gain his position. Was it to be snatched from him like this?[84]

As the summer approached the apparent schizophrenia between Simon's external calm and his inner doubts continued. He faced a speech at the National Liberal Federation meeting in Brighton in a state of near panic. He had not wanted to speak and 'hadn't the least idea how to start'.[85] Yet the speech itself was well received. The *Daily News* noticed a humanity and intensity which were not usually characteristic of him. 'Towards the close of his speech, when he was referring to the lives of the workers, his eyes glistened with moisture.'[86] In this speech Simon put a brave face on the Liberal predicament. Despite by-election set-backs he refused to concede that the Liberal party was finished as a major political force:

I do not discuss whether the Liberal Party is dead. In the long and melancholy history of the rite of burial, and of the consumption of funeral feasts, there could never have been so much time expended and so much eloquence consumed as in our interminable obsequies.[87]

At Westminster only a few days later, however, Simon's mood was very different. He was 'in deep dumps, saying he saw no future for the Liberal

party'. Charles Masterman and Wedgwood Benn tried to cheer him up.[88] In
August Simon even suggested that he might withdraw for a time from the
political scene and allow the situation to develop without him. Leif Jones, a
radical colleague from the difficult days of the War, appealed to him not to
take so precipitous a step:

Mr. A. cannot in the nature of things last much longer. . . . If you stick to the House
closely you will be chosen leader when the time comes. That is not perhaps a post to
be coveted from the personal point of view. I don't know that it will make for your
happiness. But I am sure you can serve your party and your country by taking it. How
then can you talk of withdrawing?[89]

The fall of the Labour government in October 1924 was both a relief and a
disaster for Simon and for the Liberal party. On the one hand it did at least
free the party from the intolerable position of sustaining a Labour government which the electoral arithmetic of December 1923 had imposed upon it.
Conversely the general election which followed, which the party could
hardly afford to fight in purely financial terms, revealed the extent of the
Liberal collapse that had been predictable since the party's fateful decision
to install Labour in power.

The crisis was precipitated by the celebrated Campbell Case. After the
official organ of the Communist party, the *Worker's Weekly*, published two
articles inciting members of the armed forces to disobey orders, J. R.
Campbell, the editor, was arrested and charged with incitement to mutiny.
The Attorney-General, Sir Patrick Hastings, revealed that the government
supported the arrest and prosecution, but within a few days all charges were
dropped. Though Liberal instincts might be to defend the right to freedom
of expression, the government had clearly behaved in a strange and
inconsistent manner. Simon first raised the question in a speech on 24
September in which he criticised the behaviour of the Treasury Solicitor and
implied that the government had acted improperly.[90] When parliament met
after the summer recess the Conservative opposition proposed a motion of
censure on the government's handling of the case. The Liberals, still anxious
not to bring the government down, submitted an amendment for the
appointment of a Select Committee to examine the matter. This proposal
offered the government a means of escape from the crisis which its own
actions had created. It was Simon, 'coldly chiselled'[91], who moved the
amendment. He stressed that while the Attorney-General had satisfactorily
explained his own conduct, the House was still in a state of complete
confusion over the role which the Prime Minister and other cabinet ministers
had played.[92] There was no need for the government to take the Liberal
amendment, as opposed to the Conservative motion of censure, as an issue
of confidence and Simon declared that if it did so it 'would be in the position
of a man who is asked to produce a document from his desk but prefers to
burn down his house'.[93] The speech was not one of Simon's best,[94] but the

vote upon the Liberal amendment proved crucial. The government, probably preferring defeat on this issue rather than on a proposed trade treaty
with the Soviet Union, where Liberals and Tories were also expected to go
into the same lobby, insisted on making the Liberal amendment a vote of
confidence. By 364 votes to 198 the government fell.

Events now moved swiftly towards a third general election in just two
years. Ramsay MacDonald tendered his resignation to the King and
requested an immediate dissolution. The Liberal party in the constituencies
was quite unprepared for such a contest. Finance remained a major problem. Throughout the 1924 session Donald Maclean and Viscount Gladstone
had been engaged in long and difficult negotiations with Lloyd George to
secure a substantial long-term donation from the latter's private fund. In the
end a less than satisfactory arrangement was reached for financing candidates. The party abandoned 136 seats fought in 1923 and fielded only 340
candidates. At the outset of the campaign the figure looked likely to be even
lower. As Vivian Phillipps, the Chief Whip, put it:

This was the death-blow. We had assumed that reunion meant reunion of resources
. . . We had striven at every stage to meet Ll.G.'s views in the long-drawn-out
negotiations and we now found ourselves left without the means to put more than 300
candidates in the field.[95]

In the circumstances the party could not credibly present itself as a potential
aspirant for power. Rumours abounded that Conservatives and Liberals had
engaged in an anti-socialist pact. Four of the Liberals' most prominent
figures, Asquith, Lloyd George, Mond and Simon faced no Conservative
opposition in their constituencies, but Simon alone denied that he had made
an agreement with local Tories:

For myself, I will not abate one jot or tittle of my Liberalism and utterly refuse to
merge it in Tory reaction.[96]

The impression of a pact probably did the Liberal party's cause no good in
the eyes of the electorate, particularly in view of the way that the campaign
developed. After the publication of the celebrated Zinoviev letter on 25
October, the Conservatives could convincingly present themselves as the
only effective barrier against the infiltration of Russian Bolshevism. C. P.
Scott, who seems to have believed in the existence of a Conservative-Liberal
deal, regarded both Asquith and Simon as 'certainly compromised' and felt
that without Tory support they would probably lose their seats.[97]

After an uninspiring campaign in which not even Lloyd George seemed
able to raise much enthusiasm for his party's prospects, the Liberals confronted a predictable disaster. The Conservative party secured a landslide
victory with more than 400 seats in the new House. Though Labour lost
nearly forty seats, its vote held up well. It could look back on its first period
of government with some satisfaction and its day would come again. For the

Liberals, on the other hand, there was scarcely a ray of light to relieve their electoral gloom. With just over forty seats, the party had seen nearly three-quarters of its parliamentary strength wiped out. The victims included Asquith himself. In Spen Valley, where Lady Simon had handled much of the campaign while her husband made speeches up and down the country, Simon benefited from the absence of a Conservative opponent to increase his majority over Labour to more than 4,000. But this personal achievement could not conceal the scale of the party's catastrophe. Simon tried to put a brave face on the situation. He was quite sure

that if we had four or five years of Conservative government, that at the end of that time they would find that instead of there being no use for Liberalism the cause for which they stood would be able to contribute much to the national service.[98]

Yet Sidney Webb's words were perhaps more accurate. What had taken place was 'the funeral of a great party'.[99] Nor did the election mark the end of the party's problems. Liberalism now seemed to be disintegrating as a political force in Great Britain. Winston Churchill had already left the fold, re-emerging as a senior member of the new Conservative government. In the months and years which followed many others were to take the same path, or alternatively to join the Labour party.[100]

Within weeks of the general election the final pieces in the jigsaw of Simon's discomfort fell into place. Asquith's defeat at Paisley had serious implications for Simon. While no one sought to deprive Asquith of the nominal party leadership, it could not realistically be expected that he would ever again secure a seat in the House of Commons. Indeed, early in the new year he accepted a peerage, going to the upper house as the Earl of Oxford and Asquith. In such a situation there was strong pressure to revive the post of Sessional Chairman of the party in the Commons. As the general election, unlike that of 1923, had tended to favour the Lloyd Georgeite wing of the party, the danger to Simon's position was only too clear. Wedgwood Benn first heard that Simon would take no part in the leadership controversy, 'neither proposing Ll. G., nor opposing him'.[101] But it soon became clear that Simon intended to play a more subtle game. Speaking to the National Liberal Club on 26 November he urged Liberals to forget the past and to sink their differences, but in calling for unity on Liberal issues he went on to mention every point on which Lloyd George had either dissented or sided with the Conservatives in the previous parliament. Simon, concluded Benn, was 'obviously planning to come out of his dugout'. Meeting with colleagues at the home of Godfrey Collins, the new Chief Whip, later that day, Simon urged that the post of Sessional Chairman should remain vacant, with Collins himself taking the chair at party meetings.[102] This idea was put forward when Liberal MPs met at the House of Commons on 2 December to decide the matter. It was rejected by 26 votes to 9, after which an amendment was carried to appoint Lloyd George. After the latter had taken the chair Simon appealed for unity and comradeship. He explained that intrigue was foreign to his nature – a disclaimer which was a little hard to swallow for those who knew that Simon had drafted the original motion to keep Lloyd George out, although he had neither spoken nor voted for it.[103] Lloyd George later proposed that Simon might accept nomination as vice-chairman, but the latter rejected the idea, arguing that the post was unnecessary.[104]

Losing the initiative within the Liberal movement to Lloyd George, Simon could not even claim to be at the head of the Asquithian dissidents. On the day after the party meeting ten Liberal MPs, with Walter Runciman as their chairman, formed a 'Radical Group', pledged to work with the rest of the parliamentary party, but effectively disowning Lloyd George's authority. Simon, perhaps suspicious that Runciman was attempting to usurp his position as the Asquithian heir, held himself aloof.[105] A new civil war in this most troubled era of the Liberal party's long history now seemed likely to break out. Simon, despite his status as a senior ex-cabinet minister, despite the dazzling future which had been predicted for him only a few years before, was in danger of not even having a role to play.

Notes

1 Haldane to Simon 5 Jan. 1916, SP 52 fos. 76–7.
2 See above pp. 40–1
3 Phrase attributed to Simon, J. Pope-Hennessy, *Lord Crewe 1858–1945: The Likeness of a Liberal* (London, 1955) p. 45.
4 Election Address, SP 243 fo. 2.
5 L. Jaffe, *The Decision to Disarm Germany* (London, 1985) p. 135.
6 Roberts, *Simon* p. 158.
7 *Retrospect* p. 121.
8 For an even higher estimate see K. Young, *The Diaries of Sir Robert Bruce Lockhart 1915–1938* (London, 1973) p. 129.
9 R. Holt diary 9 Feb. 1919, 920 DUR 1/11.
10 Ibid 13 April 1919.
11 B. Pimlott (ed.), *The Political Diary of Hugh Dalton 1918–40, 1945–60* (London, 1986) pp. 5–6.
12 J. Spender to Simon 3 May 1921, cited M. Bentley, *The Liberal Mind 1914–1929* (Cambridge, 1977) p. 85.
13 *Liberal Magazine* Aug. 1921.
14 A. J. P. Taylor (ed.), *Lloyd George: a Diary by Frances Stevenson* (London, 1971) p. 191.
15 M. D. Pugh, *The Making of Modern British Politics 1867–1939* (London, 1982) passim, especially chapter 10.
16 Bentley, *Liberal Mind* p. 66.
17 T. Wilson, *Downfall of Liberal Party* pp. 232–3.
18 A. J. P. Taylor (ed.), *My Darling Pussy* (London, 1975) p. 27.
19 McEwen (ed.), *Riddell Diaries* p. 297.
20 J. Ramsden (ed.), *Real Old Tory Politics* (London, 1984) p. 131.

21 Simon to H. Gladstone 26 Feb. 1921, Gladstone MSS, Add MS 46084 fo. 284.
22 S. Salvidge, *Salvidge of Liverpool* (London, 1934) p. 186.
23 Simon to Lord Mersey 21 April 1941, SP 87 fo. 196.
24 T. Wilson (ed.), *Scott Diaries* p. 438.
25 Speech at Liskeard, reported *Western Morning News* 20 Feb. 1922.
26 Speech at Eighty Club, reported *Manchester Guardian* 29 March 1922.
27 Speeches at Skipton and Heckmondwike, reported *Yorkshire Observer* 13 Feb. 1922.
28 Speech at Bristol, reported *Westerminster Gazette* 24 March 1922.
29 Speech at Leicester, reported ibid 28 March 1922.
30 Speech at Cleckheaton, reported *Daily News* 3 April 1922.
31 Simon to Alexander Brown 19 Oct. 1922, SP 57 fo. 120.
32 Speech at Gloucester, reported *Yorkshire Observer* 21 Oct. 1922.
33 Simon to Grey 30 Oct. 1922, SP 57 fos. 139–40.
34 Speech at Birstall, reported *Yorkshire Observer* 30 Oct. 1922.
35 'Final Word', SP 57 fos. 149–50.
36 Simon diary 18 Nov. 1922, SP 5 fos. 2–4.
37 Speeches in Cleckheaton, reported *Cleckheaton Guardian* 10 Nov. 1922 and *Yorkshire Observer* 14 Nov. 1922.
38 Simon diary 18 Nov. 1922, SP5 fos. 2–4.
39 Ibid 20 Nov. 1922, SP 5 fos. 5–6.
40 *Evening Standard* 13 Feb. 1923.
41 Simon diary 15 Dec. 1922, SP 5 fos. 9–10.
42 T. Wilson (ed.), *Scott Diaries* pp. 436–7.
43 Note by Simon 14 Feb. 1923, SP 58 fos. 4–5.
44 Simon to H. Gladstone n.d., (c 28 Feb. 1923), Gladstone MSS Add MS 46085 fo. 98; C. Cook, *The Age of Alignment* (London, 1975) p. 91.
45 Speech at Cleckheaton, reported *Yorkshire Observer* 5 March 1923.
46 T. Jones, *Whitehall Diary* i, 234.
47 Lloyd George to C. P. Scott 15 March 1923, Lloyd George MSS G 17/11/6.
48 *The Times* 4 May 1923; A Fitzroy, *Memoirs* ii, 803. This incident may help to explain why Birkenhead rather pointedly omitted Simon from a volume on Contemporary Personalities published the following year and why he went out of his way to denigrate Simon in the election campaign at the end of 1923. J. Campbell, *F. E. Smith* p. 649. See also *Daily News* of 31 July 1924: 'Probably most people will agree that a contemporary political portrait gallery which does not contain one of the most distinguished of politicians is lacking in an important detail.'
49 Speech at Aberystwyth, reported *Welsh Gazette* 12 April 1923.
50 Speeches at Derby and Whitland, reported *Derby Daily Telegraph* 2 Oct. 1923 and *Narbeth Weekly News* 14 June 1923.
51 *The Observer* 29 July 1923.
52 H. of C. Debates, 5th Series, vol. 161, cols. 1331–47.
53 Article on 'Democracy and War' in *Congregational Quarterly* April 1923.
54 H. of C. Debates, 5th Series, vol. 166, cols. 1897–1910; M Bentley, 'The Liberal Response to Socialism, 1918–29' in K. D. Brown (ed.), *Essays in Anti-Labour History* (London, 1974) p. 62.
55 *The Observer* 29 July 1923.

56 *Daily News* 15 Aug. 1923; *Westminster Gazette* 2 June 1923.
57 F. Hirst to Simon 29 Dec. 1923, SP 58 fo. 132.
58 T. Jones, *Whitehall Diary* i, 261.
59 B. Webb diary 19 Nov. 1923. *The Western Mail* of 26 November was even more brutal: '[Lloyd George] easily maintains his eminence among the Free Trade orators. Everybody reads him, whereas Mr. Asquith is ruthlessly cut down by sage editors, while as for Sir John Simon – where is Sir John Simon now?'.
60 D. Dilks, *Neville Chamberlain* vol. 1 (Cambridge, 1984) p. 351.
61 *Manchester Guardian* 23 Nov. 1923.
62 T. Wilson, *Downfall of Liberal Party* p. 275.
63 *Manchester Guardian* 28 Nov. 1923.
64 *Leeds Mercury* 28 Nov. 1923.
65 Lloyd George to Simon 5 Dec. 1923 and undated note by Simon, SP 58 fos. 114 and 118.
66 *Sunday Times* 9 Dec. 1923.
67 T. Wilson (ed.), *Scott Diaries* p. 450.
68 Ibid, p. 451.
69 *The Times* 19 Dec. 1923.
70 H. of C. Debates, 5th Series, vol. 169, col. 601.
71 *Morning Post* 22 Jan. 1924.
72 *The Times* 22 Jan. 1924.
73 Speech at Cleckheaton, reported *Yorkshire Observer* 25 Jan. 1924.
74 W. Benn diary 31 Jan. 1924, Stansgate MSS ST/66.
75 *Yorkshire Observer* 15 Feb. 1924.
76 W. Benn diary 27 May 1924, Stansgate MSS ST/66.
77 Ibid 20 Feb. 1924.
78 Ibid 22 May 1924 and 17 June 1924.
79 Simon to Reading 12 March 1924, Reading MSS Eur F 118/101.
80 W. Benn diary 20 Feb. 1924.
81 Ibid 13 March 1924.
82 See, for example, comments in *Daily News* 20 March 1924 and *British Weekly* 27 March 1924. In view of his critical role in the development of British foreign policy a decade later, it is interesting to note the stress he was already placing upon the loss of the traditional distinction between combatant and non-combatant in the impact of warfare. 'The House listened almost petrified', noted the *Daily News*, 'as Sir John enlarged on the horrors of indiscriminate bombing from the air to enforce his plea for international co-operation to restrain this frightfulness.' *Daily News* 21 March 1924.
83 W. Benn diary 13 May 1924.
84 *Evening Standard* 15 May 1924.
85 W. Benn diary 22 May 1924.
86 *Daily News* 24 May 1924.
87 *Cleckheaton Guardian* 30 May 1924.
88 W. Benn diary 3 June 1924.
89 L. Jones to Simon 29 August 1924, SP 58 fos. 191–2.
90 *The Times* 25 Sept. 1924.
91 Lord Winterton, *Orders of the Day* (London, 1953) p. 128.
92 H. Montgomery Hyde, *Sir Patrick Hastings* (London, 1960) pp. 154–5.

93 H. of C. Debates, 5th Series, vol. 177, col. 628.

94 W. Benn diary 8 Oct. 1924; H. Nicolson, *King George V* (London, 1952) p. 400.

95 V. Phillipps, *My Days and Ways* (privately published c 1943) p. 113.

96 Speech at Stirling reported *The Star* 11 Oct. 1924.

97 T. Wilson (ed.), *Scott Diaries* pp. 466–7.

98 Speech at Cleckheaton, reported *Yorkshire Observer* 31 Oct. 1924.

99 Beatrice Webb diary 29 Oct. 1924.

100 Simon described Churchill as 'a meteor in the political sky of whom it can safely
    be said that he will not very long remain in a fixed position. Mr. Churchill is very
    fitly included in the Conservative government, the watchword of which is
    tranquility and stability.' *The Times* 9 Dec. 1924.

101 W. Benn diary 25 Nov. 1924.

102 Ibid 26 Nov. 1924.

103 Ibid 2 Dec. 1924.

104 Simon to Lloyd George 6 Dec. 1924, SP 58 fo. 202.

105 Simon to Reading 4 Feb. 1925, Reading MSS Eur F118/101.

CHAPTER FOUR

SEEKING A NEW ROLE

I am bound to confess to you that I do not want to waste the rest of my public life, and wish I saw the road by which I might be of more general service.[1]

In just over a decade after the end of the First World War the face of British domestic politics was transformed. These years of discontinuity encompassed two periods of particular importance. Between 1918 and 1924 the Labour party became first a potential and then an actual party of government. The victim of this process was the Liberal party, yet at the end of it Liberalism remained a significant force in the land and for a brief moment Britain's electoral structure contrived to contain three major parties. The three-party structure failed, however, to survive the general election of 1929. Between 1929 and 1931 the two-party system, which would characterise the next half century, was re-created. Again the victim was Liberalism, relegated now to the sidelines and no longer a serious aspirant for power.[2] This course of events inevitably shaped Simon's career during what should have been some of his most important and creative years. For him to remain at the end of it a significant figure in British politics, he would somehow need to escape from the fate marked out for the party to which he had for so long pledged his allegiance. In fact, while the crisis of 1918–24 had threatened to destroy Simon's career, that of 1929–31 would elevate him to new heights.

The 1924 general election left Liberals without an immediate role to play. As thinking men they came in time to see that the best they could realistically hope for, especially without proportional representation, was to hold the balance rather than the substance of power in British politics. But for most that realisation probably came after the 1929 election. At the end of 1924 those who remained loyal to the Liberal faith could still dream of one day forming a government. Their time might come again. Be that as it may, a Conservative government was now firmly entrenched and Labour just as securely positioned as the official opposition. As Baldwin was most unlikely to repeat the hazardous experiment of 1923, a Conservative administration lasting a full parliament of four or five years was now the most likely development.

In the circumstances it was hardly surprising that Simon decided not to devote himself wholeheartedly to politics for the time being. Many Liberals in the 1920s seemed to enjoy acting and thinking as if they were still a party of government. But such play-acting was not for Simon. With all the potential to be a political heavy-weight, the role of supporting character – particularly in Lloyd George's shadow – held few attractions. There was always the law, which at least offered a good living if not the sort of challenge which Simon would ideally have chosen. Among Simon's cases at this time was one in which he defended the Midland Bank against a suit brought by a bookmaker, and an appearance in the Admiralty Court for an action concerning treasure trove in a wreck.[3] He also took a leading role in gathering support for Asquith's candidacy for the vacant Chancellorship of Oxford University. In this task Simon failed. Asquith's claims were eventually overtaken by those of the Lord Chancellor, Lord Cave. Some of his supporters hoped that Simon would soon return to politics full time. 'If Simon dropped the Bar and took seriously to the House,' asserted one M.P., 'he would soon outstrip competitors and become the real leader of the Liberal Party.'[4] This may or may not have been true. But the prospect of leading a 'sadly depleted band'[5] of Liberal MPs with little hope of influencing government, let along exercising genuine power, had little appeal for Simon. He could still comment on the major events of domestic and international politics. When in October 1925 the Conservative government signed the Treaty of Locarno, which many hailed as a new dawn in European diplomacy, Simon wisely commented that its success or failure would largely depend on whether it was regarded as the starting point for better things or whether the government decided instead to rest on its achievement.[6]

When he did venture into the domestic political arena, Simon's message seemed not to have changed despite the repeated setbacks Liberalism had suffered over the preceding years. 'The Liberal Party can never live on tactics or accommodations,' he told a rally at the Albert Hall. 'Its vitality depends on constancy and faith and the revival of the Liberal Party is hopeful today because the spirit upon which all depends is visibly inspiring and uniting our efforts.'[7] Speaking to an audience in Pembrokeshire he ridiculed the idea that the spirit of true Liberalism had now passed into one or other of the two opposing political parties. 'If they wanted Liberal things done, it was Liberals who had to do them.'[8] Such words no doubt went down well with the party faithful. But the faithful were a diminishing band. The prospect of a lengthy period in opposition and the enormous electoral task which thereafter awaited them were scarcely designed to add to their number.

Simon was, he told Reading, doing his utmost to keep the party together and cooperating cordially with Lloyd George, though there were 'many snags in our path' and revival would be a long and difficult process.[9] One of those snags was Lloyd George's continuing control over the Liberal party's financial resources without which the party could not contemplate fighting another election with any realistic prospect of capturing power. Lloyd George continued to insist that the conditions of the donations to his political fund prevented him from combining it with the resources of Asquithian headquarters. As a result disbursements from the fund remained rare and almost entirely at Lloyd George's personal discretion. In October 1925 Simon pointed out that a situation in which contributions from the fund were made from time to time, with the possibility of conditions being attached, was one which really could not go on.[10]

An invitation from an old friend enabled Simon to enjoy a respite from such parochial affairs. He and his wife spent Christmas and the New Year in India as guests of the Viceroy, Lord Reading. In view of the role which Simon would later play in the history of India's development towards independence, the experience was certainly important. He came back from the sub-continent, noted Leo Amery, impressed with the fact that the Oriental was not really suited to the English scheme of parliamentary government. 'I think,' commented Amery with more foresight than he could have known, 'he is rapidly becoming a Tory.'[11]

The event which brought Simon back into the centre of British politics was the General Strike of May 1926, an event which also exercised an important influence within the internal dynamics of the Liberal party. The inability of the government to settle a dispute between the coal miners and the mine owners brought the situation to the point of crisis and in the early hours of 3 May it was announced that negotiations between the government and the TUC had broke down. The General Strike began at midnight. Simon's intervention in the House of Commons on 6 May brought him into the limelight. It was eleven o'clock at night before Simon got to his feet. The majority of Labour MPs were absent and at one point two of their remaining members, Buchanan and Kirkwood, ostentatiously left the chamber while Simon was still speaking. It was an occasion when Simon's eminence as a lawyer was all-important. His natural instinct towards caution meant that he did not use words lightly and he was obviously fully aware of the significance of what he was saying. According to Simon the General Strike was not like other strikes, as the parties to it appeared to think. Indeed it was not a strike at all.

A strike, properly understood, is perfectly lawful. The right to strike is the right of workmen in combination, by pre-arrangement, to give notice to employers to terminate their engagements, and to withhold their labour when these notices have expired. . . . [On the other hand] the decision of the Council of the Trade Union Executives to call out everybody, regardless of the contracts which these workmen had made, was not a lawful act at all.[12]

Simon's belief in the illegality of the General Strike was based on the fact that it represented action not against employers but against public, parliament and government. Trade Union privileges could be used against employers, but not against the state. Consequently the General Strike enjoyed no protection in terms of legal immunity under the Trades Disputes Act of 1906, about which Simon had made his maiden speech two decades before. Any worker on strike in defiance of his contract was therefore liable to be sued for damages by his employer and, as Simon put it in the most famous passage of the speech, every trade union leader, guilty of incitement to breach of contract, was liable to damages 'to the uttermost farthing of his personal possessions'.[13]

Whether or not Simon's pronouncement represented good law remains a matter of debate. Labour's former Solicitor-General, Sir Henry Slesser, argued forcefully that it did not. He believed that the General Strike did not become illegal simply because there were individual breaches of contract. He doubted, moreover, whether any employer could prove that the strike was a conspiracy against the state. The two lawyers debated the question, with Simon making a second important speech in the Commons on 11 May. In this he relied heavily on a judgment delivered that morning in the Chancery Division by Mr. Justice Astbury.[14] The argument was later taken up in the *Law Quarterly Review* whose editor A. L. Goodhart – later to become Professor of Jurisprudence at Oxford – maintained that the General Strike was merely a sympathetic strike and that a sympathetic strike must always be designed to bring pressure to bear on a third party. The coercion of the government was merely incidental to a strike which genuinely sought to further a trade dispute.[15] Such legal niceties may properly be left for lawyers to debate, but it is interesting to note that Simon's old rival, Lord Birkenhead, devoted a dozen pages to re-examining Simon's speeches in his *Last Essays* published posthumously in 1930. In 1926 Birkenhead had dissented from Simon's judgment, but four years later he took a different view. It was, he said, necessary to take Simon's two speeches together. Then his 'exposition of the difference between a trade dispute and the General Strike is unassailable'.[16]

Irrespective of the legal opinion which he had expressed, Simon's speeches made a deep impression. The young Conservative MP Alfred Duff Cooper found them 'most important and impressive.'[17] Neville Chamberlain judged Simon's first contribution to be a great speech. The coal dispute had been thrust into the background and altogether graver constitutional issues brought to the fore.[18] It would be difficult to prove that Simon's words exercised any decisive influence in bringing the strike to an end. The idea that his speeches terrified the trade union leaders and convinced them that they might all be arrested is certainly an exaggeration. The General Council of the TUC seems not to have been affected by Simon's intervention. But many contemporary observers later concluded that the speeches had been decisive.[19] At all events Simon had effectively alienated himself from the ranks of organised Labour. 'So far as the Socialist Party is concerned,' commented the *Sunday Express*, he was 'the most hated man in England.'[20] Even so, he was keen that the Liberal party should not appear to be intrinsically opposed to 'these poor devils of miners'.[21]

Simon's involvement in the General Strike needs also to be considered in the context of Liberal party politics. Though the Liberal shadow cabinet had declared unanimously that society was obliged to secure victory over the strikers, Lloyd George from the start blamed the government for the crisis and called for a negotiated settlement. The rest of the Liberal leaders, however, supported the cabinet's stand. Many interpreted Simon's speech on 6 May as an attempt to supplant Lloyd George as the effective leader of the parliamentary party.[22] The shadow cabinet met again on 10 May and it was in response to its decisions that Simon addressed the Commons on the following day, suggesting that both the TUC and the government should act to end the conflict. Lloyd George attended neither the meeting of the shadow cabinet nor the subsequent parliamentary debate. Instead he wrote to the Chief Whip expressing his unwillingness to join in any declaration against the strike which failed also to condemn the government's handling of the situation. Lord Oxford's initial response was one of mild displeasure, but his colleagues saw in this divergence the chance of a clean break from Lloyd George. As so often since 1916 the leader's followers were ready to be more Asquithian than Asquith himself. There followed an increasingly acrimonious exchange of correspondence, most of it published in the press, which seemed to indicate that both sides were ready to push the matter to an open rupture.[23] The climax came when Simon took the lead, along with eleven other members of the shadow cabinet, in sending Oxford a public letter of support for his most recent epistle to Lloyd George. The letter amounted to an indictment of the latter's actions since reunion in 1923 and, in particular, denounced the way he had manipulated his private political fund. Lloyd George's actions during the General Strike had 'to be regarded in the light of this general position'. The letter concluded:

We have done our best in the highest interests of the cause of Liberalism to work with Mr. Lloyd George in the consultations of the party and we regret to say that we cannot any longer continue to work with a colleague who, in our judgment, is not worthy of the trust.[24]

An angry meeting of Liberal MPs took place on 3 June with Lloyd George and Simon clearly leading opposing factions. The former, however, after giving assurances that he would not ally with Labour nor support a nationalisation policy, could still command a majority.[25] A resolution was passed deploring the public display of internal party differences and Simon agreed to acquaint Oxford with the feeling of the meeting. But when Simon and Oxford spoke at the National Liberal Club the next day the situation remained unchanged. Oxford and his supporters stood firmly by their published letters.[26] With no imminent electoral necessity to bind the Liberal party together, it became clear that the reunion of 1923 had been a sham. As Oxford later put it, reunion

has turned out to be a fiction, if not a farce. The control of the Party has throughout been divided between two separate authorities; the Liberal Central Office and Mr. Lloyd George's rival machine – the former very scantily and the latter very richly endowed.[27]

All agreed that the annual meeting of the National Liberal Federation in

Weston-super-Mare on 17 June would be decisive. Less than a week before the meeting, however, Lord Oxford suffered a serious stroke which removed him from the political stage. An event which at another time might have worked to Simon's advantage now stopped him in his tracks. Simon spoke twice at Weston, 'improving his position',[28] but with Oxford out of action most Liberals saw that they needed Lloyd George. The mood was for reconciliation. To be leaderless was one thing; to be penniless was quite another. Simon's private secretary summed up the situation for his benefit:

Undoubtedly the preponderating desire of the delegates was that the recent published correspondence should not split the Party. While re-affirming its confidence in Lord Oxford as Leader, the Conference was equally emphatic that Lloyd George must be associated with the Party. How that was to be achieved I am afraid the delegates did not trouble to think about. All they were concerned with was that the Party should not be torn assunder.[29]

Simon's own position was in fact extremely delicate. 'The greatest danger arising out of the present position,' concluded this memorandum, 'is the early retirement of Lord Oxford.' But if the latter could struggle on for a while as nominal leader, despite his physical weakness, then the current wave of feeling for Lloyd George might recede. If during that breathing space Simon gradually became more and more the *de facto* leader, increasing his appeal to the party's radical wing – Runciman's Radical Group having been a casualty of the General Strike – then 'the question of leadership when Lord Oxford does retire will have practically settled itself.'[30]

Sadly for Simon, Oxford would not fall into the role assigned to him. In October he resigned the leadership. In the circumstances Simon's expressions of regret carried with them a significance beyond the realm of formal courtesy:

I feel it as a son feels the loss of his father . . . The way will be dark without you and we shall need the patience and courage you have so often inculcated if Liberalism is to have any future. But I know we shall carry with us your continued interest and good will.[31]

Yet if Oxford's relationship with Simon was that of father to son, there was little chance of the succession for the first-born. The partisan line Simon had adopted in the wake of the General Strike had offended many Liberals.[32] But more importantly if the Liberal party was to have any future at all it seemed to most of its members in late 1926 that it had to capitulate to Lloyd George, or at least readmit him once more into the Liberal fold. As the *Manchester Guardian* put it:

Many people in the party, not specifically associated with one side or the other are hoping that in the entirely different situation caused by Lord Oxford's resignation the leading signatories [to the letter to Oxford of 31 May] may find it possible to make a gesture of reconciliation.[33]

When Simon addressed the Eighty Club in mid-October he studiously avoided mentioning Lloyd George, but such an attitude was unrealistic. In November the Million Fund Administration Committee, set up after the last general election, narrowly decided to accept Lloyd George's terms for a massive grant from his political fund. In effect Lloyd George had captured the party organisation and begun to remove entrenched Asquithians from its bureacracy.

Simon was understandably disillusioned. While Lloyd George picked up the Asquithian inheritance, he returned to the bar. November saw him giving a masterly performance before the Privy Council on behalf of Newfoundland in a boundary dispute with Canada over Labrador. At Christmas time he managed to get away to Switzerland and seemed to relish his release from politics:

Here, thank God, the air is pure and refreshing and there is no thin ice.[34]

Some felt that with 'an ounce of courage and a few stray ounces of blood and a heart that beat' Simon could have blocked Lloyd George's take-over.[35] Simon himself was more philosophical. To a correspondent who urged him to fight his corner, he explained with feeling:

You speak of the necessity of others besides Lloyd George accepting the responsi-bility of taking a line of their own. I did so at the time of the General Strike and have since done so in Spen Valley, but a large number of the young Liberals look coldly on the earlier performance and have never heard of the latter, so while I thoroughly sympathise with you I do not think your exhortations are sent to the right address.[36]

To serve under Lloyd George's leadership within the diminished band of just forty Liberal MPs held few attractions for Simon. Declining Lloyd George's invitation to join an executive committee of the party and preferring 'informal cooperation' to 'artificial reorganisation',[37] Simon played his part in Liberal affairs during 1927 but without enthusiasm or commitment. He served on the Executive Committee of the Liberal Indus-trial Enquiry, a body set up with Lloyd Georgeite money. But he took little active part in the Enquiry's proceedings and agreed only at the last moment to sign its report – the famous 'Yellow Book'.[38] Simon was clearly on the lookout for more challenging tasks. He did not have long to wait. An important provision of the Government of India Act of 1919, embodying the Montagu-Chelmsford Report, had been that after a gap of ten years a Commission should be appointed to enquire into the working and efficiency of the new constitution and to report whether any further reforms were needed. Secretary of State for India in Baldwin's government was Simon's long-standing rival, Lord Birkenhead.

The choice of a chairman of the Commission was not easy. The task involved would be one of extreme delicacy and complexity. India was still seen as the jewel of the British Empire, just as it had been at the end of the nineteenth century. But the growing forces of Indian nationalism could not be ignored and the preamble to the Act of 1919 had indeed stated that the purpose of British policy was to 'provide for the increasing association of Indians in every branch of Indian Administration and for the gradual development of self-governing institutions, with a view to the progressive realisation of responsible government in British India as an integral part of the empire'. Yet if the Commission proposed too radical a solution to the sub-continent's problems, the consequences within Birkenhead's own party might be grave indeed. The Secretary of State's first choice for chairman was the Lord Chief Justice, Lord Hewart, but the latter's judicial duties precluded extended absence abroad.[39] If, by contrast, the chief requirement was for a man without major existing commitments that would have to be sacrificed, then there was an obvious candidate. Birkenhead's thoughts turned to Simon.

The relationship between these two men was never easy. Their careers had marched so closely together, yet their characters and temperaments were in marked contrast. Inevitably there was at times envy, hostility and even contempt in their attitudes towards one another. But there was also a very genuine appreciation of each other's qualities. Birkenhead had great respect for Simon's brain-power and his sheer capacity for hard work. Discussing the appointment with the Viceroy, Lord Irwin, Birkenhead noted that 'the work of chairman requires a man of great subtlety, acuteness, quickness, industry and tact. Simon possesses all these qualities in a remarkable degree.' Interestingly Birkenhead went on to remark that he had 'every reason . . . to believe that his views upon the fundamentals of the matter are very largely in agreement with my own'.[40] In all probability the Secretary of State was aware of the essentially conservative views Simon had brought back from his visit to India just over a year earlier, even though it was probably also a reasonable calculation that Simon's Liberal credentials might help endear the Commission to progressive opinion in both Britain and India.

According to Bechhofer Roberts, biographer of both Simon and Birkenhead, the invitation to Simon to serve as chairman was made during a round of golf at Tadmarten near Banbury, in which Roberts himself was the third player.[41] Simon accepted the challenge with enthusiasm. He spelt out its implications and opportunities:

I realise that this is one of the most important public duties anyone could be invited to discharge and I am very much gratified that you should think of me in connection with it. It means, I understand, abandoning politics and law entirely for five or six months next October and of course after that the writing of the Report is a very serious task indeed. But the opportunity of trying to discharge this particular service . . . would make me anxious to get over any personal obstacles.[42]

Simon's appointment was well received in the press and also by the majority of political opinion. Neville Chamberlain, the Minister of Health, was among those who saw that the opportunity was more attractive to Simon than it would have been to many politicians with a more obvious role to play in the politics of their own country. He hoped that Simon would be impressed with the greatness of the occasion and would 'soar above his own weaknesses into a higher plane than usual'.[43] Likewise the Viceroy, having no doubts about Simon's intellectual ability, judged him likely to be 'absolutely first-rate at a job like this'. Like Birkenhead, Irwin had few worries about Simon's Liberalism:

This I attribute to the influence of All Souls which has taught him that there is a great deal in theories and practices the opposite of Liberal.[44]

The Archbishop of York, Cosmo Gordon Lang, wrote of Simon's 'peculiar gifts for this most difficult task: clearness and effectiveness of brain, great capacity to unravel quickly and surely tangled issues and . . . a very great sense of our responsibility in India.'[45]

Two further matters remained to be settled. One was the composition of the rest of the Commission. Those chosen were Lords Burnham and Strathcona, Edward Cadogan, George Lane Fox, Vernon Hartshorn and Clement Attlee. Notwithstanding Attlee's later eminence, and excluding Simon himself, the members had not been drawn from the front rank of British political life. Yet it was probably a fateful decision that membership was restricted to British parliamentarians. This was a mistake against which Simon had warned:

Is there not a danger of it being boycotted by Indian native opinion? Having invited natives to take part in their country's government, I should have thought it followed that a Hindu or a Mohomedan should be on the body.[46]

It was easy to understand the government's reasoning. On a reasonably small Commission it would be impossible to include sufficient Indians to cover the wide range of native views which existed. Indian representation would also make the achievement of a unanimous report more difficult. The cabinet's original decision, therefore, was that no Indian representatives should be included, but that means should be found for securing their partnership in the Commission's deliberations by associating Indians with it as Assessors to assist in examining witnesses and deliberating with the members of the Commission, though without helping to shape its report.[47] In the circumstances Simon correctly recognised that the sensitiveness of Indians over the question of status would be a major problem. He therefore urged the need to avoid formal and official meetings of the Commission as far as possible, favouring instead informal discussions on equal terms.[48] Granted a Commission composed entirely of British parliamentarians, Simon regarded the choice of Labour party representatives as particularly important. Indeed the acceptability to the Labour party of the Commission's ultimate findings remained throughout a matter of great significance to him.[49] He hoped to get someone who would know that he personally might one day have direct responsibility for implementing the Commission's recommendations. For this reason a Labour elder statesman or too junior a figure would have been unsuitable.[50] Simon's inclination was to approach William Graham, who had served with him on the Universities Commission back in 1919. But the latter was unavailable and the choice eventually fell upon Vernon Hartshorn and Major Clement Attlee. Simon could not have known how decisive a role Attlee would play two decades later in shaping India's destiny.

The other outstanding question was the security of Simon's political future. He now decided to retire completely from the law. Only the financial aspect of leaving the bar – possibly for good – appeared to trouble him. As the press estimated his annual earnings at anything between £30,000 and £50,000 per annum, this was scarcely surprising. His likely change of income was 'alarming', but Simon was by now a rich man and he did not think that 'a man should plan his life to be immersed in forensic disputation *to the end*'.[51] Simon's political career, however, was another matter. If he gave up the bar, he 'would like to stop with the possibility of full time in front of me for other work of some sort.'[52] Before agreeing to accept the chairmanship of the Statutory Commission, Simon received as near as he could hope for in terms of an electoral guarantee. Birkenhead asked J. C. C. Davidson, Chairman of the Conservative Party Organisation, to use his best endeavours to ensure that Simon was not opposed by a Tory at the next general election, due in 1929 at the latest.[53] The argument which Birkenhead used to justify his request is interesting in that it seems to suggest that at least one leading Conservative sensed that Simon's political views were already drawing him closer to the Tory camp:

Sir John's services to the cause of stability in the speeches which he delivered in the General Strike and upon China are well within your memory.[54]

Though Davidson had to respect the autonomy of local Conservative parties, he undertook to do his best to safeguard Simon's position. For this Simon was grateful, though he was anxious to 'maintain a strictly Liberal position' and did not 'intend to abate criticism on matters where I differ'.[55]

Once Simon had accepted appointment he threw himself into his new role with commitment and took little further part in domestic politics apart from a speech in the Commons in the Prayer Book debate in December. A cruise to Latin America allowed him to recharge his energies and by the end of 1927 he was ready to embark upon his mission. The members of the Commission spent two days briefing themselves at the India Office, while Simon prepared for them a short account of the constitutional structure of the Indian Empire. Already, however, there were signs in India itself that the Commission would encounter serious problems. Once the composition of the Commission was announced, it became clear that all leading parties, including the Congress, without whose cooperation agreed political progress would be impossible, would boycott Simon's mission. Irwin reassured Birkenhead that, on arrival in India, Simon would be able to win over moderate Indian opinion, but the auguries were not good.[56] Even the Viceroy expressed doubts as to whether Simon possessed the 'simpler human qualities' which the situation would call for. Everything would depend on the personal impression Simon created.[57]

With such questions waiting to be answered the Commission set sail in late January 1928. Simon left with two words of advice from Birkenhead. The first was to give as few people as possible the opportunity of snubbing the Commission through invitations to discussions which would not be accepted. The second was to use this first visit only to gain ideas and information and not to reach conclusions.[58] To both points Simon was readily responsive. He quickly formed a good opinion of his colleagues, noting in Attlee the quick mind and unprepossessing efficiency which were to become the latter's hallmarks, and he was in an optimistic mood when the Commission landed at Bombay on 3 February.[59] It could not have been easy to sustain this mood. Even the heavy rain which attended Simon's arrival seemed an inauspicious omen. Waiting to greet him were demonstrating crowds with banners bearing the blunt message of 'Simon Go Back'. In Delhi the situation was scarcely more promising. Simon and his colleagues were taken to the Western Hotel, accommodation that was shared by many members of the Indian Legislative Assembly. But the fond expectation that this physical proximity would soon lead to relaxed social contact was rudely disappointed. The Indian leaders and their party followers treated the Commission as if it had never arrived. Simon tried to put a brave face on the situation:

We have now been in Delhi for four days and are beginning to find our feet . . . We shall of course never win over the Congress party, who are shouting loudly and proclaiming a social boycott. But as I don't ask anyone to see me or talk to me who has not asked to do so, the laugh is with us. I predict the *social* boycott will break down in a fortnight. The political boycott of the Commission is a more serious matter. . . .[60]

Simon had to work hard to counter his own ingrained prejudices:

These people are sensitive to an absurd degree and suffer frightfully from the inferiority complex. Moreover their politicians are mostly cowards, and when the extremists are very extreme everybody else is frightened out of his life and follows in their wake.[61]

But his public statements were moderate and carefully composed. He hoped that the immediate publication of a statement of the Commission's procedure, making it clear that this was not a matter for bargaining but a fixed and final resolve, would get things moving. The besetting sin of the Indian politician was 'moral funk' and 'the first sheep through the gap will bring others.'[62] But Simon was ready to make some concessions. He now proposed that the evidence presented to his Commission should be examined not only by himself and his colleagues but also by a Joint Free Conference comprising the seven British Commissioners and a corresponding group from the Indian legislature, with himself presiding. The Indians could report to their own legislature or annexe their document to the Commission's report. But, however well intentioned, Simon's offer could be construed as placing the Indians in a subordinate and inferior position. Ever ready to take offence, the Indian representatives rejected his olive branch. On 18 February, by the narrow margin of six votes, the members of the Legislative Assembly determined that the Statutory Commission was not acceptable and that they should dissociate themselves entirely from its proceedings.[63] This decision was repeated with a majority of one on the United Provinces Council.

Simon determined to carry on regardless. His reception in Calcutta and Madras was more encouraging and in the country districts the Commission was generally well received. Many of the boycotters at least joined in a dinner given to Simon by the Chief Justice in Madras.[64] A month into this first tour he advised Birkenhead that real progress was being made. Moderate Indian opinion was, privately at least, moving in the Commission's favour, but it allowed itself to be bullied and silenced by the extremists. Yet while the Commission could proceed and the actual work of producing a report would probably be easier without Indian involvement, the long-term prospects were worrying. If the report were to command acceptance in India itself, native involvement in its proceedings would somehow need to be secured.[65] Simon proposed to send another public letter to the Viceroy proposing that as some provincial legislatures had decided to cooperate and would appoint Indian Committees, while others would not, Irwin should nominate individuals to fill the vacant places. Thus it could not in the future be said that the new constitution of India, based perhaps on the Commission's recommendations, had been framed in the absence of any Indian assistance.[66] To his old colleague, Lord Reading, he was more ready to imply that the original decision to appoint a purely parliamentary commission, though entirely understandable, had been a fundamental mistake.[67]

Though his progress may have been limited, no one could fail to admire Simon's industry. Conditions were far from ideal. It was 'rather like a Midlothian Campaign in a temperature of 100° and an atmosphere of mosquitoes'.[68] Yet Simon was working 'like a perfect black', behaving with the utmost patience and refusing to be rattled by the stream of difficulties and obstructions he encountered.[69] Maintaining his composure was central to Simon's strategy. He believed that the greatest mistake would be to threaten the Indian politicians with dire consequences, for this would immediately be interpreted as one more insult to India:

The right line is the line we have been trying to follow, viz to be consistently patient and consistently firm and to leave the extremists to find out that it takes two to make a real row and we can get along without doing so.[70]

His Commission colleagues could not fail to be impressed.[71] Lane Fox, whose first impression of Simon had not been entirely favourable, finding him unctuous and over polite,[72] was now lavish in his praise. The chairman had carried out his most difficult job as well as any man could have done. His ingenious and subtle brain was admirably suited to counter the 'dishonest cunning' of the Indians step by step:

With unfailing plausibility, and a perpetual smile, he moves from group to group, assuring each one of his appreciation of its particular point of view – and earning golden opinions wherever he goes. I think the Indian enjoys being humbugged![73]

But Fox had also got sufficiently close to Simon to recognise that the latter had become depressed and dispirited by the task at hand.[74] Altogether Irwin's estimation at the end of Simon's first mission to India that he had come and gone, 'but not wholly conquered', was a fair one.[75]

Back in London Simon reported to Birkenhead on the progress he had made. In the relaxed atmosphere of the golf course the two men exchanged news and ideas. The impression Simon created on the Secretary of State was more favourable than at any time during their long association. Simon had placed the nation under a deep debt of gratitude for undertaking a task which, whether he ultimately succeeded in his mission or not, 'probably no-one in the Empire is more competent to discharge'.[76] In London the Commission resumed its sittings and began to sift the evidence gathered so far. Apart from rumblings on the left of the Labour party, the reception in Britain was good and Simon, conscious that the real difficulties still lay in the future, feared that domestic opinion might be too confident of the Commission's ultimate success.[77] The purpose of the first trip had, after all, been simply to collect evidence. Finding a solution to India's future development would be no easy matter:

I hope by dint of much patience and research the Commission may ultimately find out what it ought to recommend, but as yet illumination is denied me.[78]

The responsibility weighed heavily upon him. After dining with Simon, Lady Lee of Fareham recorded:

I got on very well with Simon . . . but found one must not even distantly refer to India, as he visibly flinches if one does, which augurs badly for its success. It is painfully evident that, so far, he does not see his way at all and is very miserable and super-sensitive about it.[79]

Picking up the pieces of his political career, Simon got some relief from the affairs of the sub-continent. From July to September he appeared on several Liberal platforms up and down the country, speaking on the mounting problem of unemployment – neither protection nor socialism offered a solution – and the need for disarmament.[80] But Simon's Indian pre-occupation would not go away and by late September he was ready to return for the second and critical stage of his mission. The task ahead filled him with a strange mixture of apprehension and excitement. It was 'difficult to avoid a feeling of being appalled at what is in front of us'.[81] Yet at the same time he was glad that the preliminaries were coming to an end at last. He felt as though 'I had been sitting in the pavilion for nine months with my pads on waiting to go in to bat.'[82] What clearly appealed to him most was that, however difficult the road to success might prove, he had at least got a chance after more than a decade away from real power, to shape events once more – 'to play my part in this tremendous business'.[83]

Birkenhead had got the impression that Simon had no more idea of the constitutional solution to India's problems than on the day he was first asked to chair the Commission.[84] But shortly before returning to India Simon gave Geoffrey Dawson, editor of *The Times*, an uncharacteristically frank insight into his thinking on the Indian situation. His report could not be expected before the end of 1929. Then in 1930 there would be a parliamentary committee of the two houses and proposed delegations from India. His prediction was that India would soon figure more prominently in British public life than for many years past. As regards a possible solution Simon had been tremendously struck by the size of the country, an 'amazing patchwork of races and creeds'.[85] It was ridiculous to think of merely transplanting British parliamentary institutions to India. The probable solution was to give the Provinces more power and to make them smaller. He thought there must be a central legislature of some sort, but not elected directly. Government from the centre would only be possible under a benevolent autocracy rather than with a representative parliament.[86]

The critical phase of Simon's mission would be carried out at the behest of a new master. In October Birkenhead resigned from the government for personal reasons and was succeeded at the India Office by Lord Peel. A further change would come the following June when a Labour government took office with the ex-Liberal, William Wedgwood Benn, holding the Indian portfolio. Yet Simon could not have predicted that his most severe problems would come from the public servant who remained in post throughout, the Viceroy Lord Irwin. For the time being, however, Simon continued with his laborious work. No matter how demanding his duties were, the novelty of India never ceased to fascinate and delight him. Even a game of golf in Calcutta provided a new experience:

Instead of bunkers the course is littered with tanks filled with filthy water, each haunted by a Bengali youth who finds the ball with his toes, and is in danger of being beaten by the caddie master if he does not.[87]

Despite the boycott he was now getting more evidence than he could easily digest, finding it difficult to fit in all the witnesses who wanted to come forward. His well-known qualities were at a premium. As Lane Fox noted:

Simon is doing his job amazingly well. His memory and grasp of detail is prodigious and his constant urbanity has kept our Indian colleagues in quite good temper and within very complete control.[88]

The Commission proceeded to take its evidence in conjunction with a seven-man Indian Provincial Committee and the nine members of an Indian Central Committee. These various representatives sat in a large horseshoe with Simon in the middle. Controlling such a body was no easy matter:

It is a difficult business to keep them all to the point and I try to combine latitude with firmness. But the sense of relevance is not the Indian's strong suit.[89]

Simon was particularly pleased with the Indian Central Committee, which was subjected to much hositility by leaders of the boycott, and he hoped to use it as a rallying ground for moderate Indian opinion.[90] Even so, as the year approached its end, Simon confessed that he was still in the dark as regards a possible solution.[91]

This sense of bafflement continued to characterise Simon's correspondence early in 1929. Before his return to India he had lightheartedly discussed the question of spiritualism. There was, said Simon, one person who had gone over to the other side with whom he would very much like to have a few words – Edwin Montagu. 'I should like to ask him what he had at the back of his mind when he introduced his reforms.'[92] He was convinced that immediate self-government would only mean anarchy. In any case he doubted whether the views of the masses in India were really represented by the leaders of the Congress who demanded independence. Whatever constitutional scheme he ultimately came up with would have to move India a stage along the path to self-government while guarding against collapse and disintegration.[93] At all events Simon was increasingly certain that Montagu's reforms had not provided a stopping place where matters could rest as they were.[94] Eventually the strain began to tell, with relations within the Commission starting to deteriorate. Simon's reluctance to delegate to his colleagues caused irritation. Lane Fox complained that Simon tended to surround himself with experts and ignore his fellow Commissioners, while the Labour representatives wrote to Ramsay MacDonald, criticising Simon's somewhat dictatorial methods.[95] A few days of rest at the beginning of March restored his equilibrium, and his smile 'which was getting rather faded is now in good bloom again'.[96] But other members of the Commission were also showing signs of strain. Attlee's health caused concern, while the elderly Lord Burnham was obliged to return early to England.

Finally, undeterred even by the throwing of a bomb into the Legislative Assembly in Delhi when Simon was guest of honour, the Commission completed its work and returned to England in April. After a total of nine months away Simon had as yet given no indication that he had resolved 'this Indian conundrum . . . the most tremendous and intractable of problems'.[97] On his return, however, Simon could not immediately devote himself to the task of writing his report. Baldwin called a general election for 30 May, and Simon immediately hurled himself into the political fray. Almost overnight he seemed to become a loyal acolyte of Lloyd George, whose imaginative plans to tackle unemployment had attracted much attention. Back in September, during the interval between his two visits to India, Simon had warned the Liberal party not to go into the next election 'like a cheap-jack in the fair,' offering a 'patent remedy' for the immediate curing of unemployment. Coming shortly after the publication of the Liberals' famous 'Yellow Book', *Britian's Industrial Future*, Simon's words had been understandably interpreted as a stricture upon his own party's proposals. Now, however, he was anxious to explain that he had been referring only to protection and socialism as spurious cures for the unemployment problem.[98] In similar vein he went to great pains to show his support for 'the remarkable man who now leads the Liberal party'.[99] Not only Conservatives such as Birkenhead found Simon's explanation less than convincing. Many Liberals too were sceptical, suspecting that his reconciliation with Lloyd George was purely a matter of political calculation.[100]

For the last time in his career Simon seems to have believed that the Liberal party had a realistic prospect of seizing power. A split in the party's ranks would remove any such prospect. In September 1928 he had accepted that the party was likely to trail behind both Labour and Conservatives.[101] But Lloyd George's policies and leadership had given Liberals a much needed shot in the arm. One historian has suggested that 'it is unlikely that the British electorate has ever been paid the compliment of a more far-sighted and responsible party programme.'[102] Simon's electoral tour convinced him that 'we have an immense opportunity before us', and he called upon Liberal luminaries such as Grey, Samuel and Reading as well as on Lloyd George, to join him in signing a joint manifesto:

We all of us want to get as many Liberal candidates in as possible and this would be a far better way of doing it than by a one-man pronouncement.[103]

Simon did not want to think in terms of pacts and alignments with other parties. He would not contemplate a repetition of what had happened in 1924 with its catastrophic effect on Liberalism:

If Liberalism has a distinct policy and attitude let us stand by these and knock on the head all this talk about Party arrangements for the election.[104]

Simon's freedom to embark on a national electoral campaign would not have been possible had he not secured Conservative cooperation to safeguard his seat in Spen Valley. Because of Simon's duties with the

Statutory Commission the selected Conservative candidate, the future cabinet minister David Maxwell Fyfe, had agreed to withdraw. Many felt that in using this concession to further the Liberal cause on a national scale, Simon was behaving dishonourably. To Churchill it seemed like 'firing from under a white flag'.[105] One Conservative commented in the sort of terms which, sadly, were not uncommon throughout Simon's long career in public life:

It is clear that everything this brilliant man does seems shifty or even worse; he has a lamentable reputation as a twister and I do not trust him. . . .[106]

Despite his optimism Simon had not appreciated the extent to which the Liberal party had already become the victim of an electoral system designed for two rather than three contestants. Its support was too thinly spread for the party ever to regain a natural majority. In 1929 the Liberals secured the backing of 23 per cent of the electorate but only won 59 seats. In Spen Valley Simon held off his Labour opponent by less than 2,000 votes. When the overall result was in, Simon saw quickly where the problem lay and how difficult it would be to put it right. On average there was one Liberal MP for every 91,000 votes; a Conservative for every 34,000; and a Labour member for every 28,000. 'You can imagine,' he told Irwin, 'that our Liberals feel rather sore about this.'[107]

There would be time enough for Simon to reflect upon these unpalatable facts and draw appropriate conclusions from them. For the time being, with a second minority Labour government installed, Liberals seemed agreed on the need for united action to safeguard their party's existence. At the first party meeting after the election Simon

smote his breast and declared that except on matters which could only be fitly decided in the sacred court of conscience – or words to that effect – no matter of opinion would induce him to do other than follow the crack of the whip.[108]

In the shorter term Simon now had to draw up the report of his Indian Commission. He still professed to being 'completely baffled' and his anxieties were increased by the recent success of the Labour party, 'for general propositions have a tremendous fascination for members of the Labour party and general propositions about India lead to no practical conclusions.'[109] The Indian problem was like a very difficult crossword puzzle. 'One read it this way and that, and then at last found in the letters at the bottom "This problem is insoluble".'[110] Ironically he looked forward to the Viceroy's forthcoming visit to England in the hope that Irwin would 'be able to give me some help'.[111]

The events which followed, culminating in the Viceroy's formal declaration at the end of October that 'the natural issue of India's constitutional progress is the attainment of Dominion Status', remain a matter of some controversy. Certainly the account given in Simon's memoirs leaves little doubt that the Commission, and Simon in particular, were treated with scant consideration and in a manner designed to undermine the authority of the Commission's report before it was even published.[112] But Simon's version of events does leave out some important details. Irwin arrived in London on 13 July bringing with him the drafts of a proposed exchange of letters between Simon and the new Prime Minister, Ramsay MacDonald. In these letters Simon would propose a Round Table Conference to discuss the findings of his Commission and the Prime Minister would reply by agreeing to the Conference and at the same time stating that the Montagu Declaration of 1917 contained an implicit commitment to the ultimate attainment by India of Dominion Status. These drafts were shown to Simon who had serious misgivings that a Round Table Conference might affect the status of his report since it might appear that it was only one among many papers to be considered by the Conference. Yet on the question of Dominion Status Irwin clearly got the impression, confirmed not only in his memoirs written thirty years later but also in his contemporary correspondence, that Simon, recognising the distinction between ultimate purpose and immediate policy, had no real objection.[113]

I remember very well when he and I had luncheon with Reading that Simon himself rather minimised the Dominion Status part of it on the lines of saying that it was academic and that if I thought it would do any good he personally did not feel strongly.[114]

On 24 September Simon placed the draft letters before his fellow Commissioners. They accepted the Conference proposal but objected to being involved in an announcement about Dominion Status.[115] Simon immediately communicated these views to Wedgwood Benn. As a result the exchange of letters went ahead with the Dominion Status statement omitted. In Irwin's mind this meant that this statement would need to go ahead independently of the Statutory Commission. Simon, in fact, had failed to convey the strength of feeling of his colleagues against the declaration. They rightly believed – and Simon seemed to have come to share their view – that such an announcement would cut the ground from beneath the Commission's report and render it stillborn. It is in fact surprising that Irwin himself did not see this to be the case. His belief that Simon's proposals on Indian constitutional advance would have a better chance of being accepted if it was made explicit that India's ultimate destiny lay in virtual independence within the Empire was curiously naïve, coming from a man who had spent four years in the sub-continent. Inevitably Dominion Status became a minimum demand rather than an ultimate goal.

What in fact had happened? It seems unlikely that both Irwin and Wedgwood Benn misinterpreted Simon's initial response to the Dominion Status proposal.[116] Yet his fellow Commissioner, George Lane Fox, suspected that this was what had occurred since Simon had 'never to me expressed anything but dislike of any such pronouncement'.[117] In all probability Simon had reacted cautiously and reservedly when first acquainted with the proposed exchange of letters in July. MacDonald's interpretation was that Simon had 'shilly-shallied all the time. Had he said at first that the Viceroy's declaration would injure his Commission, something could have been done.'[118] But the proposition that ultimate Dominion Status was implicit in the Montagu Declaration was difficult to dispute, and Simon may well have been prepared to accept such a statement if it could be shown to have all-party support in Britain. He may also have judged that to write of Dominion Status in an exchange of letters was one matter; to allow the Viceroy to make a formal and specific declaration to this effect was quite another. From the Conservative ranks Lord Salisbury put forward a plausible explanation:

I suspect that as a matter of fact Simon wobbled. At any rate I understand that until after you [Irwin] had started he had said nothing to the Government except that the Commission would *bear no responsibility* for a Dominion Status declaration. He was not consulted I believe except as to the proposed Dominion Status passage in the first draft of the correspondence, and he may have plausibly thought that to decline responsibility was all that was required in these circumstances, especially as it was effective and the passage was omitted.[119]

The correspondence was not formally submitted to Simon until September. It certainly seems likely that his opposition was strengthened by his fellow Commissioners and by figures in the Liberal party including the ex-Viceroy, Lord Reading.[120]

At all events from late September onwards Simon left little doubt as to his feelings. Even so he was more successful in getting his views across to the Conservative opposition than to the Labour government. Peel understood that Simon refused for himself and for the Commission to take any part in such a declaration either directly or indirectly and that he felt very indignant that such a statement should be issued before his report appeared.[121] At one point he even seems to have contemplated resignation from the Commission if the statement were made, but later decided to curb his feelings and conclude his report.[122] Simon and the Commission meticulously distanced themselves from the Viceroy's forthcoming statement in order to disclaim responsibility totally once it had been made. 'I do not know,' he later wrote to Irwin, 'whether you appreciated that I had no information as to what was going to be said.'[123] Stanley Baldwin even reported that Simon, protesting his ignorance of what would be said, repeatedly and indignantly refused to look at copies of Irwin's Declaration when they were offered to him.[124] Not surprisingly there were as usual those who were ready to put a less than sympathetic construction on Simon's behaviour. One Conservative peer was 'sure he has been playing a not absolutely straight game'.[125]

Irwin's Declaration caused problems not only for John Simon. Between

1929 and 1931 Stanley Baldwin's leadership of the Conservative party encountered a variety of serious problems. The Viceroy's statement only added to them. Anxious to maintain agreement on India between the two front benches, Baldwin, who was about to embark for his annual visit to Aix-les-Bains, gave his conditional approval to the Declaration on 21 September on the supposition that the Commission would agree to the course proposed. At that stage the Dominion Status Declaration was still intended to be embodied in the exchange of letters between Simon and MacDonald. When the Commission rejected the proposed draft and Irwin determined to issue his statement in a separate form, Baldwin was not informed that his condition had been ignored. According to Leo Amery – most members of the shadow cabinet were horrified by the Declaration.[126] Birkenhead wrote strongly to the *Daily Telegraph* warning that the Statutory Commission was being undermined,[127] while Salisbury urged Baldwin to try to stop the Declaration being made and convince 'Edward [Irwin] that the Party will be shaken to its very centre if we were to assent to a declaration . . . evidently intended to prejudge the issue'.[128] Dangerously exposed as far as his own right wing was concerned, Baldwin determined nonetheless to stick by Irwin and face any internal party difficulties as they arose.[129]

There seems little doubt that Simon was badly rattled by the course of events, especially as the Labour cabinet seemed to be united in support of Irwin's policy.[130] Still hoping to complete his report by the following February, he was concerned that some members of the Commission might now resign.[131] He even appealed to the King for assistance to 'keep the Indian Commission going'.[132] Lane Fox described a revealing episode:

One morning while I was in my bath I got a message to say that he wanted to come to breakfast to talk to me. I had great difficulty in persuading him to eat anything, for he would talk with part of a rapidly cooling poached egg on his fork and an equally cooling cup of tea utterly untasted.[133]

Simon had recovered his composure by the time that the House of Commons came to debate the Irwin Declaration on 7 November. He wanted to appeal to the House to let the Commission get on and finish its work.[134] His contribution was a 'most discreet and statesmanlike speech',[135] designed to damp down the strong feelings which had begun to emerge in the debate and, if possible, to stop it altogether. Lloyd George and Wedgwood Benn had already engaged in one bitter exchange before Simon rose to deliver his speech. The Chairman of the Conservative party thought Simon's an 'absolutely perfect Parliamentary performance'.[136] Rapidly Simon won the House over to his point of view and ended with an appeal that the Commission should now be allowed to proceed with its task:

Of course it is useless to pretend that the incidents leading to this debate have not for the time being added to our own difficulties, through no fault of our own, but, in fact, these things do not make the slightest difference in the determination of the Commission and of every member of the Commission to finish its task, and nothing that has happened will affect or deflect the completion of our duty or the character of our Report in the slightest degree.[137]

At least in Britain Simon felt that the moral authority of the Commission had been restored. In India, on the other hand, the reaction to the public wrangle over the Viceroy's Declaration was harder to predict.[138]

To trusted friends such as Leo Amery, Simon gave inklings of the way his mind was now moving as the Report neared fruition. Amery recorded his impression after dining with Simon:

Apparently the general line on which they are all united is giving Provincial Governors a free hand to choose their ministers in any proportion they like, white or Indian, to retain the communal franchise for the Provinces, but to elect the Central Legislature by P[roportional] R[epresentation] by the Provincial Legislatures. This will give a flexible system enabling services to be transferred boldly where conditions warranted it and to be re-transferred where Indian Ministers did not work them satisfactorily.[139]

One of the chairman's primary concerns remained to secure a unanimous report. Lane Fox observed his methods to achieve this. One aspect was his characteristic reluctance to confront major issues head on. Simon

is inclined to prefer the easy fence to the difficult one – and tomorrow we have made him agree to discuss one or two points which he had always made us leave over, until we come to a definite decision, even if we sit till late in the evening.[140]

On other occasions he would toy with his colleagues, as if he were slowly paralysing a witness in the criminal court or enjoying a debating point in the common room at All Souls:

It amuses me to watch Simon playing with Burnham. The old man will announce rather pompously that soon he will have to develop an argument on which he is afraid he is bound to be in disagreement with the rest of us. Simon, who knows exactly what is coming, purrs softly and, after some time of conversation, proves to Burnham that he is right and we are wrong, that it was very clever of Burnham to put it the way he did, that with just a slight modification we can all accept his views, leaving the old boy, who is not a very clear thinker, completely puzzled as to what it was that he wished to die in the last ditch over.[141]

By the middle of May the Report was ready and unanimity had been maintained. Simon was particularly appreciative of Burnham's readiness to compromise and of Attlee's logical mind, skill in drafting and sheer hard work. One thing that especially pleased him was that, in so far as there had been differences of opinion within the Commission, these had not developed along party political lines.[142] Simon had always believed that conflicting British opinions about the future government of India were based on general ideas which lacked sufficient knowledge of the detailed problem and all its complexities.[143] He determined therefore to publish the Commission's Report in two parts, the first of which would survey the evidence upon which the conclusions in the second were based. He feared that if the two parts had been published simultaneously attention would have focused almost exclusively upon the Commission's recommendations. Accordingly volume one appeared on 10 June 1930, with Simon taking pains to ensure that it received maximum circulation and publicity.[144] Written largely by Simon himself it consisted, in 400 masterly pages, of a descriptive and analytical survey of the Indian problem.[145] It has claims to rank among the greatest state papers of modern times and even became a best seller at the Stationery Office. The second volume containing the Commission's recommendations was published a fortnight later on 24 June. Though Simon had personally written less of this himself, his imprint was clear throughout. The Report proposed to replace the existing system of dyarchy with a new constitution giving wider powers to Indian governments in the Provinces, but still leaving a veto in the hands of the Governors and the Viceroy, 'the actual and active Head of the Government'. The hope was that Indians in the Provinces would have the opportunity of judging how far the British system of government was suited to their needs. The central government's responsibilities, over which Britain would retain final control, would be restricted to those of defence, internal security and the protection of minorities. In a proposal that would be important for the future development of the sub-continent, the Report recommended the separation of India and Burma.[146]

It all amounted to a continuing form of enlightened paternalism. Beatrice Webb noted that the Report was a mine of wisdom about Indian shortcomings:

but the assumption from start to finish [was] that the British are born rulers and the Indians are born to be ruled and that the greatest circumspection is needed before upsetting this 'natural order'. . . .[147]

That Simon's Commission should report in these terms was by no means surprising, even though the quest for unanimity may have induced an excessive zeal for caution. He had never envisaged producing a scheme for immediate Indian independence; Birkenhead who had charged him with his responsibilities, had never intended that he should. But Indian nationalism, spurred on by Irwin's Declaration of the previous October, was not in the mood for half-measures. Leaders of Indian opinion were not even prepared to weigh Simon's arguments with the care they deserved. Their reaction was prompt and hostile. In Indian eyes Simon's careful description of the slow stages which would lead to responsible self-government was already out of date. Articulate India did not accept Simon's fundamental presumption of the inevitability of gradualness. Minimum nationalist demands had already been established by Nehru and these outran Simon's cautious proposals.

The response of the Indian *Daily Mail* was harsh but predictable:

a rather badly-cooked rice pudding, strongly flavoured with the cinnamon of die-hardism.[148]

It clearly annoyed Simon that the Government of India expressed its disappointment with his Report only forty-eight hours after it had been published. He believed that the labours of his Commission could not be properly analysed in so short a time.[149] But Indians needed no more time to see that the basic framework of Simon's thinking was not theirs. In his heart of hearts Simon cannot have been altogether surprised by this reaction to his Report in India. The response of the British government and its Viceroy were of more importance to him. The reaction in traditional Conservative circles was largely favourable. Austen Chamberlain, a former Secretary of State for India, almost lost his usual composure in a fulsome expression of imperialistic support for a state paper that was worthy 'of the governing genius of our race'.[150] Conservative right-wingers saw in the Report the basis of a reasoned opposition to Dominion Status. This being the case it was unlikely that more progressive opinion would be satisfied.[151] In any case the Viceroy's thinking had moved on in advance of his party. Simon had studiously avoided any reference to Dominion Status, 'an expression the meaning and application of which are still obscure to me'.[152] This was in one sense understandable. The Commission had expressed its feelings on Irwin's Declaration in no uncertain terms and Simon still believed the Viceroy had made a mistake. But that very declaration had refocused the agenda of debate on India. Irwin believed that the omission showed an 'amazing lack of imagination on Simon's part'. The latter had made a very obvious and deliberate refusal to 'take the bandage off his eyes'. In Irwin's view the right line would have been to express sympathy with this goal of British administration in India and make proposals towards its realisation. 'But of all this in his Report not a word.'[153] Irwin was also disappointed by Simon's recommendations regarding the Central Government. He reasoned that Simon had probably felt he had gone far enough with his proposal to hand over control of law and order in the Provinces and had therefore sought to balance this by showing that there was to be 'no rot about democracy at the Centre'.[154]

If the Viceroy was disappointed, the government seemed to be indifferent. Simon received no word from Wedgwood Benn and had 'no reason to think that he has found time to read the Report'. Simon felt understandably irritated. As usual there was some logic in his position:

At the time [of Irwin's Declaration] I was told that there was no reason for me to feel disturbed, for the announcement did not in the least affect the Commission's task and was indeed merely the Government's gloss on the Montagu Declaration, so, with great difficulty, I got the Commission to go on. Now I see in certain quarters that the Report is criticised because it did not recognise that this Declaration transformed the position and created a new objective.[155]

In fact the Viceroy's Declaration appeared to have been framed to give one impression in India and a different one in Britain.[156]

The next step was for the Report to be considered by a Round Table Conference. But the government seemed determined to relegate Simon's work to minor status. It particularly annoyed him to learn that the agenda would not be restricted to the Commission's Report. By the decision to make the conference 'free', the delegates to it would be at liberty to raise any issue they wished and it was most unlikely that Indian representatives would follow Simon in studiously avoiding the concept of Dominion Status. Worse, however, was to follow. Irwin made it clear that he did not want Simon to be a member of the conference, either as chairman of the Statutory Commission or as one of the Liberal party's delegation. His stated reason – that Simon's inclusion would be interpreted, rightly or wrongly, to mean restricting the liberty of the conference by confining its discussion to an examination of the Report – did little to assuage Simon's feelings, especially in view of the inclusion of some members of the Indian Provincial Committee which Simon had been instrumental in setting up, all of whom were responsible for a share in a report or dissenting minute presented to parliament in the appendices to the Commission's Report.[157]

Simon came to the conclusion that Irwin had already decided to jettison his Report and was ready to use his exclusion from the conference to curry favour with those sections of Indian opinion which had boycotted the Commission's work or already expressed their dissatisfaction with the Report.

It would be in the end absolutely disastrous if, in the desire to please Indian critics, the Viceroy lets it be understood that the coming Conference may treat the Commission as an incubus now happily removed, so that the way is clear for some other and more advanced plan which nobody attempts to define.[158]

Seeing an advance draft of a statement to be made by Wedgwood Benn to the House of Commons, Simon noted that it began 'with the sort of flattery of the Commission which is proper if you are going to disregard its recommendations'. It went on to use language which would be understood in India as implying that at the Conference no one would need to trouble about the Commission's Report and that all that really mattered would be 'Dominion Status with reservations'.[159] To Stanley Baldwin, leader of the Conservative opposition, Simon expressed his anxiety:

I do hope [Irwin] won't, out of a desire to conciliate, use language which *in India* will be understood to be putting aside the Report and signalling to the Indian politicians that he is ready to be pushed downhill to the point where agreement is reached. That sort of agreement won't stand.[160]

Simon's correspondence at this time reveals a markedly embittered attitude towards the Viceroy and his role in the whole affair. A letter to J. L. Garvin of *The Observer* betrayed the sort of personal feelings which Simon was usually so adroit at concealing:

In spite of his going to tea with Patel and Gandhi while the Commission was being stoned in Madras, we carried on; in spite of his butting in with a declaration about Dominion Status, we produced a unanimous Report; and now he is reduced to constituting the Conference, which I had a part in suggesting, out of the rag-tag and bobtail, without the slightest prospect of it containing anybody who could secure unity or deliver the goods.[161]

Irwin was being exploited by men who were 'leading him down into the quagmire'. He was rapidly becoming 'a British Gandhi'.[162] Simon was now ready to admit that the Dominion Status Declaration had sabotaged his Report. It had ensured that every Indian politician would merely search the Report 'for the purpose of seeing if two words were used'.[163] After Irwin had attempted to explain Simon's exclusion from the Round Table Conference, Simon pointedly avoided writing to the Viceroy again.[164]

One of the most significant aspects of this whole episode was the way it brought Simon into contact with leading Conservatives. Like Simon himself many believed that his exclusion from the conference presaged the aban-donment of the Commission's Report and the adoption of a much more radical approach to India's future – one which would not be acceptable to themselves.[165] Irwin's insistence to his party colleagues that he had no wish to 'scrap all the wisdom collected by Simon and his merry men' failed to reassure them.[166] It was Austen Chamberlain who pressed most strongly for Simon's inclusion, even reading out a letter from him in the House of Commons.[167] Winston Churchill took up the theme in a speech at Thanet in August. In the hope of placating Gandhi – 'this malevolent fanatic' – the government had banished the man most capable of advising and helping such a conference. It was an abject and foolish act which reflected nothing but discredit on those responsible for it.[168] The government, however, turned a deaf ear and the Conference went ahead without Simon.

Simon's contribution to the future development of India thus ended in disappointment and disillusion. He viewed the composition of the Con-ference as finally settled with a mixture of contempt and despair. 'I should dearly like to set them an elementary examination paper . . . upon the present Constitution of India.' His own predicament left him in the wrong whatever he now did. Silence would be interpreted as acquiescence; public comment as an ill-tempered attempt to sabotage a Conference from which he had been excluded.[169] Though Irwin thought him guilty of 'injured innocence and unctuous rectitude' – 'there is something about him that never rings absolutely true'[170] – Simon was in fact genuinely hurt by the way in which his Report had been treated. He was, noted Lane Fox, very unhappy and inclined to think that everybody had tricked him.[171] He had put a tremendous amount of nervous energy into the preparation of the Report and the strain had often been intense.[172] The award of the GCSI was scant consolation for the relegation of his labours to the dustbin of history.[173] Judged within his own parameters Simon's conduct throughout the life of the Statutory Commission is difficult to fault. He was unfortunate that the rules of the game were changed in the course of his work. His initial selection as chairman had after all been due in part to the conviction that he could be relied upon to produce a 'safe' Report. The combination of the change of government in Britain and the clear advance in Irwin's thinking on India's future short-circuited Simon's work and made it inherently improbable that his Report would form a satisfactory basis for future developments. In its collection of evidence the Commission had toiled mightily and against daunting odds. It was not, after all, Simon's fault that the Commission had been restricted to British parliamentarians. In the sifting of that evidence and the deduction of a logical and clear-sighted set of conclusions Simon's twin qualities of industry and intellect were at a premium. Yet at a crucial point there is clearly a missing dimension – a failure of imagination which, if remedied, might have transformed an impressive Report into a great one. Simon could not really perceive that, in the last resort, the relationship of India to Britain could be other than one of subordination. His correspondence reveals a tendency to dismiss Indians in terms of racial stereotype. Though common among his generation, this frame of mind helped blind him to the shortcomings of his own proposals. Harold Laski, writing in the *Daily Herald*, produced a revealing commentary:

As a piece of analysis, its finely meshed structure could hardly be bettered. Its argument is closely-knit, its logical power superb. Everything is there save an understanding of the Indian mind. Nationalism gets a polite paragraph at the end, written . . . as a half-dubious peroration. Gandhi, who has set half India aflame with new dreams, is dismissed as an administrative incident. . . . You cannot deal with the hopes of a people as though they were studies in logic.[174]

With the debate over the future of the Statutory Commission's Report still raging, Simon was invited to perform another act of public service. Early on the morning of 5 October 1930 the R 101, the largest airship in the world, struck the earth near Beauvais in France after setting out on its maiden voyage to India. It immediately burst into flames. Of the fifty-four people on board all but eight perished. Among the dead was Lord Thomson, the Secretary of State for Air. At the request of Thomson's successor, Lord Amulree, Simon agreed to conduct an enquiry into the accident and its causes with the help of two assessors possessing expert knowledge of aircraft and aerodynamics. These were Colonel Moore-Brabazon, whom Simon had known since their days on Trenchard's staff during the War, and Charles

Inglis, Professor of Mechanical Sciences at Cambridge. The enquiry was held in public and lasted in all for thirteen days. After reviewing all the evidence and interviewing over forty witnesses, Simon ruled out all explanations for the accident except that of loss of gas. This seemed to be a design failing of the airship, but Simon concluded that there had probably also been a specific accident before the crash.

The report was ready in March 1931. Again it was a model of logical clarity. Amulree wrote appreciatively:

It keeps the attention of the lay reader and leads him irresistibly to one conclusion as the cause of the accident . . . It is amazing to me how you have been able to construct such a simple, straight-forward story out of such a mass of confusing detail.[175]

The government was relieved that Simon did not blame any individuals, but subsequent opinion has not been convinced that the report really found out why the R 101 crashed.[176] Most of those who had given evidence had a vested interest in the future of airship policy and some of the findings of the enquiry seemed inconsistent with the evidence given.[177] Be that as it may, the report was accepted and a parliamentary debate passed off without incident. Simon was sceptical about the whole future of airships, but was happy for the R 100 to have a further trial and hoped that later on he might go up in her himself. In the event the government's limited programme fell victim to the economic crisis of the summer.[178]

'The India Commission and the R 101 are,' wrote Simon in November 1930, 'trial trips, and if the performance is of public value, I naturally reflect a little sadly on the obstacles to helping in the wider field.'[179] Those obstacles still appeared to be formidable. Simon had now been out of government for fifteen years. The Liberal party, though it technically held the balance in the parliament created by the 1929 general election, seemed still to be a long way from real power. After the disappointments of that election many Liberals had in fact concluded that there would never be another Liberal government. Simon's fate might well be to fade out of the political limelight, carried away in the remorseless erosion of his party's strength. It was therefore of the greatest significance that while Indian affairs tended to align Simon more closely than ever before with the Conservative opposition, his own position within what was now clearly Lloyd George's Liberal party was undergoing another period of crisis.

The continuing importance of the Indian question for Simon is critical for comprehending the political metamorphosis which he underwent in 1930 and 1931 and which culminated in his membership by November 1931 of a Conservative-dominated government. The treatment of his Commission's Report and his own exclusion from the Round Table Conference continued

to rankle with him.[180] When parliament debated the activities of the conference in late January 1931, Simon intervened to chide the government for
its behaviour, giving 'the impression of a disappointed man who felt that he
had been slighted'.[181] It was the Indian question upon which Simon laid
particular stress when discussing the government's incompetence with Leo
Amery at the end of March.[182] The summer of 1931 saw him addressing a
meeting of the Conservative party's back-bench India Committee and still
ready to defend the proposals contained in his Report.[183] He had clearly not
given up hope of rescuing the labours of his Commission from oblivion at
some future date and possibly saw Winston Churchill as an ally in this
endeavour.[184]

In the early months of Ramsay MacDonald's second government Simon
followed the Liberal line that it was necessary to keep the government in
office. Lane Fox recalled an incident late in 1929 when Simon had advised a
Liberal party meeting to vote with the Conservatives against the government's Coal Bill, only after ascertaining that there were sufficient Tories
absent to ensure that the government would not be defeated.[185] But a year
later his attitude had changed. In the face of the mounting scourge of
unemployment the Labour government appeared beset by intellectual
bankruptcy. After the resignation of Oswald Mosley, one of the few
ministers who seemed to have some ideas about tackling unemployment,
Simon wrote as a 'great admirer' to express his 'great admiration'.[186] In late
October 1930, just before the opening of parliament, Simon wrote to Lloyd
George to give him advance notice of his present feelings on relations with
the Labour government. After seventeen months in power, Simon concluded, Labour had proved a complete failure in practically all departments.
The result was that while Liberals derived no benefit from the existing
situation, they were exposing themselves to the reproach that they were
trying to save their own skins by avoiding another election. Should Labour
attempt to reverse the Trade Union laws of the Baldwin government, Simon
would not be able to support them. Indeed on a vote of confidence, he would
feel obliged to join the Conservative opposition:

We are in danger of carrying offers of assistance to the point of subservience and I do
not believe that this is the way in which Liberalism is likely to become a more
effective force in national and Imperial affairs.[187]

In effect Simon had renounced the central theme of Lloyd George's strategy
since the last election. Rather than viewing each issue on its merits he had
decided that he wished to bring the government down at the earliest possible
opportunity. Lloyd George, on the other hand, continued to insist that the
government should be kept in office until there had been a revival of trade,
which would invalidate Conservative calls for protection, or until the
Liberals had extracted a commitment to electoral reform. When Simon's
letter was published in the press Liberalism entered yet another phase of its

self-destructive civil war. The extent of the party's disarray became apparent when parliament reassembled and the Conservatives put down a motion on the King's Speech. The official Liberal line was to abstain, but five Liberals including Simon and the Chief Whip, Sir Robert Hutchison (who promptly resigned his post), voted with the Tories, while four more went into the government lobby.

For the time being further attempts were made to paper over the cracks in the Liberal ranks. The leading members of the party met in Lloyd George's room in the House of Commons on 20 November to hear a plan from Lloyd George for a formal pact with Labour for two years. Simon spoke forcefully against this proposal. The Labour government was already discredited and he could see no reason to put Liberal assets into a bankrupt concern. Should a general election follow after the two-year period no Liberal candidate could expect to succeed against Labour, since he would be unable to criticise a party whose hold on power he had hitherto helped to sustain. The meeting broke up having established nothing but the extent of the party's divisions.[188] Warned that Lloyd George was scheming to capture the party for his own strategy, Simon prepared for a showdown.[189] Discussing the situation with Lord Reading before a further meeting of Liberal leaders on 27 November, Simon ridiculed the idea, now apparently favoured by Lloyd George, of a pact for a shorter period than two years in return for the introduction of the Alternative Vote. Significantly, the conversation then moved on to the possible formation of a National Government, with Reading encouraging Simon to think that he should have a place in such an adminis-tration.[190] When the meeting of party leaders began Simon and Reading opposed the whole notion of a bargain with the government. An arrange-ment for one year would in the end become a bargain for two, since after twelve months it could be said that more time was needed to secure the appropriate concessions from the government. Confusion again prevailed:

Something was said at the end by Lloyd George about the difference between an agreement and an understanding and the conference ended . . . without any clear information either as to what Lloyd George and Samuel intended to say to the Cabinet Ministers, or as to what account might hereafter be given of the result of their further conversation.[191]

Simon now appeared to have three options open to him. He could go along with a political strategy which he regarded as profoundly mistaken; he could strike out on his own in the near certainty of facing political oblivion; or he could explore the possibilities of accommodation with his erstwhile enemies in the Conservative party, with whom his recent problems over India had established a new point of contact. Yet if Simon were to con-template any sort of alliance with Conservatives beyond that needed to bring down the Labour government, he would need to experience the most dramatic intellectual conversion of his career. Whatever their internal differences, the doctrine of Free Trade – the ark of the Cobdenite covenant – remained an article of faith for all who professed to be true believers in the gospel of Liberalism. Simon had until recently been outspoken in asserting that protection offered no remedy for the country's economic ills. Now the *Yorkshire Post* gave the first indication of a possible change in his views:

Rumour has been rife lately that the state of British industry has influenced Sir John Simon, as it has so many others with knowledge of its conditions, and that he may even indicate some modification of his rigid Free Trade orthodoxy.[192]

Soon prominent Liberals became suspicious that Simon had grown ominously silent on the Free Trade issue. 'I can't make out what he is after,' noted Leif Jones. 'He seems to be bent on turning the government out, even if it involves the return of a Protectionist Government.'[193]

The first initiative seems to have come from the Conservatives. Neville Chamberlain, after securing Baldwin's assent, asked Simon to call to see him on 1 December. The two men found common ground in their belief that the most pressing need was to get rid of the present government. Chamberlain sounded Simon out on the question of protection and was pleased to note that Simon was at least open-minded on the issue. The circumstances in which Free Trade had first been espoused as a central tenet of Liberalism had now completely changed and though he was not a convinced Protectionist, Simon was ready to 'take any risks to get the Government out'. He now sought assurances and commitments from the Conservatives. It would be much easier if Liberals who took his view could know that they would not be opposed by Conservatives at the next election, and easier still if the Tories were prepared to offer some measure of proportional representation. Simon believed that in the event of the government's fall the King might well send for Baldwin to form a broadly-based government. The two men did not discuss the personnel of this hybrid administration, but Chamberlain clearly got the impression that Simon would not object to being included.[194]

Simon now seemed ready for a complete break with his Liberal colleagues. In advance of a party meeting on 11 December he warned the new Chief Whip, Archibald Sinclair, that he must insist that the party should declare itself opposed to changing the Trade Union Political Levy from a contracting-in to a contracting-out basis. If the party preferred ambiguity then he would reluctantly go his own way.[195] In the event, however, an open rupture was once again avoided at the party meeting. Simon, perhaps concerned at the amount of Liberal support he might receive, seemed reluctant to take the ultimate step. He reiterated his criticism of Liberal strategy in sustaining the Labour government, but withdrew his resolution on the Political Levy and left the meeting. Two days later he told his constituents that they must not be surprised if in future he exercised an independent judgment and followed an independent line in public affairs.

Simon's uneasy relationship with the Liberal party in general and Lloyd George in particular continued through the early months of 1931. When the government introduced legislation designed to undo the Conservative Trades Disputes Act of 1927, a clash was inevitable. Simon was understandably determined to reassert his views as to the illegality of a general strike. In a major speech Simon called for the 'humane slaughter' of the bill and clashed publicly with the man who was still nominally his party leader. In an intervention Lloyd George appeared to imply that the primary motive behind Simon's actions was his own personal advancement. Though Lloyd George felt he had 'knocked [Simon's] speech endways',[196] many Conservatives were impressed by Simon's contribution to the debate. Lane Fox doubted whether he had ever done better:

There was not a dull moment and, though very closely reasoned, his speech was not so subtle and hair-splitting as some of his speeches have been.[197]

Though the question of tariffs had still to be confronted, Simon had now become an acceptable figure in the eyes of most Conservatives. He even seemed ready to distance himself from Liberal demands for electoral reform. Austen Chamberlain was quite unequivocal:

By the speeches which you have made and above all by the public work you have done, you have become a great figure in the public life of the country, and a great figure you will remain whatever happens.

Writing as one who could himself just about claim to be a renegade Liberal from the days of the split over Home Rule in the 1880s and 1890s, Chamberlain went on to hint that Simon's rightful place was in government. He wanted him to be not merely an 'outstanding Personality but a Force'. The first step in this process would be to rally likeminded Liberals behind him.[198] The political columnist in *Punch* echoed these sentiments. Simon had become 'the biggest man and the most formidable debater' in the House of Commons. His prestige at Westminster was 'tremendous'.[199] Few men could have failed to be emboldened by such flattery. After reasserting that if Liberalism was to be merely a variant of socialism, as the party's continued support for a discredited Labour government seemed to imply, there was no reason for its independent existence, Simon renewed his negotiations with Neville Chamberlain.[200] The latter was disappointed that as yet Simon had not marshalled his forces within the ranks of dissident Liberals into a coherent whole, but noted with approval Simon's intention to speak out in public against the government and against Lloyd George's policies of increased expenditure.[201]

Simon gave the first public indication of the movement in his thinking on tariffs in an interview on the budget deficit with the editor of the *Sunday News* at the beginning of March. He had, he said, no intention of abandoning essential Liberal principles, but nor did he wish to be 'a sort of indoor servant to Socialism.' A telling sentence indicated an important change of heart:

I, at any rate, am not going to shut out of my mind the consideration of fiscal measures which may be found to be necessary, even though they involve steps which in times of prosperity and abounding trade Liberals would never contemplate.[202]

Two days later, asserting that the limits of direct taxation had been reached, he invited an audience in Manchester, in the heartland of Free Trade, to ponder on the fiscal methods they might be forced to adopt.[203] Writing to his old colleague, Lord Reading, Simon was far more explicit. His conversion to the case for tariffs was less a matter of economic doctrine than of practical necessity. The prospect of an unbalanced budget was alarming; the series of loans to the Unemployment Fund had in effect eaten up the Sinking Fund. Much as he would like to see expenditure reduced, this could not happen quickly. He had no intention of going further than this nor of professing enthusiasm which he did not feel. But

I do not think I can go to Economy meetings and talk generalities without making the observation which the very disturbing facts of the financial situation are forcing upon me.[204]

Simon's readiness to contemplate an emergency tariff for revenue purposes was reasonable enough, especially as explained in his letter to Reading. But coming from an erstwhile high priest of Free Trade, it made criticism inevitable. Lloyd George was not slow to take up the challenge. Abuse came easily to him in speaking of a man for whom he had never felt much warmth. Addressing a meeting of Liberal candidates at the Caxton Hall, Lloyd George cruelly asserted that Protection was 'one of the subjects to which Sir John has lent one of his countenances'.[205] Sadly for Simon's historical reputation it is Lloyd George's interpretation of this critical phase in his career which has found favour. One more nail was placed in the coffin of Simon's reputation for straightforwardness and political integrity. Yet while the importance of political ambition can never be discounted in Simon's career, it is worth stressing that the intellectual path which had brought him to abandon what most regarded as a *sine qua non* of true Liberalism was trodden also by many others, not least by John Maynard Keynes. If the most distinguished economist in the Liberal ranks reached the same conclusion, Simon may at least be given the benefit of the doubt as regards his motivation. Throughout these months he displayed a genuine fear about the economic consequences of the continued existence of the Labour government.

If Simon were to induce other Liberals to join him in deserting Lloyd George he would need to be able to offer some guarantees regarding the next general election. He had of course only secured his own seat in 1929 by virtue of Conservative abstention. Negotiations with the Conservatives therefore proceeded apace after his Manchester speech.[206] By the time of a meeting of the parliamentary Liberal party on 24 March, at which seventeen MPs voted against Lloyd George's proposal to support the government if pledges were given, the Chief Whip believed – probably prematurely – that Simon had the necessary assurances and that his followers would have no Tory opponents at the next general election.[207] At all events Simon seemed happy with the way matters were developing. Dining two days later with Leo Amery, one of the few leading politicians in whose presence he ever felt able to drop his guard, he talked about his plans and ideas for the future. His hope, it appeared, was to join a future government, preferably as Foreign Secretary – 'an ambition which it had never occurred to me that he cherished'.[208]

A final parting of the ways was now imminent. As Simon himself put it rather graphically, Liberals could not go on poised like Mohamed's coffin between two equal attractions, or 'rather oscillating uneasily in the valley of No Meaning'.[209] He now seemed almost anxious for issues to arise that would differentiate his own wing of Liberalism from that led by Lloyd George. On 19 May he spoke in the House of Commons against the government's proposed land tax, a cause to which Lloyd George had of course attached himself before the First World War. It seemed to Simon 'quite impossible' for a Liberal to support land taxes, except for tactical reasons. They represented a 'very definite test of our relations to Socialism.'[210] By early June one Conservative backbencher noted that Simon was 'not far from becoming a member of the Tory Party'. He had had several talks with Simon who was 'rapidly coming our way'.[211] Finally on 26 June, accompanied by Sir Robert Hutchinson and Ernest Brown, Simon formally resigned the Liberal whip. The occasion of the breach was the Liberals' confused parliamentary tactics over the land tax proposals. They scarcely merited Simon's withering indictment that the parliamentary party had by its 'pitiful exhibition' reached a 'lower depth of humiliation than any into which it had yet been led'.[212] As the Chief Whip rightly stressed in his published acknowledgement of Simon's withdrawal, the imposition of a land tax of a penny in the pound on capital values was scarcely a matter for resignation. It had been clear for more than six months that there was little common ground between Simon and the Lloyd Georgeite Liberal party.[213]

'The effect on the party is serious,' commented one Lloyd George acolyte.[214] This was a considerable understatement. What had become the Liberal 'right' now began a general exodus. Beatrice Webb was rather nearer the mark when she predicted the dissolution of the historic Liberal party.[215] Seeking re-election to the largely formal post of Vice-President of the Yorkshire Liberal Federation, Simon found himself opposed and obliged to face a ballot. Lloyd George did not miss the opportunity to condemn Simon's conduct. Seldom since the days of his Limehouse speech on the House of Lords had he used such venomous language. On 3 July, during the third reading of the government's Finance Bill, Lloyd George launched his attack, comparing Simon to a teetotaller who had turned alcoholic. He did not, he said, in the least object to Simon changing his opinions:

but I do object to this intolerable self-righteousness . . . Greater men . . . have done it in the past, but . . . they, at any rate, did not leave behind them the slime of hypocrisy in passing from one side to another.[216]

Had events been allowed to take their course, it seems likely that the Conservatives and the Simonite Liberals would have sought to eject the government when the House reassembled after the summer recess. As it was, such plans were overtaken by the dramatic internal collapse of the Labour cabinet. With the pound under severe pressure and unable to agree on a package of economy measures, the cabinet resigned in August only to find MacDonald re-emerging with the King's commission to form an all-party administration, charged with tackling the country's mounting economic crisis. When the new cabinet was announced, there was still no place within it for John Simon. Samuel and Reading represented the Liberal party and Simon could scarcely expect preferment through an organisation he had so recently renounced. For a moment it seemed that he might have badly miscalculated. Simon lost no opportunity to emphasise an almost embarrassing willingness to cooperate. Not only did he volunteer to the Prime Minister to move a vote of confidence in the new government, but he even suggested that, should MacDonald feel obliged to resign his seat at Seaham Harbour because of pressure from his constituency Labour party, he would be prepared to stand down in Spen Valley in MacDonald's favour.[217] Of more importance was his unequivocal statement to the House of Commons on 15 September in favour of an emergency tariff to deal with the deficit on the balance of payments.[218] By now about half of the Liberal MPs elected in 1929 were ready to follow him. On 23 September twenty-nine Liberals joined Simon, Runciman and Hore-Belisha in a Memorial to MacDonald, supporting any measures the cabinet thought necessary to deal with the trade imbalance.[219] Invited by Geoffrey Shakespeare and Leslie Hore-Belisha, Simon accepted the invitation of more than two dozen Liberal MPs to lead the so-called Libertal National party.[220] He sought funds to reassure Liberal MPs that in cutting themselves adrift from Lloyd George's financial aid they were not committing themselves to electoral disaster,[221] and on 5 October his group formed a separate organisation for the specific purpose of contesting the next election in alliance with the Conservatives and with MacDonald's National Labour supporters.[222] Simon was able to promise the Prime Minister the firm backing of twenty-two Liberal back-benchers.[223]

The government now decided to seek a 'doctor's mandate' from the electorate to continue its economic policies and save the pound. Potential internal cabinet difficulties were overcome by the suggestion that each party should put forward its own programme under a blanket of words supplied by MacDonald. But there was no equivocation in Simon's position. While Liberals within the government agonised over the question of tariffs, Simon argued that the game of formula-hunting had gone on long enough:

I want to use whatever powers I have to support orderly government and defeat the Opposition Socialists and I strongly think that the best thing for us to do is to support the Prime Minister.[224]

Studiously he eschewed any renewed association with his erstwhile colleagues in the mainstream Liberal party.[225] In the election campaign Simon suffered again from Lloyd George's attacks, but it no longer mattered.[226] Ill during the critical events of the summer, Lloyd George was now isolated from both the main Liberal groupings in his opposition to the National Government. Meanwhile the electoral tide was overwhelmingly behind the government. In the new House there were 473 Conservatives, 35 Liberal Nationals, 13 National Labour and 33 Liberals. Opposing them stood 52 Labour members and four Lloyd Georgeites. In Spen Valley Simon was returned with a majority of almost 13,000 in a straight fight with Labour. The only question that remained was what reward Simon would receive for his support.

Both at the time and for many years afterwards Simon's defection from the Liberal party was almost universally condemned as an example of blatant careerism. His detractors picture him manoeuvring skilfully through the slimy trail of hypocrisy painted by Lloyd George with no aspiration other than to secure advancement for himself. They seem to forget that his drift away from the Liberal party was by no means an isolated one. Many others followed the same course. In fact his actions seems to have been more principled than critics have allowed. It is certainly true that once the crisis of 1931 had broken Simon saw clearly the possibilities of personal advance and sought to take advantage of them, but he could not have predicted the course of events which culminated in the setting up of a National Government. His basic disagreement with Lloyd George over the Liberal party's attitude towards the Labour government was genuine enough. It grew out of conclusions he had rightly drawn from the experience of 1923–24. To these were added his strong feelings over the government's treatment of his Commission's Report on India. In the course of the 1920s Socialism became for Simon the ultimate political evil, just as he came also to see that the Conservative party of Baldwin and Neville Chamberlain reflected at least some of the Liberal values which he held most dear. Similarly Simon's conversion to the necessity for tariffs was no intellectual somersault. The process was slow, painful and reluctant. Many were irritated by Simon's hesitations. 'The real difficulty,' noted Edward Grigg, was that he would 'not do more than declare an open mind on the fiscal issue'.[227] But unlike many who professed to comprehend the complex arguments involved, Simon would not be rushed. 'I spend most of my time,' he wrote in September 1931, 'in trying to understand the essentials of the economic situation in this astonishingly changing world.'[228] In supporting a government which proclaimed the need for economy – the reduction of government expenditure – he could not have been more faithful to his lifelong Liberal credentials.

The Prime Minister discussed the question of government posts with Simon on 1 November. Where office was concerned Simon was not prone to false modesty. He looked for a position at the heart of affairs, international, monetary and fiscal. Questions of status precluded the post of Minister without Portfolio – he would accept nothing inferior to Samuel who was already Home Secretary. In short only the Treasury and the Foreign Office seemed appropriate.[229] MacDonald, grateful for Simon's electoral support and more especially anxious to emphasise the National character of his new administration, duly obliged. More than a decade and a half after he had last laid down the seals of ministerial office, Sir John Simon reappeared as His Majesty's Secretary of State for Foreign Affairs. Patience and persistence had had their reward.

Notes

1   Simon to Lord Inchcape 21 Nov. 1930, S P 67 fo. 23.
2   cf. S. Ball, *Baldwin and the Conservative Party* (London, 1988) pp. ix–x.
3   Roberts, *Simon* pp. 210–19.
4   'Sir John Simon' by Ben Spoor, *British Weekly* 10 Sept. 1925.
5   Simon to Reading 4 Feb. 1925, Reading MSS Eur F118/101.
6   *Manchester Guardian* 26 Oct. 1925.
7   *Daily News* 31 Oct. 1925.
8   *Pembrokeshire Telegraph* 2 July 1925.
9   Simon to Reading 4 Feb. 1925, Reading MSS Eur F118/101.
10 J. Bowle, *Viscount Samuel: a biography* (London, 1957) p. 260.
11 Barnes and Nicholson (eds.), *Amery Diaries* i, 445.
12 J. Simon, *Three Speeches on the General Strike* (London, 1926) pp. 2–3.
13 Ibid, p. 5.
14 Ibid, pp. 13–33.
15 C. L. Mowat, *Britain between the Wars 1918–1940* (London, 1955) p. 323.
16 Lord Birkenhead, *Last Essays* (London, 1930) pp. 186–7.
17 A. Duff Cooper, *Old Men Forget* (London, 1953) p. 151.
18 N. Chamberlain diary 7 May 1926, Chamberlain MSS NC 2/22.
19 See, for example, H. Macmillan, *Winds of Change* (London, 1966) p. 167: 'It had a dramatic and devastating effect on the morale of the TUC leaders.' *The Sunday Times* concluded on 16 May 1926 that the speech had a 'devastating effect on the Trade Union leaders'.
20 *Sunday Express* 16 May 1926.
21 Simon to R. Muir 12 May 1926, S P 60 fo. 76. Simon was also careful to adopt a conciliatory tone in a speech delivered in the Cleckheaton Town Hall on 20 May,

Simon, *Three Speeches* pp. 34–55.

22 See, for example, Duff Cooper, *Old Men Forget* p. 151.

23 The following year, when Lloyd George and Simon met to discuss Liberal policy towards China, Simon asked him what the expression 'Shanghaied' meant. 'It's what you and the Liberal party tried to do to me last May,' retorted Lloyd George. A. J. P. Taylor (ed.), *Lloyd George: A Diary* p. 249.

24 Simon and others to Asquith 31 May 1926 (Simon's draft) S P 60 fos. 91–3.

25 Freddie Guest, who led the effort to tie Lloyd George to specific commitments, confessed that he 'would sooner trust him than Simon'. J. Ramsden (ed.), *Real Old Tory Politics* (London, 1984) p. 227.

26 *Westminster Gazette* 5 June 1926.

27 Memorandum by Asquith 5 Oct. 1926, Runciman MSS 204.

28 Richard Holt diary 24 June 1926, 920 DUR 1/11.

29 Memorandum by J. Rowland Evans 20 June 1926, S P 60 fos. 104–7.

30 Ibid.

31 Simon to Asquith 9 Oct. 1926, Asquith MSS 35 fos. 272–3.

32 Arthur Crosfield to Reading 15 Sept. 1926, Lloyd George MSS G/5/7/5.

33 *Manchester Guardian* 19 Oct. 1926.

34 Simon to D. Maclean 27 Dec. 1926, Asquith MSS 148 fos. 220–1.

35 V. Bonham Carter to G. Murray 10 Nov. 1926, cited M. Bentley, *The Liberal Mind 1914–1929* (Cambridge, 1977) p. 108.

36 Simon to Sir Charles Mallet 18 Oct. 1926, S P 60 fo. 134.

37 Simon to Lloyd George 8 Nov. 1926, Lloyd George MSS G/18/2/3.

38 T. Wilson, *The Downfall of the Liberal Party 1914–1935* (London, 1966) p. 344; J. Campbell, *Lloyd George: Goat in the Wilderness 1922–1931* (London, 1977) p. 196.

39 J. Campbell, *F. E. Smith* p. 750.

40 Birkenhead to Irwin 16 June 1927, cited Campbell, *F. E. Smith* p. 750.

41 Roberts, *Simon* pp. 232–3.

42 Simon to Birkenhead 16 May 1927, S P 61 fo. 4.

43 N. Chamberlain to Irwin 25 Aug. 1927, Irwin MSS Eur C 152/17.

44 Irwin to N. Chamberlain 4 Oct. 1927, Irwin MSS Eur C 152/17; Irwin to Stonehaven 6 March 1928, Irwin MSS Eur C 152/18.

45 Archbishop of York to Irwin 27 Jan. 1928, Irwin MSS Eur C 152/18.

46 Simon to Birkenhead 17 June 1927, S P 61 fo. 8.

47 Birkenhead to Irwin 30 July 1927, Simon MSS Eur F 77/1/77.

48 Simon to Irwin 21 Dec. 1927, Simon MSS Eur F 77/2/25.

49 Lane Fox to Irwin 3 April 1928, Irwin MSS Eur C 152/18.

50 Sir Malcolm Seton to Irwin 20 Oct. 1927, Irwin MSS Eur C 152/17.

51 Simon to Lord Cave 24 Jan. 1928, SP 61 fo. 136.

52 Ibid.

53 R. R. James, *Memoirs of a Conservative* (London, 1969) p. 273.

54 Birkenhead's secretary to Davidson 20 Oct. 1927, cited ibid. p. 273. For Simon's speech on the situation in China, see *The Times* 28 March 1927.

55 Simon to H. Samuel 1 Feb. 1928, Simon MSS Eur F 77/7/18.

56 Irwin to Birkenhead 12 Dec. 1927, Simon MSS Eur F 77/1/203.

57 Irwin to G. Dawson 2 Feb. 1928, Irwin MSS Eur C 152/18.

58 Birkenhead to Irwin 19 Jan. 1928, cited Lord Birkenhead, *F. E.* pp. 514–15.

59 Simon to Birkenhead 1 Feb. 1928, Simon MSS Eur F 77/7/14.

60 Simon to Baldwin 9 Feb. 1928, Baldwin MSS vol. 102 fos. 198–9.

61 Simon to Wilfred Green 23 Feb. 1928, S P 61 fos. 156–7.

62 Simon to Baldwin 9 Feb. 1928, Baldwin MSS vol. 102 fos. 198–9.

63 Lord Birkenhead, *Halifax: the Life of Lord Halifax* (London, 1965) p. 252.

64 Simon to Reading 3 March 1928, Reading MSS Eur F 118/125.

65 Simon to Birkenhead 1 March 1928, Simon MSS Eur F 77/3/4.

66 Simon to Baldwin 8 March 1928, Baldwin MSS vol. 102 fos. 202–4.

67 Simon to Reading 3 March 1928, Reading MSS Eur F 118/125.

68 Simon to Lloyd George 15 March 1928, Lloyd George MSS G18/2/4.

69 Irwin to Archbishop of York 16 March 1928 and to Reading 22 March 1928, Irwin MSS Eur C 152/18.

70 Simon to Winterton 15 March 1928, Simon MSS Eur F 77/3/14.

71 Simon generally worked well with his fellow Commissioners. To Birkenhead he later wrote: 'A more loyal and pleasant set of people to deal with you could not possibly have chosen and I am deeply grateful to all of them.' Simon to Birkenhead 10 Oct. 1928, Simon MSS Eur F 77/3/76.

72 Lane Fox to Irwin 26 Dec. 1927, Irwin MSS Eur C 152/17.

73 Lane Fox to Baldwin 20 March 1928, Baldwin MSS vol. 102 fos. 205–6.

74 Lane Fox to Irwin 3 April 1928, Irwin MSS Eur C 152/18.

75 Irwin to Robert Cecil 7 April 1928, Cecil MSS Add MS 51084 fo. 58.

76 Birkenhead to Irwin 26 April 1928, cited Campbell, *F. E. Smith* pp. 754–5.

77 Simon to Irwin 17 May 1928, Simon MSS Eur F 77/4/136.

78 Ibid 28 June 1928, Irwin MSS Eur C 152/18.

79 Lord Lee of Fareham, *A Good Innings* (privately published, 1939–40) iii, 1240.

80 *The Times* 6 Sept. 1928; *Northern Mail* 24 Aug. 1928; *Daily News* 30 July 1928.

81 Simon to Irwin 18 Sept. 1928, Simon MSS Eur F 77/4/240.

82 Simon to Birkenhead 10 Oct. 1928, Simon MSS Eur F 77/3/76.

83 Simon to V. Phillipps 11 Oct. 1928, S P 62 fos. 27–8.

84 Birkenhead to Irwin 18 Sept. 1928, cited Birkenhead, *F. E.* p. 520.

85 Simon to V. Phillipps 11 Oct. 1928, S P 62 fos. 27–8.

86 Note by Dawson of conversation with Simon 26 Sept. 1928, Dawson MSS 73 fos. 101–2; J. E. Wrench, *Geoffrey Dawson and our Times* (London, 1955) pp. 266–7.

87 Simon to J. Wylie 26 Jan. 1929, S P 62 fo. 60.

88 Lane Fox to Baldwin 27 Nov. 1928, Baldwin MSS vol. 102 fos. 247–9.

89 Simon to Peel 23 Oct. 1928, Simon MSS Eur F 77/3/86.

90 Simon to MacDonald 11 Dec. 1923, S P 62 fos. 38–42.

91 Simon to Irwin 10 Dec. 1928, Simon MSS Eur F 77/4/315; Simon to Reading 12 Dec. 1928, Reading MSS Eur F 118/125.

92 Sir W. Laurence to Irwin 31 Jan. 1929, Irwin MSS Eur C 152/18.

93 Simon to Irwin 15 Feb. 1929, Simon MSS Eur F 77/5/29.

94 Simon to W. Runciman 19 March 1929, Runciman MSS 224.

95 G. Brumwell to G. Dawson 17 Jan. 1929, Dawson MSS 73 fo. 172; Lane Fox to Baldwin 3 Feb. 1929, Baldwin MSS vol. 103 fo. 11; T. Jones, *Whitehall Diary* ii, 171–2.

96 Lane Fox to Baldwin 13 March 1929, Baldwin MSS vol. 103 fo. 17.

97 Simon to Runciman 19 March 1929, Runciman MSS 224.

98 Campbell, *Goat in Wilderness* p. 230. In Simon's defence it should be stated that

he had singled out Socialism and Protection as two false panaceas for unemployment in a speech at Glastonbury in July 1928. *Daily News* 30 July 1928.

99 *Manchester Guardian* 16 May 1929.
100 Maclean to Gladstone 19 May 1929, Gladstone MSS Add. MS 46474.
101 Simon to Irwin 18 Sept. 1928, Simon MSS Eur F 77/4/241.
102 T. Wilson, *Downfall of Liberal Party* p. 345.
103 Simon to Runciman 11 May 1929, Runciman MSS 219.
104 Simon to Reading 11 Oct. 1928, Reading MSS Eur F 118/125.
105 R. R. James, *Churchill: A Study in Failure* (London, 1970) p. 183.
106 Lord Balcarres to Irwin 13 May 1929, Irwin MSS Eur C 152/18.
107 Simon to Irwin 6 June 1929, Simon MSS Eur F 77/5/56.
108 Note by D. Maclean 14 June 1929, Runciman MSS 221.
109 Simon to Irwin 27 June 1929, Simon MSS Eur F 77/5/61.
110 Lady Hilton Young diary 10 June 1929, Kennet MSS.
111 Simon to Irwin 27 June 1929, Simon MSS Eur F 77/5/61.
112 *Retrospect* pp. 150–2.
113 Lord Halifax, *Fullness of Days* (London, 1957) pp. 117–18; Irwin to Salisbury 3 Dec. 1929, Irwin MSS Eur C 152/18.
114 Irwin to Salisbury 3 Dec. 1929, Irwin MSS Eur C 152/18.
115 Lane Fox diary 24 Sept. 1929.
116 For Wedgwood Benn's opinion see Winterton, *Orders of the Day* p. 159.
117 Lane Fox to Irwin 27 Nov. 1929, Irwin MSS Eur C 152/18.
118 MacDonald diary 3 Nov. 1929.
119 Salisbury to Irwin 14 Nov. 1929, Irwin MSS Eur C 152/18.
120 Lord Lytton to Irwin 20 Nov. 1929, Irwin MSS Eur C152/18; Lane Fox diary 7 Oct. 1929; for Reading's opposition to the Irwin Declaration see Reading to Benn 27 Oct. 1929, Lloyd George MSS G 16/10/10. R. J. Moore, *The Crisis of Indian Unity* (Oxford, 1974), p. 65.
121 Peel to Baldwin 23 Oct. 1929, Baldwin MSS vol. 103 fos. 61–2.
122 Hoare to Irwin 28 Oct. 1929, Irwin MSS Eur C 152/18; Barnes and Nicholson (eds.), *Amery Diaries* ii, 52.
123 Simon to Irwin 14 Nov. 1929, Irwin MSS Eur C 152/18.
124 Dawson to Irwin 3 Nov. 1929, Irwin MSS Eur C 152/18.
125 Viscount Goschen to Irwin 4 Dec. 1929, Irwin MSS Eur C 152/18.
126 Barnes and Nicholson (eds.), *Amery Diaries* ii, 52.
127 Campbell, *F. E. Smith* p. 821.
128 Salisbury to Baldwin 23 Oct. 1929, cited Gilbert, *Churchill* v, 353.
129 Lord Templewood, *Nine Troubled Years* (London, 1954) p. 46; note by Simon for Philip Snowden 29 Oct. 1929, Baldwin MSS vol. 103 fo. 130.
130 B. Webb diary 4 Nov. 1929. It was not long before Simon began making enquiries about his likely earnings should he return to the bar. H. R. Pocock to Simon 20 Feb. 1930, S P 62 fos. 230–2.
131 Simon to MacDonald 3 Nov. 1929, MacDonald MSS, PRO 30/69/344.
132 H. Nicolson, *King George V* (London, 1952) pp. 504–5.
133 Lane Fox to Irwin 7 Nov. 1929, Irwin MSS Eur C 152/18; Lane Fox diary 29 Oct. 1929.
134 MacDonald diary 6 Nov. 1929.
135 Winterton, *Orders of the Day* p. 160.

136 R. James (ed.), *Memoirs of a Conservative* p. 309.

137 House of Commons Debates, 5th Series, vol. 231, col. 1337.

138 Simon to Reading 15 Nov. 1929, Reading MSS Eur F 118/101.

139 Barnes and Nicholson (eds.), *Amery Diaries* ii, 53.

140 Lane Fox to Irwin 2 April 1930, Irwin MSS Eur C 152/19.

141 Ibid, 19 Feb. 1930.

142 Memorandum by Simon 9 May 1930, S P 64 fos. 35–6.

143 *Retrospect* p. 148.

144 T. Clarke, *My Lloyd George Diary* (London, 1939) pp. 82–3.

145 For tributes to this work see C. Attlee, *As it Happened* (London, 1954) p. 96 and
     C. B. Fry, *Life worth Living* p. 325: 'By far the greatest exposition of India that
     has ever been produced.' Attlee always argued that the whole Report was more
     successful than is generally claimed: 'The India Bill which Sam Hoare piloted
     through the Commons [in 1935] was practically, although he didn't say so, an
     implementation of the Simon Report.' F. Williams, *A Prime Minister Remem-
     bers* (London, 1961) p. 205.

146 *Report of the Indian Statutory Commission* 2 vols (London, 1930).

147 B. Webb diary 16 June 1930.

148 G. Peele and C. Cook (eds.), *The Politics of Reappraisal 1918–1939* (London,
     1975) p. 126.

149 Note by Simon 1 July 1930, S P 65 fos. 44–7.

150 A. Chamberlain to Simon 22 June 1930, S P 64 fo. 193.

151 Ball, *Baldwin* p. 120.

152 Simon to Irwin 16 May 1930, Irwin MSS Eur C 152/19.

153 Irwin to Hoare 10 June 1930, Irwin MSS Eur C 152/19; Irwin to Benn 20 June
     1930, Irwin MSS Eur C 152/6.

154 Irwin to J. Davidson 3 July 1930, Irwin MSS Eur C 152/19. See also Irwin to R.
     Cecil 1 Oct. 1930, Cecil MSS Add MS 51084 fos. 78–9.

155 Simon to Dawson 30 June 1930, S P 65 fos. 40–1.

156 Simon to J. Buchan 2 July 1930, Tweedsmuir MSS.

157 Irwin to Simon 1 Aug. 1930, S P 66 fo. 3. As Geoffrey Dawson pointed out,
     Simon's exclusion could only be justified if his Report was to be the whole basis
     of discussion at the Conference (which had clearly been ruled out). If it was
     merely to be one of many proposals, logic demanded the exclusion of any Indian
     known to be a protagonist of any of these proposals. Dawson to Irwin 10 July
     1930, Irwin MSS Eur C 152/19.

158 Simon to J. Buchan 2 July 1930, Tweedsmuir MSS.

159 Note by Simon 1 July 1930, S P 65 fos. 44–7.

160 Simon to Baldwin 5 July 1930, SP 65 fo. 85.

161 Simon to Garvin 17 Sept. 1930, S P 66 fo. 72.

162 Simon to Professor R. Coupland 1 July 1930, S P 65 fo. 51.

163 Ibid, 5 July 1930, S P 65 fo. 96.

164 Irwin to Simon 1 Aug. 1930, S P 66 fo. 3; Irwin to Archbishop of Canterbury 9
     Dec. 1930, Irwin MSS Eur C 152/19.

165 See, for example, Lane Fox to Irwin 21 Aug. 1930, cited Gilbert, *Churchill* v,
     companion pt. 2 p. 180.

166 Irwin to Baldwin 5 Aug. 1930, Baldwin MSS vol. 104 fo. 27.

167 Winterton, *Orders* p. 163; Simon to A. Chamberlain 30 July 1930, S P 65 fo. 181.

Note MacDonald's diary entry for 31 July 1930: 'Yesterday Baldwin saw me and told me he was not supporting [Austen] Chamberlain in his attitude on Simon.'

168 Gilbert, *Churchill* v, companion pt. 2, p. 181.

169 Simon to Lane Fox 25 Oct. 1930, S P 66 fos. 132–3.

170 Irwin to Linlithgow 4 Aug. 1930, Irwin MSS Eur C 152/19.

171 Lane Fox to Irwin 29 Oct. 1930, Irwin MSS Eur C 152/19.

172 See Lane Fox diary for 20 Oct. 1929, 6 Nov. 1929 and 29 April 1930 for observations on the strain Simon was under at this time.

173 Simon to Reading 4 June 1930, Reading MSS Eur F 118/101.

174 'Sir John Simon – In the First Rank but Never the First,' *Daily Herald* 19 July 1930.

175 Amulree to Simon 29 March 1931, S P 67 fo. 165.

176 MacDonald to Amulree 6 April 1931, Amulree MSS Dep. c 386 fo. 58.

177 H. Montgomery Hyde, *British Air Policy Between the Wars 1918–1939* (London, 1976) p. 261.

178 Ibid, p. 264; Simon to Amulree 18 May 1931, Amulree MSS Dep. c 386 fo. 84.

179 Simon to Lord Inchcape 21 Nov. 1930, S P 67 fo. 23.

180 See, for example, Lane Fox to Irwin 21 Jan. 1931, Irwin MSS Eur C 152/19.

181 Ibid, 28 Jan. 1931; Peele and Cook (eds.), *Reappraisal* p. 129.

182 Barnes and Nicholson (eds.), *Amery Diaries* ii, 158.

183 Lord Butler, *The Art of the Possible* (London, 1971) pp. 41–2.

184 Churchill to Sir Mark Hunter 28 Feb. 1931, cited in Gilbert, *Churchill* v, companion pt. 2, p. 283; Lee, *A Good Innings* iii, 1290.

185 Lane Fox to Irwin 22 Dec. 1929, Irwin MSS Eur C 152/18.

186 O. Mosley, *My Life* (London, 1968) p. 249.

187 Simon to Lloyd George 25 Oct. 1930, S P 249 fo. 93.

188 Simon diary 20 Nov. 1930, S P 249 fos. 5–8.

189 D. Rowland Evans to Simon 20 Nov. 1930, S P 249 fos. 12–13.

190 Simon diary 27 Nov. 1930, S P 249 fo. 14.

191 Ibid, fos. 15–17.

192 *Yorkshire Post* 8 Nov. 1930.

193 L. Jones to R. Holt 9 Jan. 1931, Holt MSS 920 DUR 14/27/189.

194 N. Chamberlain diary 5 Dec. 1930, Chamberlain MSS NC 2/22. Simon's account of this meeting is to be found in his diary entry for 1 Dec. 1930, S P 249 fos. 45–6. The two accounts are substantially the same, although Simon makes his own position on tariffs appear less enthusiastic.

195 Simon to Sinclair 11 Dec. 1930, S P 249 fo. 106.

196 A. J. P. Taylor (ed.), *My Darling Pussy* p. 139.

197 Lane Fox to Irwin 28 Jan. 1931, Irwin MSS Eur C 152/19. The government's bill was so mangled in committee that it was withdrawn.

198 A. Chamberlain to Simon 16 Jan. 1931, S P 67 fo. 132.

199 *Punch* 4 Feb. 1931.

200 Speech at South Molton 31 Jan. 1931, *The Times* 2 Feb. 1931.

201 N. Chamberlain to Ida Chamberlain 8 Feb. 1931, Chamberlain MSS NC 18/1/725.

202 *Sunday News* 1 March 1931.

203 *The Times* 4 March 1931.

204 Simon to Reading 2 March 1931, Reading MSS Eur F 118/101.

205 *Yorkshire Observer* 27 March 1931. For Lloyd George's anger towards Simon see Clarke, *My Lloyd George Diary* p. 112.

206 Ball, *Baldwin* p. 165.

207 Sinclair to H. A. L. Fisher 20 March 1931, Fisher MSS 69 fos. 34–7; R. Skidelsky, *Politicians and the Slump* (London, 1967) p. 332. Yet, rather surprisingly, Simon still did not feel able to count on more than four supporters to vote against the government. N. Chamberlain to Ida Chamberlain 5 April 1931, Chamberlain MSS NC 18/1/733.

208 Barnes and Nicholson (eds.), *Amery Diaries* ii, 158.

209 Simon to Percy Withers 16 April 1931, S P 68 fo. 14.

210 Simon to Reading 2 June 1931, Reading MSS Eur F 118/101.

211 P. Hannon to Beaverbrook 10 June 1931, Hannon MSS 18.

212 Simon to Sinclair 26 June 1931, S P 68 fos. 92–3.

213 Sinclair to Simon 27 June 1931, S P 178 fo. 2.

214 Clarke, *My Lloyd George Diary* p. 121.

215 B. Webb diary 15 March 1931.

216 House of Commons Debates, 5th Series, vol. 254, cols. 1657–68. Yet Lloyd George's own conduct was equally open to charges of self-interested calculation. Following discussions with MacDonald the two men seem to have agreed that Lloyd George should receive a senior post in a MacDonald cabinet. F. Owen, *Tempestuous Journey* (London, 1954) p. 717.

217 Simon to MacDonald 1 Sept. 1931, S P 68 fo. 118.

218 House of Commons Debates, 5th Series, vol. 256, cols. 719–31; Amery, *My Political Life* iii, 65; R. Bassett, *1931: Political Crisis* (London, 1958) p. 255.

219 D. J. Wrench, ' "Cashing In". The Parties and the National Government, August 1931 – September 1932,' *Journal of British Studies* (1984), xxiii, 2, p. 142.

220 G. Shakespeare, *Let Candles be Brought In* (London, 1949) p. 138. Shakespeare later paid tribute to Simon's leadership of the new party: 'Although there were heavy demands for his services . . . he was never too busy to give advice or help to Members of our group. My own personal relations with him have always been intimate and I have treasured his friendship.' Ibid p. 139.

221 Simon to Lord Inchcape 24 Sept. 1931, S P 68 fos. 127–8.

222 *The Times* 5 Oct. 1931; Lord Hemingford, *Back-bencher and Chairman* (London, 1946) pp. 152–3.

223 Simon to MacDonald 5 Oct. 1931, S P 68 fo. 163.

224 Simon to H. R. Rathbone 2 Oct. 1931, S P 68 fo. 154; statement by Simon 3 Oct. 1931, quoted in Bassett, *1931* pp. 277–8.

225 Note of telephone conversation between Simon and Sir D. Maclean 30 Oct. 1931, Reading MSS Eur F118/131. After the election Simon declined to meet with Samuel to discuss the future relations of the two wings of the Liberal party, even though both had supported the National Government. The Liberal Nationals also decided to decline the Liberal whip in the House of Commons. R. Douglas, *History of the Liberal Party 1895–1970* (London, 1971) p. 223; H. Samuel, *Memoirs* p. 214.

226 *Manchester Guardian* 2 Nov. 1931.

227 Grigg to Lord Rosebery 29 June 1931, Altrincham MSS.

228 Simon to A. G. Gardiner 22 Sept. 1931, Gardiner MSS.

229 Simon to Baldwin 2 Nov. 1931, Baldwin MSS vol. 45 fos. 197–8.

CHAPTER FIVE

MAN OF MANCHUKUO

[Toby] Low asked me who was the worst Foreign Secretary [of the inter-war years]. I replied tactfully that I knew who the Office thought was the worst. Anthony asked: 'Who then?' and I replied: 'Simon'. Anthony: 'I agree.'[1]

Anyone attempting to rehabilitate or even impartially reassess the Foreign Secretaryship of Sir John Simon faces a decidedly uphill task. Simon's tenure – the longest of the decade – has been covered in a blanket indictment, with contemporaries and later historians competing with one another in hyperboles of condemnation. His appointment was 'disastrous'[2] or at least 'unexpected and unfortunate'.[3] He was 'a complete misfit', 'wholly unsuited' and 'miscast by temperament and training' for his new post[4] and, as Foreign Secretary, proved 'surely the worst of modern times'[5] or perhaps 'since Ethelred the Unready'.[6] Even governmental colleagues showed scant charity as they looked back on Simon's tenure of office. He was 'a signal failure', judged Lord Swinton; 'a hopeless Foreign Secretary' concluded Sir Donald Somervell.[7] In short Simon is seen to have initiated the least auspicious decade in the whole history of British foreign policy. He epitomised the short-comings and failures of the National Government as a whole:

Simon's advent to the Foreign Office was to commence a disastrous era in which under successive Foreign Secretaries . . . British power and influenced steadily declined and Britain was fatuously conducted towards the Second World War.[8]

The genesis of the policy of appeasement, which reached its shameful climax in 1938, is seen to lie in Simon's period at the Foreign Office. But the processes of historical revisionism, which have at least produced a greater understanding of the thinking behind the policies pursued at the end of the decade, have left Simon's tattered reputation largely unredeemed. The case for the defence has virtually gone by default.[9]

Yet the basis for a more sympathetic assessment does exist. Winston Churchill, no friend of the National Government's foreign policy and a man whose own writing had a profound effect in casting popular perceptions of the 1930s, made an important contribution to this task in a speech in the House of Commons in July 1935, shortly after Simon had moved to the less troubled waters of the Home Office:

I have criticized [Simon] and I shall probably criticize his successor, but I certainly think it is very unfair to try to pile upon a single man the blame for all the awful transformation and degeneration which has occurred in European affairs and in world affairs during the last four or five years. Certainly I feel that the late Foreign Secretary devoted to his task talents which are not easily to be rivalled . . . and a sincere, profound desire for peace . . . I hope that we shall not go about imagining that we are going to make our discussion of these matters any easier by simply trying to throw upon a single man the blame for events which all men have so far found themselves unable to contain or to control.[10]

Leo Amery took this theme much further shortly after Simon's death. Disturbed that *The Times* obituary had dismissed his old friend's Foreign Secretaryship as 'disastrous', he wrote to offer a corrective. *The Times* was 'telescoping events in a fashion which the impartial judgment of history is not likely to endorse'. According to Amery, Simon's handling of the Manchurian crisis was 'realistic and prudent'; his policy was to 'build up a containing wall of peaceful strength' against Hitlerian aggression; and had he remained in office longer 'he would have used his cool judgment and all his efforts to prevent Stresa, and incidentally the League of Nations itself, being wrecked.'[11]

If Simon's period of office as Foreign Secretary is to be understood, its context, domestic and international, must first be considered. At home this meant the unusual situation created by the existence of a National Government; abroad an environment which was being transformed by the prevailing economic crisis. In the making of British foreign policy the relationship between Prime Minister and Foreign Secretary is the single most important conjunction in government. MacDonald appointed Simon to the Foreign Office without enthusiasm. As he explained, 'the reconstitution of the Cabinet after the Election had to take more account of the representation of Parties than was possible before the Election.'[12] The Conservatives would have preferred Philip Cunliffe-Lister, but the latter was not acceptable to the Prime Minister. As an alternative Baldwin suggested Irwin, whose candidacy met with royal approval but who was himself not willing to serve. It may have been the King, who always had a high regard for Simon, who first mentioned his name.[13] Neville Chamberlain would have been happy to see Simon go to the Board of Trade instead of Runciman, but this was a post Simon would not accept because it would give him inferior status to Herbert Samuel.[14] Baldwin may have been prepared to see Simon at the Exchequer – which would probably have been Simon's own first preference – but Conservative party pressure dictated that this post be retained in Tory hands, and in any case MacDonald felt that Simon would not be acceptable as Chancellor.[15] At the end of the day, however, Simon had to be rewarded both for his personal support and in recognition of the three dozen MPs who regarded him as their leader. From MacDonald's point of view Simon had at least three merits. He was safely 'National', safely anti-Lloyd George, (which was not necessarily the case with Lord Reading, the outgoing Foreign Secretary), and at least not a Conservative. It was largely a negative recommendation, but it sufficed.

These years marked the saddest period in Ramsay MacDonald's career. disowned and reviled by the party whose fortunes he had done so much to build up, MacDonald was an increasingly pathetic figure at the head of the government. With his health, and particularly his eyesight, in decline, he increasingly owed his leading position in a government dominated by the Conservative party to Baldwin's ready acceptance of subordinate status. In domestic policy he frequently found himself overridden by his cabinet colleagues, so that it became ever more important for him to play a prominent role in the direction of British diplomacy. In his first premiership he had, of course, combined the post of Prime Minister with that of Foreign Secretary and he now found it easiest to exert an influence in this field. His diary shows that he never took to Simon at a personal level and that he became increasingly sceptical of his capacity for his post. From the outset, therefore, he sought to interfere in the work of his Foreign Secretary. Within days of his appointment Simon received clear instructions from the Prime Minister for a visit to Paris.[16] A tone had been set which was to be maintained. Neville Chamberlain illustrated the problems which this created:

The PM still thinks he has special influence with Stimson with whom he insists on exchanging telephonic negotiations while the unhappy Simon tries at the same time to carry on through the usual channels.[17]

Despite his failing strength MacDonald remained until the spring or early summer of 1934 the single most influential member of the cabinet on matters of foreign policy. Even as late as the following April he led the British delegation to the Stresa Conference, despite his by then palpable decline. He 'clung to office with the tenacity of the aged who believe that to release one's grip is to die'.[18]

Anticipating his appointment Simon had reflected that it would satisfy his 'ambition of helping about America and debts'.[19] In the press it was assumed that his appointment meant that the government intended to tackle the thorny problem of reparations and war debts which had defied final solution throughout the twenties. In fact many of the most pressing questions confronting British foreign policy makers in the early 1930s were inextricably intertwined with economic and commercial considerations. A paper drawn up inside the Foreign Office shortly after Simon took up his post neatly encapsulated the problem:

The links in the chain fall together more or less in the following order. The *monetary crisis* leads inevitably back to the *economic chaos* in Europe. The economic chaos and all attempts to deal with it involve in their turn the political questions of *reparations and war debts*. These are linked by the United States with the question of *disarmament*, and the latter, in the eyes of the French Government, depends upon the problem of *security*. The problem of security in its turn raises the question of the territorial status quo in Europe . . . which brings us to the *maintenance or revision of the Peace Settlement.*[20]

The lasting settlement of reparations and the imminent reassessment of the country's commercial relations with the Empire were the most obvious examples of pressing international issues with economic implications, but the whole aspect of the international scene had been transformed in the course of the late Labour government by the impact of the world economic crisis. The National Government owed its *raison d'être* to the impact of that crisis on Great Britain and its leading members never forgot their primary duty in this respect. Perhaps not until the very end of the decade did British diplomats assert the primacy of foreign policy over domestic economic interests. It took a long time to convince the leaders of the government that national security rather than economic prosperity was the pre-eminent national interest.[21]

All of this ensured that government ministers with economic responsibilities, and particularly the Chancellor, Neville Chamberlain, would have a prominent role in the making of British foreign policy in the early 1930s. Indeed Simon found himself effectively excluded from many of the issues with which he had confidently expected to deal. He took no part, for example, in the negotiations which led to the Ottawa agreements defining a new economic relationship between Britain and the Dominions, but expressed concern at their possible implications in the foreign arena. 'It would,' he stressed, 'be a very dangerous view that world relations in the economic field have little to do with the Foreign Office.'[22] A difference of emphasis between Simon and Chamberlain on the question of reparations and war debts was evident prior to the meeting of the Lausanne Conference in June 1932.[23] In the event it was the Chancellor who headed the British delegation, while Simon was ensconced at the Disarmament Conference in nearby Geneva. The Foreign Secretary evidently felt his exclusion keenly:

I am getting very full of interest and information about this reparation question and hope you may find it possible to transfer me from one end of the lake of Geneva to the other when we are in the thick of it![24]

Chamberlain in fact began a period of close association with international affairs which gives the lie to those who claim that the diplomatic errors of his premiership were largely the mistakes of an untrained and ignorant first minister with experience only of domestic administration.

Had Simon felt more confident of his own position within the government he might have been able to assert the rightful status of the Foreign Secretary. But owing his appointment to a Prime Minister who never had great confidence in him was not the only problem confronting Simon within the cabinet of the National Government. His personal power base was never strong. He enjoyed no close friendships in the upper echelons of the administration. Within the sea of Conservative back-benchers the 35 Simonite Liberals were little more than tokens of the government's National status, and thus a factor of diminishing importance the further events moved on from the crisis of 1931. When Samuel's Liberals withdrew their support after the negotiation of the Ottawa Agreements in September 1932, many – though not MacDonald[25] – believed that Simon had outlived his usefulness in party political terms. Little now seemed to distinguish his Liberal Nationals from the Conservatives. But, after nearly sixteen years out of government, Simon was determined not to throw away the reins of office. He trod warily even if this meant never fully asserting the authority which attached to his post.

The economic storms which had brought the National Government into being had also transformed the international environment confronting the new Foreign Secretary. 'If the world had jogged along,' suggested one critic:

Simon would of course always have put the British point of view extremely well, but he was faced with problems which required resolution and vision, neither of which he had.[26]

Yet it is difficult to envisage that any incumbent could have made a success of the Foreign Office in the circumstances of the early 1930s. This ministry proved to be a graveyard of political reputations. Had Simon become Chancellor in 1931 he might have earned the succession to the premiership as the man who presided over the restoration of the nation's finances. As it was his standing was damaged, almost beyond repair. Since the end of the First World War Britain's international position had been intrinsically vulnerable. It was a classic case of excessive commitments and inadequate resources. Left, as a result of American abdication, as the world's leading power or at least as the leading power within the League of Nations, Britain no longer had the means or indeed the will to sustain her pre-1914 role. In theory she had been saddled with the obligations of world policeman, the reluctant mainstay of an international settlement which had been founded on the presumption of whole-hearted American involvement in the post-war world. Much of Britain's diplomacy since 1919 – notically at Locarno in 1925 – had been geared towards the definition and restriction of the country's international obligations to more realistic proportions. Fortunately for her the twenties had seen no major challenges to the international settlement set up at Versailles. In the new decade all this was to change. Fostered by the economic convulsions which began in 1929 political extremism grew apace and with it challenges to the international status quo.

It was Simon's misfortune that his period of office included the single most significant date of the whole inter-war period. On 30 January 1933 Hitler became German Chancellor. Thereafter international relations entered a new era, posing problems which would certainly have tested to the full any of Simon's recent predecessors as Foreign Secretary. The gravest mistakes were made by those British politicians who failed to recognise the seismic change occasioned by Hitler's assumption of power. From a post-1945 perspective such criticism flows easily enough and Simon's culpability in this respect will be considered in due course. In his defence, however, it may be said that the evil of Hitler and his regime was a cumulative revelation and that those who had responsibility for dealing with him in the first years of the Third Reich are more easily exonerated for their misjudgments than are the men who succeeded them later in the decade, when far more evidence as to the true nature of National Socialism was available.

It has often been argued that men of greater vision, imagination and insight than Simon would have succeeded in changing the course of British diplomacy to cope with the new environment and deal with the challenges posed by the aggressor states, particularly Germany, before those challenges got out of hand. Yet the simple statement that something should have been done is easier to make than is the description of what that action should have been. Particularly in his handling of the Far-Eastern crisis of 1931–33, Simon has been subjected to a barrage of criticism which has scarcely been matched by the constructive suggestion of alternative policies. Britain's capacity to pursue a forthright foreign policy in the early 1930s was severely restricted by the condition of her armed forces. Compelled by financial necessity, public opinion and a genuine desire to respond to the disarmament commitment contained in the Versailles Treaty, successive governments had reduced Britain's armed services to a mere shadow of those assembled during the Great War. For more than a decade defence expenditure had been circumscribed by the optimism of the Ten Year Rule, the assumption that Britain would not have to fight a major war for the next ten years. Thus, when Simon took office, defence planners were still not anticipating any significant calls upon the country's military capacity before the early 1940s. The economic crisis which accompanied Simon's first months in government added further emphasis to the squeeze on defence spending. Indeed the Ten Year Rule was not abandoned until the Chiefs of Staff review of 1932 when Simon himself admitted that 'the ten-year assumption was a dangerous one.'[27]

The sorry state of Britain's armed strength was graphically confirmed in the Defence Estimates for 1932. On 7 March the First Lord of the Admiralty announced that it was his misfortune

to introduce the lowest Estimates that have been introduced since 1913, and which have obviously been framed not on what we would like but with a view to contributing, and contributing very generously, towards the nation's common effort to meet the great financial crisis.[28]

Austen Chamberlain, who had recent ministerial experience of both the Foreign Office and the Admiralty, spelt out what these estimates meant for those charged with guiding the nation's diplomacy:

I beg the House to observe that, in all that concerns the physical force that it will exert in an emergency, this country is weaker in proportion to the rest of the world than at any time within my public life. . . . If you want your Foreign Secretary to speak with the authority that he ought to have, if you want yourselves to be masters in your own house and able to decide your own policy, you must be in a position to defend yourself, you must be in a position to fulfil your obligations and to secure the respect of others for the obligations that they owe to you.[29]

The position of the army was no better than that of the navy. As the debate on the Army Estimates on 8 March revealed, financial stringency had led to a drastic suspension or retardation of many essential services. Faced with this picture of military and naval decline, and with no prospect of immediate improvement, Simon would have been guilty of wilful misjudgment had he reached any conclusion other than to avoid the sort of risks in foreign policy which could only emphasise the nation's weakness.

Out of office throughout the 1920s, Simon bore no personal responsibility for the deficiencies of national defence at the start of the following decade. Yet he could not but have been conscious of the prevailing public mood. One of the legacies of the Great War, and of the commitment to the spirit of the New Diplomacy with which it had ended, was a greater readiness than hitherto on the part of the makers of British foreign policy to listen to the dictates of public opinion. So great had been the national sacrifice in that war that diplomacy could no longer be left exclusively to expert management by a Foreign Office elite. And no one could be in any doubt what the public demanded. The supreme will of the British people, scarred by the experiences of 1914–18, was to avoid involvement in another war. The country looked for patient efforts to remove those grievances that might lead to renewed hostilities. The experience of 1914 seemed to suggest that peace and safety lay not in the building up of national defence but in disarmament. In time it would become apparent that such methods were not an appropriate response to the dictator powers, but that revelation came only slowly as the true nature of these regimes was revealed. In the context of the early thirties it was a factor which no democratic politican could possibly ignore.

Yet however strong the pacific sentiment of the country in the early 1930s, much of the contemporary criticism of John Simon's Foreign Secretaryship seems to have derived from irritation and frustration at his inability to enforce Britain's will. A cabinet colleague discussing the World Disarmament Conference put it in these terms:

Without military strength to back his policy and with public opinion set upon peace, he was expected somehow or other to reconcile the French demand for security with the German claim for equality of status, and to persuade more than fifty governments in Geneva to accept a plan of disarmament.[30]

As Britain's international impotence was increasingly revealed, discontent at its manifestation turned in the first instance on the Foreign Secretary.

Deceived by the misleading tranquillity of the late twenties and less conscious than Simon of the limitations on British power abroad, critical opinion judged that personal incompetence lay at the root of the problem. With his policies the object of a sweeping condemnation that was unaccompanied by the suggestion of a viable alternative strategy, Simon

would not have been human . . . if he had not sometimes seemed hypercritical in dealing with questions upon which the world at large preferred resounding generalities, and in analysing questions upon which scarcely anyone was ready to face the answers.[31]

★ ★ ★

Simon's appointment to the Foreign Office took most observers by surprise. The *Manchester Guardian* regarded his nomination as 'an experiment', but encouragingly reminded its readers that 'failure is not in Sir John's line'.[32] Generally the appointment was well received. Neville Chamberlain judged the new Foreign Secretary to be 'very sound', while Lord Beaverbrook wrote of a 'first-rate head of the Foreign Office in Sir John Simon.'[33] The new incumbent at least began with the valuable asset of being an accomplished linguist, able to deliver public speeches in French, Spanish, Portuguese and Italian. Additionally he could read German and had some knowledge of Russian and Hindustani.[34] Such talents apart, Simon had few illusions about the problems likely to confront him. He soon appreciated 'how difficult and delicate beyond belief this tangle is'.[35] But a letter he wrote only weeks after taking office reveals an interesting attitude towards the tasks facing him in his new post:

You spend your time writing and reading about problems which nobody quite understands and which nobody is able to solve. But a really complicated cross-word puzzle without any solution has its attractions and keeps one very busy.[36]

In time Simon's inability to come up with solutions would become the Achilles heel of his Foreign Secretaryship.

If Simon was able in the domestic context to enjoy something of the customary 'honeymoon period' which greets incoming ministers, no such luxury awaited him in the international arena. Here he certainly did not come into an enviable inheritance. In mid-September, less than a month after the National Government had taken office and when Lord Reading was still Foreign Secretary, the Japanese army in Manchuria seized the city of Mukden. Thus began an episode which rumbled on until 1933 and which came in time to be imbued with immense significance for both the history and the mythology of inter-war diplomatic relations. By its close Simon's standing has been badly damaged. The man who in the 1920s had enjoyed a reputation as an upholder of the principles of the League of Nations came now to be reviled as one of its principal enemies. As Harold Laski put it early in 1933, Simon had 'done more than any man since 1918 to destroy the prestige of the League by his scarcely concealed support of Japan in her rake's progress of imperialistic crime'. By his attitude the Foreign Secretary had 'done more to destroy the position of this country as the leader in the effort for peace than any man in our time'.[37]

In the years that followed, and particularly for those on the political left, the Manchurian episode took on the emotive guise of the decisive and tragic turning point in the whole history of the 1930s, when the cause of peace was lost, indeed betrayed. Simon, pursuing a wholly cynical and short-sighted policy, was the villain of the piece. One critic spelt out the significance of the Far-Eastern crisis in 1938:

That was the first important act of aggression in the post-war world. If it had been stopped by a united League of Nations it could have had no successors. It was, as we all know, Sir John Simon, then British Foreign Secretary, who, by using to their full strength his immense forensic powers, and, more important, of course, by using the whole influence of Britain, stopped the League from taking action.[38]

Geoffrey Mander, MP, writing a few years later, produced an even more fanciful interpretation. 'We now know,' he asserted in 1941, 'that the pathway to the beaches of Dunkirk lay through the wastes of Manchuria.'[39] Though the events concerned took place in the Far East their European implications were portrayed as all-important. Lord Cecil of Chelwood, the respected champion of the League, was clear about the relationship between Manchuria and the outbreak of European war in 1939:

Above all it encouraged aggressive Powers in Europe – first in Italy and then in Germany – to set at nought the barrier so laboriously erected at Geneva against aggression and brought us step by step to the present grave position.[40]

Though more recent and objective writers have sought to demolish the all too neat and convenient theory that events in Manchuria set in motion an inexorable process of aggression which culminated in world war, there remains a strong disposition to see the crisis as the first great test of the League of Nations and an underlying feeling that Britain, as the leading member of the League, should have taken action against a blatant act of aggression, probably by means of economic sanctions.[41]

The history of the 1930s is easily depicted in stark contrasts of black and white, of right and wrong. The presence of Adolf Hilter's unrestrained evil adds credibility to such an approach. But the Japanese invasion of Manchuria cannot be seen as a Far-Eastern version of the Prague coup of March 1939, nor even as an act comparable to their own attack on Pearl Harbour in December 1941. Only restrospectively did the Manchurian episode come to be seen as an act of naked aggression. In late 1931 Japan was widely seen to have a strong case against China. 'The right of a Government to protect its interests against barbarism and anarchy is a well-recognised one,' noted the *Daily Telegraph*, 'and if Japan is studious to keep within it her position is a strong one.'[42] Even leading figures in the League of Nations Union, such as

Professor Gilbert Murray, were doubtful whether Japanese action represented a simple case of military aggression.[43] Japan did have treaty rights in the area and, in the virtual absence of effective Chinese rule in Manchuria, could be seen as acting to rescue her interests from political chaos.[44] Furthermore, Simon must have been conscious that Baldwin's government had sent troops to Shanghai in 1927 to protect British interests, thus acting in a manner which, it could be argued, offered a precedent for Japan's military measures four years later.

It is instructive to note that the long-term significance of the Japanese attack was not immediately apparent. The Far-Eastern issue was largely peripheral to the general election campaign which preceded Simon's return to office. This was scarcely surprising. The country had no shortage of other preoccupations. If the upheaval caused by the fall of the Labour government and its replacement by a National administration were not enough, the so-called Mutiny at Invergordon had occurred only three days before the Japanese army took action in Manchuria, while two days after the Japanese coup the country was forced off the Gold Standard. In cabinet discussions in late 1931 and early 1932 the matter was often overshadowed by such competing issues as the question of tariffs, the Round Table Conference on India and the need to formulate policies on war debts, reparations and disarmament. Such factors are easily forgotten in the filtering processes of history, but they help explain not only why the country did not give its full attention to the Far-East at this time, but also why a decisive response from the British government was never a strong possibility.

Becoming Foreign Secretary on 5 November, Simon, taking his lead from the specialist advisers within his department, had formulated the main lines of British policy towards the Manchurian crisis by the time the cabinet met six days later. Even so, it is possible to argue that by the time Simon took office the crucial moment had already passed, at which Japan might possibly have been overawed by the sheer weight of united world opinion. With the security of her Empire and important trading interests to think about, Britain had much at stake in the Far East, but the crisis occurred at a time when the power and influence of the West in the area generally were in decline. At the Washington Conference of 1921–22 Britain had formally conceded local naval superiority to the Japanese. Since that time the gap between the capabilities of the two countries had probably widened, particularly following the Labour government's decision to abandon further work on the fortification of the naval base at Singapore. A contemporary critic of Simon's policies nonetheless produced an accurate statement of these important considerations:

The strategic position was such that the Japanese Empire with its insular and continental dependencies, including the newly-occupied territory in Manchuria, was virtually immune from any serious attack on the part of any foreign Power, whereas a number of important foreign holdings in the Far East were potential hostages in the hands of Japan.[45]

In the circumstances Simon had little choice but to keep the country out of any danger of war. Britain did not have sufficient interests in the political future of Manchuria to run grave risks on its behalf. Whatever they said in later years, few people in 1931 itself saw the future of world peace enshrined in the fate of this outlying province of the Chinese Empire. A Foreign Office official put the matter quite bluntly:

His Majesty's Government's interest in the territorial status of Manchuria is infinitely less than their interest in maintaining cordial relations with Japan.[46]

Economic sanctions might well have entailed war and 'had war come it would have been the most unpopular and, possibly, one of the most disastrous in our history.'[47]

The notes which Simon scribbled out at the cabinet meeting on 11 November provide an effective rejoinder to those who claim that he had no real policy at all to deal with the crisis:

Policy – conciliatory to Japan. To China. Don't rely *solely* on others: play your own part. Don't seek to transfer to Art.16 [the sanctionist article of the Covenant]. To Japan: we don't *want* to apply sanctions![48]

'The basis of the Government's policy, under Sir John Simon's direction, was, from beginning to end, conciliation through the machinery of the League of Nations.'[49] Britain might have stood completely aloof from the conflict had the Chinese not placed the whole matter before the League on 21 September, citing Article XI of the Covenant.[50] Before the rise of Hitler the Labour opposition's charge against the foreign policy of the National Government came to centre on the claim that Simon, by conniving at Japanese aggression, had sabotaged the League. Indeed a camp did emerge within the Foreign Office around Wellesley, the Deputy Under-Secretary, which sought to limit the role of the League on the grounds that any action which hinted at censure of the Japanese would only inflame the conflict and provoke Japan to further and more aggressive measures. Simon on the other hand was convinced that the League should be kept in play lest its authority be totally undermined. The problem was that, in the context of the Far East, the League effectively meant Great Britain. If coercive action were decided upon, she would certainly have to bear the brunt of the burden. 'Geneva is a place,' noted the Foreign Secretary pertinently, 'where the United Kingdom has not only got to take the lead, but to take the blame for everything that is done.'[51] As the crisis progressed it annoyed him that the strongest clamour for action against Japan came from quarters that could render little or no assistance to the League in the event of more serious trouble developing in the Far East.[52] The minor powers in the League Assembly enjoyed the luxury of denouncing aggression without having to fight it themselves. The danger always existed that in basing British policy on the League, Simon might find himself left in the lurch by his League partners and having to take action on behalf of the League of which he did not approve.

Apart from Great Britain the only other power with the potential to attempt any coercive action in the Far East was the United States, not of course a member of the League. After a decade of sometimes very strained Anglo-American relations, no confidence was felt in London of the likelihood of President Hoover's administration translating pious declarations into active steps against Japan. In part this reflected an appreciation of the deeply-ingrained isolationist sentiment in America, reinforced by contemporary economic preoccupations. But additionally the United States had much less at stake in the Far East than did Great Britain. Simon desired if possible not to upset the Americans over this matter, but he remained throughout healthily sceptical of their intentions, telling the cabinet on 11 November that 'it would be wrong to assume that [the United States] would participate in putting pressure on Japan.'[53]

We have to remember that though America expresses great surprise if we do not act with them on these occasions, if we do, they will leave us with the brunt of the work and of the blame.[54]

He was also very conscious of the problems which American non-membership of the League entailed for Great Britain:

In spite of the attempts which we have been making (a) to support the League and (b) to co-operate with the United States of America, the difficulty of co-ordinating these two efforts has tended to expose the United Kingdom at Geneva, and I daresay elsewhere, to the reproach that we were either (a) working behind the back of the League, or (b) failing to show ourselves as vigorous as the United States of America were prepared to be. There is no justification for either of these criticisms. . . .[55]

The cabinet decided on 11 November that every effort should be made at the forthcoming meeting of the League Council, 'in the interests of the League itself' – and perhaps more particularly in the interests of Great Britain – to avoid the Chinese appeal being shifted from Article XI to Article XVI of the Covenant. It was Article XVI which spelt out the commitment to impose sanctions. As Simon had warned, China then had only to prove the violation of Articles XII, XIII and XV of the Covenant to commit League members automatically to sanctions.[56] In the days and weeks which followed Simon continued to work out the details of what was, given all the circumstances, the only realistic policy open to him. Sanctions were, he minuted, out of the question, a message he repeated to the Secretary-General of the League in Paris.[57] Instead 'we ought to co-operate in any course that will preserve the moral authority of the League and a futile reference to Article XVI would surely have the opposite effect.'[58]

In Geneva Simon sought to establish good relations with both the Japanese and Chinese delegates, but became rapidly aware of the limits to the League's powers of moral persuasion. It was clear that Japan had no intention of withdrawing her troops and because of the rule of unanimity she could block any moves attempted by the League Council. Writing to the Prime Minister, Simon drew a depressing but logical conclusion. If the Manchurian situation was one which League authority could not clear up, that was a pity:

but it would be much better I think for the League to face that fact, if it is a fact, and to tell Japan that whatever may be her economic and practical case the League cannot as a League confirm the continuance of Japanese troops on Chinese territory and regrets that it is not possible owing to Japanese opposition to reach a unanimous and effective conclusion. This is not satisfactory but if all efforts at adjournment fail it is better than pretending (what nobody believes) that the League is really in a position to control the situation.[59]

Somewhat surprisingly, two days after this was written, Simon seemed to give the impression to the American observer, General Dawes, that should the Chinese invoke further articles of the Covenant the League should then proceed under Article XVI. Unless Dawes had completely misunderstood the Foreign Secretary, which seems unlikely, the most probable explanation for this apparent turn-around in Simon's attitude was that he was seeking to stress his concern for the authority of the League and at the same time to find out how far the United States might be willing to go.[60] At all events this episode may have had important consequences in laying the ground for future misunderstandings between the two countries.

The League was saved, for the time being, from a declaration of its own impotence by the decision taken by the Council on 10 December to send out a commission of enquiry to Manchuria to investigate the whole situation. Leo Amery, a senior Conservative ex-minister excluded from the National Government, was asked to chair the enquiry, but felt that he did not have the necessary time.[61] In the event the position fell upon Lord Lytton, a former junior minister and Governor of Bengal. Such an approach no doubt appealed to Simon's judicial instincts and also reflected the fact that the rights and wrongs of the case were by no means as clear cut as they were later deemed to have been. As Simon told the cabinet in early December:

There exists a widespread feeling which I believe to be justified, that although Japan has undoubtedly acted in a way contrary to the principles of the Covenant by taking the law into her own hands, she has a real grievance against China. . . . This is not a case in which the armed forces of one country have crossed the frontiers of another in circumstances where they had no previous right to be on the other's soil.[62]

In a forceful defence of his old friend's handling of the Far-Eastern crisis Leo Amery later argued that woolly-minded 'illusionists'

only saw an opportunity for the League to vindicate the new moral world order by making an example of Japan as an aggressor. That Simon failed to share that view in all its impracticable simplicity marked him out as the archtraitor to the cause of world peace, not only in the League of Nations Union circles here, but among the irresponsible crowd of busybodies, journalists, American tourists etc. – who used to flock to Geneva hoping for the excitement of a spirited League policy.[63]

Yet in the early stages of the crisis such a defence was scarcely necessary, for the most prominent spokesmen of League sentiment such as Robert Cecil and Professor Murray appear to have been entirely satisfied with Simon's performance. The Foreign Secretary was, thought Cecil, 'quite sound on the subject'.[64] Cecil stressed how dangerous 'any violent or outspoken action on our part' might be and agreed with Simon that Britain should not act unilaterally but through the League Council.[65] He dismissed press reports of a rift between himself and Simon and, as late as April 1932, emphasised that his criticism of the Foreign Secretary did not go 'very far'.[66] Only later did Cecil become significantly critical of Simon and by January 1933 was ready to describe him as the 'worst Foreign Secretary since Derby in '76'.[67] Cecil was, of course, a member of the British delegation to the League Council until February 1932. Thereafter his opposition to government policy grew, perhaps in direct relation to his ignorance of the determinants of that policy once he no longer had access to official papers.[68] In later years Cecil became understandably keen to distance himself from Simon's handling of the crisis. With the inestimable benefit of hindsight he could 'find in the timidity and shortsightedness of others the reason for the downfall of the League, the triumph of Japan and the perils that awaited the democracies'.[69]

Yet the first signs of newspaper criticism of Simon were beginning to appear before the end of 1931, particularly in the left of centre press. After Simon had spoken in the House of Commons on 25 November, the *Manchester Guardian* complained that, despite the Foreign Secretary's expressed desire not to prejudge the issue, he seemed already to have accepted some elements of the Japanese case.[70] Even the Conservative *Spectator* expressed impatience that Simon was not taking a firmer line. 'Has he been merely working for some compromise formula that would save Japan's face and deprive China of the support that she has a right to expect from her fellow signatories of the Covenant?'[71] In time these complaints would escalate into something like a personal vendetta against the Foreign Secretary.

Simon's difficulties increased early in the new year as a result of well-meaning but essentially futile gestures coming from the United States. On 7 January the Secretary of State, Henry Stimson, announced to the Japanese and Chinese governments that America stood by the open door policy in relation to China and would not admit the legality of any situation brought about by force. The American Note was sent without any consultation with the British government, but in the hope that the latter would follow suit. It immediately created problems in so far as Britain, as a member of the League, was firmly committed to a policy of conciliation and was precluded from taking further significant action until the report of the Lytton Commission had been received.[72] Two days later the British Foreign Office issued a communiqué, emphasising that it too stood by the policy of the open door for international trade in Manchuria and noting that Japan had recently reaffirmed her commitment to this same principle. The document concluded:

In view of this statement, His Majesty's Government have not considered it necessary to address any formal Note to the Japanese Government on the lines of the American Government's Note, but the Japanese Ambassador has been requested to obtain confirmation of this assurance from his Government.[73]

This statement formed the basis of subsequent accusations that Simon and the British government rejected an American offer to cooperate in resistance to Japan. The germ of a rumour took root that the United States would have taken positive measures against Japanese aggression if only Simon had been willing to cooperate. The British response to Stimson's initiative has been condemned as 'frigid'[74] and 'a plan rebuff'.[75] Certainly it was unfortunately worded and gave the impression of a lack of enthusiasm for the American gesture. But other points must be put into the balance. If the Americans desired a British response they could have prepared the ground much more carefully than they did before issuing their Note; Britain was in a difficult position, having to act in concert with other League powers – a point which Stimson later came to appreciate;[76] and it would be misleading to imagine that the American initiative presaged a more energetic response on her part to Japan's actions. On hearing of Stimson's Note Professor Murray telegraphed to Simon:

Earnestly hope Great Britain will not fail to associate herself with United States in asserting to Japan sanctity of treaties on which whole future peace of world depends.

It would, thought Murray, be an infamy if the powers of the League held back 'now that America has taken the lead'.[77] Yet there is no evidence whatsoever to suggest that the American government was now prepared to resort to an economic boycott, let alone military action against Japan.[78] Like many British Foreign Secretaries before and after him, Simon was no doubt irritated by this typical example of the American habit of invoking high-sounding principles without offering anything tangible in the way of action.

Simon's hopes soon suffered a grave setback, when, after five of their nationals were wounded on 18 January, the Japanese extended the scope of the conflict by attacking Shanghai. In contrast to Manchuria Britain had considerable economic interests in the International Settlement at Shanghai. This fact certainly made a difference to the British reaction. As Simon explained to the House of Commons on 22 February, the Government was:

in a very special degree charged with the protection and defence of British interests, and there is no part of the world in which it can be said with more complete truth than in the Far East that British interests are summed up in the words 'Peace and Trade.'[79]

In addition Simon was becoming more worried about ultimate Japanese intentions:

I have no doubt in my mind that Japan is pursuing an ambitious plan, just as she was in Manchuria, and is going to excuse herself by saying that her Navy enthusiasts have got out of control at Shanghai, just as her Military enthusiasts did in Manchuria.[80]

The incident prompted a further American initiative with Stimson suggesting British and American representations to Japan to the effect that the International Settlement at Shanghai was sacrosanct and that Britain and the United States would take the gravest view of its being the scene or source of violent conflict. With British information as yet sketchy and anxious still not to offend the Japanese too much, the Foreign Office was sceptical. But Simon was most anxious to avoid slighting the American point of view[81] and proposed as an alternative that the two countries should jointly address both China and Japan, urging China to comply fully with reasonable Japanese demands and urging Japan to exercise restraint in view of the foreign interests in the International Settlement. Unfortunately the British ambassador in Washington took it upon himself to hold up Simon's message in the belief that it was not strong enough to please the Americans, thereby giving the latter the impression that Simon was stalling. When Simon received further information to suggest that the Japanese Navy might be about to bombard the Chinese shore he acted promptly to warn the Japanese government that the International Settlement must not be made the base for operations against China. Simon hoped that 'the immediate upshot will be that Stimson . . . will be fairly well satisfied'. But he recognised the 'grave danger of falling between two stools – offending Japan without completely satisfying America'.[82]

In the event it proved possible to reach a satisfactory settlement of the Shanghai episode. After the British and American governments had protested to the Japanese and reinforced their naval forces and troops in the area, Simon began negotiations in Geneva to end the fighting. At a meeting of the League Council on 29 February the League President put forward what was really a British proposal for the re-establishment of peaceful conditions in the Shanghai area. A cease-fire was arranged in early March followed by a political settlement to remove rival forces two months later. Yet it would be dangerous to draw too many lessons from the conclusion of this aspect of the Far-Eastern conflict and apply them to the Manchurian situation. The Anglo-American forces were intended to protect the International Settlement from local Chinese elements rather than to threaten the Japanese, while the latter's readiness to reach a settlement probably reflected the fact that their naval commanders had exceeded the wishes of their political chiefs. In fact the real lesson was that the whole British position in the Far East was extremely vulnerable should the Japanese decide to attack it.

Stimson made one more effort to overawe Japan through the doctrine of non-recognition in early February. On 9 February he suggested to the British ambassador that the Nine Power Treaty of 1922 should be invoked against Japan. This seemed simply to mean that the powers should make 'non-recognition' representations to Tokyo. The proposal was then discussed with Simon in five transatlantic telephone calls during the period 11–15 February. Simon, who was in Geneva during the earlier part of this period, had the additional difficulty of trying to keep in step with thinking inside the Foreign Office and among his cabinet colleagues in London. The telephonic means of communication employed by Stimson may help explain a further incident of Anglo-American misunderstanding,[83] though it certainly appears that Simon's inherent tendency towards qualification, indeed equivocation, convinced Stimson that the British reaction was at best luke warm.[84] Accordingly, on 23 February Stimson changed course and decided to set out his government's views on the Nine Power Treaty in the form of an open letter to Senator Borah.

The Foreign Secretary was in fact balancing dangerously between the two stools of which he had earlier written. The British government had no wish to join America in the sort of indictment of Japan which Stimson was proposing:

The point that concerned him was lest, by a declaration [against Japanese actions], we might provoke a situation that precipitated Japanese resentment.[85]

But Simon was also seeking desperately, if unsuccessfully, to avoid upsetting American susceptibilities. It was this second factor which persuaded Simon to draft a paragraph including the non-recognition doctrine, which was embodied in a declaration issued by the League Council on 16 February. Simon's response to Stimson's proposal reflected a difference of methods rather than ends.

Be that as it may, in a book on the Far-Eastern crisis published in 1936, Stimson argued that the Foreign Secretary had led him to believe that the British government felt reluctant to join in the sort of *démarche* which he was suggesting. 'The British non-joinder obviously killed the possibility of any such *démarche*.'[86] This was an exaggeration. Stimson's re-writing of history caused Simon great annoyance for many years to come:

Really, retired statesmen should not write their reminiscences if much reflection on their own efforts leads them to explain their own want of success by other people's treachery. It is a form of political persecution mania.[87]

But from Simon's point of view great damage had been done. The 'story of Simon's refusal of Stimson's help was quickly elevated to the status of a dogma'.[88] Indeed, long before Stimson put pen to paper, Simon had become the *bête noire* of those who believed that the American government would have taken positive measures against Japan if only the British government had been willing to cooperate:

We on the Left all thought he was to blame for our non-intervention against the Japanese in their attack on China. . . . We now know that nothing on earth would have induced that pacifist Quaker, President Hoover, to intervene in the Far East, nor his Secretary of State, Stimson.[89]

Unrealistic expectations had been raised about the possibilities of Anglo-American action to thwart Japan's designs. Simon received a delegation from the League of Nations Union on 16 February and was advised that Japan could not resist the joint pressure from Britain, the United States and France. Britain should emphasise that she would not recognise Japan's illegal territorial gains. Simon disappointed the delegation by stressing that, even if the Americans were cooperative, the cabinet did not intend to apply sanctions under Article XVI.[90]

On 29 January China had made a further appeal to the League, citing Articles X and XV of the Covenant. As a result a special meeting of the Assembly gathered on 3 March. With Simon taking the lead the Assembly decided on 11 March that members should not recognise any situation brought about by means contrary to the Covenant. At least one of Simon's critics seemed to have been satisfied. Gilbert Murray wrote to offer his congratulations.[91] From the British point of view the League resolution was designed to show 'how great is the value to be attached to public demonstration of Anglo-American solidarity'.[92] But according to Stimson, Simon 'was not prepared to admit that the Japanese were behaving badly, but he would agree to go on record that bad behaviour was not to be recognised'.[93] The Foreign Secretary, who intervened in the debate on 7 March, remained concerned to emphasise that the central objective of British policy was unchanged. 'We should be abandoning our first duty,' he said, 'if we did not persist in pursuing the procedure of conciliation by every means in our power.'[94] Simon had little room for manoeuvre. On 5 March the cabinet's Far Eastern Committee had reiterated that sanctions against Japan were out of the question. Simon could not go beyond the expression of 'strong regrets' at Japanese action.[95] He developed his thoughts in an interview with the *Daily Mail*. The duty of the Assembly was to adopt a resolution which, while affirming the principles of the League Covenant, would enable Japan to come to an agreement with China on terms of mutual friendship.[96] Whether these two objectives would remain compatible was still unclear. Much would depend on the report of the Lytton Commission and its reception by the parties to the dispute. Simon would have another difficult role to play once the report came before the League.

★   ★   ★

By the spring of 1932 Simon was having to walk an increasingly precarious tight-rope. Once the possibility of sanctions had been excluded, there was, as the Secretary General recognised, 'a very severe limitation on what [was] possible as regards League action'.[97] But the most likely outcome of the procedure adopted was either the condemnation of Japan or the humiliation of the League. Simon relished neither prospect. Having committed Britain and the League to a policy of conciliation via the report of the Lytton Commission, he was stuck with that policy at least until the Commission reported. 'It would be quite improper,' he told the Commons on 22 February, 'for anyone to attempt to pronounce a partial or interim judgment in a matter where everything depends on the report which will have to be made by the League, recognised on both sides as proceeding from a complete sense of impartiality.'[98] World opinion, however, had moved on significantly since the previous autumn and for most people the issues were now more clear-cut than they had then been. The delay that was inherent in the setting up of a Commission of Enquiry inevitably gave the Japanese the opportunity to consolidate their occupation of Manchuria and in fact the puppet state of Manchukuo was proclaimed on the day following the Commission's arrival in Tokyo.

Simon's steadfast determination, natural in a trained lawyer, not to prejudge the issue caused mounting irritation among the growing number who had already made up their minds. His insistence that the case was complex and that Japan did have some points in her favour convinced many that he was pro-Japanese.[99] Simon was certainly anxious not to provoke the antagonism of Japan. Even after the Shanghai episode he continued, at least in public, to give some credence to Japanese assurances and rejected any suggestion of recourse to Article XVI of the Covenant.[100] To a cabinet colleague in September he stressed the need to 'avoid getting into a position of antagonism and keep in the middle of the road'.[101] But at least in Simon's thinking there was always a difference between, on the one hand, keeping an open mind and not alienating Japan and, on the other, favouring the Japanese case. If anything, the initial bases of his policy were confirmed as time went on. His perception of Japan as a united and determined country, enjoying an overwhelming military superiority in the area, re-emphasised for him the chasm between Britain's Far-Eastern commitments and her resources. Similarly, after Shanghai the Chinese Empire was increasingly viewed inside the British Foreign Office as a ramshackle edifice in which no confidence could be placed.[102] Some realistic observers sympathised with the Foreign Secretary's aims. The country was to be congratulated, argued the King's Secretary, on having a man like John Simon

to keep his fingers on the pulse of the world. It seems most important not to let Japan think that we are in any way holding a pistol at her head, but are only giving her advice as a friend and colleague in the League of Nations, and our Foreign Secretary is very firm in this attitude.[103]

If Simon's views smacked too much of *real politik*, they at least acted as a necessary corrective to those of over-enthusiastic 'Leaguers'. Gilbert Murray argued that the two 'really appalling dangers' were that Japan might successfully defy the League and that 'we might have to use violent coercion and perhaps be forced into war'.[104] That Murray believed that the powers of moral persuasion would enable both perils to be averted left Simon bewildered.

Be that as it may, Simon's critics multiplied as the spring and summer of 1932 dragged on. The very inactivity of these months no doubt increased their number. Some observers judged that a basic mistake had been made in appointing a lawyer to the post of Foreign Secretary – a complaint that would be echoed by historians down the years. For the Labour party Clement Attlee complained that 'while my house was being overrun and my family were being ill-treated, an inquiry about title deeds should have been rather cold comfort to me.'[105] F. S. Northedge has written of the 'judicial impartiality of the Foreign Secretary . . . who appeared to regard the whole transaction rather as a proceeding taking place in the Royal Courts of Justice in the Strand':

The object of the exercise . . . was to arrive at a certain legal truth, the best means to that end being the total suspension of judgment and action until the court had declared its feelings. What to do with the verdict when given, or how to prevent the situation deteriorating while the jury was out, did not seem to occupy his thoughts. . . .[106]

Simon's performances in Geneva did not create a good impression. He was judged to be devious, preferring a 'bad compromise to a straight solution'.[107] Arnold Toynbee compared his manoeuvres with the intrigues of an eighteenth-century diplomat 'deftly playing off one neighbour against another, at the least possible risk' to himself.[108] Certainly Simon's logic did not always appeal to more straightforward minds. In late March he told the cabinet's Disarmament Committee that the effect of sanctions would be to diminish the influence of the League, since Japan would accuse the great powers of bluffing if they attempted to threaten her, a claim he repeated to the House of Commons on the following day.[109] Critics noted his unfortunate habit of apparently wringing his hands during his speeches as he sought to manipulate his prompt cards. It was at this time that a parallel with Uriah Heep was first drawn.[110] 'I doubt if the old idea of "perfide Albion" has ever been more widespread,' noted Captain Liddell Hart.[111]

By the autumn Austen Chamberlain, who had begun by taking a charitable view of Simon's handling of the crisis, doubted whether the Foreign Secretary had 'any policy beyond drifting'. The British delegation at Geneva were, he thought, 'ill at ease and floundering, lacking any sure aim or certain guidance'.[112] Simon in fact was not drifting. His priorities remained clear: to be faithful to the League, but not to take the lead in futile gestures which would only antagonise Japan; to be fair to both parties to the dispute and to work to keep Japan inside the League.[113] Whether all of these objectives could be achieved was, however, another matter.

★　★　★

On 2 October the long-awaited Lytton Report was presented. The Japanese government asked for a delay of at least six weeks to consider the report and send its observations to Geneva. This request was granted. The report was a long and complicated document. It needed to be read in its entirety. Few contemporaries probably did so and many judgments upon it, then and later, were undoubtedly based upon an insufficient understanding. It contained enough evidence on both sides of the case to reinforce the existing prejudices of observers with opposite points of view. But Simon was in little doubt where most people would see the balance of the argument lying. Despite remarks in the report on the complexity of the issue, it would be very difficult, he told the cabinet, for the League to avoid pronouncing what would amount to a condemnation of Japan. That, however, would produce embarrassing and dangerous results, including the possibility of Japan leaving the League. He set out British desiderata in the full knowledge that it would require a diplomatic contortionist to secure them all:

We ought to act as a loyal member of the League and avoid, as far as possible, bringing down on ourselves the condemnation which would attach to isolated or prominent individual action. It is impossible to abandon loyalty to the League and its principles merely because Japan would prefer this: we must explain to Japan that the course we take is pro-League and not anti-Japan. Even if other considerations did not compel this course, we have to remember the serious consequences to our trade of antagonising China. In fact, we must strive to be fair to both sides. But we must not involve ourselves in trouble with Japan.[114]

The final point clearly remained the most important for him. 'Neither the interests of world peace nor the influence for good of Britain in the Far East could possibly be served by provoking an angry controversy on what is a very delicate and difficult situation.'[115]

Interestingly Simon told Commonwealth delegates in Geneva that he favoured chapters 1 – 8 of the report being made the basis of a settlement. The Commission's own conclusions were contained in chapters 9 and 10. It seems likely that Simon hoped that the vaguer, and, as far as Japan was concerned, less condemnatory chapters would be emphasised.[116] Simon underlined the potential dangers for Britain at a cabinet meeting on 30 November. The whole Manchurian question was now reaching a climax and he proposed to do his best to avoid taking a lead. If other nations attempted to pass a resolution that was unacceptable to Japan, he would stress that the report addressed the majority of its proposals to both China and Japan and did not recommend the League to do anything specific.[117]

The keynote speech which Simon made to the League Assembly on 7

December 1932 was to haunt him for the rest of his days. In some ways it was
an impressive speech. Not for the first time some listeners found themselves
irritated by the sheer persuasiveness of Simon's argument. It was certainly a
very clever speech. And, like the Lytton Report itself, the serious student
needs to read it in full.[118] But the effect created was deplorable. 'It was that
speech which made it finally impossible to take any effective action on behalf
of the central doctrine of the Covenant . . . that aggression is an international crime which must be prevented or arrested as soon as possible.'[119]
Few single moments in his long career opened Simon up to so much contemporary and later criticism. Many believed that the speech served to make the
Japanese even more intransigent. It was not his renewed assertion of
support for the Covenant which caused note, nor his admission that Japan,
by invading Manchuria, had not employed the methods of the League. What
stuck in most gullets was his continuing determination to be even-handed
and his emphasis on China's faults and the unsatisfactory condition of
Manchuria prior to the Japanese attack:

I would wish to point out that, contrary to the impression which exists in many
quarters, this report does not give a one-sided account, painting everything black on
the one side and presenting it in spotless raiments of white on the other. It makes a
measured criticism of both the side of China and that of Japan . . . For my part and
on behalf of my Government I associate myself entirely with what was so well said
yesterday by M. Benes, when he observed that he did not desire to be the judge on
either side.[120]

   Within left of centre opinion Simon's personal standing had been permanently damaged. Henceforth he would be tarred as the 'Man of Manchukuo'. According to the *Manchester Guardian* 'the speech made a bad
impression on all delegations and in all international quarters except, of
course, the Japanese and their friends who were delighted with it.'
Americans resented Simon's air of rectitude and also his reference to
Abraham Lincoln in support of the policy he had pursued. 'In short, the
whole speech was that of an advocate defending a client.'[121] Cecil later
judged the speech to be 'a forensic defence' of Japan.[122] 'Sir John Simon did
himself credit as counsel for the defence of Japan,' concluded another.[123]
   Some of the criticisms were not entirely merited. On reading a verbatim
report of the speech Cecil himself conceded that the idea that Simon was a
'thick and thin supporter of Japan' was a 'very exaggerated view of what he
said'.[124] Much play was made of the alleged remark of the Japanese delegate, Mr. Matsuoka, that Simon had succeeded in saying in a short space of
time what he had been trying to get across in ten days.[125] The story seems to
have originated in the left-wing press,[126] but so many variations of the
incident were reported, with some even suggesting that Matsuoka personally thanked Simon for his speech, that its authenticity is at least open to
question. Writing nearly forty years ago, Reginald Bassett produced an

exhaustive defence of Simon's speech which brought the latter much comfort. According to Bassett the burden of Simon's message was that the Assembly should concentrate on the task of conciliation and that he could see no basis for conciliation other than that provided by the Lytton Report.[127] But the evidence provided by Simon's remarks to the Commonwealth delegates and his warnings to the cabinet – evidence which was not available to Bassett – makes it clear that the Foreign Secretary was engaged in an exercise of damage limitation. The League was now acting under Article XV of its Covenant. Paragraph three of that article required the League to endeavour to effect a settlement of any dispute. But paragraph four required it to state the facts of the dispute and make appropriate recommendations. The cabinet was horrified by the thought that the League might leave Britain to take coercive measures against Japan and Simon was doing his best to avert this possibility. Despite Bassett's claim that Simon's speech was less out of line with those of other delegates to the Assembly than press reports suggested,[128] Simon himself admitted that

the previous debate had consisted so largely of speeches which omitted all mention of the passages of the Lytton Report which were critical of China, that I was bound to call attention to some of them.[129]

Criticism of Simon was in danger of developing into a public campaign. Gilbert Murray warned the Foreign Secretary that opinion in the League of Nations Union was getting 'greatly worked up', fearing a betrayal of the League and the 'whole new order in international politics'. Letters of indignation were pouring into the Union on a daily basis.[130] Cecil wrote in critical terms to *The Times* and tried to put into Baldwin's mind the idea that the only remedy might be 'to find some other sphere for [Simon's] activities'. 'The only explanation [of Simon's speech] which any foreigner will accept . . . is either that we have some corrupt bargain with Japan, or else that we are so afraid of her that we dare not say anything she dislikes.'[131] The second suggestion was perhaps dangerously near the mark. But at least Baldwin offered Simon some moral support. 'Of course the Bob Cecil faction denounced you as pro-Jap,' but Simon had got to keep the ship on an even keel and do his best to keep the two parties together. The Lord President expressed confidence in Simon's ability to avoid the twin pitfalls of alienating China – with the consequences this might have for £400 millions of British trade – and war with Japan.[132]

Simon succeeded in getting the Special Assembly to refer the Lytton Report back to its own Committee of Nineteen. Ostensibly the latter's task was to seek a conciliatory solution based on the report. Yet it is difficult by this stage to exonerate Simon from a charge of hypocrisy. To the American representative, Norman Davis, he stressed that he wanted to give every chance to a settlement by conciliation because peace in the Far East might depend upon it. This did not mean that he would set his face against a judgment being pronounced if attempts at conciliation failed.[133] To Baldwin, however, Simon adopted a very different tone. The purpose of Britain's continued even-handedness was to 'give no handle to Uncle Sam'. But the task of seeking a formula of conciliation was 'an impossible one'. China would hear of nothing which failed to recognise her sovereignty over Manchuria, while Japan was equally determined that the independence of Manchukuo was sacrosanct. The futile quest for compromise might drag on until the end of January 1933. Simon's real anxiety was about what would happen when conciliation was seen to be impossible. That would be the dangerous moment.[134] The time was not far distant when the Committee of Nineteen and the Assembly itself would want to proceed to judgment. 'And after judgment comes execution. . . .'[135]

If Simon did still entertain any lingering hopes of a solution by conciliation these were rudely shattered by further Japanese aggression. On 12 January Japan claimed that the province of Jehol, lying between Manchuria and the Great Wall of China, formed part of the new state of Manchukuo. By the end of the month the Japanese had succeeded in extending their authority over the whole of the disputed province. In the face of this new aggression the Committee of Nineteen resolved that its attempts at conciliation were at an end and on 24 February the League voted to accept its sub-committee's report which embodied the substance of the Lytton Commission's findings together with a recommendation that Manchuria should enjoy a large degree of autonomy under Chinese sovereignty. Japan now promptly gave notice of her intention to resign from the League.

For some time there had been mounting calls for an arms embargo on Japan. Gilbert Murray had already raised the question with Simon during a conversation on 31 December, when the Foreign Secretary's line had been that such a gesture on Britain's part would be futile while arms continued to pour into Japan from other sources.[136] The cabinet now referred the proposal to its Disarmament Sub-Committee with Simon offering four possible courses of action. The government could (a) do nothing, (b) prohibit the sale of arms to Japan, (c) announce its readiness to join in any international embargo on Japan, or (d) say that Britain could not differentiate between Japan and China, but would be happy to stop exports of arms if other nations did likewise, or in advance of other nations to set an example.[137] It was perhaps characteristic of Simon's conduct as a cabinet minister during his time as Foreign Secretary that, while outlining the problems associated with each course, he failed to make any firm recommendations in one direction. With considerable divisions of opinion inside the cabinet it was decided that, once Japan had been condemned by the League, Britain should place a temporary embargo on arms to both countries. Simon was not enthusiastic about this proposal and got Hankey, the Cabinet Secretary, to arrange another meeting on 27 February for the matter to be reconsidered. Hankey was pleased by Simon's initiative:

there and then in my presence [he] dictated a brilliant memorandum demolishing all the arguments used in favour of the Cabinet's decision . . . I was delighted.

The cabinet meeting, however, was dominated by Neville Chamberlain and the original decision was reaffirmed with the proviso that if other nations did not follow Britain's example, the embargo would soon be lifted.[138]

It fell to Simon to announce the decision to the House of Commons which was to start a debate on the Lytton Report that afternoon. It was one of the Foreign Secretary's better performances. In the course of his speech he came nearer than ever before to an honest public explanation of the motive forces behind his policy since taking office. Simon began by reiterating his belief that Japan's case did have some merits, but the most important passage came later:

I think that I am myself enough of a pacifist to take this view that, however we handle this matter, I do not intend my country to get into trouble about it . . . There is one great difference between 1914 and now and it is this: in no circumstances will this Government authorise this country to be a party to the struggle.[139]

'The House of Commons saw a very human man on Monday,' noted one reporter, 'moved deeply by the seriousness of his task. His concluding passages were scarcely audible, and when at the end he announced that under no circumstances would his country become involved in the struggle, a House that might have cheered remained silent and impressed.'[140]

The arms embargo proved to be the fiasco which both Simon and Hankey had feared. On 9 March the cabinet decided that MacDonald and Simon, who were going to Geneva, should assess whether there was any prospect of the embargo being widely supported. America possessed about a third of Japan's trade which she was not prepared to give up. And it was an odd spectacle to watch the National Government, which had been given a 'doctor's mandate' to cure the nation's economic ills, engaged upon an arms embargo which was scarcely designed to facilitate that end. On the basis of the advice of the Prime Minister and Foreign Secretary, Baldwin announced to the House of Commons on 13 March that the embargo had been withdrawn for lack of support abroad.[141] It was a sad climax to the government's handling of the Far-Eastern crisis. The whole episode of an arms embargo had been 'absurd', thought Hankey, 'the worst mistake the National Government has made'.[142]

★   ★   ★

Reginald Bassett judged that 'in the dilemma confronting the country, no greater measure of success could have been achieved and . . . seldom or never has so difficult a problem been handled with greater coolness, clear-sightedness, resolution and indifference to considerations of personal popularity.'[143] Such an assessment is difficult to sustain. Politicians are judged by results and by March 1933 Britain's policy towards the Far-Eastern crisis lay in ruins. Japan had been alienated but China's territorial integrity had not been preserved. The League of Nations had suffered a major set-back. The damage was not yet fatal, though Simon himself had put his apparently approving initials to a Foreign Office memorandum which defined the crisis as a question of whether the League of Nations was to be 'a reality or a sham'.[144] Only in the sense that it had avoided getting Britain into war with Japan, with all the consequences this would have had for her vast economic assets between Hong Kong and Borneo, may Simon's policy be deemed an unequivocal success. Some regarded this war as a very real possibility. In the draft memorandum prepared for his first biographer Simon carefully inserted a sentence in his own hand:

It was essential that Britain should not become involved in a Far-Eastern war and there were times when the danger was greater than some supposed.[145]

Sir Francis Lindley, British ambassador in Tokyo, wrote that he had 'the most awful time' in preventing 'Lord Cecil and our pacifists' getting Britain into a war with Japan:

I really thought at one time that a new world war would be started in which the whole brunt would fall on us. These fanatics will not understand that Japan is in such a state of excitement that she is perfectly ready to fight if economic sanctions are imposed; and her local position is so strong that it is quite impossible for us to do her much harm except as a result of a long and disastrous war.[146]

Certainly the Japanese attack on Manchuria posed Simon with an unenviable problem. In one of his more level-headed comments Gilbert Murray conceded that

with her trade disappearing, her unemployment increasing, and her currency off the gold standard, Great Britain simply dare not shoulder the responsibilities which she undertook when she was a strong power.[147]

Stimson admitted that 'if anyone had planned the Manchurian outbreak with a view to freedom from interference from the rest of the world, his time was well chosen.'[148] Short of a high-risk policy which could have resulted in war, there was little that Britain could do to make Japan disgorge her conquest. Even had there been an inclination to employ military measures, the Treasury would have been ready to jump in with compelling arguments about the economy and a balanced budget. But in fact the Japan of 1931 was not the nation which joined Hitler and Mussolini in alliance against Britain only a few years later. Japan in 1931, though no longer an ally of the United Kingdom, was widely perceived to be a friendly power, with whom British interests demanded continued good relations.

While League enthusiasts criticised Simon for failing to uphold the Covenant, right-wing Conservatives were ready to damn him for dealing with the League at all. One correspondent urged the Foreign Secretary to support Japan in any way possible. The latter was bound to expand some-where, 'for goodness sake . . . encourage her to do so there instead of Australia's way.'[149] In fact Simon was sufficient of a League man, without sharing the unrealistic hopes of its zealots, to want to secure a solution through the League's agencies. But as he later admitted:

It is the inevitable weakness of an international organisation, which relies primarily on the force of public opinion, that it may be set at naught by a ruthless power which calculates that it is strong enough to disregard it.[150]

Nonetheless Simon, hoping to keep Japan within the confines of the world community, went to great pains to seek some sort of settlement based on a spirit of compromise.[151]

Much of the criticism of what followed was unnecessarily personalised. This resulted in severe damage to his standing as a domestic politician, to his position among the powers of the League and to his relations with the United States. All these factors had implications for Simon's ability to guide British diplomacy in areas far removed from the crisis in the Far East. But Simon's Manchurian policy grew out of the expert assessments of his depart-ment; it was backed by the cabinet, and it had behind it the sentiment of the majority of the British people. A politician with a surer touch than Simon might have been more successful in presenting his policy. Perhaps there is something in A. J. P. Taylor's remark that Simon

lacked the air of puzzled rectitude which enabled a Grey or a Halifax to lapse from the highest moral standards without anyone complaining or even noticing.[152]

Be that as it may, some of the criticisms of Simon's policy were surely unfounded. No reading of British interests, direct or indirect, could have led to the conclusion of action against Japan. Even if British interests had been clear-cut and anti-Japanese, there was very little that the United Kingdom could actually have done. The common idea that Simon somehow prevented the League from 'taking action' is simply wrong. His reputation fell victim to men who laid claim to high ideals but bore no responsibility for concrete action. While the League's structure gave its members equal responsibility, with equal voting rights, the burden of risk in the Far East resulting from positive action would have fallen overwhelmingly, perhaps exclusively, upon Great Britain. Despite its trenchant opposition to government policy, the parliamentary Labour party never presented 'anything like a clear demand that this country should apply, or should propose to the League of Nations the application of, economic sanctions against Japan'.[153] Simon may sometimes have mishandled Britain's relations with the United States during the course of the crisis. But that is not to say that he thwarted positive American action. As Stimson himself conceded, President Hoover was 'opposed, in every fibre of his being, to any action which might lead to

American intervention in the struggles of the Far East'.[154] Indeed the President had ruled out the imposition of sanctions, economic or military, as far as the United States was concerned before Simon even arrived at the Foreign Office. In all the circumstances of the time Simon's policy was probably the best available, even though its execution could at times have been improved.[155] With an almost hopeless hand Simon played his cards with some skill. The 1930s are littered with moments at which men of principle might have made their stand for the rule of law and against aggression. Among this list of 'lost opportunities' Manchuria was far from being the issue upon which to have gone to the stake.

Notes

1 K. Young (ed.), *Lockhart Diaries* ii, 527.

2 H. Macmillan, *Winds of Change* (London, 1966) p. 314.

3 C. L. Mowat, *Britain between the Wars 1918–1940* (London, 1955) p. 414.

4 C. R. Coote, *Editorial* (London, 1965) p. 175; W. P. Crozier, *Off the Record* (London, 1973) p. 8; Lord Avon, *Facing the Dictators* (London, 1962) p. 23.

5 Sir C. Petrie, *An Historian Looks at his World* (London, 1972) p. 142; cf. Young (ed.), *Lockhart Diaries* i, 270: 'Rex [Leeper] is very bitter on Simon who he says is most unpopular and incompetent Secretary of State in modern times.'

6 M. Foot, *Aneurin Bevan* (London, 1973) ii, 213.

7 Lord Swinton, *Sixty Years of Power* (London, 1966) p. 115; Somervell MSS, typescript memoirs p. 19.

8 R. Churchill, *The Rise and Fall of Sir Anthony Eden* (London, 1959) p. 65.

9 Simon's memoirs do little for his own rehabilitation. Of somewhat more value are the relevant chapters in Bechhofer Roberts's biography which appear to have been based on memoranda provided by Simon himself. See L. A. Sanderson (Simon's private secretary) to Roberts 10 Dec. 1937, S P Adds 3 fo. 1.

10 H. of C. Debs, 5th Series, vol. 304, col. 541.

11 *The Times* 14 Jan. 1954.

12 MacDonald to Reading 5 Nov. 1931, Reading MSS Eur F 118/131.

13 K. Rose, *King George V* (London, 1983) p. 383.

14 N. Chamberlain to H. Chamberlain 7 Nov. 1931, Chamberlain MSS N C 18/1/760; Barnes and Nicholson (eds.), *Amery Diaries* ii, 225.

15 S. Roskill, *Hankey: Man of Secrets* (London, 1972) ii, 571.

16 MacDonald to Simon 14 Nov. 1931, F O 800/285.

17 N. Chamberlain to I. Chamberlain 5 June 1932, Chamberlain MSS NC 18/1/785.

18 N. Rostow, *Anglo-French Relations 1934–36* (London, 1984) p. 24; D. Marquand, *MacDonald* p. 736. As early as October 1932 Gilbert Murray expressed concern at MacDonald's physical decline: 'We could not help noticing the ill health and fatigue of the Prime Minister and his apparent inability to give a clear answer to any question . . . he did not seem equal to carrying through any difficult negotiation.' Murray to Simon 24 Oct. 1932, Murray MSS 214 fos. 230–1. But Simon himself loyally defended MacDonald against charges of unhelpful interference in the work of the Foreign Office. See, for example, J. Vincent (ed.), *Crawford Papers* p. 545 and Simon to W. Runciman 24 Dec.

1932, Runciman MSS 254.

19 Simon to Baldwin 2 Nov. 1931, S P 69 fos. 42–3.

20 Memorandum by O. Sargent and F. Ashton-Gwatkin 26 Nov. 1931, cited A. Crozier, *Appeasement and Germany's Last Bid for Colonies* (London, 1988) p. 28.

21 D. Kaiser, *Economic Diplomacy and the Origins of the Second World War* (Princeton, 1980) p. 69; H. H. Hall, 'The Foreign Policy-Making Process in Britain, 1934–1935 and the Origins of the Anglo-German Naval Agreement', *Historical Journal* 19, 2 (1976) pp. 479–80.

22 Simon to MacDonald 26 July 1932, F O 800/287. For Simon's unsuccessful attempts to exert a Foreign Office influence on the government's preparations for the Ottawa Conference, see Kaiser, *Economic Diplomacy* pp. 84–5.

23 Simon to MacDonald 2 June 1932, S P 72 fos. 50–58; B. McKercher and D. J. Moss (eds.), *Shadow and Substance in British Foreign Policy 1895–1939* (Edmonton, 1984) pp. 193–4.

24 Simon to MacDonald 18 April 1932, F O 800/286.

25 For MacDonald's concern to maintain the 'National' status of the government see MacDonald to H. Samuel 10 Sept. 1932, Samuel MSS A/89/26: 'At the head of a party government . . . I should be regarded as a limpet in office.'

26 Somervell typescript memoirs p. 19.

27 B. Bond, *British Military Policy between the Two World Wars* (Oxford, 1980) p. 96.

28 H. of C. Debs, 5th Series, vol. 262, col. 1495.

29 Ibid, col. 1515.

30 Lord Templewood, *Nine Troubled Years* (London, 1954) p. 107.

31 Ibid.

32 *Manchester Guardian* 6 Nov. 1931.

33 N. Chamberlain to H. Chamberlain 21 Nov. 1931, Chamberlain MSS N C 18/1/762; A. J. P. Taylor, *Beaverbrook* (London, 1972) p. 322. Interestingly, Beaverbrook added, 'If his character equalled his cleverness, he would be bigger than God.'

34 E. B. Segal, 'Sir John Simon and British Foreign Policy: the Diplomacy of Disarmament in the Early 1930s', University of California, Berkeley, Ph.D. thesis (1969) p. 11.

35 Simon to Lady Reading 7 Nov. 1931, Reading MSS Eur F 118/131.

36 Simon to Lady Inchcape 30 Dec. 1931, S P 70 fo. 99.

37 Cited R. Bassett, *Democracy and Foreign Policy* (2nd edn., London, 1968) p. 371.

38 J. Strachey in *Left News*, cited Bassett, *Democracy* p. 625.

39 Bassett, *Democracy* p. 5.

40 Lord Cecil, *A Great Experiment* (London, 1941) pp. 235–6.

41 Barnes and Nicholson (eds.), *Amery Diaries* ii, 267.

42 *Daily Telegraph* 23 Oct. 1931.

43 Letter to *The Times* 14 Oct. 1931.

44 In a memorandum of 23 November 1931 drawn up for the cabinet, Simon wrote: 'Japan owns the South Manchurian Railway and has been entitled throughout to have a body of Japanese guards upon the strip of land through which the railway runs. Japan's case is that, having her armed guards lawfully there, she was

compelled by the failure of China to provide reasonable protection for Japanese lives and property in Manchuria in the face of attacks of Chinese bandits, and of an attack upon the line itself, to move Japanese forces forward and to occupy points in Manchuria which are beyond the line of the railway.' *Documents on British Foreign Policy*, 2nd Series, viii, p. 945.

45 A. Toynbee, *Survey of International Affairs 1932* (London, 1933) pp. 525–6.

46 *D.B.F.P.* 2nd Series, ix, p. 31.

47 *Sunday Times* 20 May, 1934; cf. Lord Samuel, *Memoirs* pp. 271–2: 'If war came – and our information was that Japan would be more likely to fight than to yield – we could hardly risk transferring our main fleets for an indefinite time to the Far East; the European situation was too precarious.' In the autumn of 1931 the Royal Navy's C. in C. China had on station one aircraft carrier, five cruisers, nine destroyers, six sloops, eleven submarines and a number of smaller vessels – but no base with more than token defences.

48 C. Thorne, 'Viscount Cecil, the Government and the Far Eastern Crisis of 1931', *Historical Journal* xiv, 4 (1971) p. 813.

49 Bassett, *Democracy* p. 613. cf. W. R. Louis, *British Strategy in the Far East 1919–1939* (Oxford, 1971) p. 204.

50 This article made 'war or threat of war' a 'matter of concern to the whole League', but did not include sanctions.

51 *D.B.F.P.* 2nd Series, ix, p. 675; cf. Simon to G. Shakespeare 7 March 1932, S P 71 fos. 141–2, 'Everybody [at Geneva] conspires to blame . . . our unfortunate country while at the same time expecting our unfortunate country to undertake every sort of burden, leadership and responsibility.'

52 G. Scott, *The Rise and Fall of the League of Nations* (London, 1973) p. 226.

53 CAB 23/69. See also Louis, *British Strategy* p. 185.

54 Simon to MacDonald 29 Jan. 1932, S P 70 fos. 184–9. cf. Simon to G. Shakespeare 7 March 1932, S P 71 fos. 141–2, 'While America is careful to keep out of the League, her representatives are sitting in the stalls and are a little disposed to enquire why the Christians in the area do not attack the lions more vigorously.'

55 *D.B.F.P.* 2nd Series, ix, p. 675.

56 C A B 23/69.

57 *D.B.F.P.* 2nd Series, viii, p. 951.

58 Ibid, p. 885.

59 Simon to MacDonald 17 Nov. 1931, F O 800/285.

60 C. Thorne, *The Limits of Foreign Policy: the West, the League and the Far Eastern Crisis of 1931–1933* (London, 1972) pp. 191–2.

61 Barnes and Nicholson (eds.), *Amery Diaries* ii, 225.

62 *D.B.F.P.* 2nd Series, viii, p. 945.

63 Amery, *Life* iii, 154.

64 Cecil to Murray 13 Nov. 1931, Murray MSS 211 fo. 7.

65 Cecil to Simon 23 Nov. 1931, F O 800/285.

66 Cecil to Murray 28 Nov. 1931, Cecil MSS, Add MS 51132; Thorne, *Limits of Foreign Policy* p. 179; Thorne, 'Viscount Cecil' pp. 815–16. Compare the tone of Cecil's later published account of this period: Cecil, *Great Experiment* p. 227.

67 Cecil to Murray 5 Jan. 1933, cited Thorne, 'Viscount Cecil' p. 815. Even in June 1932 Cecil wrote: 'I confess I should have been glad if he had been able to play up to the Americans with rather more vigour. But I find him extremely pleasant

to deal with in other matters and always ready to listen to argument. Indeed, I find him more easy to get on with than any other Foreign Minister since Grey, even when I differ from him.' Cecil to Lord Lytton 20 June 1932, Cecil MSS, Add MS 51139 fo. 95.

68 Thorne, 'Viscount Cecil' p. 823.

69 Thorne, *Limits of Foreign Policy* p. 404.

70 *Manchester Guardian* 26 Nov. 1931.

71 *The Spectator* 18 Nov. 1931.

72 This point was emphasised by Sir John Pratt, adviser on Far-Eastern affairs in the Foreign Office, 1925–38, in a significant letter to *The Times* on 30 Nov. 1938.

73 *D.B.F.P.* 2nd Series, ix, p. 102.

74 Mowat, *Britain between the Wars* p. 421.

75 H. L. Stimson and M. Bundy, *On Active Service in Peace and War* (New York, 1948) pp. 237–8.

76 'As you know, Stimson has felt sore in the past over Simon's apparent unwillingness to co-operate over Manchukuo. He now states privately that he realises there were certain practical difficulties of which he was not aware at the time, which help to explain our attitude more clearly and he no longer feels sore.' Lord Astor to T. Jones, March 1938, cited in T. Jones, *Diary with Letters* p. 390.

77 Murray to A. Zimmern 9 Jan. 1932, Murray MSS 211 fo. 175.

78 Sir J. Pratt, *War and Politics in China* (London, 1943) pp. 217–29.

79 H. of C. Debs, 5th Series, vol. 262, col. 182.

80 Simon to MacDonald 29 Jan. 1932, S P 70 fos. 184–9.

81 Cabinet 27 Jan. 1932, CAB 23/70.

82 Simon to MacDonald 29 Jan. 1932, S P 70 fos. 184–9.

83 '[Neville] Chamberlain replied with some energy that the whole American story did a great injustice to Simon . . . (a few weeks before Eden had used the same sort of language to me). He said he had read the whole file of documents relating to that episode and he could find no basis whatever for the charge against Simon . . . Personally he would take care not to conduct any important negotiations of this kind again by telephone.' Crozier, *Off the Record* p. 68.

84 Thorne, *Limits of Foreign Policy* p. 257.

85 C. Barnett, *The Collapse of British Power* (London, 1972) p. 302.

86 H. Stimson, *The Far Eastern Crisis* (New York, 1936) p. 164. This charge was repeated in Stimson's memoirs published in 1948: 'Sir John approved of Stimson's plan in principle. In practice, however, he held back.' Stimson and Bundy, *Active Service* p. 248. Yet by this date Stimson appears to have known that his claims did not really stand up. 'I have known for some time that Mr. Stimson recognises that the statements in his book – or rather, the inference drawn from them – were unjustified, and my close friend, Lord Lothian, told me on his last visit the other day that he had had this matter out with Mr. Stimson and that Mr. Stimson appreciated what a mistake had been made.' Simon to Dr. Murray Butler 10 Feb. 1941, S P 87 fos. 96–7.

87 Simon to Sir R. Lindsay 12 March 1935, F O 800/290.

88 Macmillan, *Winds of Change* p. 381.

89 A. L. Rowse, *All Souls and Appeasement* (London, 1961) p. 18.

90 D. S. Birn, *The League of Nations Union* (Oxford, 1981) pp. 99–100; D. Wilson,

Gilbert Murray O.M. (Oxford, 1987) p. 369.

91 Murray to Simon 16 March 1932, S P 71 fo. 162.

92 *D.B.F.P.* 2nd Series, ix, p. 705.

93 Stimson and Bundy, *Active Service* p. 257.

94 F. S. Northedge, *The League of Nations: its Life and Times 1920–46* (Leicester, 1986) p. 157.

95 S. Roskill, *Hankey: Man of Secrets* (London, 1974) iii, 37.

96 *Daily Mail* 9 March 1932.

97 *D.B.F.P.* 2nd Series, viii, p. 951; J. Barros, *Office without Power: Secretary-General, Sir Eric Drummond* (Oxford, 1979) p. 350.

98 H. of C. Debs., 5th Series, vol. 262, col. 183.

99 See, for example, T. Clarke, *My Lloyd George Diary* p. 143.

100 Thorne, *Limits of Foreign Policy* p. 211.

101 Simon to S. Hoare 15 Sept. 1932, F O 800/287.

102 Thorne, *Limits of Foreign Policy* pp. 270, 234.

103 C. Wigram to H. Rumbold 18 Feb. 1932, Rumbold MSS 39 fos. 142–3.

104 Murray to Simon 16 March 1932, S P 71 fo. 162.

105 H. of C. Debs., 5th Series, vol. 270, col. 528. Attlee continued his attack on Simon in a satire preserved among his private papers and entitled *Chapters from the Life of the Bullion Family*: '[Simon] looked in and saw that Mr. Yen had got Mr. Tael by the throat with one hand and was going through his pockets with the other. Simple Simon said, "I wonder who is wrong," and went to consult the rest of the residents. After some time they decided that Mr. Yen was in the wrong. Simple Simon went back and found Mr. Tael sitting on the floor half dazed. Mr. Yen had got his watch and valuables and was making himself comfortable in the front room. "It looks to me," said Simple Simon, "that they are coming to an agreement." ' K. Harris, *Attlee* (London, 1982) p. 115.

106 F. S. Northedge, *The Troubled Giant: Britain among the Great Powers 1916–1939* (London, 1966) p. 366. Compare M. Muggeridge, *The Thirties: 1930–1940 in Great Britain* (London, 1967) p. 161: 'like an eminent counsel lunching after a case with his learned friend who had appeared for the other side, recalling points they had scored against one another, enjoying a discreet joke at the Judge's expense, perhaps even comparing fees and refreshers received, having an amiable dispute about who should pay for the lunch, each insisting: but perfectly friendly.'

107 Kordt to Dirksen 29 Aug. 1938, cited E. M. Andrews, *The Writing on the Wall* (London, 1987) p. 40.

108 A. Toynbee, *Survey 1932* p. 540.

109 Thorne, *Limits of Foreign Policy* p. 323; Birn, *League of Nations Union* p. 101; H. of C. Debs., 5th Series, vol. 263, col. 923.

110 B. H. Liddell Hart, *The Memoirs of Captain Liddell Hart* (London, 1965) i, 205.

111 Thorne, *Limits of Foreign Policy* p. 213.

112 A. Chamberlain to Ivy Chamberlain 16 Sept. 1932 and 5 Oct. 1932, Chamberlain MSS A C6/1/774, 901.

113 Thorne, *Limits of Foreign Policy* p. 294.

114 *D.B.F.P.* 2nd Series, xi, pp. 71–2.

115 Simon to George V 19 Nov. 1932, F O 800/287.

116 Andrews, *Writing on the Wall* p. 82.

117 CAB 23/73.
118 The speech is printed in Bassett, *Democracy* pp. 627–33.
119 Cecil, *Great Experiment* p. 234.
120 Bassett, *Democracy* pp. 628–9.
121 *Manchester Guardian* 8 Dec. 1932.
122 Cecil, *Great Experiment* p. 234.
123 M. Stocks, *Eleanor Rathbone* (London, 1949) pp. 222–3.
124 Cecil to Baldwin 12 Dec. 1932, Baldwin MSS vol. 118 fo. 46. See also Simon to Murray 18 Jan. 1933, Murray MSS 216 fo. 82.
125 See, for example, Notes on the Manchurian Question, Murray MSS 215 fo. 112.
126 See, for example, *New Statesman* 12 Dec. 1932.
127 Bassett, *Democracy* pp. 305–6.
128 Ibid, pp. 290–8.
129 Simon to N. Davis 13 Dec. 1932, F O 800/291.
130 Murray to Simon 14 Dec. 1932, Murray MSS 215 fo. 137; Wilson, *Murray* p. 370; Birn, *League of Nations Union* p. 104.
131 Cecil to Baldwin 12 Dec. 1932, Baldwin MSS vol. 118 fo. 46; Birn, *League of Nations Union* pp. 103–4.
132 Baldwin to Simon 21 Dec. 1932, S P 75 fo. 25.
133 Simon to Davis 13 Dec. 1932, F O 800/291. Simon made the same point when he invited Murray to visit him privately at Fritwell Manor on 31 December. Murray, however, noted Simon's reluctance to commit himself to any course of action following a judgment by the League. He feared that Simon meant the matter to rest and that the government would eventually recognise the state of Manchukuo. Murray to Cecil 4 and 5 Jan. 1933, Murray MSS 216 fos. 1, 6.
134 Simon to Baldwin 20 Dec. 1932, Baldwin MSS 118 fos. 47–8.
135 *D.B.F.P.* 2nd Series, xi, p. 124.
136 Birn, *League of Nations Union* p. 104.
137 Memorandum by Simon, 'Embargo on Arms to the Far-East', 22 Feb. 1933, Baldwin MSS vol. 120 fos. 8–10.
138 Roskill, *Hankey* iii, 73–4.
139 H. of C. Debs., 5th Series, vol. 275, cols. 58–9. Leo Amery, always sceptical about being 'tied to the Covenant' regarded the imposition of sanctions as 'illogical and . . . dangerous.' Barnes and Nicholson (eds.), *Amery Diaries* ii, 289–90.
140 *Everyman* 4 March 1933.
141 H. of C. Debs., 5th Series, vol. 275, col. 1592.
142 Roskill, *Hankey* iii, 76.
143 Bassett, *Democracy* pp. 624–5.
144 *D.B.F.P.* 2nd Series, ix, p. 239.
145 'Roberts Memorandum 2', S P adds 3 fos. 46–54.
146 Lindley to H. Rumbold 30 March 1932, Rumbold MSS 39 fos. 169–70.
147 Murray to Cecil 4 Jan. 1933, Murray MSS 216 fo. 1.
148 Stimson, *Far-Eastern Crisis* p. 6.
149 Sir W. Birdwood to Simon 6 Nov. 1931, cited Thorne, *Limits of Foreign Policy* p. 177.
150 *Retrospect* p. 192.
151 I. Nish (ed.), *Anglo-Japanese Alienation 1919–1952* (Cambridge, 1982) p. 42.

152 A. J. P. Taylor, *English History 1914–1945* (Oxford, 1965) p. 372.
153 Bassett, *Democracy* p. 551.
154 Stimson and Bundy, *Active Service* p. 233.
155 Thorne, *Limits of Foreign Policy* p. 416.

CHAPTER SIX

CHASING AN ILLUSION

This is a delightful office but it is a grind.[1]

Historians are able to analyse separately the problems which confronted John Simon as Foreign Secretary. No such luxury of course was open to the Foreign Secretary himself. Indeed one of the features of Simon's first year in office was the coincidence of major issues confronting him. It was illustrative of the crowded international agenda that the opening of the World Disarmament Conference in February 1932, which had been postponed many times since the League Assembly had first resolved in 1924 to hold such a conference the following year, was delayed for one further hour to allow the Council to meet and hear statements on the situation at Shanghai. The strain on a new minister, largely untutored in foreign affairs, and particularly one who took pride in mastering the background information on problems with which he had to deal, was intense.[2] After three months in office Simon recorded:

When I have finished reparations and disarmament and the Far East I shall need a rest cure; unless, indeed, they first finish me.[3]

In the 1920s, like all men of good will, Simon's primary interest in international matters had been to prevent another war. He was quick to see that the development of aviation meant that any future conflict might be even more catastrophic in its effects than the war which had already been endured, raising this question in the Commons as early as 1924. 'We are reaching a point,' he told an audience in 1928

when it is no longer enough to say that in a future war civilians, women and children would be exposed as much as combatants, but they will be even more exposed, because the tendency will be to strike at the centres of population.[4]

Holding such views Simon had established his credentials as a good League of Nations man, a fact which helped to ensure a favourable reception for his appointment to the Foreign Office from a wide range of liberal opinion. There was a widely held conviction that Liberals were especially keen on the League and disarmament.[5] But a price would probably have to be paid in the form of criticism from the political right if Simon's commitment to the League appeared to be too strong. As Foreign Secretary the avoidance of war remained central to his thinking. He did not, he said, envisage Britain being involved in war for many years to come, probably for the next fifty years. This was, he thought, 'the sort of attitude a Foreign Secretary has to adopt'.[6] Speaking to the Spen Valley Chamber of Commerce shortly after his appointment, he insisted that British foreign policy was no longer based on the old idea of the balance of power. Britain's contribution should be to focus the moral force of public opinion upon international problems.[7]

Since the end of the First World War British politicians had striven to abide by the spirit of the new diplomacy while, on the whole, hankering after the realism of the old. Men whose upbringing and instincts encouraged them to think of their country as a world-wide, oceanic and imperial power sought to define and limit her relationship to continental Europe, the redrawing of whose frontiers was among the more fragile achievements of the peace settlement. They needed to balance the universality of Britain's obligations as the leading member of the League against her capacity as a diminishing force in world affairs and to reach a *modus vivendi*, acceptable on the one hand to public opinion and to enduring notions of national self-interest on the other. This was a tradition which Simon continued. As Foreign Secretary he always retained a realistic conception of what the League of Nations could be expected to achieve. Its machinery must, he thought, 'be resorted to with discretion':

A judicious mixture of the new League methods and 'old diplomacy' . . . can, I feel convinced, alone achieve the practical results for which we are striving and which the League itself exists to assist us to realise.[8]

Unlike some of the League's more zealous advocates he recognised that the attempt to enforce peace through the League's sanctionist powers might first involve it in recourse to war. To parliament he explained that the League's real authority was founded upon its position as the authorised exponent and interpreter of world opinion. When this was sufficiently strong and unanimous to pronounce a firm moral condemnation, sanctions were not needed.[9] Whether Simon really believed this is by no means certain; the important point is that he would take no risks which might involve his country in an unnecessary war, and one for which she was in any case unprepared.

Ever since the end of the First World War there had existed in Britain a deeply ingrained belief, sustained by the force of economic necessity, that no safety existed in armaments. 'Whatever might be the progress of the League . . . its success continued to be judged by public opinion and by its own most devoted supporters by one test above all – the test of disarmament.'[10] If men did not always believe that the Great War had indeed been a war to end all wars, they desperately wanted to believe it and the descent back to realities was a slow process occupying most of the 1930s. Compared with many contemporaries Simon's thinking was unencumbered by flabby illusions. In restrospect Beatrice Webb's indictment of John Simon as Foreign Secretary, written at the end of 1932, appears almost to be a compliment:

The Internationalism started by Woodrow Wilson looks dead and John Simon is conducting its funeral.[11]

In time the idealism of the New Diplomacy would be revealed as a sham. But that moment had not arrived when Simon took office. For one thing public opinion still looked to a reduction in armaments for the true test of international statesmanship and the necessary condition of sustained peace. The pressures, domestic and international, for a disarmament agreement were still compelling.[12] Not least was the deeply felt need of the Prime Minister, Ramsay MacDonald, shaken by the controversy surrounding the formation of the National Government, to crown his career with an outstanding achievement in the international arena.

In a slightly different way such feelings were shared in all sections of the government where the conviction reigned that Labour must at all costs be kept out of office and that disarmament might provide the vote-catching success needed to ensure the government's continued survival.[13] As a cabinet colleague confirmed to Simon, 'I have no doubt that you are on the spot when you judge this disarmament business to be vital to the Government, certainly in the long sense.'[14] 'From 1931 to 1935,' asserted Samuel Hoare:

there was scarcely a meeting of the Cabinet or the Committee of Imperial Defence in which disarmament was not discussed in one form or another. . . . In any description therefore of the years between the wars, the pressure for disarmament is a constant factor of the first importance that must never be forgotten.[15]

With the World Disarmament Conference due to meet in February 1932 Simon had little time to prepare himself for what many anticipated would be the most important international gathering since Versailles. Writing to MacDonald less than a month after taking office, the Foreign Secretary had to confess that he did 'not see daylight at present as regards disarmament policy at all'. One of the chief difficulties was that, having led by example throughout the 1920s, Britain's armaments were already at the point where she had few bargaining counters left in relation to the other European powers.[16] In the meetings of the Preparatory Commission set up in December 1925 to clear the ground for the Disarmament Conference itself, no means had been found to reconcile Germany's demand for equality with France's insistence on security – a concept which necessarily implied the maintenance of her existing superiority in land armaments. In the French mind the themes of disarmament and security were inextricably linked. The demand for security had become a weary refrain to which no British politician had really been able to provide an answer since the time during the peace negotiations when Clemenceau had been persuaded to give up his claim for a Rhineland frontier in return for an illusory Anglo-American guarantee.

Shortly before Simon took office his predecessor had asked for a paper to be drawn up on the changing conditions in the world arena. Its conclusions were clear:

World recovery (the aim of our policy) depends on European recovery; European recovery on German recovery; German recovery on France's consent; France's consent on security (for all time) against attack.

Robert Vansittart, Permanent Under-Secretary at the Foreign Office since 1930, and a man whose later reputation would be founded on his staunchly anti-German views, urged Simon to break this unpromising chain by putting pressure on the French to convince them that they were strong enough to make concessions to Germany without endangering their security.[17] Simon, however, took his cue from the Prime Minister who feared that too firm a line with France might lead to a return to the 'Curzon regime'. Recalling the cordial Anglo-French relations which had characterised his first premiership in 1924, MacDonald reminded Simon that 'the velvet glove with firm muscles behind it is far more effective than the bludgeon in diplomacy.'[18]

Simon was clear in his own mind that France would only be satisfied by a British commitment to the continent. But such a step might involve Britain in the sort of entanglement in Eastern Europe which his predecessors such as Austen Chamberlain had sought to avoid, and for which the current state of the economy scarcely offered the prospect of increased resources. 'It might mean, for example, if we accepted that price, that British troops would be called upon to maintain the status quo of the Polish Corridor.'[19] Britain's policy, Simon explained, was to act as a sincere friend to both France and Germany, and to promote appeasement between them. But 'appeasement' in 1932 had not yet taken on any of the sinister or disreputable connotations it was later to acquire.[20]

The Conference finally opened on 2 February. With the Foreign Secretary struggling to cope with an unwanted crisis in the Far East and, from mid-December, a member of the cabinet committee set up to investigate the critical question of the trade balance, it is difficult to escape the conclusion that Simon entered the negotiations ill-prepared, his country's policies vague and incoherent.[21] Simon had approached Cecil to see whether the latter, with his great prestige in League affairs, would be willing to be one of the British delegation. Three interviews with Simon at the Foreign Office convinced Cecil that no detailed policy had been formulated. The government felt that it had already done all it could in relation to naval disarmament and did not intend to initiate any proposals relating to land and air armaments. In the circumstances Cecil decided to decline Simon's offer.[22] The opening stages of the conference served to emphasise the differences of attitude which existed between the leading powers. Tardieu for France was first off the mark in publicising proposals which would have had the effect of turning the League into a military force, but as regards the French situation he did not depart in any important respect from the line of French policy pursued since Versailles. Security must precede any substantial reduction in French armaments. Simon was determined to proceed with caution. The government seemed content to leave matters in the Foreign Secretary's hands. 'Don't worry,' stressed Stanley Baldwin:

We shall support you whatever you do providing you don't do some damned fool thing of which I hope and believe you are incapable.[23]

Whether Simon ever really expected the Conference to make substantial progress is open to question. To J. L. Garvin of the *Observer* he hinted in June that the effort to outlaw aerial bombing, which he had favoured in the 1920s, might now be too late.[24] He once admitted to the King his belief that, whatever restrictions were drawn up, a nation with its back to the wall would break them.[25] Perhaps most revealingly of all, in a Commons speech in July he seemed to draw a distinction between the Reparations Conference at Lausanne where 'something *must* be done' and that at Geneva where 'something *ought* to be done'.[26]

In the event Simon did make a promising move in suggesting that the Conference should consider what came to be known as 'qualitative' disarmament, in other words the limitation of armaments not by numbers, as had largely been envisaged by the Preparatory Commission, but by the complete abolition of certain types of weaponry, particularly those which lent themselves to offensive rather than defensive warfare. In Simon's thinking qualitative disarmament had the advantage of tending to equalise conditions in Europe and reconcile the French and German points of view since the weapons in question were largely the sort which Germany was prohibited by the Treaty of Versailles from possessing at all. Quantitative disarmament on the other hand, by which each state would agree not to have a larger number of weapons than an agreed total, might easily lead not to a reduction but to a potential increase in armaments, because the figure would not be one which a state would actually reach but only the figure which it would insist on being free to reach in case of need.[27] On the whole, however, the Foreign Secretary did not make a good initial impression at the Conference. For Geneva itself he showed an unfeigned distaste.[28] It was, he later asserted, 'a dreadful place, well worthy of Calvin'.[29] Lloyd George heard that he had been 'spineless, boneless, explaining things as if he was addressing a not very intelligent jury'.[30] He had, according to another witness, 'the most irritating set of gestures that I have ever seen in a public speaker'.[31] Not for the only time in his career, Simon's message was partly overshadowed by the unfavourable personal image he projected.

For Germany Brüning reiterated Germany's claim to equality of status, but took up Simon's theme of qualitative disarmament. This, he stressed, already existed in Germany's case and those who wanted to follow along the same road had merely to generalise the prohibitions that had been placed on Germany at the time of Versailles. For Italy Grandi put forward very much the same argument. It seemed that progress might be possible, but the domestic politics of some of the leading participants soon got in the way of a further advance. German attention was focused on a close presidential contest between Hindenburg and Hitler, while France was also on the eve of a general election. The calling of a Special Assembly on the Sino-Japanese conflict on 3 March, which occupied pride of place for more than a week, deprived the Disarmament Conference of much of its momentum and the leading delegates soon departed for a long Easter break. They left behind them their technical experts sitting on four committees with the task of classifying weapons into the categories of offensive and defensive armaments. This, thought Hugh Dalton, 'was an obvious time-wasting device',[32] but in fact the classification proved much less straightforward than had been expected. What seemed clearly to be a defensive weapon to some appeared to others to be indubitably offensive. In the Naval Committee, for example, while British and American representatives argued that the battleship was a defensive weapon and the submarine offensive, lesser naval powers put forward the exactly contrary view. By mid-June the committees were bogged down in a morass of disputed technical detail. 'It has been living for weeks on technical experts,' wrote Simon, 'and it is in danger of dying from technical experts.'[33]

All hope of success had not, however, been abandoned when the main Conference reassembled on 11 April, especially when the American delegation made a positive proposal that all tanks and mobile guns over six inches in calibre should be declared 'offensive' weapons. When both Stimson and MacDonald turned up in Geneva a few days later, optimism was again raised, and in this atmosphere Brüning put forward proposals in private conversations which, in the light of subsequent German demands, were the very essence of moderation. He wanted to increase the Reichswehr to 150,000 men, reduce the period of military service from twelve years to six and create a militia of 50,000 men serving for three months. His proposals were generally well received, but the crucial voice would, as always, come from Paris. Tardieu had returned to France for the elections and his return to Geneva was postponed when it was announced that he had contracted laryngitis. Chances of significant progress were therefore lost.

MacDonald, Brüning and Stimson had all left Geneva by 1 May and the delay consequent on the French elections and the subsequent difficulties in forming a new government meant that the central problems before the Conference remained in abeyance for several weeks. At the beginning of June, moreover, Brüning's government was replaced by a reactionary cabinet headed by von Papen. Anthony Eden later singled out the Foreign Secretary for criticism over this 'lost opportunity.' 'I should not like Simon's conscience,' he wrote in October 1933:

about the earlier part of last year when Brüning was still in power. We missed the bus then and could never overtake it.[34]

Yet it is difficult to see that Simon could have significantly affected the outcome of events. Even had the French been persuaded to consider Brüning's proposals straight away, their acquiescence could only have been bought by a British commitment to her security which Simon was in no position to give.

While the Far-Eastern crisis receded, at least for the time being, from the forefront of his concerns, Simon was able to give rather deeper thought to the question of disarmament. The prospect of aerial attack continued to cause him most worry and he was sympathetic to proposals which may have originated with Hankey to abolish all naval and military air forces. In discussions in the cabinet's disarmament committee the Foreign Office took the lead in plans to outlaw aerial bombing.[35] Simon was particularly concerned by the vulnerability of London to attack because of its heavily concentrated population:

The danger of London being heavily and suddenly bombed by way of a knock-out blow must be our main preoccupation. . . . [The Foreign Office plan] would minimise the danger of London being suddenly subjected to a heavy scale of air attack, i.e. the knock-out blow.[36]

Thus, in Simon's mind, it would be the 'ending of a nightmare' if the powers were to agree to abolish military and naval aviation.[37] His vision was not confined to the current potentialities of aerial assault. The prospect of a future war was 'appalling, particularly to civilians in crowded places':

If civil and military aviation were in a position to do what they could do after fifteen years of evolution, what were the prospects by fifty years hence?[38]

Baldwin too became a committed advocate of aerial disarmament and the cabinet agreed on 11 May to get its proposals into detailed shape and to draft a convention to put to the Disarmament Conference.[39] Two days later the Foreign Secretary urged upon the House of Commons the need for further rapid and comprehensive disarmament. In an enthusiastically received speech he stressed that only by reducing the level of arms could the dangers of a future war be averted.[40] The consequences for the world as a whole if the current efforts at disarmament failed would, he told Gilbert Murray, be 'beyond all calculation horrible'. But he was keen to strike the right balance between 'vague optimism and concrete difficulties':

I wish sometimes that there had been more public education as to the *methods* of disarmament and less public eloquence about the ideal of disarmament.[41]

Yet though Simon professed to regard it as 'a case of now or never'[42] and declared himself ready to take 'a very bold course' to rescue Geneva from the doldrums, the British proposals never made the centre of the stage. MacDonald and Simon were authorised to sound out the French and Italians on the subject, but did so very hesitantly. Cecil was concerned to learn that all the Prime Minister had in mind was 'yet another declaration of peaceful intentions by the parties to the Conference'.[43] In Geneva, and under the strain of having to commute almost daily to Lausanne to attend the meetings of the Economic Conference which began its deliberations in mid-June,[44] Simon became markedly less optimistic. It was becoming increasingly obvious that on every point of substance 'there are mountains of difficulty to be overcome'. Private conservations led him to doubt whether the French really contemplated any serious agreement. He still hoped that the British might put forward wide-ranging proposals to 'give a lead', but it was all 'an appalling job'.[45] Hankey attributed this lapse to the Prime Minister's tenderness for the Air Force and concluded that he 'blanketed the proposal . . . Simon was not the man to thwart him in this, though he believed in the plan.'[46]

It was against this background that the United States stole the limelight and attempted a fresh effort to break the deadlock at Geneva by reviving the faltering Disarmament Conference. On 22 June new proposals from President Hoover were announced simultaneously in Washington and Geneva. The essence of the American plan was the abolition of specifically offensive weapons and the reduction of the rest by one third. Those to be eliminated altogether included tanks, large mobile guns, bombers and all means of chemical warfare. Simon gave a courteous but unenthusiastic welcome to the American proposals, indicating the need for a reduction in the size of individual ships as well as in total tonnage. But sections of the British government – and particularly the Admiralty – were singularly unenamoured. Though the ten capital ships and thirty cruisers which would be left to Britain under the Hoover plan might be enough for the purposes of the United States, they would scarcely enable the Royal Navy to guarantee the security of the Empire or of Britain's vital trading life-lines. Over the next few days there was considerable friction between the cabinet in London and Simon, supported by the Home Secretary, Samuel, in Geneva. The Foreign Secretary failed to stand his ground. The trouble with both Simon and Samuel, concluded Anthony Eden, was that they were hopelessly 'chameleon' – 'the colour of the Cabinet at home, of Geneva there. They have no minds of their own, though unlimited ingenuity.'[47]

In an uncertain world, with no sign of France being ready to reduce her armed strength without fresh guarantees of her security, British caution was probably justified. But it was not long before Simon emerged as the *bête noire* of those League enthusiasts who had been expecting unrealistic achievements from the Disarmament Conference. Simon's response to the American plan was intended to 'kill it by kindness', judged one.[48] Why could he 'not have made a simple declaration, accepted eagerly the principle of a one-third cut, and intimating that a few adjustments might, in the view of the British, be necessary,' wondered another.[49] With his relations with the

United States already damaged by his handling of the Far-Eastern crisis, the American reaction was predictable:

The Americans feel that Simon has been guilty of something closely verging on sharp practice when, the other day, he asked them to postpone a three-cornered talk and then went and told the French that the Americans did not want to hold the conversations.[50]

Thus, like all those that had preceded them, the American proposals failed to make significant progress. When the Americans, British and French proposed that the Conference should adjourn until the autumn and meanwhile adopt a resolution summing up the progress made so far and setting out what should be done to prepare for the next session, it was clear that everyone was seeking to save face. Simon summed up the British position in the Commons on 12 July. His emphasis remained on the dangers of bombardment from the air. It was vital for Britain to play its part in steps to abolish 'this abominable practice of indiscriminate bombing which is threatening the whole future of the world.'[51] But while welcoming the 'interconnectedness' which had inspired the Hoover proposals, he rejected them and listed a dozen propositions which he believed the Conference could accept.[52]

Simon worked very hard to secure some sort of resolution, particularly one that would be palatable to American opinion.[53] The resolution carried at Geneva a few days later was based on Simon's outline and contained a definite commitment only to renounce chemical and bacteriological warfare, effectively a restatement of the Geneva Convention of 1925. In fact Simon recognised that further progress was unlikely until after the American presidential elections in November and was merely concerned to tide the Conference over the summer recess with a reasonably optimistic, if anodyne, resolution. To the Prime Minister Simon expressed the hope that the resolution would be 'born tomorrow, and duly baptised the next day; then it can be buried for six months and dug up again after the American elections.'[54] For the time being he regarded securing success at Lausanne on the question of reparations as of primary importance. The July resolution purposely omitted any reference to the German claim for equality since 'nothing could be more prejudicial to [Lausanne's] success than an upset of confidence in Europe.'[55]

The resolution was passed by the Conference on 23 July. The section on air disarmament reflected the influence of the Prime Minister and the air ministry. It called for the prohibition of aerial bombardment, except for purposes of 'police action' in outlying areas, which would safeguard British colonial interests. Gilbert Murray sent Simon a line of congratulations. This 'first phase . . . with all its hollow places, seems to me a great achievement'.[56] But the Foreign Secretary himself was under no illusions. 'No one pretends that the Resolution was a great achievement,' he reminded the Prime Minister, but it represented the only way out of the Americans pressing for further discussion of the Hoover Plan. The British government should not delude itself into thinking that this relatively satisfactory state of affairs would continue. If Britain stayed on the same course when the Conference reassembled, a very serious situation would result by the end of the year. At home the government would be exposed to ever-growing criticism for its failure to make the Conference a success, while 'a very nasty international position' would be developing abroad led by the United States with consequent implications for prospects of a satisfactory settlement of war debts. The Foreign Secretary therefore called for the summer recess to be used to formulate detailed British policies for the future.[57] His problems were compounded when Germany not only voted against the resolution but announced that she would cease to collaborate in the work of the Conference until the principle of equality had been recognised.

By the summer and early autumn of 1932 it was apparent that the tone of the press and of political comment in general was turning markedly against Simon. 'There seems to be a general outcry against Simon,' wrote Lloyd George, 'and a general regret that he has not been given another post.'[58] While the League trod water awaiting the report of the Lytton Commission, the Disarmament Conference seemed in danger of degenerating into futility. The Foreign Secretary had few obvious successes to which he could point. He became an easy target for those who wanted quick results. It was not the only time in his career that Simon's capacity to see the complexities and intricacies of a situation rebounded to his disadvantage. Thomas Jones heard that Simon had reduced Geneva to immobility and that the League was 'at its lowest level and almost *pour rire*'.[59] Margot Asquith, never one to mince her words, urged Baldwin to put Simon 'in any office except where he is. From the 1st day of his appointment I knew he would be a fiasco in Foreign Affairs.'[60] From another quarter the Conservative leader was pressed to move Simon to the Home Office, allowing MacDonald to become Foreign Secretary and Baldwin himself Prime Minister.[61] Typical of the press response was an article in the *Manchester Guardian* which insisted that by the time the Disarmament Conference reconvened Britain would need both a new policy and another Foreign Secretary.[62] A common theme was that Britain's policy should be more forthright in giving a lead, recognising Germany's claim to equality and going on to secure a full-scale disarmament settlement. The clear implication was that if this were not done British policy would be to blame.[63] Even Austen Chamberlain joined in the chorus of complaint. He doubted whether Simon had a policy. The Foreign Secretary was content with patchwork, when 'a very bold, strong lead is needed.'[64]

Much of the criticism was naive and ill-informed. Britain's negotiating hand was nothing like as strong as some observers fondly imagined. But the criticism clearly irritated Simon:

The keen desire of so many warm supporters of disarmament to promote its progress leads to so constant a stream of grudging and nagging comments that possibly a few words the other way would do no harm.[65]

It had fallen to Simon to present a policy which in truth represented an uneasy compromise between disparate influences within the government. According to Anthony Eden he complained:

I don't like my position. It does not seem to me fair that whatever the services want I have to defend [them] however impossible their positions.[66]

The Foreign Secretary called upon Baldwin to express the Conservative party's support for and approval of his foreign policy. 'The enemy is constantly at work whispering that I am taking a line which the Cabinet as a whole does not endorse.'[67] Of more substance perhaps were the criticisms of those who accused him of failing to stand his ground within the government. Perhaps the most perceptive of such critics was Simon's own junior minister, Anthony Eden, who had ample opportunity to view his chief's shortcomings at close quarters:

Simon's difficulty is not so much in making up his own mind as that once he has made it up – or at least has seemed to do so (perhaps that it is the truth it is not really made up). [sic] Anyway he will not fight for his own policy. He expects the Cabinet to find his policy for him. That they will never do . . . Poor Simon is no fighter. Nothing will make him one.[68]

Quite suddenly the Foreign Secretary's position looked vulnerable. His parliamentary private secretary offered an optimistic word of advice. Simon's

position can only be maintained if attention is paid to the giving of your personality, through the Press, to the world. If you can drive a wedge of Peace between the increasing 'War-mindedness' of Germany and France, and in the face of the fresh Japanese problem, preserve the League, in two or three years the very people who throw bricks, without even understanding the position, would sing loudly your praises as the 'Peacemaker'.[69]

But Simon felt himself restrained by an increasingly exposed position inside the National Government. Before the resignation of the Samuelite Liberals the government was a genuine, if unbalanced, coalition. After September 1932 it looked like a Conservative administration which happened to have a non-Conservative at its head and several other non-Conservatives among its adherents. Simon had little sympathy for Samuel's line on tariffs, believing that the latter had no effective alternative strategy to deal with the economic crisis:

It is no good prescribing a long sea voyage as a cure for persistent hemorrhage; you must try to stop the bleeding.[70]

Yet as the withdrawal of the mainstream Liberals drew near, Simon and other Liberal Nationals recognised that this might leave themselves dangerously exposed. MacDonald needed 'all the Liberal help he can get', stressed the Foreign Secretary, 'to prevent submergence in the Tory flood'.[71]

At the crucial cabinet meeting on 28 September Simon argued that the withdrawal of Samuel and his colleagues would involve a great depreciation of British influence abroad.[72] Though Simon chose to clothe his reasoning in terms of the national interest, thoughts about his own position were very much to the fore. A fellow Liberal National spelt out the problems which would arise once Samuel had resigned. The breach between the two wings of the Liberal party would then be final – 'Ottawa will be our Rubicon' – and

if we still parade the name of Liberal it will really only be by false pretences, because it must be clear to everyone that there is no future for us but ultimate absorption in the Conservative party.

The need, therefore, was for the Simonite Liberals to state their terms and conditions before consenting to the continuation of the National Government. Unless this were done, they would be handing themselves over 'gagged and bound to the Conservative Party'.[73] In the event Simon was relatively successful in protecting his group's position within the government,[74] earning the gratitude and praise of his colleagues. Geoffrey Shakespeare wrote to thank his leader for his 'terrific fight'.[75] Simon 'is real trumps'.[76] In the reshuffle which followed Samuel's resignation, a further Liberal National, Sir Godfrey Collins, joined the cabinet, while several of Simon's colleagues were promoted at junior ministerial level.

Simon's domestic political difficulties were compounded by a marked decline in his personal relations with the Prime Minister. Neville Chamberlain noted problems as early as June 1932.[77] It was widely believed that MacDonald was easily influenced by Lady Londonderry, whose husband, the Secretary of State for Air, was bitterly opposed to Simon's readiness to ban military aviation. The Prime Minister also thought that 'Simon bags his ideas and takes the credit for them himself without acknowledgement – in which there is a certain amount of truth.'[78] Hankey worked hard during the summer to reconcile the two men but, despite a personal liking for the Foreign Secretary, was exasperated by the latter's lack of drive and initiative.[79] After Samuel's resignation, however, Simon's continued presence in the government was of ever-growing importance to a Prime Minister who felt more and more his own political isolation.

★　★　★

Germany's withdrawal from the Disarmament Conference in July brought the question of that country's armaments to the forefront of the government's concerns. Despite repeated promptings from Hankey, Simon was slow to respond. He recognised that the situation could easily prove critical for the future not only of Anglo-German relations, but also Anglo-French relations and of Geneva itself. It was important to say nothing to offend the French since 'we shall need all our influence with Herriot to get the German claim for equality fairly considered.'[80]

Finally, in mid-September he produced a carefully worded statement which emphasised that the disarmament clauses of the Treaty of Versailles were still binding on Germany, deprecating any attempt by Germany to rearm, but expressing the hope that a disarmament convention could be achieved which would grant equality of status to all concerned.[81] It was perhaps an indication of the range of opinion from which criticism of the Foreign Secretary's policies might come that on this occasion Winston Churchill wrote warmly in his support. Simon's firm stand had 'done more to consolidate peace in Europe than any words spoken on behalf of Great Britain for some years'.[82] Simon was disappointed by the unfavourable response to his note in Berlin, but remained determined to seek 'a way of escape out of the mess at Geneva':

If we do not find one, I fear that the war to end war will bring another conflict in its train.[83]

The cabinet determined to hold a special meeting on 30 September to discuss disarmament. Here it was decided to summon a conference in London to consider how to bring Germany back to the disarmament negotiations. The cabinet endorsed Simon's view that it might be unavoidable to agree to Germany possessing some of the weapons prohibited under Versailles. The practical choice seemed to lie between allowing Germany to rearm within certain agreed limits, or her continued abstention from the Disarmament Conference.[84] When the French refused to come to London the cabinet accepted the recommendation of Simon and MacDonald that Britain should organise a four-power meeting at Geneva preceded by a major British initiative to try to bring about a compromise formula.[85] Drafting such a formula, however, was no easy task. Simon argued that it was essential for Britain to decide what sort of armaments she was prepared to allow Germany to have.[86] But his own proposals to offer to scrap all armaments forbidden to Germany under Versailles were badly mauled in cabinet committee by Lord Hailsham on behalf of the War Office.[87]

Near to despair Simon sought advice from Neville Chamberlain.[88] In the end he presented the cabinet with a paper which was largely the work of Eden and Vansittart. In a five-hour discussion the cabinet seemed more attracted to Chamberlain's idea that disarmament should take place in successive stages, each stage being dependent upon the good behaviour of Germany during the preceding period. The advantage was that confidence

too would proceed by stages, based on actual experience instead of promises.[89] Eden recorded his contempt for the Foreign Secretary's performance:

Simon went off to the Cabinet like a scalded rabbit, really in a pitiable state. I heard
afterwards that he was wretched in Cabinet, running round in circles. However,
ultimately a drafting committee was set up . . . It is not possible to do more than give
and make material to fight with: no one else can give him guts.[90]

When the drafting committee got to work Hankey, fearful that the Germans
were playing a game of 'heads I win and tails you lose', secured the inclusion
of a paragraph to the effect that disarmament could only be carried out by
stages as Germany proved her good neighbourliness.[91] Simon unveiled the
new policy in the House of Commons on 10 November. The fact that France
had already accepted a short-service Reichswehr was, he said, an admission
that the Versailles Treaty was not sacrosanct. Henceforth British policy
would take into account 'the fair meeting of Germany's claim to the principle of equality', while seeking a solemn declaration that the countries of
Europe would not in any circumstances attempt to resolve differences
between them by resort to force.[92] This statement was generally well
received in the British press and was repeated in Geneva on 17 November
together with detailed British proposals for disarmament, including the
immediate reduction of the air forces of the leading powers to the level of
that of the United Kingdom and a 33⅓ per cent cut all round in the world's air
forces thus reduced. Even the *Daily Herald*, one of Simon's staunchest
critics, felt able to welcome his new proposals.[93] By 11 December Germany
had been persuaded to rejoin the conference table with Simon playing a
leading role in getting the new French premier, Edouard Herriot, to accept a
compromise formula which conceded Germany equality of rights within 'a
system which would provide security for all nations'.

For the time being Simon's public standing had been partially restored.
'Your stock is right up,' assured his parliamentary private secretary. The
adverse criticism of a few months before had been quelled.[94] But finding a
formula of words was a long way from securing a settlement and Simon was
under no illusions about the tasks which lay ahead. 1932 had been a gruelling
year for him. One cabinet colleague judged that he had struggled with
situations which would have taxed the character and ability 'of even your
greatest predecessors'.[95] Another echoed the same sentiments:

I don't know when there has been such a series of insoluble Foreign problems all
coming together, but I think we have all reason to be very grateful to you for the tact
and skill with which you have handled them and brought them within reach of a
solution. . . .[96]

At Christmas time Simon summed up his feelings to a fellow Liberal
National:

This Foreign Office work of mine is an *exacting* business and I am very far from thinking that I have done it as it should be done . . . Geneva is an appalling drag and something will have to be done about it.[97]

Yet there was little time for reflection, let alone self-congratulation. 'There is plenty of trouble in front of us for 1933', he told Lord Reading, 'the Far East, Disarmament, Persia, American Debt, all sorts of things.'[98] Among the miscellaneous 'sorts of things' which may have been in the Foreign Secretary's mind was a further change of government in Germany. When it came on 30 January all existing calculations of British foreign policy would need to be remade.

Notes

1 Simon to L. Amery 19 March 1932, FO800/286.
2 One effect may have been that Simon tended to be less ready than his predecessors to engage in lengthy private correspondence with Britain's ambassadors and ministers abroad – an understandable decision, but one which inevitably caused misgivings. See H. Rumbold to Francis Lindley 24 Feb. 1932, Rumbold MSS 39 fos. 154–5. For Simon's attention to his departmental papers see Lord Gladwyn, *Memoirs* (London, 1972) p. 40.
3 Simon to Sir G. Clerk 26 Jan. 1932, FO800/286. Interestingly, the pressures upon Simon's time appear to have obliged him to abandon his diary until the autumn of 1934.
4 *North Mail* 24 Aug. 1928.
5 cf. Murray to Simon 24 Oct. 1932, Murray MSS 214 fos. 230–1: 'I expect you have had a hard task in upholding any remnant of Liberal principles against a 400 majority and any active interest in constructive peace against the social and political forces of militarism – much more militarist than the soldiers themselves.'
6 U. Bialer, *The Shadow of the Bomber* (London, 1980) p. 19.
7 *The Times* 21 Nov. 1931.
8 Simon to Cecil 28 June 1932, F.O. 800/287.
9 H. of C. Debs, 5th Series, vol. 263, col. 923.
10 F. P. Walters, *A History of the League of Nations* (London, 1960) p. 217.
11 B. Webb diary 18 Dec. 1932.
12 E. B. Segal, 'Sir John Simon' p. 74 ff.
13 Ibid, p. 80.
14 S. Hoare to Simon 16 Oct. 1932, cited ibid, p. 327.
15 Lord Templewood, *Nine Troubled Years* (London, 1954) pp. 25–6.
16 Simon to MacDonald 1 Dec. 1931, FO 800/285.
17 M. Gilbert, *The Roots of Appeasement* (London, 1966) pp. 131–2.
18 MacDonald to Simon 17 Dec. 1931, SP70 fo. 72.
19 C. Barnett, *The Collapse of British Power* (London, 1972) p. 340.
20 Simon to Rumbold 30 March 1932, *DBFP*, Second Series, vol. iii, p. 514.
21 Segal, 'Sir John Simon' p. 133. The cabinet committee on the trade balance concluded that the way to reduce imports would be to impose a general tariff of 10 per cent and a variable surtax on non-essential goods.

22 Viscount Cecil, *All the Way* (London, 1949) p. 200.

23 Baldwin to Simon 2 March 1932, cited Segal, 'Sir John Simon' p. 164.

24 Simon to Garvin 28 June 1932, SP72 fos. 127–8.

25 P. Williamson (ed.), *The Modernisation of Conservative Politics* (London, 1988) p. 254.

26 H. of C. Debs, 5th Series, vol. 268, cols. 1248–9.

27 Simon to Reading 10 May 1932, Reading MSS Eur F 118/101.

28 Notes on Sir John Simon by Alexander Cadogan, Cadogan MSS A CAD7/1. 'I, as Secretary of the United Kingdom Delegation, was in close personal day-to-day touch with John Simon and found myself occasionally depressed and feeling frustrated by chance remarks made to me by him.' A cabinet colleague confirmed, 'Of course he hates Geneva and there's a good deal here that is hateful – but it's not as bad as all that!' Ormsby-Gore to Baldwin 1 Oct. 1933, Baldwin MSS vol. 121 fos. 74–6.

29 Simon to Baldwin 11 Oct. 1933, Baldwin MSS vol. 121 fo. 86. Arthur Henderson, President of the Disarmament Conference, later complained that Simon was 'always running away back to England to attend a Cabinet meeting, leaving sometimes unimportant people to take his place'. Taylor (ed.), *Off the Record* p. 13.

30 Sir Herbert Lewis to Lloyd George 5 March 1932, Lloyd George MSS G/12/1/25.

31 Disarmament Notes 20 April 1932, Murray MSS 212 fo. 167.

32 H. Dalton, *The Fateful Years* (London, 1957) p. 49.

33 Simon to Lord Tyrrell 9 June 1932, FO 800/287.

34 Eden, *Facing the Dictators* p. 47.

35 H. Montgomery Hyde, *British Air Policy* p. 279.

36 Simon paper 14 April 1932, Bialer, *Bomber* p. 28; N. H. Gibbs, *Grand Strategy* vol. 1, (London, 1976) p. 591.

37 As note 33.

38 Cabinet 1 June 1932, CAB 23/71.

39 Cabinet 11 May 1932, CAB 23/71.

40 H. of C. Debs, 5th Series, vol. 265, cols. 2325–38.

41 Simon to G. Murray 24 May 1932, Murray MSS 213 fo. 44.

42 Memorandum by Simon 26 May 1932, cited M. Smith, *British Air Strategy Between the Wars* (Oxford, 1984) p. 117.

43 Cecil to Murray 13 June 1932, Murray MSS 213 fo. 76.

44 In Lausanne Simon seems to have played a useful role, though Neville Chamberlain took the lead. Chamberlain, in marked contrast to some of his later comments on the Foreign Secretary's performance, wrote appreciatively that 'Simon has been a tower of strength.' N. Chamberlain to Annie Chamberlain 17 June 1932, Chamberlain MSS NC1/26/460.

45 Simon to Vansittart 20 June 1932, cited G. Scott, *League of Nations* p. 267.

46 Roskill, *Hankey* iii, 63; Eden attributed 'our missing a chance' to the influence of Londonderry and Eric Drummond over the Prime Minister and believed that 'Simon ought to have refused the tentative half-measure.' Diary, 26 July 1932, cited James, *Eden* pp. 117–18.

47 Eden diary 6 July 1932, cited James, *Eden* p. 116.

48 T. Clarke, *Lloyd George Diary* p. 152.

49 Disarmament Notes 23 June 1932, Murray MSS 213 fo. 91.

50 Ibid, 1 July 1932, ibid fo. 111.
51 H. of C. Debs., 5th Series, vol. 268, col. 1247.
52 Ibid, col. 1249.
53 Drummond to Simon 31 July 1932, SP72 fo. 203.
54 Simon to MacDonald 18 July 1932, cited N. Waites (ed.), *Troubled Neighbours* (London, 1971) p. 140.
55 Simon to Rumbold 29 Aug. 1932, *D.B.F.P.*, 2nd Series, vol. iv, p. 109.
56 G. Murray to Simon 23 July 1932, SP 72 fo. 180.
57 Simon to MacDonald 26 July 1932, FO 800/287. See also Note for cabinet by Simon on the Disarmament Conference 28 July 1932, FO 800/287.
58 Lloyd George to F. Stevenson 1 Oct. 1932, cited Taylor (ed.), *Darling Pussy* p. 195.
59 T. Jones, *Diary with Letters* p. 63.
60 M. Asquith to Baldwin 27 Sept. 1932, Baldwin MSS vol. 167 fo. 215.
61 R. James (ed.), *Memoirs of a Conservative* p. 379.
62 *Manchester Guardian* 25 July 1932. For Simon's sensitivity to newspaper criticism, see Eden's diary entry for November 1932, cited James, *Eden* p. 120. Simon was sensitive to criticism throughout his career. At about this time he took the trouble to dictate a seven-page letter to a Cambridge undergraduate who had written critically of the government's disarmament policy, SP75 fos. 127–33. Another indication of Simon's desire to avoid adverse comment was his decision early in 1933 to sell his shares in ICI, one of whose subsidiary companies was involved in the manufacture of ammunition, Simon to B. Manning 31 Jan. 1933, SP75 fo. 154: 'this may seem almost pedantic and ridiculous, but one cannot be too particular. . . .' In January 1935 Simon took to the courts as plaintiff and witness for the first time in his life against a clergyman who had suggested that the Foreign Secretary was financially interested in armament firms and that this had affected his conduct of foreign affairs. 'It remains to be seen whether my denials on oath . . . will stop the slander.' Simon diary 25 Jan. 1935, SP7 fo. 15. Simon, wishing merely to clear his name, showed no malice towards the unfortunate clergyman. Victorious in his case, he sought neither damages nor costs.
63 Segal, 'Sir John Simon' p. 324.
64 A. Chamberlain to Ida Chamberlain 9 Oct. 1932, Chamberlain MSS AC 5/1/597; a month later Chamberlain wrote, 'I think his policy is just one of expedients, that he has no certain line traced for himself and can give therefore no clear guidance,' A. Chamberlain to Ivy Chamberlain 5 Oct. 1932, AC 6/1/898. Neville Chamberlain commented: 'I sympathise with his impatience but think he does Simon less than justice.' N. Chamberlain to H. Chamberlain 15 Oct. 1932, NC 18/1/801.
65 Simon to Murray 23 July 1932, Murray MSS 213 fo. 176.
66 James, *Eden* p. 118.
67 Simon to Baldwin 5 Oct. 1932, Baldwin MSS vol. 167 fo. 250.
68 Eden diary 26 July 1932, James, *Eden* p. 118.
69 E. Granville to Simon 2 Oct. 1932, SP73 fo. 125.
70 Simon to I. Macpherson 5 Feb. 1932, SP71 fos. 30–1.
71 Simon to W. Runciman 16 Sept. 1932, SP73 fo. 64.
72 Notes by Sankey, Sankey MSS, Eng. his. c. 509 fo. 130.
73 G. Shakespeare to Simon 23 Sept. 1932, SP73 fo. 79.

74 See below pp. 222–3.
75 G. Shakespeare to Simon 30 Sept. 1932, SP73 fo. 113.
76 Shakespeare to W. Runciman 27 Sept. 1932, Runciman MSS 254.
77 N. Chamberlain to Annie Chamberlain 26 June 1932, Chamberlain MSS NC 1/26/462. See also A. Chamberlain to Ida Chamberlain 9 Oct. 1932, AC 5/1/597.
78 Roskill, *Hankey* iii, 56.
79 Ibid, p. 57.
80 Simon to N. M. Butler 28 July 1932, SP 72 fos. 195–6.
81 *D.B.F.P.*, 2nd Series, vol. iv, pp. 172–5.
82 *Daily Mail* 17 Oct. 1932; M. Gilbert, *Churchill* v, 448–9.
83 Simon to Garvin 20 Sept. 1932, FO 800/287.
84 CAB 23/72; Gibbs, *Grand Strategy* p. 84.
85 Cabinet 11 Oct. 1932, CAB 23/72.
86 Memorandum on Disarmament Conference Crisis 17 Oct. 1932, cited M. Smith, *British Air Strategy* pp. 117–18.
87 Roskill, *Hankey* iii, 61.
88 N. Chamberlain to H. Chamberlain 30 Oct. 1932, Chamberlain MSS NC 18/1/803.
89 N. Chamberlain to Ida Chamberlain 5 Nov. 1932, NC 18/1/804.
90 Eden diary 31 Oct. 1932, cited James, *Eden* p. 119; Eden, *Facing the Dictators* p. 26.
91 Roskill, *Hankey* iii, 62.
92 H. of C. Debs, 5th Series, vol. 270, cols. 534–48.
93 *Daily Herald* 18 Nov. 1932.
94 E. Granville to Simon 6 Dec. 1932, SP 74 fo. 144.
95 W. Runciman to Simon 24 Dec. 1932, SP75 fo. 35.
96 N. Chamberlain to Simon 4 Jan. 1933, SP75 fos. 115–16.
97 Simon to Runciman 24 Dec. 1932, Runciman MSS 254.
98 Simon to Reading 29 Dec. 1932, Reading MSS Eur F118/101.

CHAPTER SEVEN

FACING THE DICTATORS?

The real hope for Europe [is that] while the United Kingdom should make preparations as were necessary to defend herself, she should still pursue a policy of
settlement in which Germany could take an equal share.[1]

With hindsight it is possible to see that with Hitler's assumption of power
the world entered a new era which could probably only end in one way and in
which conventional notions about the dealings of one nation with another
were largely irrelevant. The fundamental mistake was to treat Hitler as just
another German politician, a more aggressive Stresemann, a less acceptable
Brüning. There is little evidence that Simon gave much thought to the nature
of Nazism in the period before Hitler came to power. He had expressed
concern at the increasingly militant attitude of the von Papen and von
Schleicher governments and voiced his disquiet at Germany's defiance of the
armaments restrictions placed upon her by Versailles. But his reaction to
Hitler did not entail a fundamental re-thinking of British policy. His ideas
were still based on the need to undercut Germany's desire to rearm and thus
avoid the vicious circle which had led to the catastrophe of 1914.[2]

Simon's lack of vision was, of course, widely shared. The fundamental
division lay between the majority like himself and those few who recognised
that the nature of the Nazi regime, evidenced in the first instance by its
domestic aspect, was of a kind to preclude any trust being placed in its
conduct in the international arena. The Conservative elder statesman,
Austen Chamberlain, was among the few who made the necessary transition
of imagination and understanding. In the House of Commons on 13 April
1933 he begged 'the Rt. Hon. Gentleman [Simon] to beware of what he is
doing':

Europe is menaced and Germany is afflicted by this narrow, exclusive and aggressive
spirit, by which it is a crime to be in favour of peace and a crime to be a Jew. That is
not a Germany to which we can afford to make concessions. That is not a Germany to
which Europe can afford to give the equality of which the Prime Minister spoke.[3]

Simon was not completely blind to the nature of the Nazi regime. Early in
1932 he expressed a curiosity 'to know what policy in regard to the Jews the
Nazis really do intend to follow' if they were elected.[4] After January 1933
the Foreign Secretary was under few illusions, sharing the widespread
disgust at Nazi brutality. In May he informed the cabinet that current
German policy was 'definitely disquieting' and that the German government
was giving state sanction and encouragement to an attitude of mind, as well

as to various forms of military training, which could only end in one way.[5] Simon's language in a speech to the House in mid-April was so critical of the German persecution of the Jews and other minorities that a protest was received from the German government, accompanied by widespread rumours that the Foreign Secretary must himself be Jewish.[6] When Britain's ambassador in Berlin stressed the abnormality of the Nazi regime and his fears for the future, Simon noted that these warnings would be 'of great and permanent value to His Majesty's Government in determining their policy towards Germany'.[7] Then, after Germany left the Disarmament Conference for a second time in October, Simon accused the Nazi regime of preaching a doctrine 'which seemed to regard preparation for war as in itself a noble ideal pervading every aspect of national life'.[8] Writing to Austen Chamberlain he even seemed to put his finger on a central weakness in the whole policy of appeasement:

I also agree most profoundly with your reading of German psychology and with the Teutonic failing of misreading generosity and imagining that it betokens weakness rather than a warning of strength.[9]

But Simon appears not to have drawn the conclusion that the quest for an agreement with Hitler's regime was an illusion, and a dangerous illusion at that. While he recognised that the Nazis posed a threat to British security and to peace in general, there was no attempt to place the German government beyond the international pale and little move to prepare for possible conflict with it. Indeed Simon thought it necessary to continue the quest to satisfy German grievances irrespective of the character of the new regime. He seems not to have realised that even had an agreement with Hitler been reached, the latter would have regarded it merely as a temporary expedient to be discarded as circumstances dictated. 'Will he never learn what Germans are?' complained Austen Chamberlain in July 1934.[10] For this Simon stands indicted. In his defence it can only be said that his tragic mistake was shared by the overwhelming majority of his fellow countrymen.

There were those who sought to analyse the significance of Nazi ideology. Horace Rumbold, ambassador in Berlin, sent Simon a five-thousand word despatch in late April 1933. There was, said Rumbold, no need for anyone to be in ignorance of Hitler's aims and beliefs. *Mein Kampf* made clear the principles which had guided him for the last fourteen years. It would, thought the ambassador, be misleading to base any hope on a return to sanity or a serious modification of Hitler's views.[11] Yet, when the cabinet considered Rumbold's memorandum, it decided merely that Hitler should be told that 'we hope Germany will do nothing to make Europe more nervous than it is.'[12] It was a lame response based more upon hope than expectation.

In coping with the mounting problems on the international horizon, Simon could call upon the services of his parliamentary under-secretary, Anthony Eden, whose role became increasingly prominent in the course of

1933. Very early in his Foreign Secretaryship Simon had concluded that he was spending too much of his time at Geneva and the possibility of making use of a respected senior figure such as Austen Chamberlain had been discussed. [13] During 1933 Eden took on more and more of this side of Simon's duties. For the Foreign Secretary this proved to be a mixed blessing. No clear division of labour was arrived at and the scope of Eden's authority was not satisfactorily defined. [14] 'The way this Government runs foreign affairs is very surprising,' commented Robert Cecil. [15] At a personal level the relationship between the two men seems to have remained cordial, to all appearances warm. Expressions of hostility and scorn were largely confined to the pages of Eden's diary and his correspondence with trusted third parties. To begin with Eden's disenchantment was far more related to Simon's methods than to questions of policy. The younger man was irritated by Simon's over-cautious approach, his reluctance to make up his mind and perhaps still more by his failure to stand up for the Foreign Office inside the highest councils of government, particularly against the service ministries. [16] Not being himself a member of the cabinet, Eden perhaps failed to give full weight to the difficulties which Simon was bound to encounter.

Be that as it may, the working relationship between the two men certainly deteriorated in the course of 1933, though still as regards policy – and as would be the case a few years later during Eden's celebrated breach with Neville Chamberlain – their differences were of emphasis rather than fundamentals. Eden took to consulting Baldwin, whom he regarded as his political mentor, before he did Simon, his direct superior. There are enough other examples in Eden's career to assert with some confidence that, whatever Simon's failings, the younger man was not an easy person with whom to work. Yet his youth, charm and good looks guaranteed Eden a favourable press and public reaction almost irrespective of his ministerial performance. Eden seemed to exude many of the personal qualities which Simon patently lacked. 'It is [Simon's] manner that kills him here,' asserted a cabinet colleague:

I do wish we had a Foreign Secretary who was more popular here. It is most painful to have to listen to the criticisms of the Dominion delegates, the British members of the L of N staff and even of foreigners (the last veil their allusions). [17]

Increasingly Eden was seen as a better League of Nations man than his chief. [18] As Baldwin was informed:

The man who really has the international position here is Anthony Eden. Somehow or other Anthony has got the confidence – nay the adulation of all these strange animals that live in this zoo. Simon can never get it. [19]

Such successes as Britain enjoyed at Geneva tended therefore to be attributed to Eden, much to Simon's irritation. It was not long before Eden was being spoken of as a possible successor as Foreign Secretary. [20] At the end of 1933 a stressful Simon reacted angrily to press reports that Eden was about to take his place:

Simon in an awful state about press campaign. Kept pulling cuttings from his pocket about me and would talk of nothing else![21]

By the beginning of 1933 Simon seemed to be pursuing a policy towards the Disarmament Conference in which he no longer believed. From a private conversation Leo Amery judged that the Foreign Secretary was now much more sceptical than hitherto about the possibilities of success at Geneva, though concerned to avoid 'such an obvious breakdown as will do real harm'.[22] Alexander Cadogan, chief adviser to the United Kingdom delegation at Geneva, complained that Simon was reluctant even to submit his plans to the cabinet.[23] Political necessity on the other hand continued to dictate that the government should be seen to make the effort, however slim the chances of a favourable outcome. To a League of Nations man like Gilbert Murray Simon emphasised that he was still doing his best to master the whole intractable question.[24] In governmental discussions the illusion was maintained. On 19 January Simon warned the cabinet that the impetus provided by Germany's return to the Conference would soon be wasted unless a new direction and lead were given to its deliberations. In the event of failure responsibility would be placed, however unfairly, at Britain's door.[25] Eden shared these sentiments, but waited in vain for his chief to take the lead. Accordingly Eden seized the initiative himself, suggesting that Britain should put forward a Draft Disarmament Convention complete in all its details. He deliberately made his first approach to Baldwin, only informing the Foreign Secretary two days later.[26]

Eden's *démarche* helped stir Simon into action and on 1 March he presented the cabinet with a worrying picture of 'the crisis in Europe'. The European situation was deteriorating fast and the Disarmament Conference might, he said, break down within two weeks.[27] He admitted that so far there had been no agreement on any important subject and that unless there was a change of approach the Conference was doomed. Without a disarmament convention the Germans would still seek to achieve equality and this would mean German rearmament, followed by that of the other powers. Simon then painted a gloomy scenario:

In such an atmosphere, even if peace is nominally preserved, political relations will rapidly deteriorate yet further. The restoration of political confidence, in which all the economic as well as political experts insist, will be postponed to the Greek Kalends . . . It will be an atmosphere of hostility, if not hostilities, which will militate with full force against that financial and economic recovery which is essential not only to peace but to the very existence of civilisation. And the number of years for which hostilities can be staved off would, in all European opinion, be doubtful.[28]

The cabinet decided that Simon and MacDonald should travel to Geneva with the option of presenting the draft convention if they saw fit to do so. But the Foreign Secretary's warnings had taken many of his colleagues by surprise:

Simon for day or two with no implication of great urgency has indicated that things were sticking at Geneva and with other pressing things . . . the Disarmt. Conference had been ranged amongst the ordinary troubles. Now it was presented as being on its death bed.[29]

Simon's sudden concern is perhaps best explained by the wave of newspaper reports in the same week which predicted that he was about to be removed from his office.[30] There had been no real change in his thinking and privately he admitted to Baldwin that he held out no great hopes of success.[31] From Geneva he confirmed that the position was as bad as had been pictured. The committees which were sitting were simply marking time and in a state of deadlock. The alternative was between a new British initiative, 'unattractive and doubtful of acceptance as it may be', and letting the Conference 'fade away without anything material being achieved'.[32] After lengthy negotiations with the cabinet in London MacDonald formally presented the draft convention to the Conference on 16 March, including in it, as Eden had urged, specific figures of armed strength.

The British draft was generally well received although only Italy formally accepted its terms. But while in Geneva the British delegates received an invitation from Mussolini to visit Rome. The convention might at least delay the breakdown of the Conference, while Britain, France and Italy sought in private negotiations to formulate the basis of an agreement.[33] Steps were taken to reassure the French that the visit to Rome did not indicate any new orientation in Britain's foreign policy.[34] In October of the previous year Mussolini had called for a four power pact between Britain, France, Germany and Italy, who would assume a kind of directorate charged with the revision of the Versailles Treaty. Simon's reaction had not been unfavourable. But the pact shown to Simon and MacDonald in Rome on 18 and 19 March placed too great an emphasis on revision for it to be acceptable to the French. It was not difficult for the French premier, Edouard Daladier, to convince the British ministers that if, as Mussolini suggested, practical expression were given to Germany's demand for equality in the event that the Disarmament Conference broke down, the effect would be to give Germany a vested interest in seeing the Conference fail.[35] In the Commons Churchill ridiculed the Rome visit as something not to be taken too seriously.

We have got our modern Don Quixote home again, with Sancho Panza at his tail, bearing with them these somewhat dubious trophies which they have collected amid the nervous titterings of Europe.[36]

What was certainly true was that the shift of emphasis away from Geneva made further progress with the British draft convention most unlikely. As Simon recognised, the resort to private negotiations was bound to worry the smaller nations who would suspect 'a plot to dish the League of Nations'.[37] The unenviable task of seeking further progress at Geneva now devolved largely upon Eden and even his optimism soon began to flag.[38] On 12 May the Foreign Secretary instructed Eden to avoid any further discussion of disarmament details until Germany agreed to 'the principle of disarmament by stages and nothing that could really be regarded as rearmament by Germany'.[39] Simon now seemed primarily concerned with avoiding a public relations disaster at Geneva:

What I dread is that we should seem to concede a little bit in this direction [of German rearmament] only to find that Germany demands more, and the Conference breaks down after we have, by our concession, lost the overwhelming public support which would be given to a stiffer attitude.[40]

   Simon was certainly in need of lightening his work-load at this time. It is necessary to recall that while the Disarmament Conference ground to a halt, the question of an arms embargo in the Far East was coming to a head. There was little relief in the Foreign Secretary's schedule. At the end of March he hurried back to Westminster to speak in a debate on the government's India policy, where the adherence of the former chairman of the Statutory Commission was thought to be important to defuse a possible right-wing Conservative rebellion. In the circumstance Simon did as well as could be expected, expressing support for the government 'cleverly, but I thought unenthusiastically'.[41] It was in the nature of things, reported the Secretary of State for India, 'that the kind of speech that he could make was unlikely to be sufficiently definite to strengthen the waverers'.[42] Further problems arose in March when two British engineers of the Metro-Vickers Company were arrested in the Soviet Union on charges of espionage. A serious crisis in Anglo-Russian relations was in prospect. Simon took a tough line – much to the dismay of left wingers, such as Beatrice Webb, whose vision of Stalin's dictatorship was still distorted by their own misplaced idealism.[43] A powerful speech in the Commons on 5 April brought praise from the political right and a trade embargo was applied to which the Soviets replied in kind. Eventually the engineers were released and the trade restrictions lifted following conversations with Litvinov in late June at the World Economic Conference, then meeting in London.[44]

   In the circumstances it was perhaps not surprising that by the end of April the Foreign Secretary's health was showing signs of strain. The press speculated on what was wrong. Simon was said to be suffering from a chill and to be run down, and there was talk of low blood pressure. Eden expressed his concern in terms which belied his growing antipathy towards his more senior colleague.[45] But Simon was reluctant to take a break from his official duties. Since returning to government he had not taken a holiday. A parliamentary question later in the year revealed that he was out of the country on official business for 23½ weeks out of two years. By mid May his decline was evident. Eden noted that

the effect of his presence for the present is that we have no Foreign Secretary, only the appearance of one which is worse than none.[46]

A few days later Eden urged Simon to take a sea cruise to restore his health. MacDonald and Baldwin were 'clearly a little impatient of Simon's illness'. The latter agreed to go but almost immediately changed his mind:

He would not go, but would hang on somehow. I thought that if Simon were as ill as he seemed, he would be wiser to go for his cruise then, for as long as was necessary.[47]

Simon had recovered sufficiently to make a statement to the Commons on 26 May about Mussolini's proposed Four Power Pact. Listeners were reassured by his firm refusal to enter into further obligations towards the European continent. 'We take our existing responsibilities too seriously to be willing in a lighthearted and speculative fashion to enlarge them.'[48] Austen Chamberlain congratulated Simon on 'one of the most remarkable and . . . encouraging speeches that it has been in the power of any Foreign Secretary to make in this House for many years past',[49] and the press too generally voiced its approval. The pact that was finally signed in Rome on 8 June was a much weaker document than Mussolini had originally proposed. Simon's troubles, however, soon returned. On 1 June the *Daily Mail* and *Daily Express* reported that Simon had found himself in strong opposition to the rest of the cabinet on the question of abolishing the right of 'police bombing in outlying districts', and that he was ready to resign. According to Neville Chamberlain the press accounts were greatly exaggerated, but Simon was

obviously unwell and overtired and we (and particularly I) pressed him to take a holiday and not go to Geneva during Whitsun week.[50]

Still the Foreign Secretary struggled on, but by mid-June it was clear that something would have to be done. Neville Chamberlain wrote in terms designed to reassure Simon that his long-term position within the government would not be endangered by a temporary absence.

I have felt for some time that no man could go on working at the rate you have been doing . . . without presently paying for it. . . . You have been such a tower of strength to the Government that your health is a matter of the gravest concern to us all. I very much fear that you have strained it so far that nothing but a *complete rest* will save you from a bad breakdown.[51]

Eden and Vansittart shared Chamberlain's opinion and urged Baldwin to press the Foreign Secretary to take their advice.[52] Finally, in the second week of July, Simon set sail for Brazil to restore his health.

He returned in late August refreshed but perhaps not fully recovered. The

Disarmament Conference had adjourned on 10 June without a decision having been reached on the draft British convention, a tacit admission that hope of any further progress was remote. Eden had placed stress on ensuring Anglo–French solidarity before any further approach was made to Germany. At the cabinet on 5 September Simon asserted that the French were 'eager for a Disarmament Convention', providing it included a trial period during which Germany would transform the Reichswehr into a short service force, while French disarmament would commence at the completion of this period. A fortnight later he warned that if no convention were finalised Germany would then rearm as and when she liked. If other powers would not reduce their armaments as the French now proposed, Germany would have to be allowed some increase of hers. But the cabinet ruled out any possibility of Britain entering into new commitments to impose sanctions if the convention were broken.[53] On 22 September Simon emphasised this last point in conversations with Daladier in Paris.[54] Total deadlock seemed to have been reached when the Germans demanded an unspecified number of samples of weapons during the first period of any disarmament convention.[55]

Simon determined on one last effort. The Conference had become 'a squirrel's cage in which one goes on round and round without getting any further'.[56] At the end of September he drew up a revised convention as 'an honest effort, by the party to the Conference which is in the best position to do it, to mark out the necessary middle course if there is ever going to be a Convention at all'.[57] The essence of the plan, drawn up with no great hope of success, was for two stages of four years each, in the second of which the signatories would be obliged to reduce their armaments in specified stages. Behind it all was Simon's now growing conviction that, in the absence of a convention, Germany would continue to rearm in defiance of Versailles and

once the new regime in Germany settles down and becomes more respectable, there will be many people who will say that there is a good deal in the German claim that she has waited fourteen years for equality and cannot be expected to wait any longer.[58]

If the Germans were asked point blank to agree to a period of trial and waiting before the complete scheme came into operation, this would at least 'bring the Germans out into the open'.[59] Indeed bringing Germany out into the open had become the 'main point in our tactics'.[60]

On the morning of 14 October Simon presented his new plan of progressive general disarmament to the secretariat of the Disarmament Conference. From Germany's point of view the practical effect of the proposals would be to postpone substantial changes in the existing size of armies for four years. It was bound to be an important speech and Simon was understandably nervous. Eden left an unflattering description of the Foreign Secretary's mood. Simon was in a:

characteristically bad state, snappy and scared to death. It is very difficult to feel anything but contempt for the man at these times. It is not only 'nerves' at the speech which we might all suffer or excuse, but I truly believe an utter lack of moral courage.[61]

The speech itself was, as usual, lucid and elegant, but by lunchtime news had been received that the Germans were quitting the Conference and giving notice of their intention to leave the League. These decisions had been taken in advance, though the appearance suggested that they were a direct response to Simon's statement. The Foreign Secretary's enemies were ready to pounce. Margot Asquith asserted that his 'wordy, windy' speeches would have made her leave Geneva long before; the *Daily Herald* suggested that Hitler had secured a propaganda coup which would attract to his cause millions of Germans who detested Nazism.[62] 'Are you going to get rid of Simon now?' asked Nancy Astor of the Prime Minister.[63]

Simon was not unduly perturbed by what had happened. He regarded Germany's action as no more than the application to the international sphere of the shock tactics which had dominated the German government's treatment of her internal situation.[64] Time would have to be given to 'see how this works out' and time was available as Germany was still 'quite incapable of undertaking aggression'.[65] But Simon had no alternative policy waiting to be deployed. Politically speaking his options were bound to be limited by the result that month of a by-election in East Fulham which the government interpreted as a powerful indication that a policy of rearmament would see it unseated at the next general election. He rejected completely Vansittart's belief that Germany would probably have to be contained by force. Nor could he accept that Britain should now retreat into isolation by renouncing her obligations under the Treaty of Locarno. The policy of conciliation was 'the only policy to pursue', despite Germany's recent actions and indeed nothing would 'prevent us from doing our best to meet every claim that is reasonable and just'.[66] The main thrust of British policy was still to maintain European peace and this still depended on improving Franco-German relations. There was thus no alternative to seeking by international co-operation the limitation and reduction of armaments, although in the absence of Germany the Disarmament Conference would no longer be an appropriate forum.[67]

Hitler was now clearly recognised to be the major obstacle to further progress. Cold, hard, logical reason would have no effect on him other than producing 'windmill gestures and "storm" eloquence'.[68] Simon had recently described Italy as 'the real key to European peace',[69] and hoped for closer Anglo-Italian cooperation since Mussolini had denounced Hitler's withdrawal from Geneva. Like Vansittart, Simon saw that Mussolini might be able to resist German encroachments on Austria more effectively than the Austrians themselves. Not surprisingly there were little more than platitudes in his statement to the Commons on 7 November. He stressed once again that the government's policy was to work for a substantial reduction of armed forces. The door had been slammed, but should not be regarded as 'bolted, locked and barred'. The British remained upholders of the League as the best available instrument of peace.[70] It was the sort of language which would satisfy a Gilbert Murray, who sensed that it had made the international scene 'perceptibly brighter', but with greater insight Leo Amery noted that Simon had given no clear indication of what he intended to do next.[71]

A week later Simon faced a fresh personal crisis. As had happened before he found himself the victim of a sudden press campaign. The catalyst seems to have been an article in *The Times*. On 15 November this newspaper called for a new British initiative on the grounds that Simon had been wrong to agree to the French demand for a four-year probationary period and the extension of the period of the original British draft convention from five years to eight. Later that day the cabinet held two lengthy meetings at which disarmament was the main topic of discussion. As the *Manchester Guardian* put it, 'external signs were not wanting that Sir John Simon had . . . an uneasy experience.'[72] According to Neville Chamberlain the cabinet had 'had a terrible time with Simon . . . and I feel that somehow or other there will have to be a change at the FO before long.'[73] Simon surprised his colleagues by proposing that an amended Disarmament Convention should be put forward at Geneva so that Britain might not be blamed for the breakdown of the Conference. To Chamberlain this seemed to have 'every vice':

It was obviously futile with Germany away; it was almost certain to embroil us with our friends and it was moreover extremely distasteful to our own Services.[74]

Chamberlain proposed instead that the Conference should be adjourned and that attention should focus on bringing about an agreement between Germany and France:

After prolonged discussions during which Simon played a rather pitiable part being unable apparently to give a lead and always asking the Cabinet to give him instructions, the Cabinet eventually agreed on the course I had suggested.[75]

By the following day it was being widely reported that Eden would be given cabinet status as Lord Privy Seal and made something like Minister for Disarmament.[76] There were suggestions that the anti-Simon campaign had its origins in Downing Street, supported by elements inside the Foreign Office.[77] The *Evening Standard* carried a cartoon entitled 'Eve of Session Party at the Borgias' which showed Simon's colleagues trying to poison him.[78] Simon, perhaps less fit than he imagined after his rest in the summer, seemed to be living on his nerves. His standing within the government was approaching its lowest ebb.

For the time being the immediate crisis passed. Outwardly the Foreign Secretary seemed to exude renewed optimism. He was, he said, determined to achieve some regulation of armaments for the alternative of unregulated arms meant Armageddon.[79] Apparently impressed by Hitler's declarations of peaceful intent he looked forward to a definitive settlement of Western European security, which would then permit the consideration of 'conceivable ways of peacefully adjusting doubtful frontiers, possibly a cross corridor for Germany into Eastern Prussia etc'. He was becoming convinced that the time was ripe for him to make personal contact with Hitler.[80] When the Führer put forward his own proposals including an army of 300,000, an airforce of about a quarter of the combined strength of Germany's neighbours and possession of tanks and heavy artillery, the government had to work out its response. Neville Chamberlain objected to Simon's draft which appeared to accept the general basis of the German proposal while carping at the details. It was likely to send the French 'into a fit of hysterics'.[81] Chamberlain wanted to place more emphasis on the question of security, 'which really governed the extent to which disarmament was possible':

Once again Simon excited general wonderment and annoyance by his inability or unwillingness to defend his own proposals or to accept others, but in the end his draft was abandoned and another substituted which approached more nearly the line I had suggested.[82]

Once parliament rose Simon left for further talks in Paris and Rome. He was becoming increasingly convinced that German rearmament would be an accomplished fact within a few years, whether as a result of an international agreement or in defiance of one. The choice therefore was not between a disarmament convention and the status quo, but between some sort of regulatory agreement and an all-out arms race. The last, in the eyes of a generation which had lived through the First World War, spelt disaster.[83] The prospect of an unregulated competition in armaments throughout the world was, Simon told the House of Commons a few months later, 'appalling'.[84] German rearmament would necessitate British rearmament and provide a new stimulus 'to the opposition to turn the National Government out'. The loss of credit which the British government would suffer in the eyes of the public if there were no international agreement would be 'something tremendous'. His conclusion, which he introduced with the revealing remark that 'while I have no great admiration for my own judgment, I do believe in my powers of deductive reasoning', was that to break this worsening spiral Britain might be forced to make some new contribution to the security of France to move her from her present position.[85] In effect he had adopted Chamberlain's proposal as his own.

★ ★ ★

By 1934 it was difficult to find anyone with a good word for Simon's performance at the Foreign Office. His old friend Leo Amery heard that the whole cabinet regarded him as a square peg in a round hole, but did not know how to move him.[86] From late 1933 there were suggestions that Neville Chamberlain should replace Simon. Though the idea did not appeal to Chamberlain, he confessed that Simon was 'a bad Foreign Secretary for nobody trusts him'.[87] His half-brother Austen echoed that Simon was 'a very bad Foreign Secretary'.[88] Internationally the position was no better. He was, according to Lloyd George, 'a world catastrophe'.[89] With only a little exaggeration Beatrice Webb concluded that Simon was

denounced in Paris, distrusted in the USA and hated in Moscow, and disliked by the neutral powers.[90]

For good measure Vincent Massey and Jan Smuts confirmed a similar lack of confidence in Imperial circles.[91]

Dissatisfaction with Simon's conduct was founded on two main complaints. The first was his lack of achievement, a criticism based on the questionable assumption that anyone else would have done better in the unpromising circumstances in which Simon held office.[92] Of more substance was his tendency to improvise in the light of changing events instead of pursuing and standing by a clearly defined policy. His failings in this respect led to charges of moral cowardice. 'Has he', asked Austen Chamberlain, 'forgive my Saxon brutality – has he the guts for his task?'[93] He seemed only able to react rather than take initiatives himself. Throughout his life Simon was always more confident in analysing situations than in drawing conclusions from them with a view to positive action. His great intellectual power was umatched by the imaginative capacity of a Churchill or a Lloyd George. As Neville Chamberlain put it:

He can always make an admirable speech in the House – to a brief – but . . . he seems temperamentally unable to make up his mind to action when a difficult situation arises.[94]

The result was a widespread perception that Britain had no policy in relation to the central problems of European diplomacy:

Neither the officials at the FO nor our representatives abroad know what he is at or what they should try for. Everyone is without direction.[95]

In the press the anti-Simon campaign became increasingly bitter, with the Foreign Secretary becoming, as the *Sunday Times* admitted, the victim of assassination by 'paragraph and innuendo'. Pinpricks had turned into 'painful stabs in the back'.[96] Always there was the suspicion that critical articles were officially inspired and at the beginning of March, 'in great agitation', he demanded that the Prime Minister should make some public statement in his defence.[97] Simon's every word was liable to be used against him. When he made a persuasive speech on the theme of the freedom of the individual, *The Times* used it as an excuse to recommend his removal to the Home Office, an idea that was widely picked up by the rest of the press.[98] In fact, of course, the press attacks make it harder for the government to remove him without considerable loss of face.[99] But Simon's greatest strength remained MacDonald's reluctance to weaken the non-Conservative element in the cabinet. The Prime Minister did not 'mean to be absorbed in the Conservative Party'.[100] Simon himself ruled out the possibility of resignation, moved by an unresolved mixture of personal ambition and a genuine conviction that a purely party government would not be in the national interest. At the bottom line he realised that he was now a political prisoner, lacking both public and party support. If the coalition collapsed Simon had nowhere else to go and no audience to which he could appeal. Almost pathetically he clung to the illusion that he and Runciman enjoyed privileged status as members of the 'big six' at the head of the government and claimed that his influence led to an undefined erosion of the Conservatism of the government's policies.[101] 'I have no doubt that Britain can recover', he told Mackenzie King of Canada, 'but I have equally no doubt that she can only recover on broad Liberal lines. I do not care what we call them so long as we follow them.'[102]

During the first part of 1934 Simon continued to prod the flickering embers of a disarmament agreement. He was particularly pleased with the results of his visit to Rome, where he noted Mussolini's determination to impose some form of limitation on German rearmament,[103] though his enthusiasm was not shared by others.[104] It was clear, however, that Germany was enlarging its demands and consolidating its claims with every exchange of views, so Simon placed considerable importance on a British memorandum on disarmament which was completed on 25 January and presented to the Germans four days later, in the hope that it would influence a major speech which Hitler was due to make to the Reichstag on 30 January. The memorandum was

based not on what might be ideally most desirable as a maximum of disarmament, but on what we sincerely feel, after careful and prolonged study of the points of view of various foreign governments, is the best chance at present of securing an agreed Convention.[105]

It aimed to assuage French security fears, while making some concessions to Germany. The plan was phased over ten years with the major powers disarming to a level of parity with Germany after seven years.[106]

Simon discussed his White Paper with Gilbert Murray in early March. Their conversation encapsulated the difficulties the Foreign Secretary had in striking a balance between the realities of the world in which he lived and the idealism of League sentiment. The two men agreed that any disarmament treaty must have a clause obliging its signatories to combine to enforce compliance. Then Simon pointed out:

If we give this guarantee, we must have adequate forces. What will your people say to that? I said, 'Though we recognised that military power may be used in the last resort, we should object to that, as putting force in the forefront. Our great strength is economic and financial. It is that sort of pressure which we should contemplate.' Simon, after dilating on the difficulties of detail involved in either a boycott or an embargo, said, 'Suppose your embargo really squeezes Germany and she replies by a fleet of aircraft over London?'[107]

Eden was instructed to visit Paris, Rome and Berlin to assess reaction to the British document. He responded more positively to his German visit than did the rest of the government, while progress in Paris was severely hampered by domestic political crises. All the time, however, evidence mounted that Hitler's real intentions could be summed up by the word 'rearmament'. When the British ambassador in Berlin spelt this out, Simon commented that Phipps had sent 'a most illuminating document – and terrifying'.[108] Though he rounded on Churchill in the Commons for not believing in the goal of disarmament, he had in fact already conceded that the total collapse of the disarmament negotiations was imminent. Simon's own ideas were moving away from the quest for a disarmament convention and towards a rearmament agreement, which would at least set a ceiling to what was inevitable. German rearmament might thus be circumscribed within acceptable levels.[109]

On the same day that Simon and Churchill clashed in the Commons the cabinet had before it the report of the Defence Requirements Committee. This had been set up the previous November to investigate the nation's defences and to recommend remedies for the worst deficiencies. The Committee, on which Vansittart represented the Foreign Office, recommended a five year armaments plan costing £76 millions. Simon seemed reluctant to accept the Committee's conclusions and proposed further concessions to Germany and additional undertakings to France to avoid a return to prewar conditions of competitive rearmament. More discussions took place on 19 March which focused on the question of whether Germany was, as the report suggested, 'the ultimate potential enemy against whom our long range defence policy must be directed'. Simon offered some comfort by suggesting that, although Hitler was busy tearing up the Treaty of Versailles, the German menace was more likely to develop in South and East Europe than in the West.[110] There was much truth in what he said, but the conclusion to be drawn was not necessarily that which Simon implied. The idea that Hitler could be safely left to do his worst in Eastern Europe could only postpone a crisis which Simon's successors would have to face in circumstances which would not necessarily be more favourable.

Confronted by the Committee's report more starkly than ever before with the extent of the danger which faced them, British ministers first cast around for an alternative policy to the obvious one of rearmament. Simon proposed an international air pact which would outlaw bombing and oblige signatories to join in an offensive against any state which broke its promise, but Londonderry and others would not agree to a plan which might involve Britain in quarrels of no direct concern to herself.[111] Neville Chamberlain and Simon exchanged alternative proposals. The Foreign Secretary now suggested a committee representing Britain, Germany, France, Italy, Belgium, Poland and Czechoslovakia with powers to impose economic sanctions in the event of a breach of an agreed arms convention. Chamberlain countered with a proposal based on 'limited liability' by which signatories would place at the disposal of Simon's committee a force of specified strength. The committee would have to decide how much of the international force should be called up to be used on behalf of an aggrieved party.[112] But Chamberlain's plan met with no favour from the Chiefs of Staff.

When Britain enquired what guarantees the French would require before entering a convention, they limited themselves to saying that Germany would have to return to the League before any question of a convention could be considered. As this was most unlikely without substantial French concessions, the French reply amounted to putting an end to the disarmament talks.[113] The Disarmament Conference itself met on 29 May for what was to prove its last session. Anglo-French tension was only too evident. For France Louis Barthou attacked Germany and criticised Great Britain, speaking of Simon as 'mon cher collègue et presque ami'. Simon's speech contained nothing that was new. The two men's statements were as divergent in substance as they were different in delivery. Barthou committed himself and his government never to consent to any convention which involved any German rearmament or the legalisation of *de facto* German rearmament. Simon stressed that British policy was to seek an agreement acceptable to all parties.[114] For practical purposes the Disarmament Conference was dead. The quest for a general disarmament agreement ceased to be the main theme of British foreign policy.

Slowly and reluctantly Simon began to accept the need for British rearmament.[115] With Baldwin and MacDonald tied up with other matters, Simon often took the chair at meetings of the cabinet committee which considered Britain's defences. But the dominant voice was increasingly that of Neville Chamberlain.[116] Simon's emphasis lay on air rearmament in the vain hope that the Royal Air Force might be able to fulfil the role of an Expeditionary Force in terms of any future British commitment to French security.[117] Anglo-French relations were becoming an important element in this thinking. He believed that nothing was more likely to encourage German intransigence than signs of Anglo-French divergence.[118] His conciliatory attitude towards the French was still evident when Barthou came to London on 9 July and laid before the British government plans for what became known as an Eastern Locarno.

Barthou planned a comprehensive scheme of security to which a peaceful Germany could not take offence. It clearly aimed, however, at an agreement with the Soviet Union, Poland and the powers of the Little Entente for joint resistance to Nazi aggression through the League machinery of collective security and sanctions. Simon gave the plan his blessing, while persuading Barthou that France should guarantee Germany against the Soviet Union as well as the Soviet Union against Germany. He hoped thereby to avoid a new Franco-Russian alliance which would have the effect of dividing Europe up into opposing camps on the pattern of pre-1914. The concomitant was that the Soviet Union should enter the League. Simon had previously dismissed the Soviet application as sheer opportunism,[119] but he now announced in the Commons that Britain would welcome it. Privately he still wanted to make British approval dependent on a Russian promise to stop communist propaganda:

We can certainly intimate that if she is going to join the Club at Geneva we expect her to behave according to the best traditions of the best clubs.[120]

Yet it was a sign of how difficult it was for Simon to pursue a policy which escaped criticism from all sectors of the political spectrum that the right-wing press castigated him for supporting 'another of Stalin's tricks'. 'Why', asked the *Saturday Review*, 'should this country allow Sir John Simon to help pull the fat out of the fire for the benefit of the Bolshevists?'[121]

Simon was pleased with the outcome of his talks with Barthou, which he believed had improved Anglo-French relations while involving no new obligations on the part of Great Britain.[122] The reassertion of Anglo-French solidarity would have a 'damping effect on German exuberance'.[123] For a time his stock rose. Even one of his severest critics conceded that Simon had done 'really good work in his talks with Barthou, quite his best achievement since he took office'.[124] His statement to the Commons that the British attitude towards an Eastern European Security Pact was one of 'benevolent well wishes and not of actual contracting parties' pleased the House.[125] Baldwin heard 'glowing reports'. It was 'a great thing to have the House with us generally in foreign affairs'.[126] A month earlier Simon had given another effective parliamentary performance at the end of the Privilege Debate brought by Winston Churchill against the Secretary for India, Samuel Hoare.[127] The Solicitor-General wrote of 'a complete and devastating exposure by Simon of the false facts and law on which the original ruling from the Speaker was obtained'.[128] This form was maintained when Simon replied for the government at the end of July in the famous defence debate in which Baldwin had earlier declared that Britain's frontier now lay on the Rhine. Major Henry Pownall, then on the secretariat of the Committee of Imperial Defence, recorded that Simon's performance was

quite excellent, dealt with all the points and floored more than one opponent.[129]

If Simon could still rise to the parliamentary occasion, neither he nor any other member of the British government could determine the agenda of the international debate nor prevent a steady darkening of the diplomatic horizons. On 25 July Austrian Nazis murdered Dollfuss, the Austrian Prime Minister, whose position had been sustained by Italian influence and whose fall left Austria looking dangerously vulnerable to a Nazi takeover. This dramatic event occurred almost exactly twenty years after another political assassination whose disastrous repercussions Simon had by no means forgotten. For once there was no sign of the equivocation for which he was so often condemned:

We must keep out of trouble in Central Europe at all costs. July, twenty years ago, stands as an awful warning and indeed I should not be surprised if the date selected for this assassination was inspired by some memory of twenty years ago in this very week.

Britain's ties with Italy were, thought Simon, of great value. But there was an important difference between the British and Italian positions. There were circumstances in which Italy might move troops into Austria. 'There are no circumstances in which we should ever dream of doing so.'[130] Stating what would later become an important issue of policy, Simon insisted that 'I cannot conceive that we should fight for the independence of Austria', even though it was in British interests to discourage in every possible way that country's absorption into Germany.[131] Though made in a private letter to Neville Chamberlain, this statement stands as a landmark in the development of British foreign policy in the 1930s. Britain's unwanted role as the primary guardian of the Versailles settlement had been abandoned. Such *real politik* was unlikely to appeal to those who clung to the vestiges of the 'New Diplomacy'. Robert Cecil recorded his anguish:

If we only had a decent Foreign Minister much could be done. Simon will doubtless discourage any action, saying it is better to leave it to the Powers more immediately concerned, or some such dope.[132]

Yet it is difficult to argue that in the circumstances of 1934 any realistic alternative existed to Simon's strategy. 'What is so striking', said the Foreign Secretary, 'is the way in which every other country *looks to Britain*.'[133] Simon, on the other hand, looked to Italy as the best means of restraining German aggression. At least until the disastrous Hoare-Laval Pact of 1935 this policy seemed to have some chance of success.

By the autumn it was possible for Simon to abandon the last pretence that a disarmament convention was still a realistic goal. Hopes of a world-wide agreement limiting the number and type of armaments, he told the cabinet, did not exist any longer, although there were still political arguments against making a public statement to this effect.[134] Educating the country to the realities of the international situation would, however, be no easy matter. As the prospects of disarmament waned the League of Nations Union sought to convince the government of the strength of opinion which it could still command in the country by organising a Peace Ballot. Simon went out of his way to attack the ballot in a Commons speech on 8 November. It was not a debate in which he had originally wished to take part and the effect of his speech was disappointing, exposing the limits of his abilities as an orator. Conveying sincerity was never Simon's strong point. He had 'taken a lot of trouble over his speech and had persuaded himself that it was going to be one of his great efforts'.[135] But Leo Amery recorded an impression which was widely shared:

at the end Simon tried pathos at which he fails lamentably, and when he tried to quote the closing sentence of the Waterloo chapter in Vanity Fair and got to the word 'Amelia' I feared the House would guffaw.[136]

Austen Chamberlain, who had spoken in the debate in the same sense as Simon, nonetheless regarded the Foreign Secretary's speech as good grounds for reiterating his now regular call for a change at the Foreign Office.[137] The speech gave renewed life to the 'Simon Must Go' campaign which the left-wing press in particular was always ready to resuscitate.[138] To his credit Simon recognised that the speech had had an unfortunate effect and a fortnight later he made a point of intervening in the debate on the Address to deal with the matter afresh and apologise for his earlier performance.[139]

It was now clear that the European situation was deteriorating fast. The murders of Dollfuss in July and of King Alexander of Yugoslavia and Louis Barthou in October were like 'outbursts of flame in the seething crater of mid-Europe'. No one could doubt that Germany was rearming rapidly and that she would soon be strong enough openly to repudiate the restrictions placed upon her at Versailles, which she was already secretly disregarding. France, passing through a period of domestic instability, was prepared neither to try to stop Germany nor to concede to her the freedom which she would soon be able to take without asking.[140] Simon tried to warn Hitler that the effect of German rearmament was to make a peaceful and agreed solution of the international situation more and more difficult. Despite German assurances of peaceful intent, 'the psychological reaction on others is to inspire suspicion of an offensive purpose'.[141] Such warnings were, as Simon knew, essentially hollow. With a well-informed Churchill asking awkward questions in the House of Commons, the government decided to establish a small committee to evaluate German rearmament and advise on policy in connection with it. When the committee met on 22 November Simon pointed out that he could not indefinitely evade Churchill's parliamentary questions about the strength of Germany's airforce and the steps which Britain was taking to deal with it. Was the government prepared to state, he asked, that the Treaty of Versailles was not being complied with? If so, they would have to be ready to state what further steps they proposed.[142] In parliament on 28 November Baldwin made a public statement on the known extent of German rearmament, while Simon revealed in winding up that Britain had communicated her conclusions on this subject to Berlin, Paris, Rome and Washington.[143]

The Foreign Secretary was now ready to spell out the policy to which his instincts had been moving for at least a year. It was now common ground that Germany had disregarded the limitations of Part V of the Treaty of Versailles. Once the forthcoming Saar plebiscite was out of the way, she might well ask for legalisation or avow the breach. No one was going to stop her. Was there, therefore, not wisdom in getting her back to Geneva on the basis that her violations of Versailles were condoned? In the last sentence of the parliamentary debate he spoke of 'a new opportunity . . . to establish . . . a secure prospect of peace in the world'. But selling such a policy to France would be no easy task.[144]

Following the debate the cabinet committee on German rearmament met on several occasions in early December to consider further recommendations. It was Simon who set the pace and established the basis of discussion in the paper which he presented. What attitude, he bluntly asked, should Britain adopt towards German rearmament? 'If the alternative to legalising German rearmament was to prevent it, there would be everything to be said', Simon agreed, 'for not legalising it.' But preventing German rearmament by force had to be ruled out and the only alternative to legalisation was to allow Germany to continue on her present clandestine course. It could be argued that to abrogate the disarmament clauses of Versailles would only encourage Germans to advance territorial and colonial claims, but Simon doubted 'whether we should really be hastening the pace by recognising the inevitable'. In return for these concessions Germany should be obliged to return to the Disarmament Conference and to the League. This might at least prevent the polarisation of Europe between Franco-Soviet and German blocs. Britain's contribution should be a reaffirmation of her obligation to Belgium, a new statement of interest in Holland's independence and indirect support for an Eastern European pact. Britain should continue the nominal evenhandedness as between France and Germany that she had accepted at Locarno, while recognising that Nazi Germany posed problems which had scarcely existed when Locarno itself was signed. The Foreign Secretary's conclusion was that:

Germany would prefer, it appears, to be 'made an honest woman'; but if she is left too long to indulge in illegitimate practices and to find by experience that she does not suffer for it, this laudable ambition may wear off.[145]

Though some members of the government were more cautious than Simon in his readiness to scrap Part V of the Versailles Treaty, his perception of the German problem was embodied in the course of action now adopted.[146] Simon's colleagues authorised him to put his proposals to Flandin and Laval, the French premier and foreign minister. He was to make it clear that Britain could not tolerate a policy of continued drift and that Britain must insist on a full discussion with France as soon as possible.[147] In Paris on 23 December Simon emphasised the need for Anglo-French agreement before Germany made further proposals, anticipated once the Saar plebiscite was out of the way. Simon succeeded in getting a pledge that the French ministers would visit London in the second half of January after an already arranged visit to Rome for Franco-Italian discussions on Austria. In return they asked Simon to help persuade Mussolini to reach an understanding with France. Simon consented to do his best 'provided always that no new obligation on our part is in question'.[148]

Simon had laid down the outlines of a coherent and rational policy. A diary entry just before Christmas summed up what he hoped to achieve:

Our policy therefore must be to bring about agreement leading to Germany's return to Geneva while there is time: if nothing is done, in a few months it will be too late. This means that we must first persuade the French – and pay the necessary price for such persuasion – then bring in the Italians and anticipate Hitler's move after the Saar trouble is over by getting in first. The legalisation of German rearmament and the cancelling of the armament clauses of Part V of the Treaty of Versailles are a bitter pill for the French to swallow, especially as they don't believe in any German promise. But the alternative is not the stopping of German rearmament but its continuation at an ever increasing rate behind the screen. Germany is more dangerous out of the League than in it. This is the great task of 1935.[149]

If it had not been for the presence of an entirely irrational factor in the shape of the Nazi regime and its leader, this policy might have had some chance of success. But it was at least a policy in which Simon had the overwhelming support of his cabinet colleagues. In the circumstances it was somewhat surprising that the last month of 1934 saw further speculation about and discussion of Simon's place within the government. He was vulnerable less as a result of any new lapse than because past failings had not been forgotten and because he was readily identified as the weakest point in the government's increasingly vulnerable public image. From the autumn of 1934 the government's standing had slumped badly, partly because of the split in the Conservative ranks over Indian policy. 1935 was likely to be an election year and that election would probably involve the delicate task of selling to the British people a policy of increased rearmament.[150] Despite some progress on the economic front, the government still faced major problems which carried with them important electoral implications. As Simon put it:

the existence of 2 million unemployed is more eloquent than the reduction from 3 million; the plight of utterly depressed areas throws into shadow the enormous improvement elsewhere.[151]

In early December MacDonald summoned a meeting of the 'Big Six' – Baldwin, Chamberlain, Simon, Runciman, Thomas and himself. 'I do not see how we can really go on drifting,' he told Simon.[152]

   Simon's other difficulty was that he had no strong allies within the cabinet. Even Runciman, his fellow Liberal National, seemed ready to see him go.[153] David Margesson, the government's Chief Whip, had already warned the Prime Minister that Simon had become a liability and needed to be replaced, suggesting that Neville Chamberlain would be the best alternative. MacDonald ruled this out, concluding with the worrying statement that he might have to take the job on himself.[154] But Simon and MacDonald were the two principal manifestations of the continuing National character of the administration. The Prime Minister clearly felt that Simon's removal might have implications for his own position. Chamberlain recorded a meeting with MacDonald on 4 December:

It was not so much the Foreign Sec. as the Foreign policy which caused dis-satisfaction, the Govt. being credited with a desire for war. He thought some of us must get out into the country and make speeches, but he had no other suggestion to make and it was difficult to see why he had sent for me.[155]

Chamberlain himself was reluctant to force the issue – 'it would expose me to intolerable suspicions of intrigue' – though he seemed willing to consider Eden as a possible Foreign Secretary and toyed with the idea of a sort of inner cabinet of selected ministers to circumvent Simon's authority.[156] He envisaged Simon becoming a Minister without Portfolio to enable his 'gifts to be utilised in debate'.[157] Eden himself proposed that Baldwin should take over at the Foreign Office while he continued to operate from Geneva, a plan to which Baldwin was not necessarily averse.[158] But Chamberlain's commentary on the situation was very much to the point:

I can't see J.R.M. or S.B. making up their minds to sack Simon so I don't think I need worry my noddle about my future.[159]

To judge from his surviving private correspondence Simon seems to have been sublimely unaware of these discussions about his future. Instead he made speeches in the country, tried out the new opportunities offered by cinema film and took satisfaction in a series of modest successes in the international arena. These included the settlement of a quarrel between Yugoslavia and Hungary where 'I was able, behind the scenes, to make good use of the good relations established with Prince Paul at the time of the Duke of Kent's wedding.'[160] But chief among the successes for which Simon claimed credit was the arrangement of a plebiscite in January 1935 to determine the future of the Saar, an event which had been foreshadowed in the Treaty of Versailles. Yet it is interesting to compare Simon's account of his role in this episode with those of some of his governmental colleagues. According to the Foreign Secretary the idea of putting an international force into the Saar before the plebiscite originated in a paper he wrote for the cabinet on 16 November. He developed it in a private letter to Eden a few days later and presented a complete plan to the cabinet on 27 November. 'What was really remarkable was the way in which the whole Cabinet became converted to the idea.'[161]

Yet according to Eden it was he who advocated that Britain should sponsor an international police force to maintain order throughout the period of the plebiscite. He further claimed that Simon, Hailsham and Chamberlain were unenthusiastic about the scheme, and that Baldwin's intervention was necessary before it was accepted.[162] Eden, of course, was not a member of the cabinet and a more accurate version of events was provided by Neville Chamberlain. At the cabinet Simon characteristically placed four choices before his colleagues without expressing a preference. Chamberlain noted that Simon had 'very timidly and halfheartedly' brought forward a proposal for an Anglo-Italian force, but had been happy to withdraw it once it was suggested that it was inappropriate for Britain to take such an initiative. The proposal would never have got through 'if I [Chamberlain] had not urged it so strongly'. The Chancellor recorded with satisfaction the telephone call he received from J. H. Thomas:

Just to give you my congratulations and to tell you I 'ear someone is all on 'is 'eels this mornin, as though 'e'd done it all.[163]

As so often during his career, and particularly during his Foreign Secretaryship, it was Simon's failure to stand by his own policy – good or bad – with the conviction of a true believer which was most held against him.

The issue of Anglo-Japanese relations which had preoccupied Simon during the first stages of his Foreign Secretaryship reemerged into prominence in the course of 1934. Some sort of pact with Japan would be an obvious answer to British military and naval weakness in the East, particularly in the context of a worsening European situation. By the spring the Chancellor of the Exchequer, Neville Chamberlain, had emerged as the champion of such an idea. Simon was inclined to agree that a non-aggression pact with the Japanese would be to Britain's advantage. If the Japanese were to expand, such expansion would be preferable 'on the Continent of Asia rather than southward' where the British Empire lay glaringly vulnerable.[164]

But, as the Foreign Secretary recognised, there were great difficulties in the way of improving Anglo-Japanese relations, not least the fact that it 'was always difficult to know what was going on inside the anthill'.[165] 'Japan's ultimate purpose lies inscrutably hid behind their Oriental mask.'[166] Simon and Sir Bolton Eyres-Monsell, the First Lord of the Admiralty, were asked to prepare recommendations for improving Anglo-Japanese relations, but very quickly Simon changed his mind and dismissed the idea of a pact as a 'flash in the pan' which would shock opinion at home and abroad, and be represented as condoning Japanese action in Manchuria while leaving the rest of China at her mercy.[167] The Foreign Secretary was no doubt influenced by the studies of the Far Eastern Department of the Foreign Office which had concluded that any sort of renewed Anglo-Japanese alliance would be fatal to British interests.[168] But Simon's response was not sufficiently resolute to kill off the idea altogether.

Towards the end of June Simon and MacDonald, looking forward to the naval conference due to meet in 1935, had an inconclusive meeting with Norman Davis, the chief American negotiator. This convinced Simon that the best way ahead was for preliminary talks with the Japanese to try to fix the Japanese navy at a reasonable level and then to confront the Americans with the result. The latter were concerned that Britain's naval strength should not encourage Japan to build a navy large enough to threaten America, and it was possible that they would accept the British level if this meant containing the Japanese within bounds. It was a delicate task and showed 'what a delightful job we have inherited in this naval conundrum'.[169] Preliminary talks were initiated with the Japanese to assess the chances of revising or extending the Washington and London naval agreements when the naval conference met in 1935. It became clear, however, that Japan intended to give notice before the end of 1934 to terminate the Washington Treaty.[170]

Chamberlain remained convinced of the desirability of an Anglo-Japanese pact and sought the Foreign Secretary's support in terms designed to appeal to Simon's vanity. He was sure that 'this is one of those crucial points in history which test the statesman's capacity and foresight.' He sent his proposals to Simon in advance of submitting them to the cabinet because he attached 'particular weight to your cool and analytical judgment'. An agreement with Japan would stamp Simon's tenure of office with 'the special distinction that is attached to memorable historical events', while the Foreign Secretary would be remembered as 'the author of the "Simon-Hirota Pact"'. If the opportunity of investigating the possibilities of a pact was ignored:

What might not be said of us by future historians if we drifted unto unfriendly relations with Japan, lost our Far Eastern trade to them, had to look on helplessly while she marched from one aggression to another.[171]

Chamberlain's plan involved British recognition of Manchukuo in return for a Japanese guarantee not to threaten British interests. It amounted to a clear invitation to the Foreign Secretary to place Anglo-Japanese relations before Anglo-American relations and League opinion.

Simon's initial response was predictably cautious. The main political effect, he argued, would be to give Japan a free hand in the Far East so long as she respected British possessions, and it would therefore be interpreted as encouraging Japanese designs on China.[172] Simon and Chamberlain lunched together on 17 September and the Foreign Secretary, though still unwilling to commit himself, at least agreed that the admission of the Soviet Union to the League had introduced a new factor which 'made it advisable perhaps to offer the Japanese some gesture by way of counterpoise'. The two men dined together on 24 September when they were joined by Vansittart and Samuel Hoare. By this time Simon appeared much more sympathetic to Chamberlain's proposals. The upshot was that at the cabinet on the following day it was agreed that the British ambassador in Tokyo would sound out the Japanese government, while Simon and Chamberlain prepared a joint memorandum for their colleagues.[173] Simon produced his draft by early October, but it struck the Chancellor as 'one of the most miserable documents I have ever seen'. A meeting between the two of them gave Chamberlain the opportunity to tear Simon's 'paper to ribbons'. 'I should think he never had such a *quart d'heure* over any document drafted by himself.' Simon responded positively and without rancour. His second draft, embodying Chamberlain's suggestions, reached the Chancellor on 13 October.[174]

The paper which Simon and Chamberlain presented to the cabinet stressed the Imperial advantages of a Japanese pact, while enunciating what was always the strongest argument in favour of the whole policy of appeasement – the need to reduce the number of Britain's potential enemies:

if we had to enter upon . . . a struggle with a hostile, instead of a friendly, Japan in the East; if we had to contemplate the division of our forces so as to protect our Far Eastern interests while prosecuting a war in Europe; then not only would India, Hong Kong and Australasia be in dire peril, but we ourselves would stand in far greater danger of destruction by a fully armed and organised Germany.[175]

The two men hoped to secure a Japanese guarantee of Chinese territorial integrity in return for a carefully phrased statement recognising Manchukuo. In the event the project foundered because Japan was unwilling to respond, while the naval discussions ended in stalemate on 19 December.[176] Chamberlain watched helplessly as his scheme collapsed:

I wish I were in at the conversations but of course I have no status there and can only pull the strings and hope the puppets will make the gestures I want. There is no doubt that our Foreign Secretary is the weak point of the Government.[177]

As in so many other matters Simon had shown no real consistency or resolve in his attitude to the Japanese pact, always ready to listen to conflicting points of view but seldom willing to move from the indecisiveness which had become his hallmark. During conversations with Commonwealth Prime Ministers in 1935 Simon ruled out the possibility of using the recognition of Manchukuo to lessen Japanese antagonism. 'In so far as the matter was one for the League of Nations, this country would have to act as a good member of the League.'[178]

★ ★ ★

The coming year is likely to be a vital year in the sense that if European improvement is not secured and some element of German reconciliation effected, the world may enter into a most dangerous future.[179]

So wrote Simon to the King in January 1935. As Simon realised, Germany would be no easier to deal with once the outcome of the Saar plebiscite was known, as this was likely to result in an overwhelming German victory.[180] Nonetheless the first weeks of the new year gave the Foreign Secretary some cause for satisfaction. He watched as progress was made in the Franco-Italian negotiations, leading to a convention to guarantee Austrian integrity, and then sought to prepare the British position for the forthcoming French visit to London. The threat of a German aerial attack still haunted him. 'This new development', he told a radio audience, 'undoubtedly fills many people with a new foreboding of a danger which might conceivably threaten town and country alike.'[181] Simon had the opportunity for a preliminary talk with Laval in Geneva in the second week of January. He took pleasure in Laval's report of Mussolini's view that there were only three ways of dealing with the German problem – doing nothing, which was idiotic, going to war to stop German rearmament, which was impossible, and negotiating an agreement and Germany's return to Geneva. Simon restrained himself from pointing out that this was the conclusion he had reached at least a year earlier.[182] To the King he reiterated that the practical choice lay between a Germany which continued to rearm without any regulation and a Germany which, in return for recognition of its rights and some modification of the Peace Treaty, entered into the comity of nations and contributed to European stability.[183] Simon urged his cabinet colleagues to make up their minds on the issues which would arise in the Anglo-French talks. There was little hope of a positive outcome, he predicted, unless Britain was ready to offer some contributions to security. He suggested as possible British initiatives support for the proposed multilateral non-interference pact negotiated in Rome, support for an Eastern pact, a redefinition of British obligations under Locarno, a reaffirmation of Britain's commitment to the demilitarisation of the

Rhineland and a willingness to enter staff talks with France and Belgium.[184]

The cabinet, however, was very wary of anything that smacked of an increased commitment to continental Europe. MacDonald warned of the dangers of walking into a trap, while Chamberlain objected to any plan to put teeth into Locarno. The suggestion of staff talks was firmly rejected by men who still viewed those talks which had taken place between Britain and France before 1914 as significantly contributing to the outbreak of war. The cabinet even insisted that the demilitarisation of the Rhineland was not a vital British interest. It was protected under the Locarno treaties and 'in certain circumstances' Britain might fight for it.[185] In the end Britain's negotiators were authorised to state that Britain was bound by Locarno and had no intention of repudiating it.[186] Though ready to consider generous concessions to bring the Germans back to Geneva,[187] Simon was seeking to strike a balance between concessions and increased security. His version of 'appeasement' was not totally one-sided. Though it was most unlikely that Germany would agree to return to Geneva, and while Simon was wrong in his assumption that Germany wanted to be made 'an honest woman', the Foreign Secretary's proposals to increase Britain's 'continental commitment' made good sense in the context of continuing French nervousness. Simon had tried to involve Britain in a limited collective security agreement designed to deter further German aggression. But what is striking is that he put up very little fight on behalf of his own proposals in the face of the opposition of his cabinet colleagues.

When the Anglo-French conference opened on 1 February Simon acted as Britain's principal spokesman despite the presence of both MacDonald and Baldwin. He posed the same three courses of action over German rearmament of which Mussolini had spoken and arrived at the predictable conclusion that the only way forward was a general agreement by negotiation. He wanted to see simultaneous progress on the four outstanding issues of armaments, security, Part V of the Treaty of Versailles and Germany's return to the League.[188] In the afternoon the French produced a plan for a special air pact between the Locarno powers as the price they would demand for accepting cancellation of Part V. This involved a guarantee to come to the immediate help of another signatory in the event of an attack by a third party. Flandin and Simon had discussed this proposal at dinner on 31 January, with the result that the Foreign Secretary was fully prepared for the French initiative.[189] In view of the way in which his efforts to satisfy French security requirements had been thwarted by the cabinet a fortnight earlier, Simon now seemed keen to present his colleagues with a *fait accompli*. According to Hankey, Simon had already signed a memorandum on the subject (dated 29 January) before the Anglo-French conversations began, but had avoided mentioning it when dining with the Cabinet Secretary on 30 January.[190] Now Simon seemed determined to force the issue, convinced that the French plan offered a chance of approaching Germany with some hope of success. As Hankey recorded:

Simon hastily assembled a meeting in the Foreign Office at which Londonderry, the CIGS, CAS, Vansittart, several FO officials and I were present. There were many criticisms of the proposal and I in particular *urged with all the force at my command that we must be given time to consider it before being committed.*[191]

A special cabinet meeting was called for Saturday, 2 February at which Simon had the satisfaction of 'carrying all my colleagues with me in approving the scheme in principle'.[192] In a persuasive paper Simon argued that there was a grave danger that, if Britain did not respond positively to the French proposal, the conference might 'end in a meaningless communiqué'. He suggested that Britain would be the real beneficiary of the new pact. 'While the French commitment to us is plain and new, our obligations under the agreement really are in their nature the same obligations that have already been accepted under Locarno.' Without a favourable reply to the French suggestion, Britain would not get French support for the formula which the two countries were discussing as the basis for a further approach to Germany. He ended in terms which emphasised the wide-ranging importance of the issues at stake:

If we can get no terms with Germany, then we have to face rearmament on our own part on an increasing scale with financial burdens corresponding and with political results which need not be described.[193]

By the end of the day, after further sessions of the Anglo-French conference, a communiqué was ready to present to the governments of Germany, Italy and Belgium, which embodied both Simon's proposals to remove the restrictions of Part V of the Versailles Treaty in exchange for Germany's return to the League and the French plan for an air pact.[194] Hankey voiced his alarm:

Thus in 24 hours or 25 hours, without any proper examination of the proposal; without waiting for the report of the Chiefs of Staff Committee; without giving me an opportunity to be heard, the Cabinet and their representatives at the Conference had virtually pledged us to the most serious military commitment that we have entered into for centuries, if at all.[195]

Vansittart, on the other hand, was warm in his praise for Simon. Using a cricketing metaphor, he saw himself as the groundsman who had prepared a good wicket. But it was the Foreign Secretary who 'led the side':

I think the Government score will be about 400, and you have made an individual century – which, I think, has been coming to you for some time, and will be duly applauded. The match, of course, isn't over yet, but it has already been a great game from our point of view.[196]

It was central to Simon's plans that the proposal for an Anglo-Franco-German agreement should not be turned into an Anglo-French agreement against Germany.[197] The final communiqué of the conference was carefully worded to avoid any impression that Germany was to be presented with a dictated solution. After ten days the German government issued its reply, welcoming the proposed air convention without reserve – doubtless, as Simon recognised, because this would involve the recognition of Germany's air force and would 'thus be a pretty big nail in the coffin of Part V of the Treaty of Versailles'. On other matters, however, it was much more vague. But Simon was particularly interested by the passage which pressed for an Anglo-German meeting. The Foreign Secretary's reaction was that a visit to Berlin should be arranged without delay, 'but we must secure French concurrence'.[198] His enthusiasm increased when the German government assured him that all matters referred to in the Anglo-French communiqué would be open for discussion.[199] In fact Simon had been toying with the idea of visiting Hitler for some months and had recently sounded out J. L. Garvin of the *Observer* on the subject. The latter replied favourably, providing that a successful agreement was guaranteed. 'For you to go under any risk of failure is, I think, not to be thought of.'[200] From Lord Lothian, who had recently visited Germany, Simon heard that Germany would be ready to pay the price for an assured peace. A frank talk between Simon and Hitler might, it was suggested, open up a lasting political settlement.[201] Simon regarded Lothian highly, paying more attention to him, according to Vansittart, than he did to his own Foreign Office advisers.[202]

After considerable discussion the cabinet agreed that the visit to Hitler should be made. Who precisely should go was a matter of some debate, particularly when, as soon as the German visit was made public, the Soviet Union announced that it too would welcome a British visitor. There was considerable concern inside the Foreign Office about Simon's ability to bring the negotiations to a successful conclusion. Ralph Wigram, for example, feared that Hitler intended to drive a wedge between Britain and France.[203] Though Simon began by thinking that he and Eden should go together to both Berlin and Moscow, he soon came to have doubts.[204] While there was a good argument that Germany and the Soviet Union should be treated on the same footing,[205] the Russians had made it clear that, if Simon were too busy, they would be prepared to receive Eden or even Vansittart, while, as Lothian warned, to give the impression that Simon was visiting Berlin as a half-way house to Moscow would be open to misinterpretation by Hitler.[206]

With decisions about the Moscow trip still in the air, Simon attempted to prepare for his visit to Berlin by meeting Laval on 28 February. He stressed that his mission to Germany would be purely exploratory and that the demilitarisation of the Rhineland was not negotiable.[207] When, however, the British government published its Defence White Paper on 4 March, Hitler took immediate offence, claimed to have caught a cold when speaking in the open air at the Saar celebrations and postponed the visit. The White

Paper had drawn attention to existing German rearmament and criticised the spirit being inculcated in German youth, which could only spread a general feeling of anxiety. Yet it did not need much imagination to see, as the British ambassador in Berlin suggested, that the Führer's illness was a diplomatic one.[208] 'Damn Germany's impudence', wrote Austen Chamberlain:

I trust that Simon will stiffen his back. I warned him that if he took the first slap in the face quietly, he would invite another. He poohpoohed the warning. Now he knows.[209]

The cabinet, on the other hand, decided that the visit should still go ahead at a later date, although it would be pointed out that the postponement was inconvenient in view of Simon's 'other arrangements' – presumably a reference to the visit to Moscow.[210] Even so, at Neville Chamberlain's suggestion, it was now firmly decided that the Moscow visit should be undertaken by Eden alone, a decision which Chamberlain suspected Simon resented out of jealousy for the younger man.[211] The Chancellor also heard that Simon was hesitating at the idea of speaking for the government when the Commons debated the White Paper on 11 March, claiming that he personally had never agreed to its proposals and that it was unfair to be asked to incur the odium of supporting it. Chamberlain, clear in his own mind that Simon had raised no objection to the defence plans, felt that this episode cast 'an unpleasant light on Simon's character'.[212] The story had reached Chamberlain by way of the Prime Minister's doctor and it is possible that an unnecessary construction had been put on Simon's views. The latter's own diary entry reveals no significant differences between himself and the government over the White Paper. Here he admitted that he had helped prepare the original draft and that the government's case, as pre-sented in the Commons by Baldwin and himself, was 'overwhelming'. He had never heard 'a more one-sided discussion'.[213]

If Simon's position were not difficult enough, on 15 March Germany unilaterally repudiated Part V of the Treaty of Versailles and introduced conscription. On the following day the existence of the German airforce was officially admitted. The whole basis for the proposed Anglo-German talks now collapsed, as Hitler had simply taken that for which Britain and France were hoping to bargain. By these acts Hitler advertised the futility of all attempts to negotiate with him according to the normal canons of diplomatic conduct. His behaviour revealed the intellectual bankruptcy of the policy of appeasement when it was applied to an international gangster who refused to recognise that any rules and regulations should govern his actions. Such judgments are easier to make with hindsight than they were in 1935. Even so, it was one of Simon's weaknesses as Foreign Secretary that he found it difficult to react flexibly to changing situations, persisting with a redundant policy rather than exploring new options. The British note protesting at

Germany's abrogation of Part V still spoke of the desire for 'a general settlement freely negotiated between Germany and the other Powers' and armaments agreements which would 'replace the provisions of Part V of the Treaty of Versailles'.[214]

Simon's own explanation was, on the surface, reasonable enough:

We should not retort by saying that now we will not go to Berlin. After all, what ultimate end would that serve? It will not alter the German decision and it will break down whatever contact is left and destroy finally any prospect of agreeing about anything. It would be quite a different matter if excommunicating Germany would lead to a combination to stop her. On the contrary, it would have quite the opposite effect.[215]

The dangerous illusion that agreement with Nazi Germany was a realistic possibility remained the fundamental flaw in British policy at least until the spring of 1939. Even so, Simon was less starry-eyed about the prospects of success than his own behaviour might suggest. A letter he wrote to the King at this time shows a more realistic attitude. He did not believe that the German government wanted an agreement except on terms that would be intolerable for others. Neither should it be assumed that the repudiation of Part V represented the end of Germany's demands. Naval rearmament, the Rhineland, Memel, Danzig and the former German colonies could all be expected to be within the ultimate German programme. 'But Sir John feels that there is no advantage in refusing to go to Berlin, small though the prospects are of any positive result.'[216]

The French and Italian governments both expected Britain to take the lead in denouncing Germany's violations of Versailles by calling off the Foreign Secretary's visit. But so determined was Simon to go ahead that a British note condemning the German rearmament announcement, but also enquiring whether the visit would still be welcomed, was delivered to the German government without prior consultation with France and Italy. Only as a result of Vansittart's intervention did Simon see the French and Italian ambassadors just minutes before announcing to the Commons on 18 March that the note would be delivered later that day.[217] Simon's reasoning was that to delay would only serve to reveal differences between Britain, France and Italy – 'to the unconcealed delight of Germany' – as well as disappointing domestic opinion in Britain.[218] But the opposite point of view, that Simon's actions threatened to divide Britain, France and Italy in the face of German provocation, is perhaps more valid.[219] The French and Italian governments reacted with predictable anger and at one point Simon, badly rattled, proposed going to Paris to smooth ruffled French and Italian feathers. Chamberlain dissuaded him from doing so on the grounds that this would give Germany the impression that the powers were ganging up on her and thus destroy any last hopes of success. This task too would be left to Eden.[220]

When the cabinet met on 20 March Simon presented proposals for the forthcoming talks. They were ideas which seem to have originated with Chamberlain, but which Simon now adopted as his own. Hitler should not be allowed to dominate the course of the discussions, but should be told quite firmly that the way ahead was either through a system of regional pacts, on the model of Locarno, by her participation in which Germany could contribute to European security, or alternatively, and dangerously, through the division of Europe into power blocs and rival alliance systems.[221] Yet Simon had scarcely enhanced his standing among his governmental and Foreign Office colleagues by his conduct over the previous days. Rumours about his future again circulated around Westminster, with Runciman his latest projected successor as Foreign Secretary.[222] Austen Chamberlain recorded that Simon had given him three different reasons in the space of two days for his decision not to consult France and Italy before deciding to go ahead with the Berlin visit, 'and at least one of them was untrue, for it contradicted the others.[223] Neville Chamberlain's diary and letters of this period portray in Simon a figure who seemed virtually incapable of independent thought. Chamberlain expressed himself relieved that, in his view, the right things were being done, albeit in spite of, rather than because of, the Foreign Secretary. Others took comfort from the fact that Eden would be accompanying Simon to Germany, while Vansittart wrote to Phipps in Berlin to urge him to be on his guard:

I hope therefore I may count on you, Eric, to put all your weight into the maintenance of the only line which can be of any avail . . . and that this line will be maintained unflinchingly by you *all*.[224]

Simon thus went off to see Hitler 'with his ace card already trumped'.[225] He and Eden were met by von Neurath and a guard of SS troops. The latter's commander delivered a message to the Foreign Secretary from the Führer, while Simon 'looked unhappily down his nose'.[226] After friendly smiles and handshakes the talks began on 25 March. In opening Simon stressed that Britain's object was to secure peace through the cooperation of all European countries. Hitler replied that cooperation could only result from equality, but insisted that Germany had no ambitions which might threaten another state. National Socialism was not an expansionist movement and the annexation of territory would merely add to his political and economic difficulties. When, however, the discussion reached the detailed agenda, it soon became clear that an evasive Hitler was not interested in an Eastern European Security Pact and would give no guarantees regarding Austrian independence or Germany's return to the League. He seemed to stake out a claim for the return of Germany's former colonies and, when the discussion reached the question of arms limitation, almost inconsequentially made the startling assertion that Germany's air strength had already reached parity with that of Great Britain. 'There was no triumph in his tone', recalled

Eden, 'but there was grim foreboding in my heart.'[227]

Only when the question of naval armaments was brought up did Hitler become more responsive. For some time Simon had believed that it would be worthwhile to sound out Berlin about Germany's requirements for future naval building.[228] He now made it clear that what he had in mind was a general naval conference in the near future, but before then it might be useful if informal exchanges of views could take place between British and German representatives.[229] While assuring Simon that Germany did not want to pursue an unlimited race in naval armaments on the pattern of the period before 1914, Hitler nonetheless demanded a German navy 35 per cent of the size of the British navy. Though Simon insisted that the German claim would appear to be so large as to make a general agreement to limit naval strengths almost impossible, since it would only stimulate a building programme in France and Italy, he did agree to further talks in London where naval discussions on a more detailed level could be held.[230]

Simon's more extravagant hopes had not been fulfilled by his visit to Berlin, and in truth he had not really expected that they would be. The general result of the conversations, he admitted, was 'undoubtedly disappointing'.[231] Opinion was divided as to what the Foreign Secretary had achieved. Rejoicing in the end of 'the Versailles habit of mind', *The Times* suggested that public opinion was probably more solidly behind Simon than ever before.[232] By contrast MacDonald was pessimistic, asking Vansittart to prevent the circulation abroad of the notes of the Anglo-German conversations.[233] Neville Chamberlain shared Simon's disappointment. The Foreign Secretary had brought back little 'except a series of negatives' and had failed to determine whether Germany's protestations of peaceful intent were genuine or only a means of gaining time for further rearmament. Chamberlain thought that Simon might have explored the possibility of an arrangement whereby Russia and Germany would respectively guarantee the eastern and western frontiers of the countries lying between them, the Baltic States, Poland and Czechoslovakia. The Chancellor was also aware of anxiety inside the Foreign Office, particularly on the part of Vansittart, lest Simon should now do anything which might break up the common front with France and Italy. Britain's representation at the forthcoming conference at Stresa with Laval and Mussolini would clearly be critical.[234]

From Simon's point of view it was a moment to reflect upon the European situation. But his thinking revealed no clear sense of direction about the way ahead. It would not be fair to suggest that he had been taken in by Hitler.[235] 'It is as well', wrote Horace Rumbold, Britain's former ambassador in Berlin, 'that Simon – a congenital pacifist – should have seen the Führer with his own eyes and have been brought to a sense of realities.'[236] Though Simon found nothing striking in Hitler's physical appearance, as he looked at the Führer's hands he 'kept thinking of his part in the Munich assassinations', Simon recognised that Hitler's outlook and policy were not likely to be changed by argument. The Führer's first goal was to secure the moral rehabilitation of the German people after the humiliation of Versailles. The comparison which Simon drew between Hitler and a 'Joan of Arc . . . born in Austria and [wearing] a moustache' was unfortunate and is easily quoted to the Foreign Secretary's disadvantage.[237] But Simon never intended the comparison to be taken beyond the sense of nationalistic, messianic fervour which they shared. He recognised that Hitler's ambitions were 'very dangerous to peace in Europe'. The natural consequences of German policy might be 'terrible beyond conception'. Germany was determined to follow its own course in rearmament and to include all Germans within its borders, including Austria. The former German colonies would have to be returned prior to any German reappearance at Geneva. 'All this is pretty hopeless', concluded the Foreign Secretary. Europe would be certain to combine to resist Germany, and British Tories might even be seen cooperating with Russian communists, while 'the League of Nations Union thunders applause'. This might not 'prevent an ultimate explosion, but it will delay it.'[238]

In terms of his own future policy Simon was torn between a recognition of the need to maintain solidarity with France and Italy, as was pressed upon him by Vansittart, and his perception – shared by Hankey – that there remained scope for bilateral Anglo-German talks. The result was to leave British policy after the Berlin talks increasingly confused and unclear. When the cabinet discussed the Foreign Secretary's report on 27 March, Simon firmly supported further approaches to Germany about an air pact and a possible naval agreement, even though this aspect of the talks had not been reported to France and Italy.[239] In fact he deprecated abandoning all hope of a general agreement and a mere closing of ranks against Germany until this was absolutely necessary. The common line was important but would not necessarily achieve the desired result by itself:

Volcanos are singularly unresponsive to threats and this particular volcano is only the more likely to erupt if provided with a constant succession of demonstrations that threats are not followed by anything more than threats.[240]

Yet the Foreign Secretary could also assert that collective security was the 'real answer'.[241] The dilemma was real and Simon seemed incapable of resolving it. 'He is clearly confused as to what to do next,' noted Eden, 'which is not surprising.'[242] The one comforting impression Simon had got from his talks was that Hitler wanted good relations with Britain and that his ultimate enemy was Soviet communism, all of which was probably true. 'Nothing that he said from first to last suggested that German policy was addressed to the west.'[243]

One aspect of the Anglo-German talks which could not be ignored was Hitler's boast that he had achieved parity in the air. Though the accuracy of this claim was disputed inside the British government, Simon, relying on information provided by Vansittart, wrote to MacDonald to warn that Germany probably had about 3000 machines of all types. Even more worrying was the German capacity to expand at a rate of at least 200 aircraft per month 'and very probably more'. The danger was that once left behind by Germany in the air, Britain might never be able to attain a level of parity with her again. Simon wanted the whole matter submitted to the CID for an immediate report with definite conclusions:

The conclusion which might have to be drawn from the above figures, if they are correct, is that this country is seriously open to the threat of sudden attack by a continental power in a degree to which it has not been exposed for hundreds of years.[244]

The forthcoming meeting at Stresa began to take on the appearance of a critical encounter. But it was unlikely to result in a whole-hearted affirmation of collective security if Simon sought to maintain his other hand of further investigating possible Anglo-German agreements. When the cabinet concluded, in the course of a five-hour meeting, that the object of British policy should be to gain the confidence of France and Italy without isolating Germany, the difficulty was encapsulated.[245] Simon happily took up Chamberlain's idea, to be raised at Stresa, of a German-Russian pact to guarantee between them the frontiers of the Baltic States, Poland and Czechslovakia, since this would at least avoid an immediate break with Germany while, if successful, contributing to collective security. There was widespread concern that Simon should not be left in charge of the Stresa negotiations. But the difficulty was to know who should accompany him. Baldwin seemed unenthusiastic, while Neville Chamberlain was too busy at the Treasury. With Eden's heart strained during his return plane journey from Eastern Europe, it was finally decided that MacDonald – though 'tired out and incapable of decision or clear thought' – should accompany the Foreign Secretary.[246]

The conference itself was a modest success. It 'turned out well', noted General Pownall, 'in that no decisions were really arrived at'.[247] Simon recorded that the main result was to give a strong impression of 'solidarity'. Collective security had become a 'counsel of necessity'. Austrian independence was confirmed and Simon proposed to Mussolini an Anglo-Italian declaration reaffirming the Locarno treaties, which the Italian leader quickly accepted. 'Let us hope', mused the Foreign Secretary, 'that this will show Hitler that, while he repudiates Versailles, he touches Locarno at his peril.'[248] The desire to restrict British commitments was very evident when Simon and MacDonald questioned Laval over his impending Franco-Soviet pact of mutual assistance. Did it, they asked, contain anything that might, by involving France in war with Germany, drag Britain into the quarrel through her Locarno commitments. Assurances were given by the French delegates.

In the realm of Anglo-Italian relations a new problem had arisen which

Simon had little desire to bring into the open. Mussolini had never disguised his ambition to see Italy become a world power and after 1931 internal political problems increasingly drove him towards an overtly expansionist foreign policy. For reasons which went back at least as far as the defeat of the Italian army at Adowa in 1896 the ancient African Kingdom of Abyssinia seemed the predestined victim of Mussolini's aggression. After the Wal-Wal frontier incident in December 1934 a crisis became increasingly apparent. In other circumstances and at other times a British government might have turned a blind eye to Italian imperalism. The Abyssinian empire was a primitive and oppressive regime. Its record on the question of slavery was hardly likely to endear it to the humanitarian sentiments of the Foreign Secretary or indeed to those of Lady Simon, who had long campaigned against the survival of slavery.[249] But it was a member of the League and the theory of that institution did not allow for differential judgments about the rights of its member states, even though Simon might claim that such countries should 'not have been admitted so easily'.[250] The essence of Simon's policy was summed up in a letter to the King. The Italian-Abyssinian dispute would have to be handled in such a way as would not adversely affect Anglo-Italian relations.[251] Italy had come to assume too central a role in Britain's policy towards the vital issue of German expansion for the rights of a primitive African state to be allowed to intrude very far. The public pronouncement of such a policy was, however, fraught with danger in the still League-orientated atmosphere of 1935. For many Abyssinia would become another test, as Manchuria had eventually emerged, of British commitment to peace, the rule of law and the principles of the Covenant. Opinion in Whitehall, moreover, was by no means clear that Mussolini's activities in Africa represented no threat to the British position, particularly in the medium term. So, while fully recognising the nature of Italian designs and having to watch as Mussolini brushed aside his proposals for settling the Wal-Wal dispute, Simon had in January gently reminded Grandi, the Italian ambassador in London, of Abyssinia's rights as a member of the League.[252]

Before leaving for Stresa Simon had assured Eden that he was taking an Abyssinian expert with him from the Foreign Office and Eden understood that Mussolini would be warned about the consequences of a military attack in Africa.[253] Although officials did discuss the growing Italian-Abyssinian crisis, the ministerial meetings at Stresa focused on the German question and neither Simon nor MacDonald raised the non-European issue with Mussolini, except for a remark to the effect that British Somali tribesmen enjoyed certain established grazing rights on the Abyssinian side of the border. Simon, anxious not to cloud the discussion of European affairs, probably hoped to wait at least until the matter had been formally raised at the League by the Abyssinian Emperor. But in later years this omission came to assume great significance. 'Looking back at the wretched story', wrote Thomas Jones the following year:

you have the original blunder at Stresa when MacDonald and Simon funked talking straight to Mussolini because they wanted his support in Europe.[254]

The omission was, according to others, a 'hideous error', 'a disaster', 'both incomprehensible and inexcusable'.[255] Vansittart even succeeded in embellishing the Foreign Secretary's folly by inventing a story in which Mussolini had proposed adding the words 'in Europe' after 'maintenance of peace' in the final Stresa declaration, a suggestion which Simon and MacDonald meekly accepted. In fact the British record shows clearly that the words 'in Europe' were present in the original British drafts, as was only appropriate in a conference called to deal with European security.[256]

In fact, if for no other than domestic political reasons, Simon recognised that an Italian invasion of Abyssinia could not be allowed to go unchallenged. At Geneva on 15 April Simon not only succeeded in getting the Stresa resolutions accepted by the League as a whole. He also called for early progress in the Wal-Wal negotiations. Though his efforts to secure the appointment of an Arbitration Commission failed to attact Italian and Abyssinian assent, Italy could have been under no illusion that she could assume tacit British consent to her Abyssinian ambitions. Mussolini let it be known that the Foreign Secretary's intervention was decidedly 'mal vu'.[257] Returning to London, Simon enlisted the services of Austen Chamberlain, whose good relations with Mussolini dated back to the era of Locarno, to impress upon Grandi the serious view which the British government took of Italian policy in East Africa.[258] On 3 May the first formal exchange on the issue took place between the British and Italian governments. Grandi conveyed in veiled but unmistakable terms that Mussolini was now contemplating military action. Simon warned Grandi of the serious consequences for Anglo-Italian relations if Mussolini pursued his expansionist policy. He was particularly concerned about the difficult situation which would arise in parliament if awkward questions were posed to the government. Eden, whose commitment to the League was always stronger than Simon's and whose disinclination to court Mussolini was beginning to distance him from the government more noticeably than before, was unhappy about Simon's oblique warning. Grandi was only likely to draw the conclusion that 'we were troubled and uncertain in our course'.[259] But Simon was seeking to strike a delicate balance between honouring Britain's obligation to the League, which was still important in political terms, and maintaining the common front against Germany established at Stresa. To his credit he always had a clearer perception than Eden of the respective dangers posed by the two men styled by Vansittart as 'dictator major' and 'dictator minor'. The Duce's current behaviour was very annoying as far as Simon was concerned. 'Mussolini has gone mad!' he later concluded.[260]

At the cabinet on 8 May Simon made a verbal report on the serious situation which had arisen between Italy and Abyssinia. A full written report was called for, which the Foreign Secretary submitted to the cabinet a week later. As on so many other occasions during his Foreign Secretaryship Simon was much more adept at describing the implications of the situation than at pointing to a clear line of action for Britain to follow. 'It is as if a doctor, faced with the early stages of a most serious illness, is clear and unhesitating in diagnosis and prognosis, but silent as to treatment.'[261] Simon stressed the significance of the crisis for public opinion and the government's electoral fortunes. Italy was likely to undertake a military campaign against Abyssinia as soon as the climate permitted. But the strict application of League action against Italy ran the danger of compromising Anglo-Italian relations, breaking the Stresa Front and driving Italy from the League. It would, he argued, 'be hard to imagine a state of affairs which would be more welcome to Germany'.[262]

The limit of Simon's advice was that Britain should continue to urge both parties to reach an amicable settlement, while warning Italy privately of the dangers of its present policy. The cabinet, however, tended to back a more pro-League stance and Eden was given considerable discretion at Geneva to ensure that the League took an active interest in the Abyssinian situation. Eden managed to secure Italian agreement to hold a special meeting of the League Council in August if the dispute had not by then been settled. The thrust of British policy seemed to be moving away from Stresa:

We have warned Italy in plain terms that if it comes to a choice between Italy and the League we shall support the League.

The agreement at Geneva did not necessarily ensure a peaceful outcome to the dispute but, thought Simon, 'it gives peace a chance and saves the League from being flouted.'[263] Simon probably hoped that Italy could be bought off by economic concessions from Abyssinia, concessions which the British would advise the African state to make.[264] But there were few further developments in this area before Simon left the Foreign Office.

Eden's obvious success at Geneva soon had the Conservative press tipping him to be Simon's successor. It seemed to be in marked contrast to Simon's inability to bring any issue to a conclusion. After Stresa Garvin had been particularly scathing in the *Observer*:

Our Foreign Secretary once more created a curious impression – that of a man who marks time with an agility meant to look like walking. Every real problem is postponed.[265]

The Foreign Secretary was 'more unpopular than ever' in the Commons, noted Neville Chamberlain.[266] Simon even had to keep a wary eye on his old adversary Lloyd George. The latter had begun a personal crusade for a Roosevelt-style 'New Deal' which some interpreted as an opportunity for his return to government at the expense of Simon and possibly Runciman.[267] A foreign affairs debate on 2 May made public the pace at which the European situation was changing to Britain's disadvantage under the impact of Germany's violations of the Treaty of Versailles. Simon announced that Germany's front-line strength was now equivalent to Britain's front-line strength of 800 to 850 aircraft. Natural anxiety turned easily into renewed misgivings about Simon's suitability for his high office. The Foreign Secretary devoted most of his energies to helping MacDonald prepare his opening statement. By his own admission Simon's own contribution to the debate was 'rather ragged'.[268] He failed to convince all his listeners that he had been sufficiently firm in his dealings with Hitler in Berlin, while Austen Chamberlain in particular questioned whether the present regime in Germany was one with which agreement was possible.[269] 'As far as I can make out', Churchill had earlier reported to his wife, 'everyone of every party, official and political, wants to get rid of Simon.'[270] MPs were now less sympathetic to arguments about the dangers that might accrue from disturbing the existing balance of party representation in the government. In April seventy Conservative MPs had protested against keeping Simon at the Foreign Office.[271] Austen Chamberlain judged that he had become a 'positive danger . . . Nobody in any quarter has any faith in him – least of all the Cabinet and FO!'[272] Lloyd George was also busy arguing Simon's removal as essential for the betterment of the European situation, while Baldwin and Neville Chamberlain discussed the possibility of Simon becoming a Minister without Portfolio.[273] Yet still Simon clung to the Foreign Office. 'It is an unhappy situation for us all,' concluded Eden.[274]

Simon was involved in major issues of foreign policy until the day he left office. His doubts about the efficacy of the Stresa Front, together with his lingering belief that there was still scope for bilateral Anglo-German negotiations, made him look sympathetically upon the idea of naval talks as had been suggested when he visited Berlin in March, even though such negotiations appeared to have been ruled out at Stresa.[275] His vulnerable political position also left him anxious for a 'success' in the foreign arena. In his Commons speech on 2 May Simon had emphasised that 'We have kept open the door; we have tried to clear the road. We have not engaged in a senseless, endless, hopeless competition, piling armaments upon armaments to the end of time.'[276] There was always the danger that by trying to keep open the channels of conciliation with Germany, Britain would undermine the common line achieved at Stresa, and Simon had often warned his colleagues against the 35 per cent German claim and against concluding a separate arrangement with Germany rather than a general treaty to supersede the existing Washington and London naval agreements.[277] But the Admiralty, wary of the Japanese danger, was anxious for agreement, while Baldwin believed that it would be helpful to tie Germany down.

In a speech on 21 May Hitler again offered to sign a naval agreement to limit Germany's tonnage to 35 per cent of Britain's and talks finally began on

4 June. Ribbentrop made it plain that Germany would enter no real discussion until Britain had recognised the 35 per cent relationship. Simon sought to dissuade him from a demand which had every appearance of an ultimatum and at one point he left the negotiating table pleading another engagement. The cabinet, however, found the idea of tying Germany down, at however high a price, too attractive to resist. It could prevent the kind of naval race which many still held to be a principal cause of the catastrophe of 1914. Simon's own resolve now wavered and he told the cabinet that if the offer were not accepted Hitler might increase his demands.[278] On 6 June in what was effectively the last act of his Foreign Secretaryship Simon announced British acceptance of the German offer. The final conclusion of the settlement was left to his successor, Sir Samuel Hoare. Writing in 1938, Simon's first biographer could still praise the Anglo-German Naval Agreement as 'the only agreement for arms limitation which has ever been secured out of all this welter of discussion'.[279] Later judgments, made in the knowledge of the hollowness of what had been achieved, have been altogether less favourable.

★   ★   ★

Simon thus left office with the central problem of Anglo-German relations as far from solution as ever. What effect his continued tenure might have had on the course of events is difficult to surmise. Dining with Simon in 1937 – after the failure of the Hoare-Laval Pact and the collapse of the Stresa Front – Leo Amery, who was to emerge as one of the severest critics of the National Government's foreign policy, concluded:

It does look as if Simon had really been a sound foreign minister – and Stresa marked the nearest Europe has been to true peace since 1914.[280]

In addition, Amery always approved of Simon's healthily sceptical view of the potentialities of the League of Nations.[281]

After the passage of half a century British foreign policy in the 1930s can at least be observed with a detachment that was not possible for many years after 1940. It stands condemned not because it was immoral but because it failed. Simon never fully understood the interlocking connection between National Socialism and German foreign policy under Hitler, at least insofar as he never quite disabused himself of the idea of seeking a settlement with that country. Simon attempted no transformation in the conduct of British diplomacy after Hitler's assumption of power. The German leader was treated pragmatically, as his predecessors had been, with each subsequent development viewed on its merits. Yet the perception that Hitler could be reconciled to a modified status quo in Europe through the concession of legitimate demands was a basic fallacy. If this is true, it is an indictment of almost all who had responsibility for the conduct of British diplomacy in the thirties. Certainly at no time between 1933 and 1935 did the Foreign Office have an agreed view on the nature of Hitler's intentions. He was still in a way an unknown quantity, at least in the international arena. But even the most optimistic viewed his willingness for agreement as a wasting asset. On occasions Simon manifested differences of opinion from his governmental colleagues, but the substance of their views was the same. Even a figure such as Eden, whose reputation from this era still stands far higher than Simon's, diverged from him only in terms of emphasis. Returning from Moscow in the spring of 1935 Eden concluded that the basis for a general European settlement, which he had believed in a year earlier, probably no longer existed.[282] Simon was just as doubtful, but he could see no alternative to going on trying.

There was, of course, an alternative, the alternative of preparing for war. But those like Churchill and Vansittart, who probably regarded conflict as inevitable, did not in their different ways have to work within the practical constraints of democratic politics. Certain policies were politically possible in the 1930s; others were not. If appeasement was a mistake, the British electorate was an accessory to that mistake. But behind everything was Simon's conviction that war, and particularly war from the air, was so dreadful an option as to justify the exhaustive investigation of all alternative avenues, no matter how slim the chances of a successful outcome. As his Foreign Secretaryship drew to a close and with British rearmament now beginning, Simon reflected:

The fact remains that an endless competition with Germany, with its powers of industrial production and its conscripted labour, is no sure road to peace. Parity is merely a method by which air-limitation *must* be secured or we shall all be ruined together.[283]

In any case Simon deserves some credit for his recognition that Britain did need to rearm in the face of the German menace. Just over a month before he left the Foreign Office Simon warned the Ministerial Committee on Defence Requirements that the Air ministry's proposals would not be enough to maintain Baldwin's pledge of parity with the Luftwaffe.[284] 'I have to admit that he has done a good deal for the fighting services,' conceded Hankey in February 1935.[285]

No one could complain that Simon failed to put enough effort into his job as Foreign Secretary. 'You are doing much too much,' warned Neville Chamberlain in 1934. 'No man can carry on at that pace with all the cares of the FO on his shoulders.'[286] Yet however hard he worked, the outside world increasingly held Simon personally culpable for all it did not like in the government's foreign policy. According to Lloyd George, for example, it was Simon's fault, rather than the Air Ministry's, that no agreement was reached in Geneva to outlaw aerial bombing.[287] When there was something in the government's performance which merited applause, few could convince themselves that Simon might deserve the credit. When in May 1935 Baldwin delivered a well-received speech in the House of Commons, Simon wryly recorded:

I could not help wondering if the approval would have been so universal and widespread if it had been known that I wrote every word of it![288]

The Foreign Secretary's problems were exacerbated by an increasingly unsympathetic press and a weak party political base which could offer him little protection.[289]

As far as his colleagues were concerned Simon's chief defects were intrinsic to his character. What was really held against him was an inability to devise and pursue a clear-cut policy with undeviating conviction. As Churchill said:

He must trim his sails to every breeze. He must exuberate in platitudes. He must avoid any policy which any section of opinion – and there are so many – could vehemently attack. . . .[290]

'I wish Simon had more "faith",' confessed Ormsby-Gore, 'in himself and in his task – and not think quite so much what so and so in the Cabinet will say. He's astonishingly gifted, industrious and well meaning – but he's terrified of "Cabinet instructions".'[291] Simon's previous experience, and particularly his exclusion from office for a decade and a half, no doubt encouraged an inclination to caution, to follow rather than to lead. At times he resembled a diplomatic Micawber; at others he seemed reduced to dithering indecision. 'I have been trying to get decisions or action out of him about Liberia, Slavery and Elections to the Council quite unavailingly,' complained Robert Cecil.[292] 'By a process of trial and error', suggested another critic, 'he had come to believe that to accept someone else's initiative was only one degree less dangerous than to initiate a policy oneself.'[293] His problem was that while he could analyse international issues, set out the pros and cons and present every possible policy option, he could invariably see the drawbacks of any proposed course of action. 'Too penetrating a discernment and too frail a conviction', was Eden's assessment.[294]

In a sense Simon would have made an ideal permanent under-secretary, providing penetrating policy papers and leaving it to another to take the political decisions. At times this is what he seemed to do. What he liked, said Lloyd George, was that someone else should present him with a decision and then he could put up a brilliant case for it – the old complaint of a barrister working best to a brief.[295] It was not the advocate's place to take decisions.[296] Neville Chamberlain, in particular, came to regard him with something approaching contempt, so often did he end up forcing policy decisions while the Foreign Secretary hedged and trimmed. Yet Chamberlain always had his doubts as to how far Simon was 'really convinced of the wisdom of what I persuade him to do'.[297] Drained by the experience of the Manchurian crisis and the Disarmament Conference in his first year of office, Simon struggled thereafter with the increasingly intractable problems posed by Nazi Germany. In fairness to Simon it has to be said that there were no simple answers to the diplomatic conundrums of these years. It is easier to criticise him than to resolve the dilemmas with which he was confronted. 'The truth is,' said the Foreign Secretary, 'that we are living through such difficult times that criticism is the easiest thing in the world and the least useful.'[298] A measure of Simon's self-doubt might have been no bad thing for Neville Chamberlain when the latter took personal responsibility for British foreign policy later in the decade.

Notes

1 Simon 30 April 1935, cited W. J. Mommsen and L. Kettenacker, *The Fascist Challenge and the Policy of Appeasement* (London, 1983) p. 108.
2 Memorandum by Simon 20 Oct. 1933, cited M. Smith, *British Air Strategy* p. 120.
3 H. of C. Debs, 5th Series, vol. 276, col. 2759.
4 Simon to R. Boothby 19 Jan. 1932, FO 800/286.
5 Cabinet 17 May 1933, CAB 23/76.
6 H. of C. Debs, 5th Series, vol. 276, cols. 2808–12.
7 Simon to Rumbold 10 July 1933, *DBFP*, 2nd Series, vol. V, p. 407.
8 Memorandum by Simon for cabinet of 23 Oct. 1933, CAB 23/77.
9 Simon to A. Chamberlain 7 Sept. 1933, Chamberlain MSS, AC 40/5/85.
10 A. Chamberlain to Ida Chamberlain 15 July 1934, AC 5/1/670.
11 Rumbold to Simon 26 April 1933, *DBFP*, 2nd Series, vol. V, pp. 47–55. This despatch is reprinted in H. Rumbold, *The War Crisis in Berlin, July–August 1914* (London, 1940) pp. 344–58.
12 Cabinet 17 May 1933, CAB 23/76.
13 Tyrrell to Simon 3 Jan. 1932, SP 70 fo. 126.
14 Eden, *Facing the Dictators* p. 28. As late as January 1935 Eden wrote: 'I must repeat that I should be grateful if Geneva end could be left to your humble servant for a while. If each is in command at one end, it is really more easy to work, though I cannot do more than sketch this to Simon myself.' Eden to Baldwin 11 Jan. 1935, Baldwin MSS vol. 123 fo. 170.
15 Cecil to Salisbury 25 Jan. 1933, Cecil MSS Add MS 51086.
16 'I was indignant with the Foreign Secretary for making, as it seemed to me, no attempt to defend our work against the Service Departments. On the contrary, he was out-Heroding Herod.' Eden, *Facing the Dictators* p. 30; James, *Eden* p. 124. See also Eden diary entry for 7 Nov. 1934: 'Truth is he will not say 'boo' to Hailsham or perhaps he has no real convictions of his own,' cited James, *Eden* pp. 133–4.
17 Ormsby-Gore to Baldwin 8 Oct. 1933, Baldwin MSS vol. 121 fos. 83–4. The head of the Spanish delegation at Geneva later recorded: 'after the insular, enigmatic and arrogant Simon, there was at last a man alive who spoke to all comers as man to man and who needed by no means to smile in order to be open

and friendly.' S. de Madariaga, *Morning Without Noon* (Farnborough, 1974) p. 273.

18 See, for example, G. Murray to Eden 6 July 1934, Murray MSS 316 fo. 12. Leo Amery recalled: 'I had begun to be seriously alarmed by what I thought Simon's lack of control in allowing Eden at Geneva, amid general Press applause, to air what I then still supposed to be his purely personal advanced "collective security" views.' *My Political Life* iii, 168.

19 Ormsby-Gore to Baldwin 1 Oct. 1933, Baldwin MSS vol. 121 fos. 74–6.

20 A. Chamberlain to H. Chamberlain 3 July 1933, Chamberlain MSS AC 5/1/624; C. J. Hill, 'Great Britain and the Saar Plebiscite of 13 January 1935', *Journal of Contemporary History* 9, 2 (1974) p. 133.

21 Eden diary 19 Nov. 1933, cited James, *Eden* p. 129.

22 Barnes and Nicholson (eds.), *Amery Diaries* ii, 288.

23 Eden, *Facing the Dictators* p. 28.

24 Simon to Murray 1 Feb. 1933, Murray MSS 216 fo. 112.

25 CAB 23/75; Scott, *League of Nations* p. 272; A. R. Peters, *Anthony Eden at the Foreign Office 1931–38* (London, 1986) p. 32.

26 Eden, *Facing the Dictators* p. 31.

27 CAB 23/75.

28 Memorandum by Simon 28 Feb. 1933, cited A. Crozier, *Appeasement and Germany's Last Bid for Colonies* (London, 1988) p. 45.

29 MacDonald diary 2 March 1933, cited Marquand, *MacDonald* p. 752.

30 Roskill, *Hankey* iii, 105.

31 Simon to Baldwin 9 March 1933, Baldwin MSS vol. 121 fos. 40–6.

32 G. Scott, *League of Nations* p. 273.

33 Peters, *Eden* pp. 35–6.

34 Simon to George V 17 March 1933, SP 76 fo. 36.

35 *DBFP*, 2nd Series, vol. V, pp. 92–3.

36 H. of C. Debs., 5th Series, vol. 276, col. 552.

37 *DBFP*, 2nd Series, vol. V, p. 105.

38 Eden to Simon 1 May 1933, SP 76 fo. 120.

39 *DBFP*, 2nd Series, vol. V, p. 236.

40 Simon to Baldwin 12 May 1933, Baldwin MSS vol. 121 fos. 33–4.

41 Barnes and Nicholson (eds.), *Amery Diaries* ii, 291.

42 Hoare to Willingdon 31 March 1933, cited Gilbert, *Churchill v*, companion pt. 2, p. 557. Simon proved a rather difficult member of the government's India Committee which was chaired by the Secretary of State, Samuel Hoare. According to one witness Simon's approval was rigidly restricted to those aspects of the government's proposals which mirrored his own Report. J. A. Cross, *Sir Samuel Hoare* (London, 1977) pp. 155–6. But Simon gradually reconciled himself to the government's policy on India, especially when the Princes declared that they were ready to come into a federal scheme. By the beginning of 1935 he was helping to draw up the details of the Government of India Bill, 'as though foreign affairs were not enough occupation for anyone.' Simon diary 12 Dec. 1934, SP 7 fos. 9–10.

43 B. Webb diary 1 May 1933. Beatrice Webb believed that Simon intended to propose concessions to Germany at the expense of the states of Eastern Europe, with the latter receiving compensation at the expense of the Soviet Union. B.

Webb diary 7 April 1933.

44 *DBFP*, 2nd Series, vol. vii, pp. 567–76.

45 Eden to Simon 1 May 1933, SP 76 fo. 120.

46 James, *Eden* p. 128.

47 Eden, *Facing the Dictators* p. 38.

48 H. of C. Debs., 5th Series, vol. 278, col. 1454.

49 Ibid, col. 1467.

50 N. Chamberlain diary 1 June 1933, Chamberlain MSS NC 2/22.

51 N. Chamberlain to Simon 14 June 1933, SP 76 fos. 187–8.

52 Eden to Baldwin 22 June 1933, Baldwin MSS vol. 121 fo. 50.

53 CAB 23/77.

54 *DBFP*, 2nd Series, vol. V, pp. 612–21.

55 Ibid, pp. 632–5.

56 Simon to MacDonald 11 Oct. 1933, Baldwin MSS vol. 121 fos. 87–90.

57 Gibbs, *Grand Strategy* pp. 84–5.

58 Ibid, p. 85.

59 Cabinet 9 Oct. 1933, CAB 23/77.

60 Simon to MacDonald 11 Oct. 1933, Baldwin MSS vol. 121 fos. 87–90.

61 James, *Eden* p. 128.

62 M. Asquith to Baldwin 16 Oct. 1933, Baldwin MSS vol. 123 fo. 216; *Daily Herald* 16 Oct. 1933.

63 Barnes and Nicholson (eds.), *Amery Diaries* ii, 307.

64 *Simon note 14 Oct. 1933, SP 77 fo. 62.

65 Simon to George V 23 Oct. 1933, cited Nicolson, *George V* pp. 664–5. It is now clear that the makers of British foreign policy during the first years of Hitler's regime were handicapped by a poor intelligence appreciation of German intentions. 'The general expectation was that the German armed forces would be rearmed well above Versailles treaty levels but only to a strength sufficient to satisfy the demands of national security. Thus no aggressive intent was assumed from the evidence of the Versailles infractions.' W. K. Wark, *The Ultimate Enemy* (Oxford pb. edn, 1986) p. 228.

66 Simon note 14 Oct. 1933, SP 77 fo. 62.

67 Cabinet 23 Oct. 1933, CAB 23/77; Crozier, *Germany's Last Bid* p. 48; D. Kaiser, *Economic Diplomacy and the Origins of the Second World War* (Princeton, 1980) p. 116.

68 E. Phipps to Simon 26 Oct. 1933, FO 800/288.

69 Simon to A. Chamberlain 7 Sept. 1933, Chamberlain MSS AC 40/5/85.

70 H. of C. Debs., 5th Series, vol. 281, cols. 41–64.

71 Murray to Simon 8 Nov. 1933, SP 77 fo. 124; Barnes and Nicholson (eds.), *Amery Diaries* ii, 308.

72 *Manchester Guardian* 18 Nov. 1933.

73 N. Chamberlain to H. Chamberlain 18 Nov. 1933, Chamberlain MSS NC 18/1/851.

74 Ibid.

75 N. Chamberlain diary Jan. 1934, Chamberlain MSS NC 2/23A.

76 Eden's appointment as Lord Privy Seal, but without a seat in the cabinet, was announced on 1 January 1934. According to Eden, Simon was distraught at the excellent publicity the appointment received. James, *Eden* p. 131.

77 *Daily Herald* 20 Nov. 1933.

78 *Evening Standard* 21 Nov. 1933.

79 Simon to Hore-Belisha 20 Nov. 1933, SP 77 fos. 132–3.

80 Simon to Phipps 27 Nov. 1933, FO 800/288; see also Simon to Sir O. Clarke 11 Jan. 1934, SP 78 fos. 12–13.

81 N. Chamberlain to H. Chamberlain 9 Dec. 1933, Chamberlain MSS NC 18/1/853.

82 N. Chamberlain diary Jan. 1934, Chamberlain MSS NC 2/23A.

83 Some of Simon's cabinet colleagues were much slower to reach the same conclusion. As late as October 1934 Londonderry complained that Foreign Office despatches seemed to indicate a 'reversal of . . . policy' which accepted 'the re-armament of Germany as a recognised fact'. Londonderry to Simon 24 Oct. 1934, FO 800/289.

84 H. of C. Debs., 5th Series, vol. 287, col. 479.

85 Simon to Vansittart 23 Dec. 1933, Baldwin MSS vol. 121 fos. 129–35; W. N. Medlicott, *Britain and Germany: The Search for Agreement 1930–1937* (London, 1969) p. 9; *DBFP*, 2nd Series, vol. vi, pp. 326–8.

86 Barnes and Nicholson (eds.), *Amery Diaries* ii, 373; according to Cecil, while MacDonald and Simon remained Prime Minister and Foreign Secretary, 'the chances of any real success either for Disarmament or for the League are very small.' Cecil to Courtney 11 June 1934, Cecil MSS Add MS 51141.

87 N. Chamberlain diary Jan. 1934, Chamberlain MSS NC 2/23A.

88 A. Chamberlain to Ida Chamberlain 3 Feb. 1934, AC 5/1/650.

89 Lloyd George to Cecil 25 April 1934, Lloyd George MSS G/4/1/17.

90 B. Webb diary 25 May 1934. 'I will only say that, whether from his fault or his misfortune, he does not seem to be able to collect a single person who has a good word to say for him in his present office; foreigners at Geneva, Americans in the United States, officials in the Foreign Office, may I add colleagues in the Cabinet? – have only one view of his capacity as Foreign Minister.' Cecil to Halifax 27 March 1933, Cecil MSS Add. MS 51084.

91 V. Massey, *What's Past is Prologue* (London, 1963) pp. 206–7; Barnes and Nicholson (eds.), *Amery Diaries* ii, 388.

92 'I think that his defects are exaggerated and a lot of people imagine that England could in fact have done things which no Foreign Sec. could have done.' Somervell Diary, Dec. 1934.

93 A. Chamberlain to Ida Chamberlain 15 July 1934, Chamberlain MSS AC 5/1/670.

94 N. Chamberlain diary Jan. 1934, Chamberlain MSS NC 2/23A.

95 A. Chamberlain to H. Chamberlain 10 Feb. 1934, AC 5/1/651. See also A. Chamberlain to Ida Chamberlain 3 Feb. 1934, AC 5/1/650 and Barnes and Nicholson (eds.), *Amery Diaries* ii, 376.

96 *Sunday Times* 11 March 1934.

97 N. Chamberlain diary 1 March 1934, Chamberlain MSS NC 2/23A; N. Chamberlain to Ida Chamberlain 3 March 1934, NC 18/1/862.

98 *The Times* 24 Feb. 1934.

99 N. Chamberlain diary 28 Feb. 1934, Chamberlain MSS NC 2/23A.

100 MacDonald to Sankey 15 July 1934, Sankey MSS Eng. hist. c511 fos. 82–3.

101 Simon to Lord Willingdon 29 Sept. 1933, SP 77 fos. 43–4; M. Cowling, *The*

Impact of Hitler (Cambridge, 1975) p. 41.

102 Simon to Mackenzie King 23 Oct. 1934, SP 79 fo. 116.

103 *DBFP,* 2nd Series, vol. VI, pp. 243–6.

104 Compare Simon to Drummond 22 Jan. 1934, SP 78 fos. 26–7 and A. Chamberlain to Ida Chamberlain 3 Feb. 1934, Chamberlain MSS AC 5/1/650.

105 Simon to G. Murray 26 March 1934, Murray MSS 219 fos. 158–9.

106 Gilbert Murray sent 'warmest congratulations'. 'Of course one would have wished for a greater reduction of armaments, but if you can get general agreement on these lines it will be a great achievement and a real blessing to the world.' Murray to Simon 2 Feb. 1934, FO 800/289.

107 Murray to Cecil 9 March 1934, Murray MSS 219; D. Wilson, *Murray* pp. 375–6.

108 *DBFP*, 2nd Series, vol. VI, p. 366.

109 Crozier, *Germany's Last Bid* pp. 49–50.

110 Cabinets of 14 and 19 March 1934, CAB 23/78. Another comforting illusion which Simon seems to have cherished at this time about the intentions of Germany was that there might be possibilities in a gesture of colonial appeasement. Lord Cecil gathered that he would be willing to offer Hitler Liberia – which would, of course, have been at no cost to any of the other colonial powers. Note of conversation with Simon 14 June 1934, Cecil MSS Add MS 51082.

111 Hyde, *British Air Policy* p. 302.

112 N. Chamberlain diary 25 March 1934, Chamberlain MSS NC 2/23A; N. Chamberlain to H. Chamberlain 24 March 1934, NC 18/1/865.

113 F. S. Northedge, *The Troubled Giant: Britain Among the Great Powers* (London, 1966) pp. 382–3.

114 Eden, *Facing the Dictators* p. 92; Carlton, *Eden* p. 50; *The Times* 31 May 1934.

115 Bialer, *Bomber* pp. 45–6.

116 N. Chamberlain to Ida Chamberlain 12 May 1934, Chamberlain MSS NC 18/1/870.

117 N. Rostow, *Anglo-French Relations 1934–36* (London, 1984) p. 20.

118 Simon to Londonderry 14 June 1934, FO 800/291.

119 *DBFP*, 2nd Series, vol. vii, pp. 669–70.

120 Ibid, p. 711.

121 N. Thompson, *The Anti-Appeasers: Conservative Opposition to Appeasement in the 1930s* (Oxford, 1971) p. 65.

122 Simon to George V 10 July 1934, FO 800/289.

123 Simon to Londonderry 14 June 1934, FO 800/291.

124 A. Chamberlain to H. Chamberlain 21 July 1934, Chamberlain MSS AC 5/1/671.

125 H. of C. Debs., 5th Series, vol. 292, col. 697.

126 Baldwin to Simon 15 July 1934, SP 79 fo. 27.

127 H. of C. Debs., 5th Series, vol. 290, cols. 1764–75; Hoare to G. Stanley 15 June 1934, cited Gilbert, *Churchill* v, companion pt. 2, p. 810.

128 Somervell diary 17 June 1934.

129 B. Bond (ed.), *Chief of Staff: The Diaries of Lieutenant-General Sir Henry Pownall, 1933–1940* (London, 1972) p. 49.

130 Simon to MacDonald 27 July 1934, SP 79 fos. 39–40.

131 Simon to N. Chamberlain 7 Aug. 1934, SP 79 fos. 49–52.

132 Cecil to Murray 29 Aug. 1934, Cecil MSS Add MS 51132 fo. 194.

133 Simon to Baldwin 2 Aug. 1934, Baldwin MSS vol. 122 fos. 108–9.

134 Cabinet 29 Oct. 1934, CAB 23/80.

135 N. Chamberlain to Ida Chamberlain 10 Nov. 1934, Chamberlain MSS NC 18/1/895.

136 Barnes and Nicholson (eds.), *Amery Diaries* ii, 388.

137 A. Chamberlain to N. Chamberlain 11 Nov. 1934, Chamberlain MSS NC 1/27/119. *The Sunday Times* commented: 'He is too severely relevant to the immediate matter in hand; perhaps he lacks imagination or is too cautious. A calculated indiscretion sometimes, some bold essay in construction, or thinking aloud every now and then would do much to correct the impression that his dialectical skill creates. He does not make sufficient allowance for the ordinary man's impatience to feel that the solution of questions is making definite advance.' *Sunday Times* 11 Nov. 1934.

138 Simon even appealed to the American Secretary of State, Cordell Hull, to help him get kinder treatment from the American press in order to prop up his domestic position. Simon to Hull 23 Nov. 1934, cited Thorne, *Limits of Foreign Policy* p. 401.

139 H. of C. Debs., 5th Series, vol. 295, cols. 296–7.

140 Simon diary 20 Nov. 1934, SP 7 fos. 2–3.

141 *DBFP*, 2nd Series, vol. xii, pp. 253–4; record of Simon's statement to German ambassador, ibid pp. 259–61.

142 Gilbert, *Churchill* v, companion pt. 2, p. 934.

143 H. of C. Debs., 5th Series, vol. 295, col. 980.

144 Simon diary 28 Nov. 1934, SP 7 fos. 5–6.

145 Simon memorandum 29 Nov. 1934, cited Crozier, *Germany's Last Bid* pp. 51–2; *DBFP*, 2nd Series, vol. xii, pp. 271–6; M. Smith, *British Air Strategy* pp. 146–7; Kaiser, *Economic Diplomacy* p. 122; Cowling, *Impact of Hitler* p. 73; Rostow, *Anglo-French Relations* pp. 46–7.

146 Hall, 'Foreign Policy Making Process' pp. 486–8.

147 Cabinet 19 Dec. 1934, CAB 23/80.

148 Simon diary 23 Dec. 1934, SP 7 fo. 12; Gibbs, *Grand Strategy* pp. 143–4.

149 Ibid 21 Dec. 1934, SP 7 fo. 11.

150 Simon had himself argued in favour of holding a general election in 1934.

151 Simon diary 20 Nov. 1934, SP 7 fos. 2–3.

152 MacDonald to Simon 30 Nov. 1934, SP 79 fo. 174.

153 N. Chamberlain diary 5 Dec. 1934, Chamberlain MSS NC 2/23A.

154 Ibid 3 Dec. 1934, NC 2/23A.

155 Ibid 4 Dec. 1934, NC 2/23A.

156 Ibid 11 Dec. 1934, NC 2/23A.

157 Ibid 13 Dec. 1934, NC 2/23A.

158 Ibid 17 Dec. 1934, NC 2/23A.

159 N. Chamberlain to H. and Ida Chamberlain 9 Dec. 1934, NC 18/1/898.

160 Simon diary 11 and 14 Dec. 1934, SP 7 fos. 9–10.

161 Ibid, 9 Dec. 1934, SP 7 fo. 8; CAB 23/80.

162 Eden, *Facing the Dictators* pp. 100–7.

163 N. Chamberlain to H. and Ida Chamberlain 9 Dec. 1934, Chamberlain MSS NC 18/1/898.

164 Cabinet 14 March 1934, CAB 23/78.
165 C.I.D. 9 Nov. 1933, cited P. Haggie, *Britannia at Bay* (Oxford, 1981) pp. 51–2.
166 Simon diary 22 Nov. 1934, SP 7 fos. 4–5.
167 S. L. Endicott, *Diplomacy and Enterprise* (Manchester, 1975) p. 65.
168 Ibid, pp. 67–8.
169 Simon to Baldwin 27 June 1934, Baldwin MSS vol. 131 fos. 129–31.
170 Simon diary 20 and 22 Nov. 1934, SP 7 fos. 2–5.
171 Chamberlain to Simon 1 Sept. 1934, SP 79 fo. 60.
172 Simon to Chamberlain 7 Sept. 1934, SP 79 fo. 73; Simon to MacDonald 3 Oct. 1934, FO 800/289.
173 N. Chamberlain to H. Chamberlain 29 Sept. 1934, Chamberlain MSS NC 18/1/890; N. Chamberlain diary 9 Oct. 1934, NC 2/23A.
174 N. Chamberlain to Annie Chamberlain 11 Oct. 1934, NC 1/26/502; N. Chamberlain to H. Chamberlain 21 Oct. 1934, NC 18/1/892; N. Chamberlain diary 17 Oct. 1934, NC 2/23A.
175 *DBFP*, 2nd Series, vol. xiii, pp. 61–5; Andrews, *Writing on Wall* p. 152; Louis, *British Strategy in the Far-East* pp. 212–4. See also Warren Fisher to Simon 30 Oct. 1934, cited S. Roskill, *Naval Policy between the Wars* (London, 1976) ii, 296, in which Fisher asked what would happen if, on Germany's 'next venture . . . she could find England distracted with a hostile Japan'.
176 Simon diary 19 Dec. 1934, SP 7 fos. 10–11; Haggie, *Britannia* p. 65; Mommsen, *Fascist Challenge* pp. 362–3.
177 N. Chamberlain to H. Chamberlain 17 Nov. 1934, Chamberlain MSS NC 18/1/896.
178 C. Barnett, *Collapse of British Power* p. 348.
179 Simon to George V 14 Jan. 1935, FO 800/290.
180 Simon diary 8, 15 Jan. 1935, SP 7 fos. 13–14. Nonetheless Simon probably wanted to get the Saar plebicite out of the way as quickly as possible in order to move on to the serious business of bilateral negotiations with Germany.
181 Bialer, *Bomber* p. 76.
182 Simon diary 13 Jan. 1935, SP 7 fo. 14.
183 Simon to George V 14 Jan. 1935, SP 81 fo. 24.
184 Gibbs, *Grand Strategy* p. 146; Rostow, *Anglo-French Relations* pp. 87–8.
185 Cabinet 14 Jan. 1935, CAB 23/81.
186 *DBFP*, 2nd Series, vol. xii, pp. 410–14.
187 Ibid, pp. 397–400.
188 Ibid, pp. 458–63.
189 Simon diary 5 Feb. 1935, SP 7 fos. 15–16a.
190 Roskill, *Hankey* iii, 156–7; N. Rose, *Vansittart: Study of a Diplomat* (London, 1978) p. 141.
191 Roskill, *Hankey* iii, 157.
192 Simon diary 5 Feb. 1935, SP 7 fos. 15–16a; CAB 23/81.
193 *DBFP*, 2nd Series, vol. xii, pp. 475–7; Smith, *British Air Strategy* p. 149; Gibbs, *Grand Strategy* pp. 148–9.
194 *DBFP*, 2nd Series, vol. xii, pp. 477–84.
195 Roskill, *Hankey* iii, 158. When, shortly afterwards, Simon sought Hankey's support for his retention of the Foreign Secretaryship in any cabinet reshuffle, Hankey noted: 'I don't feel inclined to support him after this terrible gaffe of the

Pact'. Ibid p. 161. Simon could not understand Hankey's strength of feeling against the air pact. 'The only cases to which the Air Pact would apply are cases in which our aid is already promised under Locarno; the condition that there must be "unprovoked aggression" by air leaves us, as Locarno leaves us, with the right to decide for ourselves whether there is "aggression" which is "unprovoked", and the real value of the Air Pact would be that it would operate as a *deterrent* and so render it less, and not more, likely that we should be called upon to honour our Locarno obligations.' Simon diary 25 Feb. 1935, SP 7 fos. 20–21.

196 Vansittart to Simon 4 Feb. 1935, SP 81 fo. 149.

197 Simon to Garvin 7 Feb. 1935, SP 81 fo. 176; Simon to Reading 11 Feb. 1935, Reading MSS Eur F 118/101.

198 Simon diary 15 Feb. 1935, SP 7 fo. 20.

199 Ibid, 25 Feb. 1935, SP 7 fos. 20–21.

200 Garvin to Simon 10 Feb. 1935, SP 81 fo. 207.

201 D. C. Watt, *Personalities and Policies* (London, 1965) p. 127; J. R. M. Butler, *Lord Lothian* (London, 1960) p. 203.

202 MacDonald diary 3 March 1935.

203 D. Dilks (ed.), *Retreat from Power* (London, 1981) i, 88.

204 Eden, *Facing the Dictators* p. 125.

205 Garvin spelt this out in the *Observer* on 3 March.

206 Lothian to Baldwin 28 Feb. 1935, Baldwin MSS vol. 123 fo. 35.

207 Rostow, *Anglo-French Relations* pp. 130–1.

208 *DBFP*, 2nd Series, vol. xii, pp. 601–2.

209 A. Chamberlain to Ivy Chamberlain 6 March 1935, Chamberlain MSS AC 6/1/1036c. For a similar statement of opinion see Ormsby-Gore to Baldwin n.d., Baldwin MSS vol. 123 fo. 54.

210 Cabinet 6 March 1935, CAB 23/81.

211 N. Chamberlain diary 8 March 1935, Chamberlain MSS NC 2/23A; N. Chamberlain to H. Chamberlain 9 March 1935, NC 18/1/908. The decision to send Eden rather than Simon to Moscow seems to have pleased Maisky, the Soviet Ambassador in London, who 'dislikes Simon intensely, mainly because he feels that, in this slippery lawyer, the USSR has an enemy.' B. Webb diary 16 March 1935.

212 N. Chamberlain diary 11 March 1935, Chamberlain MSS NC 2/23A.

213 Simon diary 11 March 1935, SP 7 fos. 21–2. Whatever the truth about this episode, Simon's speech was not among his better performances. Bond (ed.), *Chief of Staff* p. 65; N. Chamberlain to Ida Chamberlain 16 March 1935, Chamberlain MSS NC 18/1/909.

214 Cabinet 18 March 1935, CAB 23/81.

215 Note by Simon 17 March 1935, cited Crozier, *Germany's Last Bid* p. 53.

216 Simon to George V 18 March 1935, FO 800/290. Compare Simon's Commons statement on 21 March 1935: 'The object of British policy has been . . . to help bring this great State back into the councils and comity of Europe on terms which are just to her and which are fair and secure for all of us, so that she, with her great talents and resources, may contribute . . . to the task which every good European who wants peace has got to share.' H. of C. Debs., 5th Series, vol. 299, col. 1409.

217 *DBFP*, 2nd Series, vol. xii, p. 663.

218 Simon diary 21 March 1935, SP 7 fo. 23.

219 A. Chamberlain to Ida Chamberlain 24 March 1935, Chamberlain MSS AC 5/1/693.

220 N. Chamberlain diary 21 March 1935, NC 2/23A; N. Chamberlain to Annie Chamberlain 19 March 1935, NC 1/26/507.

221 CAB 23/81; N. Chamberlain diary 21 March 1935, NC 2/23A; N. Chamberlain to Annie Chamberlain 21 March 1935, NC 1/26/508; N. Chamberlain to H. Chamberlain 23 March 1935, NC 18/1/910; Note in Simon's papers described there as 'PM's note', SP 82 fo. 32.

222 Barnes and Nicholson (eds.), *Amery Diaries* ii, 393.

223 A. Chamberlain to Ida Chamberlain 24 March 1935, Chamberlain MSS AC 5/1/693.

224 Vansittart to Phipps 22 March 1935, cited Rose, *Vansittart* p. 116.

225 Smith, *British Air Strategy* p. 149.

226 Eden, *Facing the Dictators* p. 133.

227 Ibid, p. 141.

228 Gibbs, *Grand Strategy* pp. 156–7; 164–5.

229 Ibid, pp. 157–8.

230 *DBFP*, 2nd Series, vol. xii, pp. 703–46; Hall, 'Foreign policy making' p. 492.

231 Simon to George V 27 March 1935, FO 800/290.

232 *The Times* 4 April 1935.

233 Rostow, *Anglo-French Relations* p. 142.

234 N. Chamberlain diary 2 April 1935, Chamberlain MSS NC 2/23A; N. Chamberlain to Ida Chamberlain 30 March 1935, NC 18/1/911.

235 See, for example, I. Kirkpatrick, *The Inner Circle* (London, 1959) p. 69; Barnett, *Collapse of British Power* p. 403; Ormsby-Gore to Baldwin 29 March 1935, Baldwin MSS vol. 47 fo. 36.

236 Gilbert, *Rumbold* p. 393.

237 Simon to George V 27 March 1935, FO 800/290.

238 Simon diary 27 March 1935, SP 7 fos. 24–5; Simon to Dr. S. Berry 5 April 1935, SP 82 fos. 38–9.

239 CAB 23/81.

240 Simon to Phipps 5 April 1935, FO 800/290. 'I am very far from believing', Simon told Garvin, 'that the "united front" is all that is needed to secure European peace, but I am very profoundly convinced that we need to show Germany in her present mood that she need not hope to divide us.' Simon to Garvin 18 April 1935, SP 82 fos. 58–60.

241 Note by Simon on telegram from Sir G. Clerk of 28 March 1935, cited Hall, 'Foreign policy making' p. 494.

242 Eden, *Facing the Dictators* p. 187.

243 Simon to George V 27 March 1935, FO 800/290. The idea of Germany's eastern expansion clearly gave Simon considerable comfort: 'If she acts, it is surely better than she should act to the East. That will at worst occupy her energies for a long time and may well prove a lesson and not a stimulus.' Notes written by Simon on the aeroplane returning from Stresa and Geneva, 17 April 1935, SP 82 fos. 48–57.

244 Simon to MacDonald 10 April 1935, Baldwin MSS vol. 1 fos. 160–3; Bialer,

Bomber pp. 70–1.
245 Cabinet 8 April 1935, CAB 23/81.
246 N. Chamberlain diary 8 April 1935, Chamberlain MSS NC 2/23A; N. Chamberlain to H. Chamberlain 6 April 1935, NC 18/1/912; Cecil to Murray 15 April 1935, Murray MSS 222 fo. 85. MacDonald himself noted that he ran 'Great risks of being unequal to the task and of making a failure.' Marquand, *MacDonald* p. 772.
247 Bond (ed.), *Chief of Staff* p. 68.
248 Simon diary 11–14 April 1935, SP 7 fo. 26.
249 Lady Simon's book *Slavery* was published in 1929.
250 *DBFP*, 2nd Series, vol. xiv, p. 137.
251 Simon to George V 21 Feb. 1935, cited Nicolson, *George V* p. 528.
252 *DBFP*, 2nd Series, vol. xiv, pp. 136–8; G. Thompson, *Front-Line Diplomat* (London, 1959) p. 95.
253 Eden, *Facing the Dictators* p. 179.
254 T. Jones, *Diary with Letters* p. 187.
255 E. Phipps quoted in Roskill, *Hankey* iii, 178; Lord Gladwyn, *Memoirs* (London, 1972) p. 48; Amery, *Life* iii, 167.
256 Lord Vansittart, *The Mist Procession* (London, 1958) p. 520; Lord Vansittart, *Lessons of my Life* (London, 1943) p. 46; G. Baer, *The Coming of the Ethiopian War* (Harvard, 1967) p. 122; Rose, *Vansittart* p. 162; *DBFP*, 2nd Series, vol. xii, pp. 910–11.
257 Crozier, *Off the Record* p. 39.
258 Sir C. Petrie, *A Historian Looks at His World* (London, 1972) p. 142.
259 Eden, *Facing the Dictators* p. 204.
260 Simon to Reading 24 May 1935, Reading MSS Eur F 118/101.
261 F. Hardie, *The Abyssinian Crisis* (London, 1974) p. 120.
262 *DBFP*, 2nd Series, vol. xiv, p. 251.
263 Simon diary 27 May 1935, SP 7 fo. 30.
264 Crozier, *Off the Record* p. 41.
265 *The Observer* 14 April 1935.
266 N. Chamberlain to H. Chamberlain 12 May 1935, Chamberlain MSS NC 18/1/915.
267 E. Grigg to Lloyd George 11 Jan. 1935, Lloyd George MSS G/141/20/9; Taylor (ed.), *Lloyd George: A Diary* p. 300; Simon diary 20 Jan. 1935, SP 7 fos. 14–15.
268 Simon to Eden 7 May 1935, SP 82 fo. 77.
269 D. J. Dutton, *Austen Chamberlain: Gentleman in Politics* (Bolton, 1985) p. 313.
270 Gilbert, *Churchill* v, companion pt. 2 p. 1140.
271 N. Thompson, *Anti-Appeasers* p. 65.
272 A. Chamberlain to H. Chamberlain 5 May 1935, Chamberlain MSS AC 5/1/698.
273 T. Jones to Baldwin 16 May 1935, Baldwin MSS vol. 47 fo. 1; N. Chamberlain diary 29 April 1935, Chamberlain MSS NC 2/23A.
274 Eden, *Facing the Dictators* p. 187.
275 Gibbs, *Grand Strategy* p. 159.
276 H. of C. Debs., 5th Series, vol. 301, col. 688.
277 Gibbs, *Grand Strategy* p. 166.
278 Cabinet 5 June 1935, CAB 23/81; D. C. Watt, 'The Anglo-German Naval Agreement of 1935', *Journal of Modern History* xxiii, 2, (1956) pp. 167–8;

Roskill, *Naval Policy* ii, 303–4.

279 Roberts, *Simon* p. 291.

280 Barnes and Nicholson (eds.), *Amery Diaries* ii, 451. Simon himself seems to have placed less faith in the Stresa Front than Amery came to believe. Shortly before leaving office he noted: 'The "united front" of France, Italy and Britain makes no difference in this respect [of German rearmament] at all. As the united front won't intervene to stop her, why should it make any difference?' The value of Stresa was 'not so much that it diverts and restricts Germany's present action as that it is our only security *if* Germany turns nasty.' Note by Simon 17 April 1935, SP 82 fos. 48–57.

281 See, for example, Amery, *Life* iii, 154.

282 Peters, *Eden* p. 90. 'On the whole Eden and Simon were in agreement on policy up to mid-1934, their differences being those of temperament when the younger man was impatient to achieve results.' J. C. Robertson, 'The Origins of British Opposition to Mussolini over Ethiopia', *Journal of British Studies* (1969) p. 125.

283 Simon diary 22 May 1935, SP 7 fos. 29–30.

284 Gilbert, *Churchill* v, 640–1.

285 Roskill, *Hankey* iii, 161.

286 N. Chamberlain to Simon 14 March 1934, SP 78 fo. 111.

287 A. J. P. Taylor (ed.), *Lloyd George: A Diary* p. 259.

288 Simon diary 22 May 1935, SP 7 fos. 29–30.

289 Murray to Simon 17 May 1935, SP 82 fos. 84–5.

290 Gilbert, *Churchill* v, companion pt. 2, pp. 825–6.

291 Ormsby-Gore to Baldwin 1 Oct. 1933, Baldwin MSS vol. 121 fos. 74–6.

292 Cecil to Murray 5 Jan. 1933, Murray MSS 216 fo. 2. See also Crozier, *Off the Record* p. 15.

293 A. Campbell–Johnson, *Eden: The Making of a Statesman* (New York, 1955) p. 75.

294 Eden, *Facing the Dictators* p. 219.

295 Crozier, *Off the Record* p. 20. 'He would produce a paper setting out all the pros and cons of a question but reaching no conclusion. He would look to his colleagues for a decision. When a point of view was expressed, and then only, he would bring into play his brilliant powers of criticism – but in a purely destructive way.' J. Colville, *Fringes of Power* (pb. edn., London, 1987) ii, 60.

296 A. J. Sylvester, *Life with Lloyd George* (London, 1975) p. 97.

297 N. Chamberlain to Ida Chamberlain 27 Oct. 1934, Chamberlain MSS NC 18/1/893.

298 Simon to Willingdon 5 March 1935, SP 82 fo. 9.

CHAPTER EIGHT

DOMESTIC INTERLUDE

Simon has disappeared from the Foreign Office an acknowledged failure.[1]

'There are two reasons,' wrote Simon to Sir John Anderson in 1940, 'why Ministers are given new offices. 1. because they filled the old one so well, 2. because they filled the old one so badly.'[2] In Simon's case in 1935 there could be no doubt that it was the latter situation which prevailed. For more than two years his continued tenure of the Foreign Secretaryship had been under question and the cabinet reshuffle, though long postponed, had as one of its primary objectives to remove him from his existing post.[3] The other pressing factor, of course, was the evidently failing health and capacity of the Prime Minister. As one cabinet minister put it to Stanley Baldwin, 'I can't disguise from you that I don't think we can carry on with Ramsay as Prime Minister or Simon at the FO.'[4] Serious discussions between the six leading members of the government about a cabinet reconstruction got under way in the second week of February 1935. Simon recorded that 'the Wavertree by-election, the muddle over the Unemployment pay-regulations, Lloyd George's reappearance and (truth to tell) an increasing impression that the Government lacks drive and direction have brought matters to a head.'[5] The principal decision reached was that MacDonald and Baldwin should change places. The latter, noted Simon, would make 'an entirely acceptable chief – he represents our general outlook completely and there is nothing of the high and dry Tory about him.'[6] Little more was then done for two months.

When the changes did finally take place Simon was in some ways lucky to hold on to cabinet rank, so loud and widespread had been the criticisms of him. What to do about Simon, said Neville Chamberlain, was Baldwin's chief difficulty.[7] When MacDonald again discussed the forthcoming recon-struction with Baldwin on 30 April, the latter said that the Foreign Secretary would either have to be moved or go altogether.[8] A fortnight later, however, Baldwin was ready to let Simon take a sinecure office, 'look after defence and be Deputy leader H of C'.[9] In the event Simon did even better, returning to the Home Office, a post he had briefly held twenty years before. It was largely a reflection on the continuing importance of maintaining the National character of the government that he received such favourable treatment. indeed it was part of the bargain finally struck with Baldwin that the elevation of a Conservative to the premiership should be balanced by the addition of an extra Liberal National – Ernest Brown as Minister of Labour – to the cabinet.[10] Steps were also taken to give the public appearance that

Simon was not being demoted – 'done in' as Hore-Belisha put it[11] – by including the deputy leadership of the Commons, previously held by Chamberlain, with the Home Office. Chamberlain speculated that Simon would regard the deputy leadership as a means of re-establishing his stature in the House of Commons and as a possible stepping-stone to a future premiership, on the ground that a minority leader might be required to preserve the character of the National Government. But the Chancellor of the Exchequer professed not to be worried for his own ambitions:

In this Simon deceives himself and I need never be jealous of him because I know now that he lacks certain qualities essential to a leader. The House will I believe accept him for the present, because they will be glad to get rid of him from the FO, but though he will I believe do us very useful service in setting out our case (which no one can do better) that won't mean that he will be any the more acceptable to the House in person. The fact is the House detests him; he hasn't a friend even in his own party. . . .[12]

Nonetheless, Chamberlain, who did not consider Simon entitled to the concession of the deputy leadership 'to soften his fall',[13] took the trouble to secure Baldwin's assurance that the arrangement was only temporary, to last until the general election.[14]

Almost four years had now elapsed since the crisis which had given birth to the National Government. Irrespective of his status within the cabinet, it could scarcely be said that the position of Simon and those who followed him in the Liberal National group had grown stronger in that period. Essentially they had become the prisoners of the Conservatives, the overwhelmingly largest element in the governing coalition. As an independent movement it was unlikely that the Liberal Nationals could command a base in popular support if the government collapsed or if the Conservatives decided that they could dispense with their services. Lacking genuinely close relations with his senior cabinet colleagues, Simon was understandably nervous about his own position and that of his followers throughout MacDonald's premiership. At a constituency level it was only too clear that the political survival of the Liberal National movement depended on the tolerance and indeed the active support of the Conservative party organisation. In July 1932 the Simonites had set up the Liberal National Council with Lord Wimborne as president, Leslie Hore-Belisha as chairman of its General Committee and Lord Hutchison chairman of its Executive Committee. The aims of the Council were to co-ordinate the efforts of Conservatives and Liberal Nationals at electoral level, publicise the role of the Simonites inside the government and raise funds to support Liberal National candidates at by-elections and the next general election.[15]

The fundamental predicament of the Liberal National group was forcefully underlined when the Samuelite Liberals left the government in September 1932. Relations between the two Liberal groupings had worsened steadily since the formation of the National Government, and the refusal of the Simonites to stand by Samuel in his opposition to the Ottawa agreements appeared to rule out any possibility for the foreseeable future that the Liberal Nationals could be readmitted into the mainstream of Liberal politics. The cost of severing links with the Samuelite Liberals had to be a clearer definition of relations with the Conservatives. Simon confronted the problem shortly afterwards in a letter to Baldwin:

Now that Samuel and co. are withdrawing, the position of these friends of mine in their constituencies will be much more difficult and they will very soon be exposed to every sort of attack and pressure from the organisations who approve Samuel's *démarche*. At the same time, they sincerely desire to continue to show themselves, as they have shown themselves in the past, amongst the stoutest defenders of the National Government, which I am sure is what you wish. Yet, unless they can be assured that they are going to have, so far as official Conservatism is concerned, a free run in their constituencies at the next election, they stand to be shot at from both sides.[16]

Baldwin took almost a month to reply and, respecting the independence of local Conservative associations, was unable to give as firm a commitment as Simon would have liked. But

I, as Leader of the Party, and the Chairman, who directs the Conservative Party Headquarters, will exercise all the influence and authority we possess to see that those who play a patriotic part receive the full support of our party in the constituencies they now represent.[17]

Simon seems to have been happy with this assurance and did not press the matter further, but it is interesting to note that he reacted unenthusiastically a little later to the idea that the Liberal Nationals should publish a newsletter. Simon feared both that the enterprise might fail, thus revealing the intrinsic weakness of the movement, and that to attempt it might be interpreted in Conservative quarters as excessively partisan.[18]

The test of the Simon-Baldwin agreement would come at the next general election. This event was not likely to be long delayed after the cabinet reconstruction of June 1935. Several members of the government, and particularly the Chancellor Neville Chamberlain, were anxious in view of the worsening European situation to secure a new mandate for a policy of moderate rearmament. Chamberlain found that Simon was in agreement with him that rearmament should be the central issue, but judged a speech made by the latter on the subject 'so vague and nebulous' that he felt obliged to take the lead himself.[19] Despite resistance from MacDonald and an equivocal attitude on the part of the new Prime Minister, the Chamberlain-Simon line carried the day and an election was called for mid-November.[20] The Liberal Nationals fought the election in complete accord with their Conservative allies and were nowhere opposed by them. Simon busied himself to strengthen the organisation of his party and embarked upon an extensive speaking tour which took him from Peterborough to Aberdeen and from Manchester to Devizes. Meanwhile Lady Simon played a leading role in the campaign in Spen Valley where she addressed over forty women's meetings. Whatever he believed about the pressing needs of national defence, Simon chose to concentrate on domestic issues, stressing once again the dangers of socialism. In his radio broadcast he appealed to Liberals to recognise that their political beliefs were broader than the present Liberal party and argued that all Liberals could trust Baldwin.[21]

It was as inevitable as anything in politics can be that the National Government would lose some ground to Labour after the landslide result of 1931, though with an overall majority of 255 seats its position remained secure. In the event two government ministers, Ramsay MacDonald and his son Malcolm, went down to defeat. Simon, in what proved to be the last election he fought, scraped home in Spen Valley by a mere 642 votes against a Labour opponent, while his band of Liberal National followers returned 35 members, the same as in 1931. Indeed the Home Secretary took comfort from the fact that proportionately his group had retained its strength better than either of the other components in the National Government.[22] It was the first time since the War that a government, after a long term in office, had appealed to the country and been confirmed in power. This Simon attributed to the reassuring personality of the Prime Minister, the success of the government both internationally and domestically, the divisive policies of the opposition and the fact that the concept of a 'national' administration – 'the way of cooperation rather than of conflict' – appealed to the outlook of the ordinary voter.[23]

★ ★ ★

Though Simon occupied the Home Office – for many a political graveyard – for less than two years, his tenure did much to restore his political reputation, particularly among his cabinet colleagues. Within a matter of months many of those who had been most critical of his handling of the nation's diplomacy had come to appreciate once again Simon's intrinsic qualities. It was, of course, a department with which he was fully familiar and one where his innate liberalism came into play. His handling of the ministry's affairs proved to be firm and sensible. Simon himself claimed to be well content with his change of office, particularly as it would enable him to spend more time in the House of Commons, and, after three and a half years of trying to grapple with the intractable problems of the international situation, there seems little reason to doubt his sincerity.[24]

Among the ministerial duties associated with the Home Office are those relating to the monarchy and royal family. In general these are of a largely ceremonial and formal nature, and Simon's first public function as Home Secretary was to accompany King George V and Queen Mary on the fourth and last of their Jubilee drives through London. Simon recorded with satisfaction 'boundless enthusiasm, immense crowds [and] perfect weather'.[25] Four months later there was a less conventional task to perform:

The Home Secretary attends Royal Births and I was fetched out of my bed soon after mid-night to attend at 3 Belgrave Square and await the arrival of the Duchess of Kent's baby. The news reached us downstairs, after the fashion of less exalted households, by the excited father bursting in with the words 'it's a boy!' after which I went up to inspect.[26]

One of Simon's last duties as Home Secretary in the spring of 1937 was to supervise the arrangements for the coronation of King George VI, for which services the new monarch favoured him with the award of GCVO.

But not all of Simon's royal preoccupations were of so light a character. Three kings occupied the throne in the course of 1936 and the year also witnessed the gravest crisis to confront the British monarchy in the course of the twentieth century. Credit for the successful conduct of the events which culminated in the abdication of Edward VIII has for long, and rightly, been given to the Prime Minister, Stanley Baldwin. His patient and sensitive handling of a most delicate situation, both from the point of view of the King himself and of the British electorate, helped to preserve the monarchy and the unity of the Empire. It also enabled Baldwin to take his leave of the political stage in something approaching a blaze of glory, a rare distinction for a retiring premier in modern times. Yet there were aspects of the crisis – legal and constitutional – for which Baldwin was not ideally equipped, and it is well to note Hankey's comment that it was Simon, the Home Secretary, who had 'become a very great strength to the Cabinet' and 'who steered us through the Duke of Windsor crisis and its many pitfalls'.[27] Though many of the most important documents relating to the Royal Abdication remain closed to historians, it is nonetheless possible to discern the Home Secretary's hand at almost all stages in the dramatic weeks of late 1936. Simon was, by virtue of his previous close connection with constitutional questions and long experience of government, marked out to become one of Baldwin's principal lieutenants in the handling of the affair, but events conspired to make his role critical. The government's other distinguished lawyer, Lord Hailsham the Lord Chancellor, was absent for much of the year following a stroke and the Attorney-General, Sir Donald Somervell, was, by comparison with Simon, a political novice. Not surprisingly 'when the crisis started, Simon rather took over the major constitutional issue.'[28]

From the outset of Edward VIII's brief and ill-fated reign Simon had the gravest doubts as to his suitability to occupy the throne. At the end of the crisis Simon was even to offer the opinion that the King 'wasn't sane'.[29] Notwithstanding his undoubted popularity in the country, 'there were sides to his nature which seemed never to have developed to the stature of manhood.'[30] Reacting from the formal and unloving correctness of his parental upbringing, Edward 'favoured frivolities which a circle of light-hearted friends were always ready to encourage'.[31] The ceremonial functions of a modern constitutional monarchy held no attraction for him and questions were being asked about his commitment to his duties even before the matter of his intended marriage came to the fore. After the celebrated interview between King and Prime Minister at Fort Belvedere on 20 October 1936, Simon was one of three or four senior ministers in whom Baldwin confided and with whom each subsequent step was concerted. On 16 November Edward made known his determination to marry the American divorcee, Wallis Simpson, and his readiness to give up the throne in order to do so. This statement created a constitutional predicament for which there was no precedent in British history, for the title to the throne is defined in the Act of Settlement and Simon believed it impossible for the succession to be modified by the mere declaration of the present incumbent. Certainly parliamentary confirmation would be necessary to exclude any of Edward's direct descendants from the succession. A further complication had been imposed as a result of the passing in 1931 of the Statute of Westminster, which recognised that the assent and approval of the Dominions would have to be given to any law modifying the devolution of the Imperial Crown.

Though in retrospect there seems to have been no alternative to the King's abdication, many strove for as long as possible to avoid this inevitable conclusion. On 23 November the newspaper magnate, Esmond Harmsworth, sought an interview with Baldwin at which he unfolded a remarkable plan whereby the King should marry Mrs. Simpson and remain on the throne, while she should not become Queen. Morganatic marriage is unknown to English law, so further legislation would have been necessary to enact such a solution. But, as Simon rightly saw, Harmsworth's plan failed to take into account 'what ordinary citizens would think of a proposal to treat the King's wife as a welcome choice, though quite unfit to be Queen'.[32] Baldwin buried the proposal on 4 December when answering Attlee in the House of Commons in a statement largely drafted for him by Simon:

The lady whom [the King] marries . . . necessarily becomes Queen. She herself therefore enjoys all the status, rights and privileges which, both by positive law and by custom, attach to that position, and with which we are familiar in the cases of Her Late Majesty Queen Alexandra and of Her Majesty Queen Mary, and her children would be in the direct line of succession to the Throne. The only possible way in which this result could be avoided would be by legislation dealing with a particular case. His Majesty's Government are not prepared to introduce such legislation. Moreover, the matters to be dealt with are of common concern to the Commonwealth as a whole, and such a change could not be effected without the assent of all the Dominions. I am satisfied from enquiries I have made that this assent would not be forthcoming.[33]

On the morning of 4 December, before making his parliamentary statement, the Prime Minister summoned the cabinet to discuss the King's request to broadcast to his subjects. Edward clearly hoped thereby to win popular support for his cause. There was, however, general agreement that it would not be possible for him to make any public utterance the details of which had not been approved by his ministers, for while Edward remained on the throne his ministers were constitutionally responsible for his words. Again it was the Home Secretary who drafted a paper to this effect. 'Simon has his legal uses,' noted Thomas Dugdale, Baldwin's parliamentary private secretary.[34]

The King now made his final decision to abdicate, but matters were further complicated when his legal adviser, Walter Monckton, proposed that, as a concession to the monarch, Mrs. Simpson's divorce from her husband Ernest should be made absolute immediately. Baldwin spent seven hours with Simon on 5 December discussing this proposal. The Home Secretary judged that while it might be practically possible to satisfy the King's wishes, to offer such favours to a woman whose role in the crisis had already engendered considerable hostility would not be politically acceptable. This view was confirmed at a meeting of senior ministers the following day.

Only the details of the Act of Abdication now remained to be settled. Again, Simon's hand is clearly in evidence. As Monckton recorded on 9 December:

Then we went back to Downing Street and Simon played the part of Chief of Staff . . . Sir John gave us complete orders to ensure that the Instrument of Abdication and the Messages should be distributed at the right time and place throughout the Empire and that there should be no breakdown in the machinery. I have seen many staff officers but none so competent.[35]

Simon also helped the King compose his public broadcast which explained the reasons which had obliged him to take his fateful decision.[36] One final detail of the crisis saw Simon contribute to a controversial decision whose repercussions were to ripple through the following years. This was the refusal to grant the style of Her Royal Highness to the Duchess of Windsor after her marriage to the ex-king in June 1937. Though Simon, Hailsham and Somervell seem to have been happy about the legality of this step, later opinion has been divided.[37] Simon was perhaps moved less by constitutional correctness than by the practical worry that the Duchess, having already divested herself of two husbands, was not beyond dropping a third and that her status as Her Royal Highness could be an embarrassment in the event of a fourth husband being found. Yet there seems a strong argument that the Duke of Windsor, as a royal prince (indeed he was clearly styled as such at the time of his national broadcast after the Instrument of Abdication had been signed) had, as of right, the status of Royal Highness which automatically passed to his spouse, whosoever she might be. At all events Monckton warned Simon of the offence which would be created by this decision and what was clearly a snub to the Duchess remained as a wounding thorn in relations between the Windsors and the British Royal Family for the remainder of their lives.[38]

★ ★ ★

Those who, like Simon, bore responsibility for the outcome of the Abdication Crisis of 1936 possibly held within their hands the fate of both the monarchy and the Empire. At a less elevated but no less serious level one of the most dreadful and uneviable duties of the Home Secretary was to decide whether convicted murderers should be hanged or reprieved. It was not a task which Simon took lightly. Inside the Secretary of State's office was a framed card containing the names and details of all pending cases until the fate of each was decided. To this Simon added a line from Juvenal: Nulla unquam de morte hominis cunctatio longa est.[39]

As a classical scholar Simon was fully aware that the sentence was open to two interpretations – either counselling reflection and caution or warning against letting time slip by.[40] This text appears to have been removed by Samuel Hoare, Simon's successor at the Home Office, but it was there again during the Second World War and was not finally taken away until the 1950s when R. A. Butler became Home Secretary.[41]

Simon seems to have adopted an attitude towards capital punishment which, if maintained by his successors, might have averted some of the controversy of the following decades. Hitherto Home Secretaries had tended to argue that as death was the penalty prescribed by law for murder, there had to be some mitigating circumstances to justify setting it aside. Simon followed a subtly different approach. In his view the large number of cases in which the criminal was reprieved suggested that society was ready to accept a policy in which capital punishment was only imposed in the worst cases of murder. He therefore looked for an aggravating feature such as premeditation or the fact that the murder was committed in conjunction with another crime before placing an individual case in this category. In other circumstances the Home Secretary was ready to exercise clemency.[42]

Simon was not responsible for any major legislative reforms during his time at the Home Office, although some useful measures were put on the Statute Book. Perhaps the most significant was the Public Order Act which passed quickly through all its stages and became law on 1 January 1937. The excesses of Sir Oswald Mosley's British Union of Fascists were causing concern, particularly when clashes occurred with left-wing opponents. The Public Order Act took some of the steam out of Mosley's movement and was widely applauded. It had four main provisions. It banned the wearing of political uniforms except on private ceremonial occasions; it stopped the use of stewards at open-air meetings; it strengthened the existing law on the use of insulting language; and it gave the police power to ban marches and processions. Simon handled the measure with skill throughout. Of one parliamentary performance the correspondent of *The Spectator* was particularly enthusiastic:

I cannot recall ever having witnessed a more skilful performance than Sir John Simon's conduct on Monday of the Committee stage of the Public Order Bill. Always urbane, never at a loss for the right argument, ready to meet points when they were sound, never wavering on essentials, he disarmed his opponents, encouraged his friends and succeeded through a gruelling Parliamentary day in avoiding a division on any of the questions that seemed likely at one time to raise controversial issues.[43]

Simon's Factory Act of 1937 was a valuable piece of legislation whose provisions were long overdue, while another important measure for which Simon had responsibility was the Ministers of the Crown Bill. This revised the salaries of cabinet ministers, giving £10,000 a year to the Prime Minister and bringing up all other cabinet salaries to the normal level of £5,000. It also provided a pension of £2,000 a year for former Prime Ministers and instituted a salary of £2,000 for the Leader of the Opposition.

The work of the Home Office inevitably brought Simon back into closer contact with the House of Commons than had been necessary, or indeed possible, during his Foreign Secretaryship. There was an unfortunate incident in July 1936 when Simon, winding up for the government after a three day debate on new regulations for unemployment assistance, stressed that a Means Test was inevitable. One opposition MP interjected that the Home Secretary was a liar and the rumpus which followed led to the suspension of three members.[44] In general, however, Simon quietly reasserted his position. The *Daily Dispatch* commented in July 1936 on the 'increasing dominance' which he was exercising over the House:

During the past few weeks a new Sir John has been evolved – a hard hitting and unambiguous Sir John, mincing no words, but letting the Opposition have it straight from the shoulder. It used to be deprecatorily said of the Home Secretary that he was too legalistic, almost too 'precious', as a front bench man. . . . But that style has virtually vanished. In its place is a sparkling competence, with a sense of humour, especially at Question Time.[45]

The possibility of Simon succeeding Baldwin at 10 Downing Street was even mentioned.[46] Overall, then, Simon's period as Home Secretary must be judged a success, both in terms of intrinsic achievement and as regards restoring his own standing among his governmental colleagues. 'Simon good at the Home Office', judged Sir Samuel Hoare and, a little more informatively, 'good in cabinet as long as he did not have to give a lead'.[47] 'His conduct as Home Secretary', noted the *Sunday Times*, 'has won the respect of the whole House and the liking of most of it . . . Sir John Simon has become a great political success.'[48]

Simon obviously exercised no direct control over the conduct of British diplomacy once he left the Foreign Office in June 1935. Nor did his departmental responsibilities as Home Secretary permit him to wield the very considerable influence in this area which he regained during his period as Chancellor of the Exchequer between 1937 and 1940. Nonetheless Simon remained a senior cabinet minister, an ex-Foreign Secretary, at a time when the preoccupations of the National Government of which he was a member were coming to focus more and more on the worsening international situation. In addition he still, on occasions, spoke for the government on questions of foreign policy in the House of Commons.

In view of the widespread dissatisfaction at Simon's performance as Foreign Secretary, particularly during his last months in office, it was not surprising that Samuel Hoare enjoyed something of a honeymoon period after taking over from him. At the first cabinet meeting of the new government Baldwin passed MacDonald a note, saying that he found it 'very refreshing to hear "I strongly advise . . ." from the FO!'[49] Eden too was pleased with the change, enjoyed working under Hoare and noted that 'the difference in the FO is incredible.'[50] Yet the problems of the international situation were no more capable of instant resolution by the new Foreign Secretary than by the old, and Hoare's reputation was to collapse even more dramatically than Simon's had done. The latter would not have been human had he not felt a slight feeling of satisfaction as difficulties began rapidly to envelop his successor. In July 1935 he wrote:

My successor at the Foreign Office has not had long to wait before finding out how difficult it is to handle international affairs to the general satisfaction.[51]

The issue which proved to be Hoare's undoing was one which had clearly been simmering when Simon was at the Foreign Office. After the Wal-Wal incident in December 1934 Italian military preparations throughout the first half of 1935 left the British government in no doubt that Mussolini intended to begin the conquest of Abyssinia, probably in the autumn. Simon was under no illusions about the threat which Italian aggression would pose to the League of Nations:

If zeal for the League of Nations is the test I greatly fear that Abyssinia is going to provide a much more concrete trial than ever Manchuria did.[52]

The League was unlikely to survive if it stood by as an ineffective witness of Italian aggression. That would expose it as an instrument which could bully a small and weak state, but which would look the other way when a permanent member of the Council stole territory from another country. But would the League be able to act?

France, following discussions between Laval and Mussolini early in January 1935 and only recently shaken by Britain's bilateral naval negotiations with Germany, was unlikely to attempt to obstruct Italian designs and 'we cannot act alone as policeman of the world.'[53] On the other hand the Stresa accords indicated the importance which Simon and the government placed on good relations, with Italy in a European situation where Germany had been positively identified as the major threat to the peace. Simon indeed had already posed the unpalatable choices which these conflicting pressures placed upon the British government:

If they support against Italy the practical application of League principles, their action is bound greatly to compromise Anglo-Italian relations and perhaps even to break the close association at present existing between France, Italy and the United Kingdom . . . On the other hand, if the United Kingdom acquiesces in a misuse of League machinery, His Majesty's Government will undoubtedly lay themselves open to grave public criticism.[54]

Hoare had as little chance as Simon would have had of constructing a viable policy out of the ambivalent combination of overt support for the League and concern to keep Italy friendly in Europe. Attempts to effect a compromise between June and September, including a plan for Abyssinia to receive the port of Zeila in British Somaliland in return for ceding the Ogaden to Italy, came to nothing and in the early hours of 3 October Italian forces launched their long-anticipated invasion. The League now acted with some speed. Italy was designated the aggressor and Article 16 was invoked on 7 October. By 19 October the Assembly Committee of Eighteen, with the support of the British government, had adopted a series of sanctions proposals against the aggressor. Significantly, these did not include the vital commodity oil. Meanwhile the Italian occupation proceeded with the speed and success which were to be anticipated in view of the wide disparity between the contending parties.

The calling of a British general election for 14 November inevitably posed an additional complication. In particular the suspension of cabinet meetings for over a month left Hoare and his colleagues in the Foreign Office very much to their own devices in attempting to work out a solution. But the British government seemed committed to a policy of economic sanctions. Shortly before the dissolution of parliament Simon assured the House of Commons that no arrangement with Italy was being contemplated:

We are neither going behind the back of the League, nor have we ever contemplated for one moment doing so . . . we have no intention of wavering in giving effect, as a member of the collective system, to our obligations under the Covenant.[55]

In his election address, moreover, Simon sought to emphasise Britain's continuing commitment to the League of Nations. 'The best guarantee of peace', he argued, 'is co-operation with other peace-loving nations with a view to collective security.'[56]

Hoare, in poor health and in desperate need of a holiday, arranged to see his French opposite number, Pierre Laval, in Paris *en route* to Switzerland in early December. Prior to his departure the cabinet met on 2 December and gave the Foreign Secretary virtual *carte blanche* to conclude an agreement with Laval, emphasising the need to take a generous view of Italian claims in Abyssinia. In Paris the two foreign ministers reached agreement on a plan which would bring about the partition of Abyssinia. The principal and most

valuable areas would go to Italy, while the Emperor Haile Selassie would
retain a limited kingdom with access to the sea via a narrow corridor. To
begin with the cabinet seemed ready to acquiesce in Hoare's proposals.
Simon recorded:

We met in haste on Monday night to consider the rather imperfect report contained
in a telegram from Paris. The terms proposed involved an exchange of territory
which would give Abyssinia a port on the Red Sea, League assistance to bring about
internal reform, and economic monopoly for Italy over a large area south of Addis
Ababa. This seemed very much like 'rewarding the aggressor', but the Cabinet felt
that it was hardly possible to throw over the Foreign Secretary in his absence. So we
contented ourselves with insisting (contrary to Laval's wishes) that the terms must be
submitted with equal fulness to both sides – it seemed very improbable that Abyssinia would accept them – and with refusing to agree (as Laval urged) that oil
sanctions were impossible if Abyssinia rejected the terms.[57]

But, confronted with a hostile reaction in the press and the rumblings of a
serious revolt on the Conservative back-benches, the government's mood
quickly changed. On 10 December

the full gravity of the proposal became more evident. We learned for the first time
that it was not intended to allow Abyssinia to construct an independent railway to the
port and *The Times* attacked the scheme in a leader headed 'A Corridor for
Camels'.[58]

By the following day Simon was ready to ditch the plan:

At the Cabinet today I took the lead in reexamining the plan and, though Baldwin
remained silent and Chamberlain was cautious, there was a general feeling that it
would never do. Sam Hoare is being sent for from Switzerland.[59]

   Hoare returned to England though illness prevented him from attending
the vital meetings at which the cabinet finally decided to renege on its
original decision to back his proposals. Crucially it was agreed that Eden
should prepare a draft statement for the meeting of the League Council on
18 December making it clear that the British government would not recommend acceptance of the Hoare-Laval agreements if they did not meet with
the approval of all parties concerned. Simon wrote to Eden to express his
relief:

He told me he was horrified at the idea that Hoare should defend us by saying, in
effect, that the peace terms were necessary as an alternative to war. He did not
believe it, and to say so would be to give Mussolini the biggest score of his life and
make Italy intolerable in the future.[60]

By now there was a strong and growing feeling in the cabinet that Hoare
should resign. Simon hinted that his own position might otherwise become
impossible as he could not defend Hoare's proposals.[61] Chamberlain, who
visited Hoare in his sickbed, reported to the cabinet on what the Foreign

Secretary proposed to say in defence of his pact. To Simon and the majority of the cabinet this seemed 'very disconcerting'. The parliamentary position had become extremely difficult. The Chief Whip advised that nothing short of Hoare's resignation would meet the situation, while the Opposition was ready to move a vote of censure on 19 December denouncing the Hoare-Laval scheme as an attempt 'to reward the declared aggressor at the expense of the victim, destroy collective security and conflict with the expressed will of the country and the Covenant of the League of Nations'. As Simon warned the Prime Minister, 'this was very nearly what the Cabinet felt.'[62]

While Simon busied himself concocting an amendment to the vote of censure, assuring the government of unswerving support for the policy declared in its last election manifesto – a move which was likely to bring potential rebels into the government lobby – Hoare bowed to the inevitable and agreed to resign. One observer, present when the news of the Foreign Secretary's fall came through, noted Simon's reaction – 'a huge smile on his face'.[63] If true, this story displays an unattractive side to Simon's character. The former Labour Chancellor of the Exchequer, Philip Snowden, provided corroboration:

I hear that Simon makes no secret of his gratification at the recent Foreign Affairs episode. He seems to think that the disgrace of Hoare and Baldwin is some compensation for his own treatment.[64]

Not surprisingly Thomas Jones heard that Simon was one of two ministers for whom the fallen Foreign Secretary felt resentment.[65] Yet Simon's motivation is not easy to discern in the course of this crisis. It is difficult to picture as the idealistic champion of the League of Nations the same man who had presided over Britain's handling of the Manchurian affair. Nor is it likely that Simon felt particular sympathy for Abyssinia, granted that country's record on the question of slavery, where his wife's preoccupations, if not his own, would have determined his attitude. But, to his credit, Simon was not one of those cabinet ministers who stood on their heads between accepting Hoare's proposals on 9 December and demanding his resignation just over a week later. Chamberlain singled Simon out as one who had expressed his 'surprise and even consternation' at the cabinet meeting at which the Foreign Secretary's proposals were first examined.[66] The most likely explanation is that Simon's sensitive political antennae told him that Hoare's proposals would never be acceptable in Britain's existing League-orientated climate of opinion.

★ ★ ★

Under the Foreign Secretaryship of Hoare's successor, Anthony Eden, the international questions confronting the British government multiplied in both variety and complexity. In March 1936 Hitler reoccupied the demilitarised Rhineland. The British and French governments, pointing to one another's inertia to explain their own unwillingness to act, stood on the sidelines, comforting themselves with the illusion that Germany was merely re-entering her own backyard. Simon even opposed holding staff talks with the French, making his disagreement so widely known that Eden and Chamberlain had to ask Baldwin to speak to him.[67] In July civil war broke out in Spain, carrying with it the haunting spectre of a wider European war and of a fundamental clash of incompatible ideologies. In the background Germany steadily increased her military potential to challenge the existing order of European affairs. It was 'beyond question' that 'Germany is putting herself in a position where she can act as she pleases and fears no one's veto.' In August Simon noted:

Our major preoccupation has been the relentless march of German rearmament . . . Meetings of the CID and of the Defence Requirements Committee have been frequent and important, our own expenditure on armaments is increasing so considerably that after this year we shall have to meet it by loan. . . .

But it is interesting that Simon went on to take some comfort from the fact that German ambitions lay in the first instance in areas outside the traditional sphere of British influence:

Her eyes are turned East and South-East – not West. The Cyclops paid Odysseus the compliment of promising to eat him last.[68]

One somewhat half-hearted gesture of recognition towards the growing threat posed by Nazi Germany came with the creation in March 1936 of a Ministry for the Co-ordination of Defence. Called in to discuss the filling of this post, Simon exerted his influence to help exclude Hoare and the job eventually fell to Sir Thomas Inskip, 'safe but not inspiring' and until then Attorney-General.[69]

The growing German menace convinced Simon that British strength should not be dissipated in a vain attempt to punish Italy for her Abyssinian adventure. When the Opposition moved a vote of censure on 23 June for the government's lifting of sanctions, Simon, to whom the main defence was entrusted, made a brilliant reply, effectively crushing the Opposition's case and ruthlessly exposing the inconsistencies of a speech by Lloyd George. 'If multitudes of congratulations mark success,' noted Simon, 'this was a successful speech.'[70] But one sentence in particular stuck in the gullets of the advocates of collective security through the League. He was not, he said, 'prepared to risk a single ship to preserve Abyssinian independence'. This, thought Robert Cecil, was an advertisement to the aggressor powers and to the neutrals that the Covenant meant nothing to Britain. It was the deathblow to collective security and indeed to the League as a guarantee of peace. 'It breathed the essential spirit of appeasement.'[71] But appeasement was never as simple or as supine a policy as contemporaries and many subsequent historians imagined. As Simon recognised, in a hostile world Britain could not afford the luxury of antagonising Italy in a cause that was probably already lost, while the altogether more frightening spectre of German aggression loomed just over the horizon.[72] The remedy, Simon believed, lay in steady British rearmament. He put his case to an audience in Plymouth in March 1937:

A stronger Britain is not a threat of war but a contribution to world peace. Our object continues to be to promote international agreement on the subject of armaments, but I am convinced that we are far more likely to promote this object if we make it plain that our democracy, devoted to world peace as it is, is prepared and able to shoulder this additional expenditure and will never consent to allow our country and our Empire to be without adequate defence.[73]

Few Prime Ministerial change-overs have been so smooth and well planned as that effected between Stanley Baldwin and Neville Chamberlain in May 1937. Baldwin, never the most energetic of politicians, was all but exhausted after fourteen years at the head of the Conservative party, most of them in government. He had been ill for much of 1936 and would probably have resigned earlier but for the constitutional crisis of that year and his determination to see a new monarch safely crowned. Chamberlain, only nineteen months younger than Baldwin, was nonetheless restless with energy and prepared the way for his own government with the administrative diligence and efficiency that had become his trademark. His close friend Samuel Hoare urged Chamberlain to make the new cabinet as different as possible from that of his predecessor,[74] but in the event ministerial changes were quite limited. It was testimony to the restoration of Simon's political standing since June 1935 that the talk now was not of whether he would survive the ministerial reshuffle, but of which great office of state he would occupy next. Late in 1936 it was rumoured that he might succeed the ailing Hailsham on the Woolsack,[75] but in the New Year Simon let it be known to Chamberlain via the Chief Whip that he was not prepared to go to the House of Lords. His preference was for Chamberlain's own post at the Treasury, a job he had hoped for back in 1931. If this were not available he would consider retiring from politics and turning his hand to writing. 'All ambitious politicians,' noted Chamberlain with some insight, 'like to say this at such moments.'[76] As it happened Chamberlain's mind was already moving in the same direction, a clear indication of the extent to which his opinion of Simon had mellowed since the latter's days at the Foreign Office. Discussing the forthcoming changes with Baldwin in mid-January he revealed that his preferred choice for Chancellor had switched from Hoare to Simon. It would, commented Baldwin, be 'most valuable' to have the Liberal leader fully satisfied.[77] By March Hoare was writing of rumours 'carefully circulated' that Simon was bound to go to the Treasury. In newsreels Simon was being projected as Chamberlain's possible successor. Hoare, who had anticipated that the job would be his, toyed with the idea of joining the Midland Bank, but was eventually happy to settle for Simon's post at the Home Office.[78] It was therefore no surprise when in the middle of March Chamberlain sent for Simon and told him that he wished him to become Chancellor. He had been chosen, said Chamberlain, because 'we had worked so happily and effectively together.'[79] Simon, delighted, said that he approached his new office 'with humbleness'. 'Not a bad qualification to start with,' retorted the Prime Minister designate.[80]

Notes

1 Lloyd George to Smuts 31 July 1935, Lloyd George MSS G 18/6/8.
2 J. Wheeler Bennett, *Sir John Anderson* (London, 1962) p. 256.
3 A. J. P. Taylor (ed.), *Off the Record* p. 47; R. R. James, *Victor Cazalet: a portrait* (London, 1976) p. 167; S. Roskill, *Hankey* iii, 173.
4 Ormsby-Gore to Baldwin n.d. [Feb. 1935], Baldwin MSS vol. 47 fo. 14.
5 Simon diary 14 Feb. 1935, SP 7 fos. 18–20.
6 Ibid.
7 Chamberlain diary 17 May 1935, Chamberlain MSS NC 2/23A.
8 D. Marquand, *MacDonald* p. 774.
9 MacDonald diary 13 May 1935, Marquand p. 775.
10 Simon diary 4 June 1935, SP 7 fos. 31–2.
11 Taylor (ed.), *Off the Record* p. 47.
12 N. Chamberlain to H. Chamberlain 22 May 1935, Chamberlain MSS NC 18/1/918.
13 Ibid.
14 Chamberlain diary 3 June 1935, Chamberlain MSS NC 2/23A. In the event Simon retained the post.
15 T. Stannage, *Baldwin Thwarts the Opposition* (London, 1980) p. 30.
16 Simon to Baldwin 28 Sept. 1932, Baldwin MSS vol. 46 fos. 59–61.
17 Baldwin to Simon 26 Oct. 1932, SP 73 fos. 200–1.
18 Stannage, *Baldwin* p. 39.
19 N. Chamberlain to H. Chamberlain 22 Sept. 1935, Chamberlain MSS NC 18/1/934.
20 Simon diary 22 Oct. 1935, SP 7 fo. 38.
21 Stannage, *Baldwin* p. 179.
22 Simon diary 16 Nov. 1935, SP 7 fo. 40.
23 Ibid, 5 Dec. 1935, SP 7 fo. 40.
24 Simon to Reading 12 June 1935, Reading MSS Eur. F 118/101.
25 Simon diary 8 June 1935, SP 7 fo. 33.
26 Ibid, 8 Oct. 1935, SP 7 fo. 37.
27 S. Roskill, *Hankey* iii, 277. See also T. Jones, *Diary with Letters* p. 291.
28 Somervell Diary of Abdication, Feb. 1937.
29 C. Stuart (ed.), *The Reith Diaries* (London, 1975) p. 192.
30 Undated Simon memorandum on the Abdication, SP 8 fos. 1–17.

31 Ibid.
32 Ibid.
33 House of Commons Debs, 5th Series, vol. 318, cols. 1611–12.
34 Diary of Nancy Dugdale 3 Dec. 1936, from data supplied by Thomas Dugdale, quoted *The Observer* 7 Dec. 1986.
35 Monckton's account of the Abdication, cited Lord Birkenhead, *Walter Monckton* (London, 1969) p. 149.
36 Stuart (ed.), *Reith Diaries* p. 192.
37 See, for example, introduction to *Debrett's Peerage* for 1973.
38 F. Donaldson, *Edward VIII* (London, 1974) p. 344.
39 Simon to Sankey 15 Oct. 1941, Sankey MSS Eng. hist. c 519 fo. 132. Simon's own translation was 'You can never hesitate too long before deciding that a man must die.'
40 Simon diary 1 July 1935, SP 7 fo. 35; Simon to D. T. Holmes 20 June 1935, SP 82 fos. 151–2.
41 S. Hoare, notes on 1935–7, Templewood MSS X: 5; Simon to Sankey 15 Oct. 1941, Sankey MSS Eng. hist. c519 fo. 132; Lord Butler, *The Art of the Possible* (London, 1971) p. 201.
42 R. Heuston, *Lord Chancellors* ii, 51–2, citing evidence of Terence FitzGerald, former Assistant Under-Secretary at the Home Office.
43 *The Spectator* 27 November 1936.
44 Simon diary 11 Aug. 1936, SP 7 fo. 58.
45 *Daily Dispatch* 1 July 1936.
46 Ibid; cf. *Liverpool Post* 29 March 1937: 'One of the personal features of the session . . . has been Sir John Simon's rise in reputation and prestige.'
47 S. Hoare notes on Baldwin's Third Government and on 1937–39, Templewood MSS IX: 3 and X: 5.
48 *Sunday Times* 29 Nov. 1936.
49 Baldwin to MacDonald 26 June 1935, Templewood MSS VII: 1.
50 N. Chamberlain to H. Chamberlain 1 Sept. 1935, Chamberlain MSS NC 18/1/930.
51 Simon diary 7 July 1935, SP 7 fo. 35.
52 Simon to Bishop of Pontefract 15 July 1935, SP 82 fo. 180.
53 Simon diary 7 July 1935, SP 7 fo. 35.
54 J. Cross, *Hoare* p. 201.
55 House of Commons Debs, 5th Series, vol. 305, col. 458.
56 Election address, SP 250 fo. 17.
57 Simon diary 11 Dec. 1935, SP 7 fos. 41–2.
58 Ibid.
59 Ibid.
60 Avon, *Facing the Dictators* p. 309.
61 N. Chamberlain diary 17 Dec. 1935, Chamberlain MSS NC 2/23A.
62 Cabinet meeting 18 Dec. 1935, CAB 23/90B; Simon diary 18 Dec. 1935, SP 7 fo. 42.
63 K. Young (ed.), *Lockhart Diaries* i, 335.
64 Snowden to Lloyd George 31 Jan. 1936, Lloyd George MSS G 18/7/14.
65 T. Jones, *Diary with Letters* p. 161.
66 N. Chamberlain diary 15 Dec. 1935, Chamberlain MSS NC 2/23A.

67 Avon, *Facing the Dictators* p. 360.
68 Simon diary 11 Aug. 1936, SP 7 fos. 51–2.
69 N. Chamberlain diary 11 March 1936, Chamberlain MSS NC 2/23A.
70 Simon diary 11 Aug. 1936, SP 7 fo. 51; R. R. James (ed.), *Chips: the Diaries of Sir Henry Channon* (London, 1967) p. 87; H. Macmillan, *Winds of Change* p. 458.
71 Cecil, *Great Experiment* p. 278.
72 Simon diary 11 Aug. 1936, SP 7 fo. 51.
73 Speech in Plymouth 19 March 1937, SP 193 fo. 80.
74 Hoare to Chamberlain 17 March 1937, Templewood MSS IX: 2.
75 T. Jones, *Diary with Letters* p. 273.
76 N. Chamberlain diary 11 Feb. 1937, Chamberlain MSS NC 2/24A.
77 Ibid, 17 Jan. 1937, NC 2/24A.
78 S. Hoare, Notes on Baldwin's Third Government, March/April 1937, Templewood MSS XI: 3.
79 N. Chamberlain diary 19 March 1937, Chamberlain MSS NC 2/24A.
80 *Retrospect* p. 227.

CHAPTER NINE

GUILTY MAN

Discussed the politicians who were criminally responsible for war and should be hanged on lamp-posts of Downing Street. Not many candidates. Nearly everyone agreed that sinner No. 1 was Simon.[1]

Over a weekend in 1940 as Britain prepared to face its gravest challenge of the Second World War, three left-wing journalists combined to produce a polemical tract which sold in many thousands of copies and played a major role in determining the popular history of the 1930s.[2] Despite half a century of more scholarly historiography, some of the legends which this book created have still not been entirely erased from the public consciousness. *Guilty Men* sought to show how the crisis of 1940 was the direct creation of the policies, and perhaps more particularly the personalities, of the previous decade. It begins by listing the *dramatis personae* of this sorry tale, the cast list of those who had played their part in reducing the country to its present predicament. Inevitably the name at the top of this list is that of Neville Chamberlain, the man whose premiership saw both the highpoint and the collapse of the policy of appeasement. For Chamberlain, then recently replaced by Winston Churchill as Prime Minister but still a member of the latter's War Cabinet, the authors of *Guilty Men* display a particular scorn. The second name on their list is that of John Simon.[3]

Other contemporary critics produced slightly different hierarchies of culpability, but Simon's name is never absent. Robert Boothby, a consistent opponent of the National Government whose views on the thirties never wavered throughout his long life, told Lloyd George shortly after the outbreak of war that 'four men have landed us in this deplorable situation – Chamberlain, Simon, Halifax and Hoare'.[4] Clement Attlee, leader of the Labour party from 1935, looked back on the prewar years and concluded that MacDonald, Baldwin, Simon and Chamberlain were 'mainly responsible'.[5] Events conspired to elevate Simon to this position of dubious distinction among those thus indicted. No one could deny his close association with the policies of the National Government. A major political figure throughout the decade, he had successively held the three great offices of state beneath the premiership. An increasingly close personal association with Neville Chamberlain had become apparent. After six months at the Exchequer Simon's relations with Chamberlain seemed far removed from the uneasy days of the early thirties. At Christmas 1937 the Prime Minister sent a warm seasonal message:

It has been the greatest pleasure to me to work with you in such complete harmony and your quick mind and unrivalled power of analysis have been a tower of strength. May our association long continue.[6]

As Chamberlain's standing fell in later years, Simon was inevitably tarred with the same brush. Indeed his reputation became submerged beneath the torrent of invective which dragged down the politicians of the National Government, condemning them almost without exception as time-serving mediocrities who presided with complacency or indifference over the declining fortunes of Great Britain, while in Europe the perils of fascism mounted apace. He was pictured as one of that country house party associated with Lady Astor, whose vacuous chatter drowned out the warnings of those few brave men – Winston Churchill *et al* – who sought to open the nation's eyes to its imminent danger. Beatrice Webb expressed what became in time a common point of view:

But the 'Cliveden coterie' – Lady Astor, Samuel Hoare, Simon, Inskip, Halifax with Garvin and Geoffrey Dawson in attendance are die-hard pro-German and, in their hearts, desire Germany to extend her territory and her influence in the near east, to the detriment of the Soviet Union. They would like to see the new social order disappear, by foreign invasion and renewed civil war: even at the cost of imperilling the British Empire.[7]

At a slightly more subtle level Simon's handling of the Far-Eastern crisis came, as has been seen, to assume a growing, if largely unwarranted, significance with the passing of the years. As the decade unfolded and Japanese aggression was followed by that of Italy and Germany, international affairs slipped all too easily into a pattern – a pattern which, in the eyes of governmental critics, could most easily have been broken at the outset. In other words the events of 1931–3 took on the appearance of a lost opportunity – the fateful moment at which the peace-loving nations of the world could and should have acted to stop the aggressor in his tracks. Not to have done so – and for this Simon as Foreign Secretary was held to bear primary responsibility – was to invite Mussolini and Hitler to copy the example of Japan and undo the international settlement by force, confident in the knowledge that the western democracies would not lift a finger to stop them. As the 'Man of Manchukuo'[8], Simon took his place alongside the Men of Munich who had failed to see the essentially futile and self-destructive nature of the policies they sought to pursue towards aggressor states.

Simon's sins as Foreign Secretary in the first part of the decade were seen to be compounded by the role which he played at the Treasury during Chamberlain's premiership. When men came to ask why the British army had been reduced in June 1940 to the degradation of Dunkirk, the figure of the parsimonious Chancellor of the Exchequer offered an easy explanation. One critical ministerial colleague put the matter with commendable simplicity:

John Simon was the *fons et origo mali* before and during the early stages of the war of the slow pace of rearmament. He would not sanction the expenditure.[9]

The authors of *Guilty Men* were just as confident in their assertion of where blame should be placed.

[Simon] spoke on these matters in the counsels of the Cabinet. He represented the views of the Treasury. And he was successful in war as in peace in carrying through the Treasury policy of ensuring that expenditure should be vigorously limited.[10]

Critics were quick to draw the simple equation between Simon's jealous guarding of the nation's finances and that same nation's patent unpreparedness for war. And, in the context of 1939 and 1940, what might normally have been excused as the characteristic caution of any Chancellor became tantamount to criminal negligence. As early as October 1938 Alfred Duff Cooper, only recently resigned from Chamberlain's government, had claimed that rearmament was being held back by the 'paralysing hand of the Treasury'.[11] Yet while not all of Simon's actions as Chancellor may have been wise, his motivation was altogether more complex and creditable than contemporary critics were ready to concede. The unravelling of the Treasury's role in the late 1930s has been among the more significant recent contributions to the ever expanding historiography of appeasement.[12]

Simon recorded that he responded to Chamberlain's offer of the Exchequer with the modest disclaimer that he had 'no special knowledge of finance'.[13] Such a comment was always likely to be used to his own disadvantage,[14] but the remark, if made, did scant justice to the deep interest, displayed in his public speeches, which he had shown in the problems of national finance since the end of the Great War and particularly since 1929. He had indeed considerable qualifications for the post, not least his brilliant legal mind and a temperament well suited to working within the limits imposed by the financial realities of the day. Simon as Chancellor may have done little to alter the course already charted by Neville Chamberlain, his predecessor at the Exchequer, but the continuity of policy along the lines that Chamberlain had set since 1931 reflected less a lack of understanding of the subject on Simon's part than the all-pervading nature of the economic orthodoxy of the day. The context of the National Government, even six years after its formation, remained important. That government had been created in 1931 with the specific purpose of rescuing the British economy, believed at the time to be on the verge of catastrophic collapse. Those who had sat in the cabinet during the ensuing years would not lightly jeopardise the dearly won gains in the economic sphere. The Treasury strove mightily in the 1930s to balance the national budget as the essential pre-requisite of a sound economy. In 1933, 1934, 1935 and 1937 this was achieved. Chamberlain and Simon had an absolute horror of inflation and regarded excessive government expenditure as the primary engine of such a disaster.

Any temptation to experiment with an alternative economic strategy was unlikely to survive the evidence provided in the first months of Simon's tenure of office. The remarkable achievements of the United States and its New Deal ran out of steam in the summer of 1937 and over the next nine months America experienced one of the worst recessions in its history. With production falling by a third and unemployment rising again to 10 millions, the American experience could only confirm that the Treasury's fundamentally deflationary instincts were well founded. Later commentators, moreover, have sometimes drawn too neat and clear a distinction between the cautious orthodoxy of the thirties and an adventurous Keynesian alternative based on deficit financing, which would have enabled much larger funds to be devoted to national defence. But the contemporary Keynes, as opposed to his later disciples, was less out of line with government thinking on this matter than has sometimes been supposed. The fear that rapid rearmament would produce severe inflationary pressures was one which Keynes himself shared. It would in fact be difficult to show that the rearmament programme would have been any more intense had Keynes been in charge of the Treasury.[15]

Any reassessment of the Exchequer's role during the Chamberlain-Simon era must also take into account that the Treasury was not simply making a value judgment between a sound economy and military preparedness for European or World War, and opting for the former. The two were not seen as competing alternatives but as complementary aspects of the same problem. As a Treasury official noted, economic stability was 'a fourth arm of defence . . . without which purely military efforts would be of no avail'.[16] As in so many other ways the men of the thirties drew their lessons, real and imagined, from the First World War and concluded that an essential prerequisite of a future British victory would be the economic capacity to sustain a long drawn-out conflict. There was, however, an important contrast with 1914. In the years immediately before World War Two the Treasury saw little prospect that American finance would be available on anything like the same scale to help Britain prosecute another war with Germany. To damage the economy with excessive expenditure on defence before war actually came might well mean jeopardising the country's long-term capacity to fight that war to a successful conclusion. Rapid rearmament could exhaust the government's ability to raise credit, destabilise the economy and drain the reserves of gold and convertible currency. The Treasury's task was to ensure the economic base for a long war. There was then an unenviable dilemma to be faced. The more prepared Britain was to protect herself from Germany's initial attack, the less able she might be to sustain herself later on. Simon, as Chancellor, had a critical role to play in determining where the balance should lie. The Exchequer thus enjoyed a much wider brief than simply trying to save money. Especially in the absence of a fully-blown Ministry of Defence it came to assume considerable responsibility for determining where the thrust of Britain's defence effort should be placed.

The move from the Home Office to the Exchequer allowed Simon, still struggling to get through the Committee stage of his Factory Bill containing 151 clauses, little scope for respite. Becoming Chancellor on 28 May 1937 Simon immediately took to his bed with an attack of bronchitis.[17] But he was anxious to move the second reading of Chamberlain's Finance Bill himself, not least in view of the poor reception accorded to the former Chancellor's proposals for a National Defence Contribution on the lines of the old Excess Profits Tax. Simon recovered sufficiently to speak in the House on 31 May before returning to his sickbed. He showed himself ready to reconsider Chamberlain's proposals, responding to the pressure of business interests which offered to find the same revenue by the simpler method of an additional tax on business profits themselves rather than on the growth of profits. Simon's new proposals were introduced on 21 June and were generally welcomed, allowing the Finance Bill to pass into law by 16 July.[18] It was the first time for many years that an important budget taxation proposal had been fundamentally changed as a result of parliamentary opposition.[19] Simon's early weeks at the Treasury were also occupied with the technical question of increasing the resources of the Equalisation Fund Account by £200 millions. Again, the Chancellor's proposals were well received and the matter was settled without difficulty by early July.[20]

Chamberlain's proposals for a National Defence Contribution reflected his growing concern during his last months at the Exchequer with the cost of the country's defence programme and he had set up a long-term review of this cost in relation to the totality of national resources. It was Simon who inherited this review and brought it to fruition. The new Chancellor gave his first impressions of the financial implications of the current defence programmes in a letter to Lord Swinton, the Air Secretary, on 22 June. He viewed the situation as one of the utmost seriousness. Estimates had risen steadily since 1934 and there was no sign that they were levelling off. Even allowing for the Defence Loans Act of February 1937 the annual cost of maintaining the defence forces would be more than ordinary revenue could bear. The country was in danger of being swamped by an impossible burden of defence expenditure.[21] A week later Simon presented his report to the cabinet. Combining the revenue available from taxation with the authority to borrow £400 millions under the Defence Loans Act, Simon concluded that a total of £1500 millions in all would be available for the three defence services in the five years until 1942. But, he warned, 'if there is a set-back in trade, indeed if prosperity does not increase, the sum available is likely to be less and even very substantially less.'[22]

Simon could not but be worried by the fact that the cost of defence programmes undertaken and planned was constantly rising from their original estimates. For example the cost of new naval construction for 1936 and 1937, previously estimated at £64 millions, had now almost doubled. The Chancellor's conclusions were sober in the extreme.

Figures such as these indicate the pace at which the cost to be met continues to grow and show that there is at present no trace of finality. We are running the gravest risks if we do not resolutely insist on correlating the rising total burden of Defence liabilities to the whole of our available resources. Indeed the means of correlation is, under existing practice, rapidly breaking down.

Accordingly Simon argued that it was now necessary for a general review of the rearmament question and to introduce a new procedure to regulate current and future defence expenditure.[23] To achieve this tighter control over expenditure Simon submitted four main proposals. The defence departments were to submit new estimates of the time and money required for the completion of their programmes. These estimates were to be reviewed and commented on by the Treasury. The estimates and Treasury comments would then go the Defence Policy and Requirements Committee of the cabinet which would have the power to determine priorities between conflicting claims and recommend to the cabinet maxima for the yearly expenditure of each department. Finally decisions on new projects of major importance would be postponed until these procedures had been completed.[24]

Simon's plan provoked surprisingly little opposition within the cabinet considering that it involved the lengthy reassessment of issues that had already been extensively discussed and meant the assertion of a major role for the Treasury in fixing not just the size but also the shape of the nation's defences. The impact of the new regime soon became apparent. In July Hore-Belisha, Secretary of State for War, requested new equipment for the Territorial Army. The request was turned down. Simon was 'quite firm that at present there should be no increase in the cost of the Army's programme', though he implied that Hore-Belisha's proposals might be acceptable if he could make economies elsewhere.[25] The forecasts of the Service Departments together with Simon's comments were considered by the cabinet at its meeting on 27 October. With the Prime Minister indisposed, Simon took the chair and opened the discussion. Simon played a restrained role at this stage, summarising the evidence presented to him but leaving the financial and military implications to be deduced by his colleagues. But the Chancellor drew attention to 'the magnitude of the defence requirements asked for by the fighting services'.

At that moment, he did not propose to mention a figure which the nation could afford. He only wished to draw attention to a consideration which increased the gravity of the situation, namely that it was not going to be so easy to borrow the necessary money as had been contemplated.[26]

Worried that the DPRC might take too long to sort out conflicting claims, Simon succeeded in having the whole matter referred to Inskip. He proposed 'to take full advantage of the existence and functions of the Minister for Coordination of Defence and to refer the memoranda before the cabinet to him'.[27]

Inskip's report 'Defence Expenditure in Future Years' was considered by the cabinet on 22 December. The hand of the Treasury was only too apparent. Inskip again emphasised that a sound economy was vital for the overall effectiveness of national defence. Asserting that £1500 millions was the most that the country could afford over the period 1937–41, especially in view of the rising costs of maintenance after 1941, the minister proposed drastic revisions in the plans of the service ministries. The most severely hit was the army and it was significant that Inskip succeeded in relegating to fourth position in the scale of Britain's defence priorities – 'which can only be provided after the other objectives have been met' – cooperation in the defence of the territories of any allies in war. In effect this meant finally abandoning the concept that the British army would have any significant role to play in a future continental war. Simon welcomed the report. He later said that it contained 'a classic statement of the elements that made up our strength for national defence'.[28] The change in the army's role would enable savings of many millions to be made. He asked the service ministers to provide early defence estimates as he would need to consider what part could be met out of taxation and what out of loans. The estimates would need to be published by the end of February 1938. But Simon warned that 'until that total was known, we did not know whether the programmes would be within the financial capacity of the country to carry them out.'[29]

The system of defence rationing was now effectively in place. It represented a considerable upheaval in the balance of power and influence within the government as regards questions of national defence. Hitherto the service ministries had been able to argue that, irrespective of financial implications, the government had to provide the resources to meet the country's defence commitments. Now it appeared that under the impact of rationing those defence commitments might have to be modified. It was a sign of the times when, just before Christmas 1937, the First Lord of the Admiralty, Duff Cooper, sent Simon a detailed account of why the navy would need an extra £55½ millions for the coming year. He received a 'discouraging response'.[30]

★　★　★

By the beginning of 1938 and until early 1939, when the Treasury's control became markedly weaker under the impact of a rapidly worsening international situation, Simon stood at the zenith of his career. As late as March

1939 one disgruntled official noted that 'Unless PM or Simon say "yes" nothing counts at all and it's a waste of time having meetings with other ministers.'[31] More powerful within the British government than at any time before or afterwards, he ranked second in the cabinet behind the Prime Minister. 'Incredible as it may seem', noted one hostile observer within the Foreign Office, 'he also believes that he can become Prime Minister.'[32] But 1938 marked also the zenith – or perhaps it should be said the nadir – of the policy of appeasement. Simon would require all of his very considerable political skills to emerge from it with credit.

While awaiting Inskip's second report, the Chancellor maintained his pressure upon the service ministries. 'My principal aim,' he told the Prime Minister early in the new year, 'has been to avoid allowing departments to embark on expenditure which would prejudice the review of our defence programmes now being carried out by Sir Thomas Inskip.'[33] The defence estimates submitted to the Treasury added up to £357 millions – an increase of £79 millions on those authorised in 1937. Simon insisted that they should be reduced by £12 millions. Hore-Belisha – 'this knocked me out' – and Duff Cooper – 'I don't see how it can be done' – recorded their disquiet.[34] But the Chancellor's priority remained 'to see the fall in armaments expenditure after reaching this appalling peak'.[35] Even before the crucial meeting of 16 February at which the cabinet considered Inskip's second report, Simon had effectively asserted his authority over the Admiralty. He refused to accept a programme on anything like the scale proposed and claimed that the Admiralty was trying to telescope a seven year scheme into three years in carriers, destroyers and submarines. By 10 February Duff Cooper had to tell the Admiralty Board that he had been obliged to accept a figure in line with Simon's wishes, even though this meant deliberately slowing down the speed of the country's rearmament.[36]

Reporting to the cabinet on 16 February, Inskip pointed out that the service estimates now appeared to be running at about £2000 millions instead of the £1500 millions previously envisaged. He proposed a total defence budget of £1650 millions, of which £1570 millions were to be devoted to the defence ministries themselves, and suggested that the question of allocation should be the subject of discussions between Simon, the Defence Ministers and himself. Inherent in Inskip's proposal was the continuing idea of the economy as the fourth arm of defence. As the Chancellor said, 'the Treasury really ought to be included as one of the Fighting Departments, as their contribution was as great as that of any.' Simon, warning that the question at hand was as serious a matter as any cabinet had ever had to face in time of peace, accepted Inskip's revised figures with reluctance. They would place a terrible strain on the national finances and could not be increased without financial disorganisation to an extent that could weaken the country. Yet he was ready, 'with a heavy heart', to agree also to an enquiry two years hence as he thought it would be wrong for a government to say rigidly that it could not spare more than a fixed amount for defence irrespective of the prevailing international situation. After considerable discussion the cabinet accepted Inskip's report.[37]

The cabinet's critical decisions on defence spending carried important implications for the direction of the country's foreign policy. As Inskip put it at the meeting held on 22 December:

In the long run the provision of adequate defences within the means at our disposal will only be achieved when our long-term foreign policy has succeeded in changing the present assumptions as to our potential enemies.[38]

In February he reiterated that it was beyond Britain's resources to make proper provision in peace for the defence of the Empire against three major powers (Germany, Italy and Japan) in three different theatres of war.[39] The developments of British foreign policy through 1938, which culminated in the infamous Munich settlement and in which Simon played no small part, are inexplicable unless this crucial link between defence spending and diplomacy is appreciated. In the Chancellor's thinking on defence expenditure the danger was that Britain might bankrupt herself in the attempt to sustain the arms race, unless agreement with the dictator powers could be quickly reached. Significantly the voice of Anthony Eden, the Foreign Secretary, had been among the more critical and sceptical at the two decisive cabinet meetings. In December he expressed his concern at the proposed change in the role of the British army, while in February he suggested that Inskip and Simon were projecting an unnecessarily pessimistic worst-case scenario in which Britain would have to face her enemies without allies. He, on the other hand, believed that much assistance would be forthcoming from France and the United States. Not surprisingly Simon and Eden found themselves at odds in those events which climaxed in the latter's resignation.

The first serious indication that Eden was out of step with the majority of his colleagues came in January 1938 when President Roosevelt sounded out the British government about a possible peace initiative. Eden was understandably enthusiastic, but Simon reflected the views of the majority of the government when, in a significant diary entry, he noted the other side of the question. The cabinet's Foreign Policy Committee had discussed the President's message and 'its bearing on our conciliatory plans to improve our relations with Italy'.[40] Chamberlain, Simon, Halifax and Inskip were hostile to Roosevelt's plan. They argued that, notwithstanding the President's fine words, America would never do anything practical to help Britain, while by contrast there was now a real possibility of improving relations with at least one of the European dictators, which Roosevelt's intervention was only likely to thwart.[41] 'May it be', asked Simon

that Italy thinks it is time to disentangle herself from the Spanish adventure and get her troops back? The news from Germany, that von Blomberg's resignation is accepted and Fritsch dismissed and that Hitler becomes supreme War Lord, with Goering a Field Marshal, may well make Mussolini anxious about Austria.[42]

Conventional historiography, conditioned on the one hand by the years of the war-time Special Relationship and on the other by Eden's later close association with Winston Churchill, has tended to support the Foreign Secretary's line in this governmental dispute. Yet, realistically, logic lay with Simon and the Prime Minister. America's neutrality legislation and the state of public opinion in the United States, not to mention the problems of Anglo-American relations over the preceding two decades, meant that few could legitimately expect Roosevelt's proposals to bear fruit.

Eden was temperamentally disinclined to negotiate with Mussolini, though strangely he had fewer qualms about Hitler. On the other hand Simon, like Chamberlain, believed that concrete gains were there for the taking. Not only might Italy pull out from the Spanish Civil War, but Italian troops might leave Libya and relations between Britain and Italy be improved in the Middle East and the Red Sea. The cost would involve no more than British recognition of the Italian conquest of Abyssinia, which was after all now an established fact. In an ideal world Simon's attitude might be characterised as unprincipled *real politik*, but the circumstances of 1938 were far from ideal and the government's policy options were extremely circumscribed. The Chancellor's thinking may not have been heroic; but it was realistic:

My view is that a friendly understanding with Italy, promptly arrived at, is of the greatest importance. We cannot prepare to fight Germany, Japan and Italy all at once: let us at any rate get rid of *one* potential enemy.[43]

Simon's relationship with Eden is among the more curious personal features of British history in the 1930s. His own papers display none of the animosity which leaps from the pages of Eden's diary. Indeed there is some evidence of warmth and affection.[44] Nonetheless contemporaries clearly believed that Simon was party to attempts to undermine Eden's position in the government from the autumn of 1937 onwards, particularly by spreading rumours about the state of the Foreign Secretary's health.[45] Yet Simon seems to have been taken by surprise by Eden's resignation the following February. As late as 12 February he was discounting press speculation that the question of negotiations with Italy would lead to a serious cabinet crisis.[46] Simon certainly seems to have appreciated that the resignation of as popular a minister as Eden might have had serious consequences for the National Government. J. P. L. Thomas, Eden's parliamentary private secretary, recorded a curious episode just before the Foreign Secretary decided to leave the government.

[Simon] opened by saying that he was as fond of Anthony as if he had been his own son, that he was becoming more and more depressed in watching A.E. at Cabinet Meetings and in realizing that he was both physically and mentally ill. Nothing but six months' holiday could restore him and that it was very important that I should go away with him. During this period he and his Cabinet colleagues would keep his seat warm for him and look after foreign affairs. I replied that Anthony had just returned from a good holiday in the South of France and that his health had indeed never been better. Simon then told me that resignation would be 'fatal to the Government, the country, nay the peace of the whole world'; that all this lay in my hands and he begged me to be sensible and take Anthony away. On my direct negative he popped his hat on his head, walked down the stairs and did not speak to me again until he had become Lord Chancellor in May 1940.[47]

The crucial meeting of the cabinet took place on 19 February. Developments on the continent ensured that the majority of ministers including Chamberlain and Simon would stick to their guns even if this meant losing their Foreign Secretary. In Austria the enforced appointment of the Nazi, Seyss-Inquart, as Minister of the Interior presaged a complete Nazi takeover of that country. The upshot, thought Simon, was that Italy would now be more anxious than ever to open conversations and follow up the personal approach which Chamberlain had made to Mussolini the previous July. Chamberlain and Simon were determined to respond, whatever objections Eden might raise. 'The international and the financial situation alike make it essential to reduce the risk abroad.'[48] Invited by the Prime Minister to speak after Eden in the cabinet discussion, Simon seized on the Foreign Secretary's admission that the difference between himself and Chamberlain was a question of method. 'We were all agreed that there should be Anglo-Italian conversations and the only query was on timing.' If the talks succeeded a great step would have been taken towards assuring peace and reducing Britain's liabilities. If they failed, nothing would really have been lost. But at all events Britain badly needed to take some positive action to give the smaller countries of Europe a sense of confidence in Britain and to show Hitler that Britain was 'not without resource'. Even though Italian good faith could not be taken for granted, it was worth taking the risk and giving Mussolini the benefit of the doubt. Mussolini had been keen on opening conversations for some time, so it could not be said that he was simply seeking to recover prestige after recent events in Austria.[49]

Despite further emergency meetings of the cabinet on Sunday, 20 February, Eden was now resolved to leave the government. His cabinet colleagues were surprised that he was ready to take so drastic a step when no insurmountable obstacles seemed to divide him from the Prime Minister.[50] But Eden now suggested that broader issues were at stake than had previously been implied. Simon spoke for the majority. He felt

rather disturbed and surprised at the extent of the ground of differences of opinion as stated by the Foreign Secretary. He had had special opportunities to observe these matters, and he had never realised the width of the breach.[51]

Contemporary bewilderment has been followed by historical uncertainty.

Subsequent writers have continued to place subtly different interpretations upon the Foreign Secretary's thinking and actions.[52] Visiting the Foreign Office, Simon said that he could not see that any point of principle was at stake. It was merely a question of timing,[53] but his contemporary diary reflections were perhaps more acute and perceptive:

The explanation of the trouble does not lie in any fundamental difference of policy but largely in the contrast between the temperament and methods of Stanley Baldwin and Neville Chamberlain. When Baldwin was Prime Minister he left the conduct of Foreign Affairs to Eden, and his own contribution was much more one of general reflection than of specific suggestion. Chamberlain is much more clear-cut and exercises the privilege of supervision and direction. . . .[54]

When the dust had settled and Chamberlain had appointed Lord Halifax to take over at the Foreign Office,[55] Simon sent Eden a personal letter. Denying that he had ever suggested that problems of health were at the root of Eden's decision, Simon ended in terms which the younger man must have found it difficult to accept at face value.

As we have been so closely associated at the FO, at Geneva and in the Cabinet, may I add this? You know, I think, that I have never failed you in comradeship and championship, and perhaps you may even remember that I did all I could to give you the first full opportunities of displaying your great qualities. All this makes me feel sad over the break beyond expression – though like everybody else in the Cabinet I am completely convinced that N.C. is right in opening conversations.[56]

In the event Eden's withdrawal from the government failed to create the shock waves which Simon had feared. No doubt in part this was because the retiring Foreign Secretary, keen not to cut all his ties with the government, declined to move into a position of outright opposition in the House of Commons, while his resignation speech left MPs as confused as his cabinet colleagues had been about the real reasons for his decision. Nonetheless Simon personally faced an uncomfortable situation when, on the Monday after the resignation, he answered Foreign Office questions in the Commons, only to be met by booing from the opposition benches.[57]

Eden's resignation opened the way for Chamberlain to exercise an increasing domination over the course of British foreign policy. Had Eden remained in office he might have exercised a moderating influence over the Prime Minister's single-minded commitment to his chosen course. As it was, the policy of appeasement, misguided if understandable, was pursued to its inevitable and tragic conclusion. It was founded upon the probably mistaken premise that a point of compromise must exist at which the dictator powers would be satisfied and content to live in peace with the other nations of the world – that their leaders were rational men capable of reaching a reasonable solution to outstanding issues. As 1938 progressed British diplomacy was more and more determined by a small group of men around the Prime Minister. The full cabinet was progressively eclipsed, first by its own Foreign

Policy Committee and latterly by an inner cabinet of Simon, Halifax, Hoare and Chamberlain himself. Samuel Hoare had urged Chamberlain at the outset of his premiership to utilise a small group of this nature to give a dynamic thrust to his administration and emphasise the contrast with the more lethargic ways of Stanley Baldwin.[58] Certainly the Inner Cabinet was a perfectly constitutional device, even though it largely failed to provide a critical examination of Neville Chamberlain's ideas. Its members have frequently been criticised for their supine acquiescence in the will of the Prime Minister, compounded, particularly in Simon's case, by sycophantic flattery.[59] In reality Chamberlain had surrounded himself with like-minded men who shared all the basic tenets of his own approach to the international situation. They shared by instict, training and experience the Prime Minister's aims, assumptions and methods. All remained convinced to the end of their lives of the fundamental correctness of what they had tried to achieve. All recognised the dangers posed by the dictators, particularly Hitler. Yet all believed that an agreement with them was possible, for all regarded the alternative – war – as an unacceptable option. What might have been a mechanism for the articulation of alternative ideas thus became merely a means of underlining the Prime Minister's personal control.

The generation in power in Britain in the late 1930s was a generation which had experienced at first hand the horrors of World War One. By this date these had been compounded in both the public and the official mind by the addition of aerial warfare and the bombing of civilians. In a war Britain was likely to face a combination of hostile powers with her own defences inadequate, her allies uncertain, her Dominions determined to make their own decisions as to intervention on behalf of the mother country and with an economy only recently and painfully nursed back to health. That war might indeed come, but, believed Simon and those who thought like him, the interests of humanity demanded that all alternatives should first be explored and, if it did come, that British diplomacy should by then have ensured that it involved the least threatening combination of enemy powers. Ultimately appeasement failed, and there is no better illustration of the maxim that history is the story of the victors than the debate carried on at the time and subsequently in much historical commentary between the appeasers and their critics. Yet Churchill's devastatingly sweeping comment that 'there never was a war more easy to stop'[60] is easier to repeat than to defend. Appeasement may not have been a wise policy. It was not an heroic policy. But it was not as dishonourable a policy as has so often been said, and it was one which made sense to the majority of people alive at the time.

Within a week of Eden's resignation Simon commented on 'an immense swing-over to the PM's side in all quarters where the vaguest idealism does not obscure realities'.[61] But if Chamberlain was now well and truly in charge of British diplomacy, British diplomacy in the late 1930s was never in a position to determine the agenda of the international arena. On 13 March

1938 Hitler's troops were welcomed into Austria and the strategic situation of Central Europe was transformed overnight. Czechoslovakia, its landmass now sliding tantalisingly into a voracious Nazi jaw, would clearly be the next object of Hitler's attention. The Anschluss had brought war much nearer, but it made Simon's position as Chancellor no easier. His task remained to strike a balance between financing rearmament now and retaining the economic strength to sustain a war later on. Simon expressed his dilemma graphically to his cabinet colleagues on 14 March:

At the present moment we were in the position of a runner in a race who wanted to reserve his spurt for the right time, but did not know where the finishing tape was.[62]

His own view was that recent events in Europe were not important enough to warrant a change in the policy agreed as recently as February. Certainly they had done nothing to increase Britain's financial resources nor to diminish the vital importance of those resources as an element in Britain's defensive strength.[63]

Such thinking determined the Chancellor's response to further proposals to expand the RAF. On 14 March Swinton urged the immediate adoption of the Air Ministry's Scheme K. But, as Simon noted, this would raise the total defence budget to £1735 millions and 'the danger was that we might knock our finances to pieces prematurely.'[64] Three weeks later Swinton was seeking approval for Scheme L, but Simon remained unmoved. It was, he said, a question in which every member of the cabinet had a responsibility and not one department alone, and he repeated his previous arguments about the importance of Britain's economic strength.[65] Before the meeting of the cabinet on 6 April Simon circulated a trenchant paper to his colleagues. He argued at two levels. From the financial point of view he believed it was possible to accelerate the completion of the existing Air Force programme including some increase in the first line strength of fighter aircraft without wrecking the overall financial limitations imposed by the cabinet less than two months before. In the second place Simon questioned whether the additional labour force required would be obtainable at the required dates and in the necessary numbers. Such a scale of industrial transference would be impossible unless the economy were put on a war footing. He believed that the wisest course would be to concentrate on improving the readiness for war of the force already authorised and to build up reserves behind the first line. As he reiterated at the cabinet on 6 April, it would 'be better to adopt the sound business method of not expanding the business until we were in a position to do so'.[66]

Inherent in Simon's thinking was the conviction that it would be futile to try to match Germany in terms of defence expenditure. He must have sent a shiver down the spine of his fellow ministers when he asserted that spending at the German level would require Nazi-like powers to control wages, enforce loans and avoid inflation. Higher defence expenditure could not be reached 'unless we turned ourselves into a different kind of nation'.[67] Simon's liberalism still burned too strongly for this to be an option while he was at the Treasury. His point may have been exaggerated, but it was certainly true that the British Chancellor of the Exchequer faced far more restrictions than his German opposite number. No British government could afford, for example, to neglect the social security system or cancel foreign debts with the mere stroke of a pen.[68]

With the Chancellor so reluctant to move his ground, it was impossible for the cabinet to reach any firm agreement on 6 April. At the end of the meeting Scheme L was submitted for further consideration to an informal committee of four ministers, Chamberlain, Simon, Inskip and Swinton. The matter was finally resolved on 27 April when the cabinet endorsed the recommendation of the informal committee that Britain 'should aim at the dual purpose both of securing acceleration of suitable types now in production and of bringing into production as early as possible the latest improved types' of aircraft. The Air Ministry appeared to have done quite well. But the actual excess over the rationed total was restricted to two years and the five-year total defence programme remained pegged at £1650 millions. The control of Simon and the Treasury remained as firm as before.[69]

Undaunted by the experience of the Air Ministry, the Admiralty too sought to challenge the Chancellor's authority. Duff Cooper's exchanges with Simon during the spring of 1938 became increasingly acrimonious. The First Lord launched a devastating attack on the whole principle of rationing in a paper sent to Chamberlain, Simon and Inskip on 28 April. It was, he said, the government's first duty 'to ensure the adequate defence of the country'.[70] Simon believed that the Admiralty had not even tried to cooperate in the rationing scheme and urged Cooper to itemise all the Admiralty's proposals.[71] Cooper and Simon met to discuss the matter on 9 May but 'the result of my conversation with the Chancellor . . . was, as I anticipated, Nil.'[72]

The worsening international situation determined the tone of Simon's second budget in April 1938 – 'our annual problem play presented in three acts'.[73] Inside the Treasury Sir Richard Hopkins had advised that the Anschluss had given an opportunity to win over public support for rearmament which would make it possible to raise more money by taxation or possibly by borrowing.[74] Estimated expenditure for the coming year stood at £1034 millions; estimated revenue on the present basis at £914 millions. Simon had already provided for the borrowing of £90 millions for defence expenditure. 'The all-important question,' he now told the House of Commons, 'is whether the gap is to be closed by resorting to fresh taxation or by resorting to further borrowing.'[75] Gasps went up when the Chancellor announced a rate of 5s. 6d. for income tax – 'a great shock to previous expectations'[76] – and Simon also increased the duty on oil and tea. In due course the budget was generally well received[77] and it is instructive to note the reaction of Harold Macmillan, generally a consistent backbench critic of the National Government. This was, thought Macmillan, the first budget which had confronted the country with any serious attempt to finance defence spending.[78] But, as Simon appreciated, the financial position was bound to deteriorate. 'There is a fearfully difficult budgetary conundrum preparing for next year.'[79]

★   ★   ★

The question of Czechoslovakia loomed ever larger on the horizons of British policy makers as 1938 progressed. Historical attention has focused inevitably and inexorably upon the ill-fated Munich Conference in September. Yet the broad outlines of British policy had been fixed much earlier in the year, particularly at important meetings of the cabinet's Foreign Policy Committee in March.[80] Here it became clear that the British government in the last resort would not fight for Czechoslovakia and would therefore not join in the French guarantee of that country. These conclusions formed the basis of Neville Chamberlain's statement to the House of Commons on 24 March. Criticism of the British government's policy can never be fully overcome. At the end of the day Britain did, at the behest of Hitler's threats and dictation, participate in the dismemberment of a sovereign state, a member of the League of Nations, which Britain herself had helped to create at the end of the First World War. But there was and there remains another side to the argument which merits consideration. Czechoslovakia was not, Simon believed, worth a war. Britain's primary objective remained to avoid a conflict with Germany and all the suffering and misery which that would entail. In his memoirs he described Czechoslovakia as 'an intense strain in the centre of Europe which, if it was not to lead from bad to worse, could only be relieved by a concession'.[81] Simon firmly believed that the Czech stated lacked legitimacy. It was indefensible not just militarily but also morally. He frequently wrote of 'Czecho-Slovakia' to emphasise the country's disunity. In March he had described it as 'a modern and very artificial creation with no real roots in the past'. He was, he said, 'much struck' by a report from the British Minister in Prague that even after a successful war against Germany the allies 'could certainly not contemplate the re-creation of Czechoslovkia'. It would simply fall apart. The *raison d'être* of a policy of resisting Hitler's demands for the Sudetenland was grounded in sand and could not be sustained.[82] The Sudeten Germans did, moreover, have a legitimate grievance. They had been incorporated into the Czech state in defiance of the principle of national self-determination which was supposed to underpin the whole of the Versailles settlement. 'I have been reading the documents placed before the Peace Conference by those who sought to establish the present

Czecho-Slovakian state,' wrote Simon at the height of the crisis in September. 'It is curious to contrast the assurance in these documents that Sudeten Germans would receive absolutely equal treatment in all respects and could have no possible grievances, with the facts as disclosed in Lord Runciman's report.'[83]

None of this, of course, constitutes a total vindication of the British government's line. It leaves Adolf Hitler and the National Socialist movement out of the Czech equation. If for no more serious reason Simon and those who thought like him stand indicted for a failure of imagination. Blindly they failed to recognise that a policy of concession and conciliation, which might have made good sense in normal times, performed only the service of whetting the insatiable appetite of the German dictator. The inherent nature of the Nazi regime should have precluded the sort of gentlemanly diplomatic dialogue in which the appeasers placed such faith.

Simon summarised the government's Czech policy in a diary entry towards the end of May:

We are endeavouring, at one and the same time, to restrain Germany by warning her that she must not assume that we could remain neutral if she crossed the frontier; to stimulate Prague to make concessions; and to make sure that France will not take some rash action such as mobilisation . . . under the delusion that we would join her in defence of Czechoslovakia. We won't and can't – but an open declaration to this effect would only give encouragement to Germany's intransigence. It is difficult to see a happy issue and a renewal of war in Europe never seemed more threatening.[84]

Despite this gloomy conclusion the avoidance of war remained Simon's guiding principle. 'J.S. takes our view strongly,' noted Sir Alexander Cadogan, the new Permanent Under-Secretary at the Foreign Office. 'We can't go to war.'[85] In public the Chancellor remained optimistic. Addressing an audience in Lincolnshire he said that he repudiated altogether the outlook which said that war was inevitable. He would rather hold the view that if we did our utmost to remove causes that might lead to war and tried to meet in a fair spirit the difficulties that arose from whatever quarter they came, then war was not inevitable.[86] But time was running out for a peaceful solution and, as the summer progressed, British policy became increasingly frantic. In August Lord Runciman headed a supposedly independent but government-encouraged mission to Prague to try to persuade the Czechs into making the sort of concessions which would satisfy both Hitler and the Sudetendeutsch. 'If you succeed,' wrote Simon to his old colleague, 'you ought to become the Earl of Marienbad-cum-Karlsbad.'[87] Simon regarded the Runciman mission as in keeping with the positive policy which the cabinet had pursued since Eden's resignation, though he feared that it would be difficult to maintain the mediator's independent status and that his position could prove embarrassing for the government. Nor was he over-optimistic of success. Any proposals were likely to alienate one side or the other and 'either way we are in danger of becoming involved'. But whatever happened he remained sure that the British people and their government meant to 'keep out of things'.[88]

As a member of Chamberlain's Inner Cabinet Simon played an increasingly important role as the Czech crisis moved towards its denouement. His relationship with Chamberlain became closer than ever before. He was 'a wonderful help . . . through all these difficult times', noted Chamberlain's wife.[89] The Prime Minister who, like Simon himself, had few intimates in politics, appreciated the support which Simon gave him. When, later in the year, the Chancellor was indisposed, Chamberlain expressed his feelings:

I confess that in these difficult times I do occasionally feel rather lonely and if you should become hors de combat I should miss terribly your counsel and support.[90]

At least as far as public consumption was concerned Britain appeared ready to stand firm. In August stories of German mobilisation prompted the government to reiterate the essence of Chamberlain's Commons statement of 24 March that if war broke out it would be impossible to say where it would end and which governments might become involved. As Simon had a long-standing engagement to address a rally in Lanark on 27 August, the task of stating government policy was entrusted to him. The Chancellor set out less to warn Hitler than to keep him guessing:

In the modern world there is no limit to the reactions of war. This very case of Czechoslovakia may be so critical for the future of Europe that it would be impossible to assume a limit to the disturbance that a conflict might involve, and everyone in every country who considers the consequences has to bear that in mind.[91]

Reactions to Simon's words were predictably varied. *The Times* and the *News Chronicle* praised the speech.[92] In the Foreign Office Cadogan thought it 'all right', though he warned that 'we mustn't dare Hitler to be humiliated too much.'[93]

The German press on the other hand was suitably hostile, while in Britain governmental critics such as Churchill and Boothby did not think that Simon had gone far enough towards issuing Hitler with an open public warning.[94] But it was no part of Simon's design to threaten Germany. As he himself explained:

It is quite certain that this country would never 'go to war for Czechoslovakia', but France is bound by treaty to defend her if she is attacked . . . and if Germany and France came to blows, no one can say whether we should not be drawn in. We therefore have to do everything we can to *dissuade* Hitler; hence my firm tone. At the same time, Benes must be helped or induced to make *large* concessions to the Sudeten Deutsch . . . We must act on the assumption that H. has *not* decided on invasion: we must leave him guessing as to our intentions; but we *must keep out*.[95]

If the Czech situation became too threatening Chamberlain had for some time been nurturing a bold plan based on personal diplomacy. At the beginning of September he confided to Simon and Halifax that if things got worse he would, at the appropriate moment, visit Hitler in person. The scheme was christened Plan Z so that it could be referred to in telegrams without being identified. But events moved so quickly that on the evening of 13 September Chamberlain sent a message to Hitler saying that he intended to come to Germany the next day and it was not until 14 September that the full cabinet heard of what had been decided. At this meeting Simon played that role of chief flatterer which, throughout his career, served to alienate him from so many of his colleagues. The Prime Minister was subjected to a shower of compliments from his Chancellor. Chamberlain's plan was 'brilliant'; his absence from Britain even for forty-eight hours would be 'grievous'; but if he returned with the seeds of an honourable peace it would be 'the greatest achievement'. 'Somehow or other,' noted Inskip, 'coming from Simon's lips they give an impression of soapiness and flattery which they do not deserve.'[96]

The history of the Prime Minister's dramatic trilogy of visits to Germany – visits which came to epitomise the very idea of 'appeasement' – has been related on numerous occasions. Emphasis here will be placed on identifying Simon's role in the story. At the Berchtesgaden meeting on 15 September Hitler insisted upon the right of self-determination for the Sudetenland. Chamberlain personally was ready to accept this solution if appropriate procedures were followed, but could not commit his government without further consultation. He proposed therefore to return to London and then visit Hitler again. It was also necessary to secure French approval. Daladier and Bonnet came to London for a conference on Sunday 18 September at which Chamberlain asked Simon, Halifax and Hoare to be with him throughout. Simon recorded:

It was quite evident that the French were at their wits end what to do in view of their treaty promising aid and assistance to Czecho-Slovakia.[97]

The British delegates retired to a separate room in 10 Downing Street to settle what they could offer and after three hours returned with the text of a proposed telegram to be sent by the French and themselves advising Czechoslovakia to transfer the territory and offering, if she did so, to join in an international guarantee of the new boundaries of the Czech state against unprovoked aggression. The French accepted this proposal 'with the greatest show of gratitude that I have ever seen in a spokesman of France'.[98]

Despite some misgivings the British cabinet also concurred and a plan was devised to provide for the cession to Germany of all areas of Czechoslovakia containing more than fifty per cent Germans. Unlike some of his colleagues Simon was clearly anxious to impose no restrictions upon the Prime Minister before he left for his second meeting with Hitler:

The Prime Minister was the only person who was in a position to compare what Herr Hitler said on the first occasion with what he might say in the resumed conversations.

It was therefore essential, at the outset at any rate, that [the negotiations] should be carried on by the Prime Minister.[99]

Indeed it was Simon's almost total faith in Chamberlain's capacity to cope with the situation singlehandedly which has most exposed him to subsequent criticism. Yet for a while Simon seemed unready to dance to the Prime Minister's tune. Before Chamberlain left for his second meeting with Hitler at Godesberg, Simon sent him a personal letter, stressing the extreme gravity of any plan for admitting German troops into the area before everything had been settled.[100] But both men were taken by surprise when Hitler stepped up his demands. At Godesberg a truculent Führer insisted upon the immediate German military occupation of the Sudetenland. Shaken and upset, yet still convinced that a settlement opening the way to improved Anglo-German relations was possible, Chamberlain returned again to London. Simon well captured the dilemma which now confronted the government:

On Chamberlain's return we had the most agonising of all our problems to solve. The cession of Sudetenland was agreed; the only question that remained was how it should be done. We had proposed a method of territorial transfer providing first by agreement for any inhabitants in the transferred territory, who did not wish to belong to the Reich, to opt and remove themselves and their belongings. Hitler proposed, instead, immediate occupation with the manifest probability that unpopular minorities would come under the Nazi heel and the worst features of the Austrian occupation might be repeated. Was this only a difference of method, in which we must give way, or was it not a difference so fundamental as to merit resistance even to the point of war?[101]

During Chamberlain's absence at Godesberg Simon had appeared ready to stand firm. In consultation with Halifax and Hoare he decided on 23 September, despite protests coming from the Prime Minister, that it was not possible to maintain the Anglo-French embargo on Czech mobilisation while that country seemed in imminent danger of invasion.[102] Later that day the Chancellor brought some of the other members of the cabinet up to date with the situation. Duff Cooper found him 'in a robust mood, prepared for the fray', but wondering how Chamberlain would react to the impasse. 'If the worst comes to the worst, will he be ready to go to war?'[103] When, however, on the following day Chamberlain reported back to the Inner Cabinet, Simon seemed to have lost his nerve. Cadogan, present at the meeting, recorded his impressions with some bitterness:

J.S. – seeing which way the cat was jumping – said that after all it was a question of 'modalities', whether the Germans went in now or later! Ye Gods![104]

Yet there was a certain logic in Simon's line. Apart from the brutality of the operation, the essentials of Hitler's new demands were not significantly different from the Berchtesgaden plan which had already been conceded.

Daladier and Bonnet returned to London for further discussions on 25 September, at which Simon sought to manipulate them into a confession of military hopelessness. Subjecting Daladier to the sort of cross-examination he usually reserved for the accused in a court of law, Simon finally extracted from the French premier an admission that on her own France could probably do little more than hold the Maginot Line, attempt probing operations against the Siegfried Line and make some demonstrations in the air. This exchange between Daladier and Simon could be said to encapsulate the whole debate over the rights and wrongs of appeasement. The French premier said that he was more interested at the moment in the moral issue than in strategy. The Berchtesgaden proposals had been bad enough, but where were they going to stop? He could not agree to the Godesberg demands as they stood. But Simon had no time for moralistic niceties. He remained convinced that there was no realistic alternative to accepting Hitler's demands. He persisted in asking whether, if the present plan were rejected, the decision would be to fight Germany and, if so, how.[105] Gamelin came over to London the following day to give further details, but made it plain that if German forces were now to invade Czechoslovakia, Czech resistance was likely to be of very short duration. Simon 'did not believe . . . that the French really intended any offensive operations against Germany at all.'[106]

Even if the French could be browbeaten in this manner, a large number of the cabinet were determined to call a halt. Simon, while recognising that Hitler's proposals were 'a shocking document', was ready to back the Prime Minister – 'urging further retreat' as Churchill put it.[107] But majority opinion, sustained now by Lord Halifax as Foreign Secretary, was against accepting the Godesberg demands.[108] While Chamberlain sought to keep the doors of negotiation open via his special emissary, Sir Horace Wilson, the nation prepared for war. What happened next would have constituted pure theatre had the stakes not been so high. While the Prime Minister was on his feet addressing the House of Commons on 28 September news came through that, under Mussolini's mediation, Hitler was ready to meet Chamberlain again at Munich. Alec Dunglass, the Prime Minister's Parliamentary Private Secretary, handed the message to Simon who was sitting next to Chamberlain on the government front bench. The scene which ensued has often been described, but Simon's account is worthy of repetition for its vividness and also for the sense of mistaken optimism which it conveys:

I waited for some time with the necessary sentences on a piece of paper in my hand, for I did not want to interrupt the current of his argument or throw him off balance by suddenly interjecting the joyful piece of news. At last during a burst of cheering I managed to whisper to him that Hitler's answer had come and gave him the passage to be inserted later on. This was to give him time to prepare for the announcement, which might make the difference between peace and war, before the actual moment came to make it . . . Then came the passage which suddenly turned gathering gloom into new hope and indeed may alter the course of the history of the world. It evoked a demonstration . . . the like of which has never been witnessed in Parliament . . . Chamberlain sat down beside me while most of his supporters and many other Members crowded round to wring his hand. It was incomparably the greatest piece of real drama that the House of Commons has ever witnessed.[109]

On Simon's suggestion the whole cabinet turned up at Heston airport to see the Prime Minister off on his fateful journey. Chamberlain returned having secured minor modifications to the Godesberg demands together with an Anglo-German declaration that the two countries would continue efforts to remove sources of difference by negotiation. The mood of emotional relief in the government and the nation at large was understandable enough. In the aftermath of the condemnation to which Munich has since been subjected, it is all too easy to forget what was majority opinion at the time. Simon expressed it at the first meeting of the cabinet after the Prime Minister's return. He thought the occasion justified a departure from normal procedure and, before the Prime Minister spoke, he expressed the cabinet's profound admiration for the unparalleled efforts Chamberlain had made and for the success he had achieved. He added that ministers were proud to be associated with the Prime Minister as his colleagues at this time.[110] Seen through the perspective of 1939 and 1940 Simon's words may seem hollow, but they were real enough when war had been so narrowly averted, as the crowds which lined Chamberlain's route from the airport and his postbag amply testified.

In later years Simon adopted a more balanced attitude towards Munich. It was, he told Duff Cooper shortly before his death, 'an inglorious episode' and he claimed to have been shocked by Chamberlain's injudicious remark about 'Peace for our Time' as the Prime Minister waved aloft the scrap of paper upon which he had secured Hitler's signature.[111] But Simon never wavered from his belief that Munich did constitute a positive achievement and that Chamberlain deserved well of his country for having secured it. It gave the nation another twelve months in which to prepare for Armageddon; it enabled the country to enter the war united in 1939, convinced by then that no other option remained; and it served to open the British people's eyes to Hitler's true character.[112] Yet in a revealing passage written in 1942 Simon put his finger on his own culpability in the whole affair:

Where there is grave reason after the event for reproach and repentence is in the refusal of the country and of great bodies in Parliament to face up to the need for great rearmament sooner than it did.[113]

It seems not to have occurred to him that the country and parliament needed to be led in the 1930s to accept the unpalatable truth about Hitler and the threat which he posed and that, as a prominent member of the National

Government after 1931, he bears his share of responsibility at the bar of history for creating the situation of 1938 which made the Munich settlement inescapable.

It fell to Simon on the third day of the parliamentary debate on Munich to make a major speech defending the settlement and moving that the House of Commons should approve the policy of the government by which war had been averted and support its efforts to secure a lasting peace. Chamberlain's speeches had necessarily been devoted mainly to a description of his negotiations with Hitler. Simon sought to show that what had been done was right. It was by all accounts one of his most impressive performances. 'The best speech I've heard you make and that's saying something,' wrote a governmental colleague.[114] 'Chips' Channon thought it 'magnificent'; Chamberlain described it as a masterpiece of close-knit argument and persuasive reasoning. 'The Opposition were quelled by it and kept silent.' From his retirement Baldwin wrote to congratulate Simon on 'a very great speech indeed'.[115] In the course of it Simon posed what was the central dilemma.

How many amongst us are there who, if we could, would undo what was then done, would reject the settlement to which the Prime Minister put his hand on Friday, and instead – because it was the only alternative – would fling the world into the cauldron of immediate war?[116]

Whatever they may have said in later years, few of Simon's critics were ready at the time to take up his challenge.

The pace of British rearmament did increase after Munich, though never to the extent that would fully justify the settlement as a dearly-won breathing space in which to gain time to face an inevitable conflict when Britain was better prepared. Thomas Jones suspected that Chamberlain and Simon were against an all-out programme of rearmament because of its effects on Britain's foreign trade. 'They are much more optimistic than I am about the good behaviour of the Dictators.'[117] After Munich the Treasury was less inclined than before to fix ceilings for defence expenditure, nor were departments asked to tailor their plans in accord with strict financial limits. Cases now tended to be considered on their merits. Yet, notwithstanding the government's increased awareness of the need for rearmament, Simon continued to exercise considerable control.[118] A month after Munich Simon argued strongly against the revived notion of a continental army, telling the cabinet committee on defence programmes and acceleration that Germany was extremely unlikely to violate Belgian neutrality and that the Maginot Line was probably 'the strongest system of fortification that had ever been constructed'.[119] 'Simon didn't like the cost; one could hardly expect him to,' noted the Director of Military Operations.[120]

When the Air Ministry put forward proposals to improve its position vis à vis potential enemies, Simon was ready to play his traditional role. Inside the Treasury Simon's senior advisers were clear that the Air Ministry's Scheme M threatened to destroy the country's economic viability.[121] Even Kingsley Wood conceded that the cost of his proposals would be staggering. Simon pointed out that if the proposals went forward without modification the Air Ministry would be spending in the five years to April 1942 a sum exceeding by nearly £350 millions the portion of the aggregate of £1650 millions allotted to it in February. The programme would have 'literally stupendous' results on the country's financial stability. This was at a time when the economy was slowing down and revenue sagging. The Chancellor painted a gloomy forecast. Excessive borrowing would lead to higher costs, higher wages and higher interest rates. Substantially increased imports and substantially reduced exports would worsen the already serious balance of payments situation. In the end Britain's monetary reserves might be exhausted and 'we should have lost the means of carrying on a long struggle altogether.'[122] The Chancellor was not quite as assertive and confident as he had been a year earlier. Simon no longer claimed that purely financial considerations could have priority over the urgent and definite needs of material defence. The two things had to be considered together. 'But the worst of all results would be to reach a position hereafter in which defence plans should be openly seen to have been frustrated by the financial and economic situation.'[123] Simon therefore urged concentration on producing the desired target of fighter aircraft by 1940 but only enough bombers to avoid substantial dismissals in the factories concerned. As his senior civil servant advised, parity with Germany was

an objective which we cannot attain and don't need. What we do need is to be a sufficiently unattractive hedgehog . . . [so that] the Germans will think many times before they ignore, and still more, attack us.[124]

With the Prime Minister again backing him, the main themes of Simon's advice were once more accepted by the cabinet at its meeting on 7 November. Simon calculated that current defence proposals would require £725 millions to be met either from borrowing or increased taxation over the next three years. 'The real question was whether this task was within our powers.' The cabinet, while agreeing to increase fighter strength by thirty per cent, decided to re-examine Kingsley Wood's appeal for an expanded bomber programme.[125]

In the first weeks of 1939, partly out of conviction and partly out of no more than hope, senior ministers seemed to be competing with one another in the optimism of their public statements on the international situation. Typical was Simon's speech to the British Iron and Steel Federation in February:

There is an increasing feeling all over the country that the prospects of peace are becoming more secure. We earnestly hope that this feeling may be well founded . . . You feel this growing confidence in the atmosphere. It is influencing the City. It is giving more encouragement to traders.[126]

Some regretted that the apparent improvement on the diplomatic front made it easier for Simon to reassert financial control. 'It is increasingly difficult,' noted the Director of Military Operations, 'to get big projects through, as the financial side comes heavily to play at once.'[127] By contrast with the European situation, the state of the domestic economy was causing Simon grave concern. In the middle of January he made an important statement to the cabinet. Since the previous April there had been a massive flow of funds from Britain largely because of anxious foreigners withdrawing capital to America because of the threatening international climate. Something like £150 millions of gold had been lost between the beginning of April and the end of September 1938, and not even the Munich settlement had altered the situation. 'It appeared only too evident that the view continued to be persistently held abroad that war was coming and that this country might not be ready for it.' He ended by drawing a chilling comparison between the existing situation and that which had obtained immediately before the financial crisis of 1931.[128] In such circumstances Simon was not going to sanction additional expenditure on armaments without a struggle. 'Large new additions to defence expenditure are still being proposed almost daily,' he complained a few days later. The Chancellor asked the Service Ministers to scrutinise their estimates closely and make the maximum possible reductions.[129]

The tide, however, was turning. Important to Simon's ascendancy had been the co-operation he had received in maintaining the Treasury's line from Sir Thomas Inskip as Minister for Coordination of Defence. But in January Inskip was succeeded by Lord Chatfield, an Admiral of the Fleet and former First Sea Lord, who made it clear that he intended to side with the service ministries.[130] After further discussions at the beginning of February on the role of the army, Simon concluded that none of his colleagues – with the significant exception of the Prime Minister – now placed much importance on finance as the fourth arm of defence.[131]

The Director of Military Operations marked the change of mood:

We got some admirable support from Halifax, who in response to Simon's bleats on finance said he would sooner be bankrupt in peace than beaten in a war against Germany.[132]

At the cabinet on 2 February Simon repeated all his forebodings. In the ensuing year there would be a vast gap to bridge between the sum available for defence from the budget and a defence expenditure of over £500 millions. He did not dispute that the Army's proposals could be represented as both urgent and necessary, but they had to be set against other competing claims. Once again the spectre of 1931, the *raison d'être* of the National Government itself, was trailed before the cabinet's eyes:

Once a loss of confidence showed itself on a wide scale, there would be no means of arresting it. We might be faced with a financial crisis as grave as that of 1931, but with . . . the foreign situation . . . far more serious.[133]

A compromise was reached. General approval was given for the provision of all twelve infantry divisions of the Territorial Army with full training equipment. But further discussion of War Office recommendations was deferred pending examination of the whole question by Simon, Hore-Belisha and Chatfield.[134] Perhaps sensing the way the argument was going Simon now secured cabinet approval for a Defence Loans Bill which would increase the government's borrowing powers by a further £400 millions.[135]

Finally, after lengthy ministerial discussions, the cabinet made its decision on the army's future on 22 February. Simon now had to concede that 'other aspects in this matter outweigh finance', and the cabinet accepted a Field Force of two mobile divisions, four regular and four Territorial Army divisions. As a sop to 'placate the Chancellor'[136] minor economies were announced including the postponement of two new colonial divisions. 'This indeed is a great victory!' purred General Pownall. The dominating influence of the Treasury in the shaping of Britain's foreign and defence policies was at an end.[137] The balance of power within the Chamberlain cabinet had thus shifted decisively before dramatic events in the international arena provided the *coup de grâce* to the whole policy of appeasement. On 15 March German troops marched into Prague and the independent Czech state, guaranteed by Britain at the time of the Munich settlement, ceased to exist. The moral basis of the National Government's foreign policy – if it had ever truly existed – collapsed at a stroke. Hitler, who had given assurances that he had no further territorial demands in Europe, could no longer claim that his ambitions were restricted to the incorporation of German peoples within the Reich. The unpalatable truth of naked Nazi aggression was revealed with brutal clarity. Simon, as closely associated as Chamberlain himself with the government's now discredited policy, would never be as powerful a force again.

Notes

1 K. Young (ed.), *Lockhart Diaries* ii, 42.
2 'Cato', *Guilty Men* (London, 1940).
3 Mr. A. J. P. Taylor, describing the refusal of the Labour party in September 1939 to join a government which contained Chamberlain and Simon, has written 'The objection to Chamberlain is easy to understand. But why Simon? Was it his conduct during the Manchurian affair? Or his later acts as Chancellor of the Exchequer? Perhaps only that he was a symbol of the National pretence as leader of the Liberal National Party.' D. Butler (ed.), *Coalitions in British*

Politics (London, 1978) p. 122. One of the aims of the present chapter is to answer this question.

4 Boothby to Lloyd George 10 Sept. 1939, Lloyd George MSS G/3/13/10.

5 F. Williams, *A Prime Minister Remembers* (London, 1961) p. 19.

6 N. Chamberlain to Simon 24 Dec. 1937, SP 84 fo. 170.

7 B. Webb diary 13 Dec. 1937.

8 Interestingly Dalton used the phrase 'Man of Manchukuo' in a House of Commons debate as late as July 1939.

9 A. H. Brodrick, *Near to Greatness* (London, 1965) p. 232. Cf. C. Wilmot, *The Struggle for Europe* (London, 1952) p. 35: 'The promised expansion of Fighter Command was delayed by the Treasury's reluctance to finance it. Simon, now Chancellor of the Exchequer, had evidently forgotten what he had learnt as Foreign Secretary from Hitler's own mouth.'

10 *Guilty Men* p. 100.

11 *Evening Standard* 26 Oct. 1938.

12 For the best analysis of this subject see G. C. Peden, *British Rearmament and the Treasury 1932–1939* (Edinburgh, 1979).

13 Simon diary 20 May 1937, SP 7 fo. 60; *Retrospect* p. 227.

14 See, for example, Peden, *Rearmament and Treasury* p. 18.

15 G. C. Peden, 'Keynes, the Economics of Rearmament and Appeasement' in W. Mommsen and L. Kettenacker (eds.), *The Fascist Challenge and the Policy of Appeasement* (London, 1983) pp. 142–56.

16 Inskip's Interim Report of Dec. 1937, cited Peden, *Rearmament and Treasury* p. 65.

17 He did not in fact move into the Chancellor's official home, 11 Downing Street, until October 1938.

18 Simon diary 15 Jan. 1938, SP 7 fo. 60; D. Jay, *Change and Fortune* (London, 1980) p. 69.

19 B. Sabine, *British Budgets in Peace and War 1932–1945* (London, 1970) p. 112.

20 Simon diary 15 Jan. 1938, SP 7 fo. 61.

21 Simon to Swinton 22 June 1937, cited M. Smith, *British Air Strategy between the Wars* (Oxford, 1984) p. 181.

22 Cabinet 30 June 1937, CAB 23/88; Gibbs, *Grand Strategy* pp. 279–81.

23 Ibid.

24 I. Colvin, *The Chamberlain Cabinet* (London, 1971) p. 44; K. Middlemas, *Diplomacy of Illusion* (London, 1972) p. 119.

25 R. Minney (ed.), *The Private Papers of Hore-Belisha* (London, 1960) pp. 35–6.

26 Cabinet 27 Oct. 1937, CAB 23/90A.

27 Ibid.

28 Cabinet 16 Feb. 1938, CAB 23/92.

29 Cabinet 22 Dec. 1937, CAB 23/90A.

30 J. Charmley, *Duff Cooper: The Authorised Biography* (London, 1986) p. 108.

31 B. Bond (ed.), *Chief of Staff* p. 194.

32 J. Harvey (ed.), *The Diplomatic Diaries of Oliver Harvey* (London, 1970) p. 51. Simon's perception of himself as the next Prime Minister was not widely shared. In March 1939 Gallup found that, of those who supported the government, 38 per cent would have chosen Eden to succeed Chamberlain, 7 per cent Halifax, 7 per cent Churchill and only 4 per cent Simon. G. Gordon, *British Seapower and*

Procurement between the Wars (London, 1988), p. 171.

33 Simon to Chamberlain 15 Jan. 1938, cited M. Gilbert, *Churchill* v, 895.

34 Minney, *Hore-Belisha* p. 87; A. Duff Cooper, *Old Men Forget* (London, 1953) p. 215.

35 Simon diary 23 Jan. 1938, SP 7 fo. 62.

36 Cooper, *Old Men Forget* p. 216; Roskill, *Naval Policy* ii, 423.

37 Cabinet 16 Feb. 1938, CAB 23/92.

38 Cabinet 22 Dec. 1937, CAB 23/90A.

39 Cabinet 16 Feb 1938, CAB 23/92.

40 Simon diary 23 Jan. 1938, SP 7 fo. 62.

41 Harvey, *Diplomatic Diaries* p. 74; Avon, *Facing the Dictators* p. 561.

42 Simon diary 5 Feb. 1938, SP 7 fo. 64.

43 Ibid 12 Feb. 1938, SP 7 fos. 64–64 bis.

44 Compare Eden's comment on Simon on 14 Oct. 1933: 'in characteristically bad state, snappy and scared to death. It is very difficult to feel anything but contempt for the man at these times,' (cited James, *Anthony Eden* p. 128) and Simon's friendly postscript on a formal letter to Eden the following June: 'This is according to Protocol. More briefly, "Dear Anthony, meet me at Geneva, Yrs. Cleopatra." 28 June 1934, FO 800/289.

45 R. James, *Eden* p. 180; Harvey, *Diplomatic Diaries* p. 61. 'Jim [Thomas] told H[orace] W[ilson] how Cartland had told him that Beverley Baxter . . . had been visited by both Simon and Hoare separately to explain that A.E.'s flu was the beginning of the end for A.E., that strain was too great and he would soon go.'

46 Simon diary 12 Feb. 1938, SP 7 fos. 64–64 bis.

47 Cited Avon, *Facing the Dictators* p. 585.

48 Simon diary 18 Feb. 1938, SP 7 fos. 64 bis –65.

49 Ibid 19 Feb. 1938, SP 7 fos. 67–8; CAB 23/92.

50 Lord Hailsham, the Lord Chancellor, told his son: 'I can't tell you why Anthony resigned because I couldn't make out myself.' N. Thompson, *The Anti-Appeasers* (Oxford, 1971) p. 145.

51 Cabinet 20 Feb. 1938, CAB 23/92.

52 Compare, for example, the accounts given by Eden's two most significant biographers: D. Carlton, *Anthony Eden*, chapter 4; R. R. James, *Anthony Eden*, chapter 5.

53 Harvey, *Diplomatic Diaries* pp. 94–5.

54 Simon diary 20 Feb. 1938, SP 7 fos. 68–9.

55 As Halifax was in the Lords, Simon now resumed responsibility along with the Prime Minister for speaking from the government front bench in the Commons on major questions of foreign policy.

56 Simon to Eden 23 Feb. 1938, SP 84 fos. 180–81.

57 Amery, *My Political Life* iii, 234; Winterton, *Orders* p. 230.

58 Hoare to Chamberlain 17 March 1937, Templewood MSS IX:2.

59 Cf. Liddell Hart's diary entry for 12 Sept. 1938. 'So far as [Eden] could see the determination of policy lay with Neville Chamberlain . . . Simon, Sam Hoare and Halifax. Chamberlain seemed disquietingly complacent, while Simon and Hoare had an underlying lack of virility. Thus too much depended on Halifax.' Liddell Hart, *Memoirs* ii, 163.

60 W. Churchill, *The Gathering Storm* (London, 1949) p. viii.
61 Simon diary 27 Feb. 1938, SP 7 fo. 70.
62 CAB 23/92.
63 Smith, *British Air Strategy* p. 204.
64 CAB 23/92.
65 Cabinet 6 April 1938, CAB 23/93.
66 Gibbs, *Grand Strategy* pp. 577–9; J. A. Cross, *Lord Swinton* (Oxford, 1982) p. 199; CAB 23/93.
67 CAB 23/93. Simon reiterated this theme later in the year at a meeting of the CID. Industrial mobilisation on the German scale was only possible in peacetime with a Hitler. Britain could adopt such practices only 'if we had a "Hitler" and a population prepared to accept a "Hitler".' W. Wark, *Ultimate Enemy* pp. 171–2.
68 Mommsen, *Fascist Challenge* p. 114.
69 CAB 23/93; Smith, *British Air Strategy* p. 204; Middlemas, *Illusion* p. 221.
70 Charmley, *Duff Cooper* pp. 111–12.
71 Haggie, *Britannia at Bay* p. 124.
72 Roskill, *Naval Policy* ii, 424.
73 H. of C. Debs., 5th Series, vol. 335, col. 43.
74 Peden, *Rearmament and Treasury* p. 93.
75 H. of C. Debs., 5th Series, vol. 335, col. 60.
76 Simon diary 26 April 1938, SP7 fo. 74a.
77 Peden, *Rearmament and Treasury* p. 92; Simon diary 8 May 1938, SP 7 fo. 74a.
78 H. of C. Debs., 5th Series, vol. 335, col. 241.
79 Simon diary 3 Aug. 1938, SP 7 fo. 75.
80 The members were Chamberlain, Simon, Hoare, Inskip, Halifax, Hailsham, Malcolm MacDonald, Ormsby-Gore and Oliver Stanley.
81 *Retrospect* p. 241. A. L. Rowse describes Simon's defence of Chamberlain and Munich in *Restrospect* as 'the poorest performance in advocacy that the famous advocate ever made.' *All Souls and Appeasement* pp. 57–8. This judgement seems a little harsh.
82 Colvin, *Chamberlain Cabinet* p. 110; Gilbert, *Churchill* v, 921. At the end of the crisis Simon reiterated that Czechoslovakia was an artificial, unstable structure, 'part of a French plan to keep Germany under control.' Simon to J. A. Spender 10 Oct. 1938, SP 85 fos. 77–8.
83 Simon diary 29 Sept. 1938, SP 10 fos. 1–7.
84 Ibid 22 May 1938, SP 7 fo. 74a.
85 D. Dilks (ed.), *The Diaries of Sir Alexander Cadogan* (London, 1971) p. 79.
86 *The Times* 28 May 1938.
87 Simon to Runciman 30 July 1938, Runciman MSS 292.
88 Simon diary 3 Aug. 1938, SP 7 fo. 75.
89 Annie Chamberlain to Simon 6 Oct. 1938, SP 85 fo. 61.
90 Chamberlain to Simon 16 Dec. 1938, SP 85 fo. 93.
91 Cited Dilks, *Cadogan Diaries* p. 90.
92 Gannon, *British Press* pp. 175, 207.
93 Dilks, *Cadogan Diaries* p. 91.
94 Gilbert, *Churchill* v, companion Pt. 3, p. 1147; Lord Boothby, *I Fight to Live* (London, 1947) pp. 156–7.

95 Simon diary 31 Aug. 1938, SP 7 fo. 77.

96 CAB 23/95; Inskip's diary 14 Sept. 1938, cited Heuston, *Lord Chancellors* i, 593.

97 Simon diary 29 Sept. 1938, SP 10 fos. 1–7.

98 Ibid.

99 Middlemas, *Illusion* p. 363.

100 Simon diary 29 Sept. 1938, SP 10 fos. 1–7.

101 Ibid.

102 Lord Birkenhead, *Halifax* p. 398.

103 Cooper, *Old Men Forget* pp. 233–4.

104 Dilks, *Cadogan Diaries* p. 103.

105 Lord Strang, *Home and Abroad* (London, 1956) p. 141; Dilks, *Cadogan Diaries* p. 105.

106 Simon diary 29 Sept. 1938, SP 10 fos. 1–7; *DBFP*, 3rd Series, vol. 2, no. 1093; Hoare noted that Simon's cross-examination of the French was 'resented'. Notes on 1937–39, Templewood MSS X:5.

107 Cabinet 25 Sept. 1938, CAB 23/95; Nicolson, *Diaries* i, 367.

108 Cabinet 25 Sept. 1938, CAB 23/95.

109 Simon diary 28 Sept. 1938, SP 10 fos. 11–12.

110 Cabinet 30 Sept. 1938, CAB 23/95.

111 Simon to Lord Norwich 30 Sept. 1952, SP 100 fo. 196.

112 Simon to Bechhofer Roberts 13 Nov. 1940, SP 87 fo. 27; Simon to T. Duffill Denman 31 Dec. 1942, SP 92 fo. 68a.

113 Simon to T. Duffill Denman 31 Dec. 1942, SP 92 fo. 68a.

114 E. Wallace to Simon 5 Oct. 1938, SP 85 fo. 39.

115 R. James, *Chips* p. 216; N. Chamberlain to Ida Chamberlain 9 Oct. 1938, Chamberlain MSS NC 18/1/1071; Baldwin to Simon 6 Oct. 1938, SP 85 fo. 52. *The Times* (6 Oct. 1938) enthused that Simon had returned 'to a parliamentary form which he had not touched since his famous speech during the General Strike'.

116 H. of C. Debs, 5th Series, vol. 339, cols. 349–50.

117 T. Jones, *Diary with Letters* p. 418.

118 Gibbs, *Grand Strategy* p. 296.

119 Gilbert, *Churchill* v, 1014.

120 Bond, *Chief of Staff* p. 167.

121 Peden, *Rearmament and Treasury* p. 133.

122 Cabinet 7 Nov. 1938, CAB 23/96. Concern about the balance of payments and Britain's gold and currency reserves determined the Chancellor's attitude towards requests from foreign governments for loans at this time. See, for example, cabinet meeting of 3 Oct. 1938, CAB 23/95. When Poland requested a loan, Simon reminded Chamberlain that 'further depletion of our gold stocks means a reduction of the time for which we could feed our people during a war.' Undated letter PREM 1/357, cited D. Kaiser, *Economic Diplomacy and the Origins of the Second World War* (Princeton, 1980) p. 306.

123 Gibbs, *Grand Strategy* pp. 296–8.

124 W. Fisher to Simon 5 Nov. 1938, cited Peden, *Rearmament and Treasury* p. 133.

125 CAB 23/96; Colvin, *Chamberlain Cabinet* p. 174; Smith, *British Air Strategy* pp. 218–20; R. Parkinson, *Peace for our Time* (London, 1971) pp. 77–8.

126 SP 250 fo. 26.
127 Bond, *Chief of Staff* p. 186.
128 Cabinet 18 Jan. 1939, CAB 23/97; Colvin, *Chamberlain Cabinet* pp. 178–9; Parkinson, *Peace for our Time* p. 92.
129 Gibbs, *Grand Strategy* p. 298.
130 Lord Chatfield, *It Might Happen Again* (London, 1947) p. 170.
131 Peden, *Rearmament and Treasury* p. 148.
132 Bond, *Chief of Staff* p. 185.
133 CAB 23/97; Colvin, *Chamberlain Cabinet* p. 183; Parkinson, *Peace for our Time* p. 100.
134 Cabinet 2 Feb. 1939, CAB 23/97; Gibbs, *Grand Strategy* pp. 510–11.
135 Cabinet 9 Feb. 1939, CAB 23/97.
136 Bond, *Chief of Staff* p. 189.
137 CAB 23/97; Peden, *Rearmament and Treasury* pp. 104, 148; Middlemas, *Illusion* p. 428.

CHAPTER TEN

NOT THE MAN FOR THE JOB

I am simply saying that opinion runs in a particular way and I do not know how it is to be combatted as long as the Chamberlain-Simon combination is the best that England can do.[1]

There seems little doubt that the German invasion of the rump Czechoslovak state on 15 March 1939 occasioned a major change in the means, if not necessarily the purpose, of British foreign policy. The avoidance of war with Germany remained the ultimate goal. Yet the British government was forced to concede that there were circumstances in which the country's interests would oblige it take up arms. A repetition of any-thing like the Munich settlement was probably impossible. Whatever Chamberlain and those who surrounded him might have preferred to do, the prevailing atmosphere in parliament, the press and the country conspired to limit their options and compel the Prime Minister in a significantly different direction. Yet, even now, Simon seemed reluctant to accept a change of course. Moreover, so closely associated was he with a line of policy which was now widely perceived to have failed that his own position in the government began to look more vulnerable than at any time since his last months as Foreign Secretary. As Britain moved ever closer to war with Nazi Germany, Simon looked an increasingly inappropriate figure to occupy the second place in the government.

The post-Prague change was not immediate.[2] When the cabinet met to consider the situation Simon wanted Chamberlain to make it clear that Britain was no longer bound by the guarantee to Czechoslovakia given at the time of the Munich settlement.[3] The Prime Minister agreed and the two men spoke in this vein in a heated House of Commons debate later that day. Their words were not what the House wanted to hear. Throughout the debate speakers urged that the events in Prague must persuade the govern-ment to abandon the policy of negotiating with probable enemies and institute instead a policy of allying with potential friends. From opposite sides of the chamber Eden and Dalton urged the creation of a system of mutual security to check any further aggression on Hitler's part. Duff Cooper, labelling Hitler a 'thrice-perjured traitor and breaker of oaths', was enthusiastically cheered. But Simon, winding up the debate, conveyed the impression that appeasement was still alive. His argument was based upon the sort of legalistic nicety which might have provoked a wry smile from an appreciative judge in a court of law, but which only created anger in the anxious House of Commons. Simon's point was that, as the state of Czechoslovakia had ceased to exist as a result of the Nazi invasion, there was nothing left for Britain to guarantee. 'It was indeed impossible to suppose that a guarantee to maintain the State of Czecho-Slovakia could have any meaning at all.' He deprecated any extension of Britain's commitments which would place the control of her destiny outside her own hands. Britain must be careful, he stressed, not to enter into any

extensive, indefinite commitments with the result that the control of our own action, and to a large extent the control of our own foreign policy, will depend not on this country, on this Parliament, on these electors, but upon a whole lot of foreign countries.[4]

In the abstract there was something to be said for Simon's words. They reflected the traditional concern of British foreign policy makers not to commit the country to unrealistic objectives and highlighted in advance the hollowness of the barrage of guarantees that the country would issue within the next few weeks. Yet in the context of the mood created by Hitler's latest treachery, Simon's speech was a miserable performance. He seemed to feel no responsibility for what had happened to Czechoslovakia, no doubts about the wisdom of the Munich settlement and he gave no sign that the government recognised that a review of its existing policies was needed. Not surprisingly the House of Commons responded with anger and resentment. 'The Chancellor's reply seemed to me deplorable and all in my group thought the same,' recalled Anthony Eden.[5] For once in his parliamentary career the communist, Willie Gallacher, spoke for a wide range of opinion in the House. Never, he stormed, had a government minister 'given such an exhibition of complete and hopeless political bankruptcy.'[6]

A radical change of temper, reflecting it seemed an explosion of public disquiet, immediately appeared in the British press. Simon was singled out for particular criticism. The *Daily Telegraph*, commenting on the Chancellor's Commons speech, pointed out that

the purpose of any commitment now envisaged is to aid the victim of an unprovoked aggression, and it is surely not the victim who decides whether there shall be an aggression. In a word, we find ourselves in a situation which demands a realistic not a legalistic view of our undertakings. The firmer and more decisive the policy of the Government the more certainly will they be assured of the unstinted support of the country.[7]

With pressure upon him coming also from parliament, the Conservative party, the Chiefs of Staff and the Foreign Office, Chamberlain prepared to change course. He adopted a significantly different tone in a speech in Birmingham on 17 March. No new policy was yet spelt out in detail, but Chamberlain revealed an awareness of the dangerous implications of Hitler's latest moves and declared himself ready to resist the domination of the world by force. On the following day he told the cabinet that Hitler's attitude 'made it impossible to continue to negotiate on the old basis with the Nazi regime'.[8] After two further rather frantic weeks the international situation and Britain's place within it had been transformed.

Simon had no alternative but to follow where the Prime Minister led. 'To my surprise,' noted Alexander Cadogan after a meeting of the cabinet's Foreign Policy Committee, 'no strong objections – even from JS – to our guarantee of Poland and Roumania.'[9] Harold Macmillan recorded that some of Chamberlain's colleagues had a legitimate grievance over the suddenness of his conversion.

Simon, for instance, like an old priest at some pagan altar, went on mumbling the obsolescent ritual of appeasement to a rapidly diminishing congregation.[10]

With greater accuracy it might be said that Simon's words and actions, more clearly than those of some of his colleagues, showed that while the mechanics of British policy had changed, its ultimate purpose – the avoidance of war – had not. All the measures that were now taken, including the guarantee of Polish independence issued on 31 March followed by similar guarantees to Greece and Roumania in April, aimed less to create a coalition to meet Germany in an impending and inevitable conflict than to restrain Hitler and possibly bring him again to the negotiating table. Indeed the wording of the Polish guarantee, covering as it did the country's independence rather than its territorial integrity, confirmed that further diplomatic initiatives towards Germany were not ruled out. Neither Chamberlain nor Simon yet perceived war to be unavoidable, though both recognised it as increasingly likely. As Simon stressed as late as June 1939, 'we are not preparing for war, we are constructing a peace front.'[11] Never in the period between March and September did he regard the state of the British economy as being ready for war.[12] If for no other reason a settlement with Germany, however distasteful, still made good sense to him.

In public Simon appeared steadfast. In the House of Commons he stressed that the government's pledge to Poland was perfectly straightforward and unequivocal: 'I do not think it was capable of being given some refined or unnatural meaning.' The government would throw its whole strength into the essential work of making the country stronger and more united.[13] Similarly, after the Italians moved into Albania in April, Simon defended the government against charges of hesitation and dawdling, and reemphasised that momentous changes had taken place in British policy.[14] In private, however, his tone was rather different. One of the concerns which Simon voiced at the time of the guarantee to Poland was that Britain might find herself at war solely because of a decision of the Polish government.[15] His hesitations were also evident when, with Chamberlain absent in Scotland, members of the cabinet met on 8 April to consider the situation created by the Italian invasion of Albania. It seemed clear, he said, that the present juncture did not justify Britain in taking steps which would result in European war:

It was, however, necessary that we should so conduct ourselves that we should not appear to condone aggression while, at the same time, we should not indulge in such strong rebukes as to make ourselves appear in a weak position.[16]

Two days later Simon urged procrastination in the face of calls for a guarantee of Roumania. If that country were to be invaded the government could at least say it was in consultation with Poland.[17] He only agreed to the idea of declarations of support for Greek and Turkish independence as it would make it easier to acquiesce in what had taken place in Albania.[18]

Changes in the nation's diplomatic commitments inevitably encouraged a reassessment of corresponding defence arrangements. The refusal to entertain a continental commitment now looked increasingly unrealistic, and indeed a Field Force of six divisions had been accepted at the end of February, before the Prague coup. Staff conversations with the French began at the end of March. When the cabinet considered Hore-Belisha's plans to raise the Territorial Army from 130,000 men to its war strength of 170,000 and then to double its size, Simon offered no opposition. He was, he said, impressed by the arguments put by Lord Halifax in favour of this expansion. The problem had to be looked at from a wider point of view than that of the Exchequer. It was all a far cry from the heyday of rationing a year earlier, though the Chancellor did set his face against the idea of adding a further 50,000 men to the regular army. 'He felt, that it was impossible for him . . . to accept this further very large commitment. The total liability thus involved was more than we could possibly bear.'[19] For the most part the tone of Simon's correspondence showed that he no longer had the whip hand. On 13 April Chatfield wrote, urging the desirability of fully equipping a ten-division Territorial Army of perhaps a quarter of a million men. 'Would it not be wiser,' asked Simon, 'to limit the initial programme to 8 divisions as something less unmanageable?' Significantly, however, he added, 'If you say that you are satisfied yourself in this I shall not oppose the ten divisions.' His worries remained, but he could only voice them. His word was no longer final:

What is really happening is that we are receiving a great change in the role of the Army and acting on that assumption without having really discussed and decided it. Is it possible to maintain a great Fleet and an immense Air Force requiring a vast labour force behind it, to sustain the dislocation of continued bombardment from the air, to provide munitions at a rate contemplated for allies as well as ourselves, and at the same time to fight with an unlimited Army on the continent backed by an unlimited supply of materials?[20]

When conscription was introduced at the end of April, Simon had 'an eye prepared to pick holes', but admitted that the case presented by Hore-Belisha was unanswerable.[21]

In the likely time available only limited progress was possible towards closing the military gap between Britain and her future enemies. As an ever increasing body of opinion appreciated, the only way to give substance to the country's new diplomatic initiatives was through closer association with the Soviet Union. In guaranteeing countries as far away as Poland and Roumania, Britain was involving herself in parts of Europe where traditionally, and even at the height of her power in the golden days of the *Pax Britannica*, her writ had never run. The Soviet Union alone had the military potential to make a British guarantee in Eastern Europe any more than a pious declaration of intent.

But closer association with communist Russia would require some deeply ingrained fears and suspicions to be overcome, not least in the minds of the Prime Minister and his Chancellor. Indeed, on the day after his Birmingham speech, Chamberlain followed Simon's advice and declined to support a Soviet proposal for an international conference of anti-Axis powers.[22] Once again, however, the government's public face was rather different. In the parliamentary debate on the Polish guarantee on 3 April speakers from all parties stressed that 'Russia is obviously the key.'[23] Simon replied that the opposition under-estimated the degree of difficulty in negotiating with the Soviet Union, but assured the Commons that the government would strive to conclude an agreement with her.[24] After the invasion of Albania, Dalton for the Labour party raised the question again, asking whether an Anglo-Franco-Soviet military alliance had been proposed to Moscow, and, if so, whether it had been rejected. Simon, answering for the government, tried to evade the question but, when pressed, stated that the government had no objection in principle to such an alliance.[25] His answer delighted Maisky, the Soviet ambassador in London.[26]

A. J. P. Taylor has written that 'if British diplomacy seriously aspired to alliance with Soviet Russia in 1939, then the negotiations towards this end were the most incompetent transactions since Lord North lost the American colonies.'[27] This is certainly an exaggeration, but many contemporaries saw Simon as responsible for the lack of enthusiasm with which Britain certainly pursued these talks. Hugh Dalton, for example, blamed him for introducing unnecessary complications at a late stage in the negotiations.[28] Contemporary evidence on the other hand does not support this view. The secretary's minutes suggest that Simon played no significant role in the cabinet discussions on Russia in May and behind the scenes he may even have helped to overcome the Prime Minister's reluctance to proceed with the talks.[29] Be that as it may, rumours of Simon's role indicate the extent to which opponents were ready to saddle him with responsibility for all that they disliked in government policy. Such innate hostility would be an important factor in determining Simon's fortunes in the crisis of May 1940.

That the Soviet talks proceeded at all was probably an indication that the Prime Minister's grip over the administration was slackening. One historian has argued that, by contrast with the period up to Prague, 'in the summer of 1939 Chamberlain no longer controlled foreign policy.'[30] Certainly, after Prague Chamberlain's position was never as dominating as it had been throughout 1938. As yet his control over the Conservative party machine remained unbroken and while this was the case his premiership was under no serious threat. For some of his senior ministers, on the other hand, the picture was less reassuring. Simon now became the subject of more hostile comment than he had experienced at any time since leaving the Foreign Office. It is impossible to escape the conclusion that he was a failing force within the government. His own health at the beginning of 1939 was not good; that of his wife was a source of constant concern. With the Treasury's grip over defence spending almost entirely relaxed – Warren Fisher wrote of the Treasury 'being progressively put out of action'[31] – Simon seemed to have lost his self-confidence, particularly inside the House of Commons.[32] Significantly the period between the Prague coup and the outbreak of war is covered in the most cursory fashion in his memoirs. From inside the Foreign Office Oliver Harvey had already urged Eden to use the deteriorating financial situation as grounds for pressing for Simon's removal.[33] On 3 April Archibald Sinclair, the Liberal party leader, launched a particularly strong attack upon the Chancellor:

For more than seven years the Chancellor of the Exchequer has been the evil genius of British foreign policy. It will be difficult for a Cabinet of which he remains a member to present that aspect of unity and resolve which the need of inspiring confidence in our friends imperatively demands. Men like the Chancellor of the Exchequer and the Home Secretary [Hoare], who have already once sabotaged the policy of collective security, ought to make way for men like Mr. Eden and Mr. Churchill, who have consistently advocated it.[34]

Some of the criticism was particularly selective. After talking to Vansittart, Hugh Dalton concluded that two out of the four members of the Inner Cabinet were 'not too bad', but that of the other two 'one is PM and the other [Simon] the snakiest of them all.'[35]

Calls for a reconstruction of the cabinet were becoming more common. One MP noted

a growing demand that Winston should be included in the Government . . . The real objection, of course, is that Simon and Sam foresee that all possible hopes of the Premiership for them are gone if Winston is in the Government.[36]

If Simon did still entertain such an ambition, he was almost alone in seeing it as a realistic possibility. Hailsham, now retired, regarded the very idea of 'such a person leading the Tory party' as 'too distasteful to contemplate'. Even Lord Alness, a life-long Liberal, was ready to consider Inskip, Hoare, Halifax or Kingsley Wood becoming Prime Minister – 'but Simon – impossible'.[37] By the summer Chamberlain himself admitted that Simon was neither liked nor admired.[38] The premier, for whom personal survival was always the most important consideration, may even have been contemplating replacing his Chancellor. Certainly he gave Maurice Hankey to understand that Simon had 'very much deteriorated'.[39]

Simon's standing was further damaged in the spring of 1939 by his insensitive handling of a controversy concering Czech gold. It became clear that at the end of March, in other words after the German seizure of Prague, the Bank of England had handed over to Germany £6 millions of Czech gold deposited on behalf of the Czech National Bank by the Bank of International Settlement. The story ran for several weeks and Simon, while denying that he had ever been consulted on the matter, faced difficult parliamentary questions in May and June. Technically the Chancellor's answers were all correct. The BIS and the Bank of England could not refuse to comply with the orders of a depositor; Simon as Chancellor had no authority over the BIS which had been specifically created as an autonomous financial organisation; the British government could not prevent the Bank of England from transferring the gold; and the Governor of the Bank, Montagu Norman, was not required to consult the government about such transactions. Yet it was easy enough to condemn Simon for the immorality of apparently rewarding the Nazis for their conquest and for the stupidity of lining the German war coffers. The Chancellor's handling of the question struck many as excessively legalistic, cynical and insincere.[40]

While others planned, predicted or speculated upon Simon's downfall, the Chancellor himself was busy producing his second budget. Income tax remained unchanged at 5s. 6d. in the pound, though surtax was raised. Modest increases in indirect taxation on cars, tobacco and sugar covered the anticipated deficit between income and expenditure, which was itself a direct consequence of the defence budget. It was in no sense a war budget and this fact opened up it and its author to much subsequent criticism. But the budget was reasonably well received at the time. *The Times* thought it 'exceedingly sensible', striking a reasonable balance between the general desirability of the country paying its way and the temporary impossibility of doing so.[41] Similarly the *Daily Telegraph*, generally no friend of the National Government, found little cause to criticise the Chancellor either for the proportions in which he had elected to charge his defence expenditure as between taxation and borrowing, or for the distribution of the new burdens of taxation.[42]

The motivation behind Simon's caution was no doubt complex. He remained concerned not to overstrain the economy when the nation's timetable of future requirements was still uncertain. War might come within a matter of weeks; it might not come for a year or more; it might still be avoided. As he told the cabinet in July:

It was impossible to say when war might break out. If it should break out some years hence it was important that those who were responsible for policy should realise that our financial strength was then likely to be much weaker than it was today.[43]

Above all, however, it is still possible to detect the reluctance of a man of peace to accept the fact of imminent war. His public pronouncements remained optimistic. 'As the weeks and months go by,' he told an audience in June, 'I get increasing confidence that our efforts for peace will succeed. We have been through much worse weather than we have to face today.'[44] Simon's own later assertion that the six months before the outbreak of war saw 'a redoubling of effort in every department to meet what was destined to come' represents an exaggeration of what the National Government achieved at this time.[45] Be that as it may, it was not long before Simon was contemplating an autumn budget with large increases in taxation.[46]

Though the Treasury could no longer force ministers to choose between strategic priorities, Simon tried hard to reassert some of his old authority. On 23 May the cabinet considered a paper from the Chancellor entitled 'Control of Expenditure' which drew attention to the seriousness of the financial situation and asked for 'closer control of ordering and spending'. There was, Simon said, a grave danger that within six or twelve months the country would find itself in a very serious position. Resources were being expended at an alarming rate and the limit to the rate at which money could be raised had already been reached. With backing from the Prime Minister Simon's paper and his proposal for a Committee of Control were accepted.[47] Another success for the Chancellor came over the issue of financial assistance to Poland. 'The real question,' said Simon, 'was how much was it within our power to do, even at the cost of weakening our own position.' The cabinet agreed that proposals for political loans and credits to other nations should be submitted in the form of a statement by the Foreign Secretary to the Chancellor.[48]

Lying behind Simon's attempts to resurrect a modicum of financial restraint was his mounting anxiety about the state of the economy. The estimate made in February of £580 millions for defence expenditure in the financial year 1939 had been increased to £630 millions in April and to £750 millions in July. The calculations contained in Simon's budget statement soon looked irrelevant. The Chancellor placed his concern before the cabinet in two papers presented on 5 July. The first dealt with the country's financial situation and began with an examination of the 'war chest'. There were, it said, four possible sources from which Britain might pay for imported goods in wartime – exports, sterling balances and stocks of gold, foreign securities owned by British subjects and loans from abroad. None of these elements could be viewed as satisfactory. The balance of trade was far less strong than it had been in 1914. Sterling balances and gold reserves were falling as a result of overseas purchases for the rearmament programme. Available foreign securities totalled only about £200 millions. The potential for borrowing was also limited. Under the terms of the Johnson Act Britain would not be in a position to borrow from the United States as she had done during the last war. Simon's comparisons with 1914 were particularly telling not just because the experience of the Great War was indelibly imprinted upon the mind of the ruling elite of the 1930s, but also because they came from one of only two members of the present cabinet who had held comparable rank at the outbreak of the previous conflict.[49] 'We should realise,' Simon concluded, 'that we were steadily reducing our war chest.' In essence the Chancellor was reiterating his long-held belief that Britain could not afford a major war or a protracted arms race.

Simon's paper went on to consider the money available for defence spending. His conclusion was that to maintain the present scale of rearmament quasi-wartime controls over the economy would soon be necessary. He was clearly seeking to fix new ceilings on defence expenditure:

Further expenditure on armaments in this country cannot be undertaken without counting the cost in gold. . . . Indeed, as there is a prospect of the continuance of the present armed peace, if not of the outbreak of war, finality of expenditure (unless for overmastering reasons) should now be declared.[50]

Simon's second paper dealt with the 'German Financial Effort for Rearmament'. Its purpose seemed to be to make the British situation appear even more alarming. Though based on sketchy intelligence information, the paper concluded that Germany had a larger sum to spend on armaments than Britain and that she could probably maintain spending on this basis for a long time. Germany was now reaping the fruits of her long-term policy to create a self-sufficient economy. 'The question of the means of payment for overseas imports in war – an ever present anxiety in our case – scarcely arises in Germany.'[51] Though some members felt that the picture drawn was too gloomy, the cabinet agreed to take note of Simon's papers.

Simon's tune had scarcely changed when the cabinet reassembled in late August after an unusually short summer break. Sombrely he told his colleagues that the loss of British gold reserves had become a flood, amounting to £30 millions in one day. It would soon be necessary to take drastic action since the amount of gold remaining in the Exchange Equalisation Account had to be regarded as the minimum required for the War Chest. The Chancellor secured the cabinet's authority to change the existing exchange rate of the pound if this proved necessary.[52] Events on the international front, however, were now moving with a speed which would invalidate all the Treasury's calculations. On 21 August Anglo-French negotiations with the Soviet Union broke down on the question of transit rights for the Red Army through Poland and Roumania. On 22 August news came through that Nazi Germany and Soviet Russia were about to sign a pact of non-aggression. On 1 September the forces of Germany moved speedily into Poland. The world waited for the British government to honour its treaty of guarantee.

★ ★ ★

The war crisis of 1939 involved one of the most important and surprising episodes in Simon's career. A. J. P. Taylor has written that 'the man who had been on the point of resigning in protest against the First World War gave the final push into the second.'[53] Two events on 1 September underlined the paradox of Simon's position. While his role was crucial in getting Britain into war against Germany, some still regarded his membership of the executive as unacceptable. On that day Chamberlain invited the Labour party to join his government. According to Hugh Dalton Labour could not enter a cabinet in which Chamberlain and Simon were numbers one and two.[54] Elsewhere that day Simon encountered the Polish Ambassador in London, Count Raczynski, and grasped him by the hand. 'We can shake hands now,' he said, 'we are all in the same boat. . . . Britain is not in the habit of deserting her friends.'[55]

In Berlin Sir Nevile Henderson delivered a note to the German government which warned that unless Britain received satisfactory assurances that Germany had suspended all aggressive action against Poland and was prepared to withdraw her forces from Polish territory, 'His Majesty's Government will without hesitation fulfil their obligations to Poland.'[56] That statement was clear enough and there seems little doubt that Chamberlain himself now accepted that war was inevitable.[57] His overriding concern, however, was to keep in step with the French government and in straining to do so the inevitable delays gave rise to the belief that the Prime Minister was once again seeking to extricate himself by diplomatic means. Thus the warning delivered to Germany had contained no time limit. With Chamberlain busy negotiating with France, it was arranged that Simon should go in his place to make a statement on the situation to the House of Commons at 2.45 p.m. on 2 September. Simon's statement was to indicate that no reply had been received from Hitler and to stress that Britain would not be prepared to wait more than a very short time longer. Two or three minutes before the House met, however, a message reached Simon via Halifax and Oliver Harvey that a communication had just been received from Italy proposing a conference. Halifax and Simon decided that they must postpone the Commons statement and consult the Prime Minister. But Simon agreed with the Foreign Secretary that no conference could be contemplated while German forces were on Polish soil and added his belief that the proposal was a 'plant to gain time and allow more ships out, etc'.[58] Accordingly, parliament was told to await a later statement by the Prime Minister himself.

The cabinet met later that afternoon to hear of the Italian proposals and the reaction to them of the Prime Minister and Foreign Secretary. It appeared that Chamberlain and Halifax favoured an armistice in Poland with the forces on both sides halted where they were in order to give

Hitler until noon on the following day to consider the proposal for a conference. But the conference itself was only to be entered upon if Hitler agreed to withdraw German troops from Poland. Simon was 'horrified' at what he regarded as the first instance of bad judgment by Chamberlain and Halifax.[59] The Chancellor felt it impossible to concede to Hitler the right to remain on Polish soil merely in order to give him time to reflect on the conference proposal. Majority opinion in the cabinet was with him. No terms could be acceptable which did not include the immediate withdrawal of German forces, which had after all been a condition laid down in the message which Henderson had delivered to Ribbentrop the previous night. In the end the cabinet concluded that Britain could not countenance any delaying tactics and that, in the absence of a satisfactory German under-taking to withdraw, the country ought to be at war by midnight.[60]

Before the Prime Minister addressed the Commons at 7.45 p.m., it had become clear that the French were still not ready to adopt as prompt a time-table as the British cabinet had just agreed. As a result, Chamberlain's statement appeared to go back on the cabinet decision of only two hours before as he studiously avoided mentioning any deadline. 'We expected one of his dramatic surprises,' noted Harold Nicolson. 'But none came.'[61] The reaction among both MPs and cabinet ministers was extreme. Arthur Greenwood, acting leader of the Labour party, declared to cries of 'Speak for England' that he was gravely disturbed:

The moment that act of aggression took place one of the most important treaties of modern times automatically came into operation. . . . I wonder how long we are prepared to vacillate at a time when Britain and all that Britain stands for, and human civilization, are in peril.[62]

Inevitably Chamberlain's speech had given the impression that 'we are weakening on our undertaking to Poland and that the French were ratting.'[63] Simon had never seen such a sudden reversal of feeling in his thirty years' experience in the House of Commons.[64] Ironically, in view of the role which the Chancellor was now to play, Dalton recorded:

In the Lobbies afterwards there was a terrific buzz. It almost seemed that, on a free vote, Chamberlain and Simon would have been overthrown.[65]

When the Commons rose something like ten members of the cabinet assembled in Simon's room in the House of Commons.[66] What followed was as near to a cabinet revolt as ever occurred during Chamberlain's premiership.[67] On the whole the rebels were the less senior members of the cabinet and it is at first sight surprising that they should have chosen Simon, with his long-standing reputation as the government's arch-appeaser, as their standard bearer. But the Chancellor had made his own position clear at the meeting of the cabinet that afternoon and ministers would have known that his very loyalty to the Prime Minister made him more likely than anyone else to be able to influence Chamberlain. All the rebels expressed their surprise that Chamberlain's Commons statement had differed so fundamentally from the earlier cabinet decision and yet had been announced without another cabinet being called. Even the guarded words of Simon's diary account cannot conceal the anger which the Prime Minister's actions had aroused:

The language and feelings of some of my colleagues were so strong and deep that I thought it right at once to inform the Prime Minister, who was still in his room at the House. He asked me to bring in the protesting and disappointed Ministers and invited me to state the difficulty. I did so very briefly and moderately, and I think I conveyed to the Prime Minister the undoubted fact that this was no exhibition of disloyalty or disunity, but proceeded from a deep concern lest the policy announced had these grave implications [of dejecting the Poles and being exploited by German propaganda.][68]

The Prime Minister 'seemed a little rattled and his face was deeply lined'.[69] But he reacted calmly and sought to explain the difficulties he had experienced over coordinating British action with that of France. Immediately after this meeting Simon and the dissenting ministers gathered again and authorised the Chancellor to write to Chamberlain rehearsing their anxieties and stressing their view that, at the outside and only as the price of securing synchronisation with the French, the expiry of an ultimatum to Germany should extend to noon on 3 September. At 10 p.m., while the Simon group were in further discussions in the Chancellor's room at the Commons, a message came from Downing Street asking Simon to go over immediately. On arrival Simon found the Prime Minister with Halifax and Corbin, the French ambassador. It was clear that Chamberlain expected him to explain to the ambassador that French delays were creating a most serious political situation for the British Prime Minister. Simon responded dutifully:

For the first time since the crisis loomed up there were signs of cleavage in the House and the Prime Minister's position as leader of the whole nation was in danger of being challenged.[70]

Despite French protests Simon insisted that, as parliament was due to meet at noon on the following day, it was imperative that Chamberlain should be in a position to make a definite announcement – either that Hitler had agreed to withdraw or that a state of war existed. When Corbin had gone the Prime Minister decided to hold another meeting of the cabinet. Ministers were hastily assembled, some from their beds, and the meeting began at 11 p.m. Governmental unity had now been restored. At Simon's suggestion the expiry time for the British ultimatum was moved to 11 a.m. rather than midday, so that when the Prime Minister spoke there would be no problem in announcing whether or not the country was at war. This was agreed. 'So

ended this remarkable day,' recorded Simon, 'the last day of peace, possibly, that I shall ever see.'[71]

   Simon clearly played a decisive role at this most important moment in his
country's history. Had the details been more widely known at the time, his
position within the government would surely have been strengthened. Yet
even some of those who were aware of what had happened could not bring
themselves to make a charitable interpretation of Simon's actions.
Channon, for example, supposed that the Chancellor 'saw his chance of
becoming PM.'[72] In later years, when Simon came to write his memoirs,
this was clearly an episode upon which many writers in the same position
would have dwelt, perhaps at the expense of the reputation of Neville
Chamberlain, by then long dead. But it was to Simon's credit, and indicative
of one of the more admirable sides to his character, that he made no attempt
in his published version of events to draw credit upon himself.[73] Even in his
contemporary diary account Simon showed charity towards Chamberlain
over the difficult decisions which the Prime Minister had had to take:

The real credit of the conclusion rests with Chamberlain, whose patience under
almost unbelievably trying conditions is a marvel and who never for a moment
misunderstood the differences expressed by his colleagues as anything but genuine
efforts to help him.[74]

Simon felt that Chamberlain had misjudged the situation, but no more. No
doubt remembering the response of the House of Commons to his own
similar error of judgment after the Prague coup, he recognised more clearly
than did the Prime Minister that parliament should not be given the impression that Britain would in any way backtrack on her obligation to Poland.

With the outbreak of war Chamberlain followed the lessons which had
been so painfully and slowly learnt in the Great War and immediately took
steps to streamline the government. A War Cabinet was created of nine
members, although Labour refused an invitation to join a coalition. Simon
retained his post as Chancellor of the Exchequer and his status as
Chamberlain's number two. It was an important position. As Simon himself
put it, 'Practically everything of importance which is decided in carrying on a
war involves finance.'[75] But with Churchill now restored to the ranks of
government as First Lord of the Admiralty, the Chamberlain cabinet would
never again be the supine body controlled by the Prime Minister that it had
sometimes appeared before. That, however, is not to say that Churchill
found himself seriously at odds with the men who were now his colleagues,
but of whose policies he had previously been so critical. A month into the
War Chamberlain wrote that he had not constructed his cabinet according to
any theory governing its size or nature. His sole purpose had been to

construct an executive which would work. This meant that '*personalities* must be taken into account and in that I seem to have been successful.'[76] It was a view Simon shared. He wrote of the War Cabinet as 'an extremely united body, with no internal strain of any kind' and added that the Prime Minister had proved 'absolutely first-class' in promoting team work.[77] One of the striking features of this period was the close cooperation between Chamberlain and Churchill and their growing mutual respect for one another, a neglected and perhaps significant aspect of the history of these years.[78]

It was, of course, the period of the 'Phoney War'. While the German forces overran Poland, there was little that the Anglo-French alliance could do. Poland's salvation could only come at the end of a long and successful conflict with Germany. It was a difficult decision to take, but Simon was confident that it was correct. Gestures at this stage might appear heroic, but they could prove foolhardy. 'The squandering of resources in a vain effort to give immediate proof of our willingness to aid would only lose the war in the end.'[79] Simon captured the government's dilemma:

It is very difficult to decide whether, in order to demonstrate the reality of our intervention, we should stage some positive attack on Germany by air at this moment. The trouble is that there is nothing that we can do to help Poland in her extremity by sending supplies etc. And that has always been recognised. It looks as though Germany is being as careful as she can to attack only military objectives in Poland and we do not want to be the first to be involved in damaging civilian populations.[80]

Thus Britain waited for the 'real' war to begin and the country's first experience of hostilities was nothing like as painful as had been predicted. All-out conflict was unlikely before the following spring:

Our troops are steadily assembling in France and Gamelin has a very large French army facing the Siegfried Line. But it is difficult to believe that a major attack on either side will take place soon, and winter is advancing.[81]

Simon feared that as soon as Hitler had over-run Poland he would turn westwards, not with arms but with an offer of peace, inviting France and Britain to accept the new situation and to realise that any further warfare would be of their creation.[82] When, however, Hitler's 'peace offer' arrived, Simon agreed that no trust could be placed in any promise the Führer might make and that a peaceful settlement was unlikely while the present German government was in power. Along with Chamberlain, Churchill and Halifax, Simon helped draft Britain's rejection of Hitler's overture. The conclusion was stark but inescapable:

I fear we are forced to the horrible conclusion that unless Hitler, owing to internal pressure, climbs down (which at this stage seems most unlikely) there is no choice but to undergo the dreadful trial of intense warfare. And then, out of the ruins of the

world, there may be some brave and farsighted people left who would build a better
one.[83]

For Simon the fact of phoney war was doubly significant. In the first place
it gave men time for recrimination. The government's foreign policy had
self-evidently failed, war had indeed come, and yet those who had presided
over the drift into that conflict were still in office. Past failings would not now
be forgotten. Anthony Eden, restored to government as Dominions Secretary but without a seat in the War Cabinet, recalled that Simon and Hoare
were particularly criticised for their earlier policies. 'The Dominion High
Commissioners would voice their feelings about them to me, vigorously if
unofficially.'[84] Robert Boothby spoke for many. Chamberlain, Simon, Halifax and Hoare had 'landed us in this deplorable situation. . . . Why should it
be supposed that they can get us out of it?'

I am convinced that if the poison which now infects the body politic . . . is to be
removed; and if the nation is to go forward with full strength, resolution and
confidence; then the authors of our present misfortunes . . . will have to go. . . .[85]

Hugh Dalton harboured similar thoughts. A number of ministers, he told
R.A. Butler, Under-Secretary at the Foreign Office, should be sacked as
incapable of running the War. 'I suggested that Simon should be shot first.'[86]
Though the period of phoney war was probably vital in giving Britain time to
prepare herself for sterner trials ahead, it appeared to many that the country
was once again losing the initiative – just as she always had done throughout
the decade. Richard Law, son of the former Prime Minister, well captured a
common feeling of the time in a speech to the House of Commons in March
1940:

In the last few years I and every hon. Member have witnessed one or other prominent
member of the Government – the Prime Minister or the Chancellor of the Exchequer
or the Lord Privy Seal [Hoare] – come down to the House and stand at that Box in the
midst of the wreckage of some policy or other, and explain that there was nothing
that could possibly have been done. That has happened time after time. . . . I am
convinced that the country today is not getting the leadership, drive, determination
and decision which it deserves.[87]

Some predicted that the formation of a Churchill government was only a
matter of time and that this would mean the end of Simon's ministerial
career.[88] Others foresaw that when the period of phoney war ended public
opinion would compel the formation of a Coalition. It was evident, noted
Harold Nicolson, that none of the opposition leaders would enter a cabinet
which contained Chamberlain, Simon and Hoare.[89] In the second place the
absence of full-blown military operations inevitably directed attention away
from the service ministries and towards those such as the Treasury which
were expected to put Britain in a position to win the War when fighting
began in earnest. Thus Simon's conduct as Chancellor was scrutinised more

closely than ever before; and perceptions were generally unfavourable. Even in the first month of the War R. A. Butler remarked that 'if any Department was losing the War, it was the Treasury.'[90]

As Chancellor in the first stages of the War Simon warned of the dangers of inflation and appealed to the nation to save and to lend its money to the government. He brought his concerns to the War Cabinet on 11 September. Here he called for the restriction of unnecessary imports, especially those involving payments in scarce currencies, the encouragement of exports, the reduction of payments by the Defence Services, particularly in North America, to the absolute minimum of essential and speedily available resources and the maintenance of firm controls over demands on the country's exchange resources from her allies, particularly France. As far as curbing inflation was concerned, the cabinet accepted Simon's view that now was the time for introducing heavy increases in taxation to deflate the economy.[91] Many of the Chancellor's preoccupations were unchanged from the pre-war era. He was still concerned that the country should husband its resources so as to survive a long conflict.[92] On 22 September the War Cabinet considered a three-year plan involving a great increase in the size of the Air Force and Army. Simon presented a memorandum showing the effect which so great an additional effort would have on expenditure and particularly on dollar reserves, as there would have to be immense buying of machine tools from the United States. Total expenditure was already higher than it had been in 1918. The supplying of 55 divisions, when added to the Air Programme for an output of 2550 aircraft a month, would involve very serious difficulties in regard to dollar exchange by the end of the second year of war. Simon's logic was probably impeccable, but in a sense it was irrelevant. The government now had no alternative but to prepare itself militarily as best it could. Simon well captured the balance of the discussion:

The deductions from my figures could not be challenged, but, as the Prime Minister said, it is the uncertain factor which we must not forget, and if the war did last for three years, we must hope that American aid would go far to meet the immediate financial difficulty. The only thing that matters is to win the war, even though we go bankrupt in the process. There would be no comfort if we lost the war in the reflection that we still possessed a credit balance in dollars. On this basis I agreed to the decision, treating it rather as a target to be aimed at than as a scheme well within our present powers.[93]

With daily meetings of the War Cabinet and various cabinet committees as well as his Treasury work, Simon was fully occupied. But his most important task was to prepare an emergency budget and present it before the end of September.[94] At 3.45 p.m. on Wednesday 27 September he rose to present it to the House of Commons. His custom as Chancellor during budget speeches was to sip a mixture of honey, brown sugar, lemon and water. In the circumstances of the day it seemed an appropriately sober concoction. Reiterating that finance was the nation's fourth arm of defence, his theme was that 'if the price of victory is high, it is worth paying.' The need was to propose additional taxation for the possibility of a three-year war. He aimed also to avoid a competitive scramble for goods in which prices would rise and the value of money fall. The arrangement of his speech was something to which Simon gave considerable thought. Early on in his relatively short 1¼-hour speech he announced that the standard rate of income tax would rise to 7s. 6d. in the pound. The news was greeted with a gasp. 'The crowded House was dumbfounded, yet took it good-naturedly enough.'[95] Thereafter his other measures seemed light by comparison:

Having sustained the initial shock of the increase in income tax, Members were almost hilarious over the later proposals. It was as though they had been suffering from very bad tooth ache and took refuge in laughing gas.[96]

Allowances were to be reduced and there were increases in the duty on alcohol, tobacco and sugar. Trades benefitting from the War would pay an excess profits tax of 60 per cent. Altogether Simon added £107 millions to the present year's revenue and £226.5 millions to that of the following year. Even so this still left £1000 millions to be raised by borrowing before 31 March, 'and that is a stupendous task'.[97]

Churchill had urged the Chancellor to bring in a severe budget based upon 'the broad masses of the well-to-do'.[98] Judging by the reaction of 'Chips' Channon, a representative of that class, he had succeeded:

Simon . . . practically demolished the edifice of capitalism. One felt like an Aunt Sally under his attacks . . . blow after blow. . . . It is all so bad that one can only make the best of it and reorganise one's life accordingly.[99]

Reactions generally were more favourable, although the Labour party opposed the increase in the sugar tax, while editorials in *The Times* and the *Economist* questioned whether the Chancellor had gone far enough.[100] The Prime Minister approved, convinced that Simon was right to begin now to get a substantial addition to tax revenues 'while the going is good'.[101]

With the Finance Bill safely enacted, much of Simon's time in the autumn was taken up with co-ordinating economic relations with the French. His broad aim was to persuade them to shoulder an equal share of the financial burden of the War with Britain.[102] But his French opposite number, Paul Reynaud, argued that as the wealth of France was only a third of that of Britain, aid to the allies of the two countries should be paid out in the same proportions.[103] Most outstanding matters were successfully concluded at talks in Paris between the two men at the beginning of December.[104]

On the domestic front co-ordination of economic policy was also a priority and by early October Chamberlain had appointed Simon to chair a ministerial committee charged with this task. It included Hoare as Chairman of the Home Policy Committee and a number of other ministers who were not members of the War Cabinet. It would not, thought Simon, be easy to reconcile all the conflicting forces in the economic field.[105] The Treasury also secured the help of a number of academic economists and business men. It was attempting to manage the economy through the normal peacetime methods of interdepartmental conciliation and consensus, but opinion was growing that Simon was not up to the burden of the work involved. Despite the apparent mark of favour by the Prime Minister in giving Simon the chairmanship of the Co-ordinating Committee, his position was increasingly under attack. The Prime Minister's private office and close advisers were quietly discussing possible alternative Chancellors, including even Reginald McKenna, who had last held the job in 1916. The Chief Whip, regarding Simon as an 'egotistic intriguer', was even ready to consider his own claims to the post.[106] With Chamberlain frequently laid up with gout, Simon took the chair at several meetings of the War Cabinet. It was scarcely a position in which he was likely to shine. 'The Cabinet was not so well run as usual' was General Ironside's verdict on one such occasion.[107]

The Chancellor's reluctance to take decisive action or to give a lead was never more damaging to his standing than in these first months of the War. One supporter, commending the 'quiet display of restraint and breeding', felt that the 'Chamberlain-Simon method [had] given us a strength beyond the understanding of those who like flagwagging and epigrams', but this was not a common sentiment.[108] 'The present front-bench are an uninspiring crew,' remarked Boothby. 'I should say that neither Simon nor Hoare has any following anywhere.'[109] *The Times* picked up a remark which Simon made that 'most of the economic problems in conducting a war consist of a conflict of arguments'. These words, so typical of Simon's whole approach, were, thought *The Times*, the strongest reason for putting economic policy in the hands of someone who could take decisions, instead of stating a case, however admirably, on both sides.[110] It is interesting to note two conflicting accounts of the Prime Minister's Mansion House speech in November. With Chamberlain laid low, Simon had to speak in his stead. Simon himself recorded:

Chamberlain is a very methodical person and he had written out every word of his speech last night. So instead of any impromptu effort on my part, I read his manuscript and did it well enough to evoke great enthusiasm.[111]

Chamberlain's private secretary left a very different account:

Simon proved obstinate, unbelievably unhelpful and ended by leaving half of the speech behind. Arthur Rucker pursued him with it to the Mansion House in a taxi.[112]

At some point the desire for a new face at the Exchequer reached the Prime Minister himself. Possibly Chamberlain had never forgiven Simon for his role in the war crisis. Certainly he felt very bitterly towards those ministers who had taken part in the cabinet revolt on 2 September.[113] Be that as it may, by late December very secret soundings were being made regarding the possibility of an enabling bill to allow a peer to speak but not vote in the Commons, so that Lord Stamp, the economist and businessman, whose standing in the Treasury had grown considerably during the autumn, could succeed Simon. The latter might become Lord President in a cabinet reshuffle.[114] This peculiar episode, which may have originated in the mind of Montagu Norman, the Governor of the Bank of England, has left little documentary evidence behind it. But Sir John Colville recalled Norman, 'wearing a black cloak and, with his short beard, closely resembling Mephistopheles', arriving after dark for meetings with Horace Wilson to discuss the details of the plan. 'It was usually my job to let him in, because even our respectable messengers must not be allowed to see him.'[115] Chamberlain saw Stamp at the beginning of January, but the latter was reluctant to become Chancellor. The planned governmental reconstruction also involved Leslie Hore-Belisha whose position at the War Office had become untenable as far as senior generals were concerned. One idea was that Hore-Belisha should move to the Board of Trade. This he was only prepared to consider if it involved control of economic coordination, which Simon refused to countenance.[116] The Chancellor also seems to have blocked Sam Hoare's appointment to a similar position.[117] In the event the fact that Hore-Belisha left the government altogether may have persuaded Chamberlain not to press Stamp any further over the Exchequer.[118] Like Simon, Hore-Belisha belonged to the Liberal National group and the demotion of both men might have had unfortunate consequences for the loyalty of the thirty or so Liberal National MPs supporting the government.[119] At all events Simon seems to have been blissfully unaware of the plans for his removal and for the time being the Chancellor remained at his post.[120]

Still, however, Simon found it difficult to avoid controversy. Almost all his actions and pronouncements caused resentment somewhere. 'A Chancellor of the Exchequer expects to be cursed,' he announced and this was certainly the case in wartime.[121] As Chancellor his duty remained to warn his colleagues of the financial consequences of their war strategy,[122] but in doing so he risked being accused of a half-hearted approach to the quest for victory. His wireless broadcast urging people to save and not waste money on Christmas presents was criticised for damaging trade.[123] Calls for increased welfare benefits filled him with alarm. In November he told the War Cabinet that 'we should be lucky if we were able to get through the war without a reduction in the standard of our social services.'[124] In January, however, Simon had to bow to increased political pressure and introduce a scheme of supplementary allowances with age concessions for insured women. The additional assistance took the form of a supplementary pension paid through the Post Office after the application of a means test.[125] Inflation was another continuing concern. The government was spending about £1 million a week to stabilise prices, but Simon was ready to abandon this strategy if trade unions failed to moderate wage demands. His hope was to boost exports in traditional commodities in order to earn the foreign exchange needed to buy war materials from the United States. With foresight he also appreciated that such a strategy would have long-term benefits. Britain's post-war trading position would be gravely weakened if pre-war markets were lost as they had been after the last war.[126] Lying behind all these difficulties was Simon's clear conviction that the financial demands of the War were going to get far heavier. 'Nobody realises yet', he told John Colville, 'what privations we have got to face.'[127]

In February 1940 the Opposition picked up the idea of economic coordination, with Herbert Morrison calling in the House of Commons for the creation of a new ministry. In part this sortie was directed against Simon personally. The Chancellor rose to the challenge and delivered what Colville heard was 'the speech of his life'. The gist of his argument was that it was impossible to distinguish between economic and financial policy and that only the Chancellor could have overall control.[128] For Simon to retain this ascendancy it was essential that his spring budget be well received. The Chancellor approached his task with some trepidation. His budget was 'perfectly horrifying' and he could only hope that the German attack on the Western Front would coincide with Budget Day to distract attention![129] Nor was the climate favourable. After the collapse of Finland in March, Oliver Harvey noted that the government's stock was 'very low indeed, especially Simon and Hoare'.[130] There was probably little Britain could have done to help the Finns, except at the risk of starting a conflict with the Soviet Union, but the impression created by British inactivity was nonetheless unfortunate.[131] In these circumstances, and on St. George's Day, Simon delivered his last and longest budget speech of two hours and nine minutes.

The Chancellor estimated expenditure for the year at £2667 millions. Existing taxes would produce £1133 millions to which he now added a further £101 millions. Income tax was confirmed at 7s. 6d. in the pound, tax allowances were reduced all round and there were increased duties on postal charges, tobacco, alcohol and matches. This still left £1433 millions to be found during the year. Simon rejected Keynes' plea for a forced loan and pinned his faith on voluntary savings. It was again a fairly cautious budget and reactions were mixed. Simon himself predicted that there would be those who would criticise him for not estimating for enough expenditure and for not raising enough in taxation.[132] He was not mistaken. A *Punch* cartoon pictured a tax-payer declaring: 'I tell you income tax at 7 and 6 pence is outrageous – it should have been ten shillings at least!'[133] One of the most trenchant critiques came from his old friend Leo Amery, who regarded the budget as 'yet one more proof of the complete incapacity of the Government to realize the seriousness of the situation or the kind of effort required to meet it'. Amery told the Commons that Germany was still spending fifty per cent more than Britain on the War. The budget was no more than provisional, a stop-gap budget which had not even stopped that year's gap and which would require to be supplemented later in the year.[134] From the Labour benches Aneurin Bevan made his attack more personal. It was a bad business, he said, that after eight months of warfare the country should have a budget which disclosed so appalling a failure to organise the whole of the resources of the country. 'We have a Chancellor of the Exchequer . . . whose name is despised throughout the world'.[135] To begin with press reaction to the budget was reasonably favourable. The *Daily Telegraph* described it as 'bold and realistic'.[136] But as the days passed opinion began to change. The *Manchester Guardian* wrote of 'too little courage' and *The Times* shifted its line after publication of a damning letter from Maynard Keynes. The latter complained that Simon had grossly underestimated the nation's capacity for sacrifice. 'I marvel how little the country understands (and how shamefully little the Chancellor does to enlighten it) what sacrifices victory will require.'[137]

Much subsequent opinion has been far more sympathetic to Simon's handling of wartime finance.[138] To an extent he was the prisoner of the slow momentum of war production, which was largely outside his control. Expenditure was only one of the factors which governed the rate of armaments production. Simon's gradualist approach to increases in taxation made the task of his successor later in the War much easier. Indeed, it is clear that Simon himself was ready to raise more money when he deemed the moment to be right. In May he told a National Savings Association lunch that

We will put no limit on that which we have to spend, because we must at all costs put forward our maximum possible effort for the purpose of winning the war. There is no other limit than that.[139]

The proposals made in the budget were in fact more imaginative than Simon was given credit for. Three achievements of this, his last, budget stand out. It legislated for the taxation of excess rents; it provided for the introduction of purchase tax; and it refined his earlier Excess Profits Tax.[140] None of this, however, counted for much in the spring of 1940. In the minds of a substantial number of people Simon had once again displayed his incapacity for high office.

The catalyst for change would come when the phoney war ended and genuine hostilities involving Britain got under way. Even so there was some irony in Simon's position being so vulnerable to a change in military conditions, since he adopted a far more realistic attitude towards the future than did the Prime Minister. While Chamberlain repeated in both public and private his unfortunate belief that Hitler had 'missed the bus', Simon warned against complacency. A broadcast he made in March was typical. The greatest danger facing the British people, he said, was that of drawing the false conclusion that because the full rigours and hardships of war had not yet touched them, victory would be cheaply and easily secured. This was 'a most dangerous delusion'. The only wise course was to resolve to face the strength of Germany for as long as was necessary and to vow that the only possible conclusion of the War was the disappearance of Hitlerism.[141]

Unbeknown to Chamberlain the Germans had been planning the conquest of Scandinavia. On the night of 8/9 April German troops landed at all the main Norwegian ports, including Narvik in the far north. At the same time the Germans launched an invasion of Denmark, largely by land. Though Denmark was lost, Simon accepted the need to try to turn the enemy out of Norway, most importantly because otherwise they would become sole controllers and exporters of the iron ore from the north of Sweden.[142] There ensued a period of open struggle between the British and German navies along the coast of Norway. Troops were despatched a few days later but by the end of the month it was clear that the Allied operation could not succeed. The enemy was too firmly entrenched while British forces were short of artillery and aircraft. In late April, after less than two weeks of fighting, orders were given for the evacuation of central Norway. Though Simon had noted at the beginning of the month that the Prime Minister's position was stronger than it had ever been,[143] these developments set in motion events which culminated in the fall of the government.

Simon appears not to have anticipated the pent-up emotions which were now released. The Norwegian episode, he assured a gathering of his Liberal National followers, would not become a matter of political controversy. The government had the situation well in hand and was ready at the right moment to explain the whole matter frankly and fully to the British people.[144] It was a grave misjudgement. The reality of the German menace now looked much more real than hitherto. One dissident Tory complained of the 'terrible complacency' of Chamberlain, Simon and Hoare:

We all behave as if we had three years or more in which to win the war, whereas it is certain that it is in the next 4 or at latest 5 months that Hitler will stake his all in an attempt to administer a knock-out blow.[145]

Elsewhere knives were being sharpened. Dalton told an audience in Cambridge that for prestige abroad and confidence at home to be restored, there had to be drastic changes:

Mr Chamberlain and Sir John Simon are our two greatest liabilities both at home and abroad. They would best serve their country by resigning now.[146]

A two-day House of Commons debate on the Norwegian campaign was held on 7 and 8 May. Critical to the future of the government was Labour's decision to table a motion of censure and ultimately to press it to a division.

In the course of these two days what began as a critique of a specific military operation – from which Churchill as First Lord of the Admiralty might logically have expected to incur most hostility – became a thorough-going denunciation of the government's conduct of the War as a whole, with Chamberlain, Simon and Hoare as the primary targets. Simon captured the irony of what was taking place:

Really the Government's case is unassailable so far as the actual operations in Norway are concerned . . . It will certainly be an odd result if Churchill . . . who is more directly responsible for recent decisions on tactics and strategy in Norway than any of his colleagues, should be elevated into the PM's place.[147]

Some speakers took the argument even further back and produced an indictment of the whole of the National Government's foreign policy since 1931. All Labour's bitter resentment over the failure of successive governments to uphold a policy of collective security before the War now came out. On 8 May Herbert Morrison spoke from the Labour front bench.

We have felt that the whole spirit, tempo and temperament of at least some Ministers have been wrong, inadequate and unsuitable. I am bound to refer, in particular, to the Prime Minister, the Chancellor of the Exchequer and the Secretary of State for Air [Hoare]. I cannot forget that in relation to the conduct of British foreign policy between 1931 and 1939, they were consistently and persistently wrong. I regard them as being, perhaps more than any other three men, responsible for the fact that we are involved in a war which the wise collective organisation of peace could have prevented, and just as they lacked courage, initiative, imagination, psychological understanding, liveliness and self-respect in the conduct of foreign policy, so I feel that the absence of those qualities has manifested itself in the actual conduct of the war. I have the genuine apprehension that if these men remain in office, we run [a] grave risk of losing this war.[148]

As Simon saw, such arguments could only strengthen Churchill's position. The latter 'has the advantage that he has no responsibility for anything which occurred before the war'.[149]

It was a debate of virtuoso performances. Leo Amery, Lloyd George and Roger Keyes, the last resplendent in the uniform of an Admiral of the Fleet, all made dramatic contributions. Amery's withering attack on the Prime Minister has often been quoted, but he also had harsh words for Simon, repeating his earlier criticisms of the Chancellor's management of the war economy and arguing that the gap between Britain and Germany was continuing to widen.[150] After the first day of the debate deep gloom pervaded the Prime Minister's camp. Plans were hatched to reconstitute the government, including an offer to Labour of a coalition in return for dropping Simon and Hoare while Chamberlain retained the premiership.[151] Alec Dunglass, the Prime Minister's Parliamentary Private Secretary, and the government whips dropped hints to dissident backbenchers that Simon and Hoare would be sacked if the government got safely through the vote in the division.[152] Conservatives such as Patrick Hannon encouraged the Prime Minister to believe that he could survive providing these two ministers were eliminated.[153] The formation of a truly National Government seemed now to be the need of the hour and it soon became clear that a change in the premiership would be a precondition of Labour's entry into a coalition. It took Chamberlain some time to realise that he would not be able to save his own skin simply by throwing his most unpopular ministers overboard.[154] The Prime Minister seemed 'determined to stick on', noted Dalton:

like a dirty old piece of chewing gum on the leg of a chair, as someone said – but is offering to get rid of Simon, Hoare and, if need be Kingsley Wood, if this would propitiate critics. It will not.[155]

Dalton was personally prepared to draw a distinction between Simon and Hoare in the latter's favour, but no one seemed ready to see the Chancellor remain in office:

In our view Chamberlain and Simon had failed so often, both in peace and war, and had such long crime sheets, that they must go.[156]

The debate ended with a government majority of 81. In technical terms this constituted a victory, but as the government's normal majority was about 200, it was clear that there had been a very serious revolt. Simon had sought out dissident Conservatives in the Lobbies and the Commons Smoking Room and warned them, without success, that a bad result for the government might prompt Hitler to strike westwards. Chamberlain, who had been having urgent talks with Halifax and Churchill, asked to see Simon at 4 p.m. on 9 May. Only Simon's account of this conversation survives. According to the Chancellor, he urged Chamberlain to stand firm, but to carry out a substantial reconstruction of the government:

I proposed to him therefore that he should at once get rid of myself and of Sam Hoare; if that would stop the rot nobody would cheer more loudly than I should. The PM said 'that is just like you John', and I was glad to feel that he was really moved.[157]

But Chamberlain had now come to see that the essential outcome of the crisis was that Labour should come into the government and that for this purpose it was necessary for someone else to be Prime Minister. Reluctantly Simon agreed. Chamberlain's inclination during his interview with Simon was to resign and advise the King to send for Halifax, but later that afternoon he saw Halifax again and the latter effectively ruled himself out of contention by raising objections to his own position as a peer. In such a situation the way was opened for Winston Churchill to assume the highest office of state.

Simon could only await his fate. When news came through that Germany had indeed attacked in the West, he thought for a moment that changes in the government might be delayed.[158] It was not to be. His own future now looked bleak:

The Labour Party have been put in a position where they can almost name their own terms, for they have been told that they are indispensable. . . . I should think that the next condition will be to be presented with the head of John Simon on a charger and I shall most cheerfully comply.[159]

Lady Simon, still in poor health, was already preparing to leave London and 'I expect I shall follow in my new character as a purely private citizen before the day is out.'[160] Yet fate – or Winston Churchill – determined otherwise and a last and not undistinguished chapter in Simon's long political career was about to open up.

Notes

1 T. Jones, *Diary with Letters* p. 434.
2 Interestingly, this fact is glossed over in Simon's memoirs, where Chamberlain's Birmingham speech on 17 March is made to appear the government's first reaction to the Prague coup. *Retrospect* p. 251.
3 Cabinet 15 March 1939, CAB 23/98; S. Newman, *March 1939 : The British Guarantee to Poland* (Oxford, 1976) p. 100.
4 House of Commons Debates, 5th Series, vol. 345, cols. 435–564.
5 Lord Avon, *The Reckoning* (London, 1965) p. 46.
6 House of Commons Debs, 5th Series, vol. 345, col. 559.
7 *Daily Telegraph* 25 March 1939; F. R. Gannon, *The British Press and Nazi Germany 1936–1939* (Oxford, 1971) p. 243.
8 Cabinet 18 March 1939, CAB 23/98. Chamberlain now excused his earlier line by saying that it had been unfortunate that Opposition demands had made it necessary to hold a parliamentary debate 'immediately on the heel' of the Czech coup.
9 Dilks, *Cadogan Diaries* p. 164.
10 Macmillan, *Winds of Change* p. 566.
11 Colvin, *Chamberlain Cabinet* p. 216.
12 See below pp. 276–8.
13 H of C Debs, 5th Series, vol. 345, cols. 2581–8.
14 Ibid, vol. 346, cols. 131–40.
15 Cabinet 30 March 1939, CAB 23/98; S. Aster, *1939: The Making of the Second World War* (London, 1973) p. 104.
16 Cabinet 8 April 1939, CAB 23/98; N. Gibbs, *Grand Strategy* p. 708.
17 Foreign Policy Committee 10 April 1939, Aster, *1939* p. 139.
18 Cabinet 10 April 1939, CAB 23/98; Aster, *1939* p. 134.
19 Cabinets 29 March 1939 and 5 April 1939, CAB 23/98; Aster, *1939* pp. 98–9; Peden, *Rearmament and Treasury* p. 148; Parkinson, *Peace for our Time* pp. 131–2; Minney, *Hore-Belisha* pp. 188–9.

20 P. Cosgrave, *Churchill at War* (London, 1974) pp. 44–5.

21 Minney, *Hore-Belisha* p. 197.

22 B. Gilbert, *Britain since 1918* (London, 1980) p. 113.

23 The quotation is from the Liberal leader, Archibald Sinclair. H of C Debs, 5th Series, vol. 345, col. 2493.

24 H of C Debs, 5th Series, vol. 346, col. 136.

25 Ibid, cols. 138–40; Dalton, *Fateful Years* pp. 248–9; W. R. Rock, *Appeasement on Trial* (Hamden, 1966) p. 254; F. Williams, *A Pattern of Rulers* (London, 1965) p. 188.

26 Pimlott (ed.), *Dalton Political Diaries* p. 259.

27 A. J. P. Taylor, *The Origins of the Second World War* (London, 1961) p. 229.

28 Dalton, *Fateful Years* pp. 254–5; Pimlott (ed.), *Dalton Political Diaries* pp. 262–4.

29 M. Cowling, *Impact of Hitler* p. 303; R. Manne, 'The British Decision for Alliance with Russia, May 1939', *Journal of Contemporary History* 9, 3, (1974) pp. 22–4.

30 M. Cowling, *Impact of Hitler* p. 303.

31 Fisher to Wilson 15 May 1939, cited Peden, *Rearmament and Treasury* p. 44.

32 See, for example, James (ed.), *Chips* p. 201: 'John Simon is taking the Foreign Affairs debate tomorrow [26 May]. . . . It was a struggle to induce him to do so, and he insisted that Rab should "hold his hand", a monstrous stipulation. Peter Loxley and I had so hoped to get poor Rab off this added and unnecessary chore – but Simon, always bloody-minded, insisted, and was in fact adamant.'

33 Harvey, *Diplomatic Diaries* p. 237.

34 H. of C. Debs, 5th Series, vol. 345, col. 2490.

35 Pimlott (ed.), *Dalton Political Diaries* pp. 262–3.

36 R. James, *Victor Cazalet* p. 211.

37 J. Vincent (ed.), *Crawford Papers* pp. 596–7.

38 Notes by Lord Camrose of conversation with Chamberlain, Gilbert, *Churchill* v, companion part 3, p. 1545.

39 S. Roskill, *Hankey* iii, 413.

40 P. Einzig, *In the Centre of Things* (London, 1960) chapter 19; H. Macmillan, *Winds of Change* pp. 596–7; D. Jay, *Change and Fortune* p. 70; M. George, *The Hollow Men* (London, 1965) p. 180.

41 *The Times* 26 April 1939.

42 *Daily Telegraph* 26 April 1939.

43 Cabinet 5 July 1939, CAB 23/100.

44 *Eastern Daily Press* 9 June 1939.

45 *Retrospect* p. 232.

46 Peden, *Rearmament and Treasury* p. 103.

47 Cabinet 23 May 1939, CAB 23/99.

48 Cabinet 21 June and 28 June 1939, CAB 23/100.

49 The other was Walter [by then Lord] Runciman.

50 Cabinet 5 July 1939, CAB 23/100; Barnett, *Collapse of British Power* pp. 568–9; Colvin, *Chamberlain Cabinet* pp. 229–30; Kaiser, *Economic Diplomacy* pp. 308–9; Parkinson, *Peace for our Time* pp. 160–1. Simon's two papers are

included with the cabinet minutes.

51 F. H. Hinsley, *British Intelligence in the Second World War* (London, 1979) i, 69–70.

52 Cabinet 22 Aug. 1939, CAB 23/100; Colvin, *Chamberlain Cabinet* p. 236; Parkinson, *Peace for our Time* p. 182.

53 A. J. P. Taylor, *English History 1914–1945* (Oxford, 1965) p. 452.

54 B. Pimlott (ed.), *Dalton Political Diaries* p. 297.

55 Ibid, p. 292; Aster, *1939* p. 369; E. Raczynski, *In Allied London* (London, n.d.) p. 25.

56 *DBFP*, 3rd Series, vii, p. 488.

57 See cabinet of 1 Sept. 1939, CAB 23/100, when Chamberlain said that 'the event against which we had fought so long and so earnestly had come upon us.'

58 Simon diary 2 Sept. 1939, SP 11 fos. 3–17; James (ed.), *Chips* pp. 211–12; Aster, *1939* p. 375; Harvey, *Diplomatic Diaries* pp. 314–15.

59 Notes on 1937–39, Templewood MSS X:5.

60 Simon diary 2 Sept. 1939, SP 11 fos. 6–7; R. A. C. Parker, 'The British Government and the Coming of War with Germany, 1939' in M. R. D. Foot (ed.), *War and Society* (London, 1973) pp. 8–9. This article quotes extensively from Simon's diary.

61 H. Nicolson, *Diaries and Letters* i, 419.

62 H. of C. Debs, 5th Series, vol. 351, cols. 282–3.

63 Minney, *Hore-Belisha* p. 226.

64 Simon diary 2 Sept. 1939.

65 Dalton, *Fateful Years* p. 265.

66 Elliot, de la Warr, Wallace, Anderson, Stanley, Colville, Burgin, Dorman-Smith and Hore-Belisha. Euan Wallace's diary speaks of nine, apart from himself, going to Simon's room.

67 Interestingly when the Minister of Agriculture, Sir Reginald Dorman-Smith, recalled these events a quarter of a century later he placed the leadership of the dissenting group with Sir John Anderson rather than Simon. (*The Sunday Times* 6 Sept. 1964). According to Simon's diary, corroborated by other sources, Anderson was one of the rebels and he drove Simon to Downing Street later in the day and 'waited to take me back', but played no more significant role. It seems almost as if Dorman-Smith's memory could not accept Simon in the sort of role which he actually played.

68 Simon diary 2 Sept. 1939; see also Minney, *Hore-Belisha* pp. 226–7 and E. Wallace's diary entry for 2 Sept. 1939, MSS Eng. hist. c.495 fos. 18–19.

69 Inskip diary, cited Heuston, *Lord Chancellors* i, 602.

70 Simon diary 2 Sept. 1939.

71 Ibid.

72 James (ed.), *Chips* p. 213.

73 *Retrospect* p. 252.

74 Simon diary 2 Sept. 1939.

75 Ibid, 7 Oct. 1939, SP 11 fo. 35.

76 N. Chamberlain to Ida Chamberlain 8 Oct. 1939, Chamberlain MSS NC 18/1/1124.

77 As note 75.

78 D. Dilks, 'The Twilight War and the Fall of France: Chamberlain and Churchill in 1940', in D. Dilks (ed.), *Retreat from Power* (London, 1981) ii, 36–65. Simon, too, appreciated Churchill's value to the government. 'His real qualities of statesmanship have come out strongly in cabinet council during the past month,' he wrote in October. Simon diary 7 Oct. 1939, SP 11 fos. 35–39. On occasions Simon even sided with Churchill against Chamberlain. See, for example, discussion of action in the event of a German invasion of the Low Countries, War Cabinet 9 Nov. 1939, CAB 65/4. But by the spring, when Churchill assumed the chair of the Military Co-ordination Committee, Simon was becoming irritated by Churchill's tendency not to present full details of military operations to the War Cabinet. P. Addison, *The Road to 1945* (London, 1975) p. 90; P. Cosgrave, *Churchill at War* p. 165.

79 Simon diary 23 Sept. 1939, SP 11 fos. 27–31 bis. Simon's diary at this time contains some remarkably prescient forecasts of the future course of the War. This particular entry went on to consider the dilemma which Britain would face when Germany turned to the West. 'If Germany were to force back the French line and use the new technique [of blitzkrieg], Gamelin is certain to call urgently for British Air Forces to help to stem the tide and then will come one of the gravest problems of the war; whether we are going to denude our own air strength in order to supplement the air resistance of our ally.'

80 Ibid, 10 Sept. 1939, SP 11 fos. 21–2.

81 Ibid, 21 Sept. 1939, SP 11 fos. 26–7.

82 Ibid, 10 Sept. 1939, SP 11 fo. 21.

83 Ibid, 13 Oct. 1939, SP 11 fos. 40–2,

84 Avon, *Reckoning* pp. 72–3.

85 Boothby to Lloyd George 10 Sept. 1939, Lloyd George MSS G 3/13/10.

86 Dalton, *Fateful Years* p. 282.

87 H. of C. Debs., 5th Series, vol. 358, cols. 1879–81.

88 James, *Victor Cazalet* p. 219.

89 Nicolson, *Diaries and Letters* ii, 38.

90 Dalton, *Fateful Years* p. 282.

91 War Cabinet 11 Sept. 1939, CAB 65/1.

92 Cf. Cato, *Guilty Men* p. 100: 'He was successful in war as in peace in carrying through the Treasury policy of ensuring that expenditure should be rigorously limited.'

93 War Cabinet 22 Sept. 1939, CAB 65/1; Simon diary 23 Sept. 1939, SP 11 fos. 6–7; Minney, *Hore-Belisha* p. 243.

94 Simon diary 14 Sept. and 18 Sept. 1939, SP 11 fos. 24 bis and 25.

95 James (ed.), *Chips* p. 222.

96 Simon diary 28 Sept. 1939, SP 11 fos. 32–32 bis.

97 Ibid.

98 Churchill, *Gathering Storm* p. 361.

99 As note 95.

100 E. Wallace diary 27 Sept. 1939, MSS Eng. hist. c. 495 fo. 66; Hemingford, *Backbencher* pp. 211–12; *The Times* 28 Sept. 1939; *The Economist* 7 Oct. 1939.

101 N. Chamberlain to H. Chamberlain 1 Oct. 1939, Chamberlain MSS NC 18/1/1123.

102 War Cabinet 15 Nov. 1939, CAB 65/2.

103 Ibid, 30 Nov. 1939, CAB 65/2.

104 Simon diary 6 Dec. 1939, SP 11 fos. 53–4.

105 Ibid, 7 Oct. 1939, SP 11 fos. 35–9.

106 J. Colville, *The Fringes of Power* (London, 1985) p. 47.

107 R. Macleod and D. Kelly (eds.), *The Ironside Diaries* (London, 1962) p. 157.

108 Sir E. Benn to Simon 2 Oct. 1939, SP 85 fo. 177.

109 Note on war aims by Robert Boothby 31 Oct. 1939, Lloyd George MSS G 3/13/18.

110 *The Times* 1 Dec. 1939.

111 Simon diary 9 Nov. 1939, SP 11 fo. 50.

112 Colville, *Fringes* p. 50.

113 N. Chamberlain to I. Chamberlain 10 Sept. 1939, Chamberlain MSS NC 18/1/1116.

114 Colville, *Fringes* pp. 60, 64–5; J. Colville, *Man of Valour* (London, 1972) p. 164; J. H. Jones, *Josiah Stamp: Public Servant* (London, 1964) pp. 337–8; A. Booth, 'Economic Advice at the Centre of British Government, 1939–41', *Historical Journal* 29, 3 (1986) p. 660.

115 J. Colville, *Footprints in Time* (London, 1976) p. 73. For confirmation of Montagu Norman's low opinion of Simon, see Stuart, *Reith Diaries* p. 240.

116 Barnes and Nicholson (eds.), *Amery Diaries* ii, 579.

117 Notes by S. Hoare, Jan. 1940, Templewood MSS XI: 2; Cross, *Hoare* p. 312.

118 Chamberlain may have been referring to this episode when he told his sister that 'the reason why I abandoned the daring project of which I told you was because when I broached it to the individual for whom I had designed the hero's role, he showed such a very unheroic trepidation at the prospect that I saw he would be hissed off the stage.' N. Chamberlain to I. Chamberlain 20 Jan. 1940, Chamberlain MSS NC 18/1/1139.

119 Addison, *1945* p. 68. Hore-Belisha did not feel that he received much support from Simon during the crisis which led to his leaving the government, A. J. P. Taylor (ed.), *Off the Record* pp. 130, 150–1. When Hore-Belisha began openly to criticise the government, a difficult situation arose and Simon was relieved when Hore-Belisha agreed in March 1940 to resign as Chairman of the Liberal National party. Simon diary 20 March 1940, SP 11 fos. 70–1.

120 Colville, *Fringes* p. 65; Jones, *Stamp* p. 338. There is, though, evidence that Simon found out enough of what had been planned to keep a wary eye on Lord Stamp and Montagu Norman. He objected to the plans of the Ministry of Information under Lord Reith – 'a self advertising ass' – to use these two men in its publicity operations. Stuart, *Reith Diaries* p. 242; Colville, *Fringes* p. 95. The whole Stamp episode had a curious sequel. Stamp was killed by an enemy bomb in 1941. His belongings, including a note detailing the abortive plot, scattered into the street. The note was found by an air raid warden who brought it to John Colville in Downing Street. Colville, *Footprints* p. 73.

121 Colville, *Fringes* p. 53.

122 See, for example, discussion of Middle-Eastern military policy, War Cabinet 15 Jan. 1940, CAB 65/5.

123 Colville, *Fringes* p. 53; E. Turner, *The Phoney War on the Home Front* (London, 1961) p. 136.

124 War Cabinet 29 Nov. 1939, CAB 65/2.

125 Simon diary 23 Jan. 1940, SP 11 fos. 58–9.

126 Colville, *Fringes* p. 78; E. Wallace diary 31 Jan. 1940, MSS Eng. hist. c 496 fo. 53.

127 Colville, *Fringes* p. 53; see also Simon's New Year message to his constituents, *Spenborough Guardian* 1 Jan. 1940.

128 H. of C. Debs, 5th Series, vol. 356, cols. 1422–32; Colville, *Fringes* p. 79.

129 Colville, *Fringes* p. 102.

130 Harvey, *Diplomatic Diaries* p. 341. Harvey also heard from Eden that Simon was anxious to leave the Exchequer and take on another post, ibid, p. 345.

131 For Simon's very fair appreciation of the Finnish situation, see his diary for 13 March 1940, SP 11 fo. 67.

132 Simon diary 23 April 1940, SP 11 fos. 79–80.

133 *Punch* 29 May 1940; Turner, *Phoney War* p. 213.

134 Amery, *Political Life* iii, 356; H. of C. Debs, 5th Series, vol. 360, cols. 245–55.

135 J. Campbell, *Nye Bevan and the Mirage of British Socialism* (London, 1987) p. 95.

136 *Daily Telegraph* 24 April 1940.

137 *The Times* 25 April 1940. See also *The Times* editorial of 26 April. The budget was 'a most painstaking effort to balance the national accounts . . . rather than the programme of a chief Economics Minister for harnessing all the productive resources of the country to the task of winning the war'.

138 B. Sabine, *British Budgets in Peace and War 1932–1945* (London, 1970) pp. 171–3.

139 *Daily Telegraph* 8 May 1940.

140 Sabine, *British Budgets* p. 172.

141 *Sunday Times* 3 March 1940.

142 Simon diary 12 April 1940, SP 11 fo. 77.

143 Ibid, 4 April 1940, SP 11 fo. 72.

144 *The Times* 4 May 1940.

145 Lord Lloyd to son 7 May 1940, cited Gilbert, *Churchill* vi, 290.

146 Dalton, *Fateful Years* p. 303.

147 Simon diary 8 May 1940, SP 11 fos. 81–7.

148 H. of C. Debs, 5th Series, vol. 360, col. 1264.

149 Simon diary 9 May 1940, SP 12 fos. 1–7.

150 H. of C. Debs, 5th Series, vol. 360, col. 1146.

151 Colville, *Fringes* p. 118.

152 Nicolson, *Diaries and Letters ii*, 79; Barnes and Nicholson (eds.), *Amery Diaries* ii, 610–11.

153 Hannon to Chamberlain 9 May 1940, Hannon MSS.

154 At the end of the crisis, Chamberlain still did not see the extent to which the parliamentary revolt had been directed against himself. He stressed that 'the

personal dislike of Simon and Hoare had reached a pitch which I find it difficult
to understand.' I. Macleod, *Neville Chamberlain* (London, 1961) p. 291.

155 Pimlott (ed.), *Dalton Political Diaries* p. 343; see also Boothby to Churchill
9 May 1940, cited Gilbert, *Churchill* vi, 302.

156 Pimlott (ed.), *Dalton Political Diaries* p. 342.

157 Simon diary 9 May 1940, SP 12 fos. 1–7.

158 Avon, *Reckoning* p. 97.

159 As note 157.

160 Ibid.

CHAPTER ELEVEN

THE WOOLSACK – AT LAST

How seldom things turn out as they should and how splendid it it is when they do. . . .[1]
[Simon on Lord Cave's appointment as Lord Chancellor in 1924.]

When, a quarter of a century earlier, Simon had declined to become Lord Chancellor, he had done so with a characteristic display of wit: 'the sack rather than the Woolsack'.[2] In May 1940 he knew that the stark choice which faced him was between the Woolsack and complete loss of office and – unlike 1915 – there could now be no realistic prospect in Simon's mind of his ever becoming Prime Minister. Opposition to him within the Labour party was sufficently strong to block his presence at any other ministry within the Coalition government. Acceptance of Churchill's offer was therefore automatic and immediate. The new Lord Chancellor kissed hands on 13 May and made his first appearance in the upper house the following day, taking the title of Viscount Simon of Stackpole Elidor, the Pembrokeshire village where his father had been born. Many though were surprised to see Simon's name in the new list of government ministers. Channon viewed the appointment as 'rather unexpected'.[3] Maisky regretted that Churchill had not made a clean sweep of all the Chamberlainite old guard[4], while even a month into the new regime Boothby sensed that public opinion nurtured 'a savage hatred' of the new Lord Chancellor.[5] This appeared to be confirmed following the publication in July of the short, vitriolic volume *Guilty Men*, which was to do such lasting damage to Simon's reputation. In the short term its impact was to encourage the demand for the early retirement of all the surviving Chamberlainites from the government. A Gallup Poll in the *News Chronicle* showed that more than half of those with an opinion felt that Simon should go.[6]

Yet there can be little doubt that the appointment was a wise one on Churchill's part. On the one hand it removed Simon from the mainstream of political life and from the higher direction of the War. 'Thank God he has [been] sidetracked' was Horace Rumbold's reaction.[7] This was clearly a pre-condition of Labour's entry into government, which Churchill correctly recognised as the pressing need of the hour. On the Woolsack, noted Attlee, Simon 'will be quite innocuous'.[8] On the other hand Simon had at last been installed in that great office of state for which, whatever he thought himself, his qualities so well fitted him. The greatest barrister of his age now stood at the head of the English judiciary. Churchill, moreover, clearly recognised that, whatever hostility he might have incurred in the past, a man of Simon's ability should not be lost to the national service at this great moment of crisis. His political skills could still be of value in defence of the government's cause in the House of Lords after three decades of experience in the Commons.

Simon himself approached his new post with little evident enthusiasm. Fitted out with a new full-bottomed wig, he felt like 'a long retired actor who has just been appointed dramatic critic by the former editor of the *Daily Express*'. But like everyone in the crisis of May 1940 Simon saw the crucial need to 'defeat the enemy and save the liberty of the world' and was therefore willing to do any job which might conceivably help a little towards this end.[9] In fact the Woolsack proved more congenial than expected and Simon soon settled into his new duties, including that of presiding over debates in the upper house. One of his distinctive habits as Lord Chancellor was to pass witty and spontaneously composed epigrams from the Woolsack to his fellow peers during the course of Lords' debates. After speaking on the question of day nurseries and evacuee children, Lord Mersey received the following:

> Clive Bingham tells the House of Peers
> He's twenty children under five.
> Their Lordships marvel; it appears
> That bigamy is still alive.[10]

As the weeks passed Simon began to warm to his task, recognising that the Lord Chancellorship is a multi-faceted ministry, whose duties are by no means restricted to legal matters. There was 'a great deal more of importance to do (apart from Law) than I had supposed'. He had, he noted with some pleasure, wound up a secret session debate on foreign affairs in the Lords 'to Edward's [Halifax] satisfaction'.[11] July saw him take the Emergency Powers Bill through Committee 'with skill and diplomacy'.[12] He also came to appreciate the fact that the House of Lords is more inclined to be swayed by good argument than is the Commons.[13] But, not being a member of Churchill's War Cabinet, Simon was not privy to many of the critical decisions which had to be taken in the momentous spring and summer of 1940. He was 'simply staggered' by Churchill's proposal in June for an indissoluble union between England and France. Inevitably his legal brain seized upon the constitutional ramifications of such a move. 'What happens to the Dominions or to the King?' Of one thing he was certain. Nothing would serve but a British resolve never to yield to the enemy. Contrary to what has sometimes been suggested, Simon set his face against any thought of a compromise peace in the summer of 1940, although he did seem to believe that meaningful negotiations might be possible once Hitler's position had been undermined militarily or inside Germany.[14]

The ancient office of Lord Chancellor involves a strange mixture of duties, a combination of functions, as Simon noted, 'quite indefensible according to de Toqueville but working quite well according to the British Constitution'.[15] Its incumbent is head of the judiciary, a senior cabinet minister and the nearest equivalent in the Lords to the Speaker of the House of Commons. Yet it is the only cabinet office which cannot be occupied by an amateur, no matter how gifted his civil servants.[16] Simon, of course, was no amateur in legal matters and for five years he filled his office with great distinction. It was in many ways the most successful stage of his long and varied political career and one which, despite his early misgivings, came perhaps to give him his greatest satisfaction. By 1942 he was 'really enjoying' the job.[17] Simon's Lord Chancellorship was not a period of great legal reforms. The War precluded such an undertaking which would not in any case have been Simon's forté. Nonetheless two important measures did find their way on to the Statute book – the Law Reform (Frustrated Contracts) Act of 1943 and the Law Reform (Contributory Negligence) Act of 1945. Simon prepared the way for these reforms by correspondence with leading academic lawyers and personally steered the bills through the House of Lords. But it was as a judge that Simon was outstanding.

From his early days as a young barrister Simon had been involved in the highest class of litigation across the whole spectrum of the law. He could move with easy mastery from one field to another and a remarkable memory had helped him retain the law which he had learned over so many years, even though he had not practised at the bar for more than a decade. His redoubtable scholarship meant that his judgments were invariably superbly argued, yet without unnecessary displays of elaborate erudition, and were presented in a polished literary style. As Lord Porter later put it:

If the duty of a judge is to make certain that he has followed and appreciated an argument, given it due weight and felicitously expressed the reasons for his decision, Lord Simon will stand high in the ranks of those who sit to clarify the law.[18]

His combination of intellectual and political power proved forbidding. Early on in his tenure of office Simon delivered several important judgments which became landmarks in the history of the English Law. These related, *inter alia*, to the principle upon which damages as regards expectation of life should be calculated in cases of death by negligence; the putting of the law relating to frustration of contracts on to a new and juster basis; and in the case of Mancini – one of the few murder cases to reach the House of Lords – the principles upon which a jury should be directed in a murder case where there is a possible alternative defence of manslaughter.[19] Simon's political instincts remained strong as when, in 1942, he wisely dissuaded the Law Lords from developing the law of conspiracy in relation to trade unions. He was assisted in this period by an unusually distinguished body of Law Lords but his own personal contribution is unmistakable. They dissented from his speeches only with trepidation. Simon worked tirelessly, presiding as often as he could in the House of Lords and in the Judicial Committee of the Privy

Council, 'producing judgments like a sausage machine'.[20] The Law Reports for 1943 contain no less than twenty-three of his judgments. As the Dictionary of National Biography aptly noted, Simon's occupancy of the Woolsack gave him 'an assured place among the greatest jurists' who have been Lord Chancellor.[21] If any of his judgments are to be criticised it is perhaps on the grounds that he continued to act as an advocate in the presentation of his decisions, with an occasional tendency to gloss over difficulties with the use of beautifully phrased arguments. But to criticise Simon in this area is to counsel perfection.[22] On his death in 1954 the then Lord Chancellor, Lord Simonds, delivered an appropriate tribute:

A long and wide experience in the law, a scholar's passion for accuracy, and a compelling sense of the judicial oath drove him to sustained and unremitting efforts in the preparation of judgments which will be his most enduring monument. I sometimes thought that in that work he found his greatest happiness.[23]

Though Hankey's view that he became merely 'a cypher'[24] is perhaps an overstatement, Simon was not normally involved in the central questions of war policy during the Churchill coalition. Briefly, however, in the spring of 1941 he re-emerged into prominence. On 10 May Hitler's deputy Rudolf Hess climbed into a fighter plane in Augsburg in southern Germany and, after a flight of eight hundred miles, parachuted on to the estate of the Duke of Hamilton near Glasgow. Hess claimed to have a specific set of peace proposals to present to the duke in the belief that the latter would quickly pass them on to Churchill. Though Churchill seemed at first uninterested in Hess's mission, discussions in the cabinet and with senior officials of the Foreign Office persuaded him that Hess should be brought to London. As Alexander Cadogan recorded: 'PM agreed we ought to draw Hess by pretending to negotiate and he came out with my idea of J Simon for the part.'[25] Simon was vaguely acquainted with the Deputy Führer from his visit to Berlin in 1935, but more importantly the forensic skills of the lawyer-statesman might be able to ascertain the true purpose behind Hess's flight and in particular to clarify whether Hess had been sent by Hitler as part of a peace initiative. To prepare for his interview Simon was given all available documentation including the monitoring reports of Hess's private conversations with the guards who had watched over him since his arrival in Britain.[26] The whole episode was veiled in almost comical secrecy. Even the private letter from Foreign Secretary Eden, confirming the Lord Chancellor's task, was couched in the most oblique terms:

I would be grateful if you could see your way to interview the man of whom we spoke. We [Eden and Churchill] feel sure that it is in this way that we are most likely to obtain advantages helpful to the common cause. We do not rate the chances high, but we are confident that this is the best method we can devise.[27]

Simon was to be accompanied by Ivone Kirkpatrick, a Foreign Office official now seconded as Controller of European Services at the BBC, who had interviewed Hess soon after the latter's arrival in Britain. In order to maintain secrecy Simon and Kirkpatrick assumed the names of Drs Guthrie and Mackenzie and were described to the guards as well-known psychiatrists. They were received by two specially detailed German speaking officers who were party to the secret. In the event, however, the three hour meeting which took place on 9 June at a house near Aldershot was little short of a fiasco. To begin with Hess seemed to have cold feet at the prospect of meeting Simon and on the morning of the interview declined to get up from his bed. Eventually he appeared in airforce uniform and jackboots and after formal introductions the interview began at 2.30 p.m.

Rather surprisingly the meeting was dominated by Hess who bombarded his visitors with a mixture of distorted history, cajolery and thinly veiled threats. The Nazi leader spoke in terms which were hardly likely to endear him to his listeners:

The reason for my flight was that among the leading personalities, the leaders of Germany, we were absolutely convinced that England's position was hopeless.[28]

Simon interrupted Hess's monologue only occasionally, but at length his patience clearly began to run out:

I am waiting – I say it with great respect – I am waiting to be informed of the matter for which I was invited to come down here. And now I have been waiting, I suppose, for two hours. . . .[29]

Hess continued to pour out a long discourse to the effect that British reports of success against German U-boats were greatly exaggerated and that Germany had every chance of starving Britain into submission through the destruction of her supply routes. Finally Hess implied that any peace settlement would necessitate the return of Germany's former colonies and the recognition of continental Europe as a German sphere of influence. At half past five Hess requested to be left alone with Simon and then proceeded to allege that he had been maltreated in custody. He complained that he had been subjected to great noise and that his food had been tampered with. By the end of the interview Hess seemed on the verge of hysteria. Kirkpatrick later recorded:

Suffice it to say that Simon did his best to lift the conversation on to a reasonable plane . . . But it was no good. We abandoned the unequal struggle and went home as secretly as we had come.[30]

Simon concluded that Hess was 'of a very second-rate intellectual ability' and incapable of acting a part.[31] He was almost certainly deranged and the flight to Britain had probably been his own scheme. The Lord Chancellor gave an account of his meeting with Hess to the cabinet on 16 June, but little more was heard in public of the episode until the Nuremberg trials of 1945–6. Hess himself began that long incarceration from which he was freed only by his suicide in 1987.

As one of the government's principal spokesmen in the House of Lords Simon was sometimes called upon to make important policy statements. In March 1943, a few weeks after the Allies had enunciated the policy of 'unconditional surrender', he defined the nation's war aims as the destruction of the Hitlerian state, the punishment of war criminals and the overthrow of the German army. But, he stressed, an Allied victory would not mean the end of Germany, the extinction of the German race, the breakdown of society or a return to chaos:

We are not seeking to deny Germany a place in the Europe of the future . . . but the German nation can be saved only by the German people and they would be foolish . . . to believe Goebbels' stupid falsehood that their best chance rests in supporting the Nazi rule.[32]

That same year it was Simon who had to dampen down the calls that were coming, particularly from Lord Beaverbrook, for a second front to relieve the military pressure on Britain's Soviet allies. Simon rebuked the press baron for stirring up 'ill-founded clamour' and dismissed the call for a second front as 'a seriously misleading catchpenny phrase'.[33] The Lord Chancellor's speech a few days later on the Beveridge Report – 'one of the greatest . . . plans for social reform that has ever been promulgated' – evoked an almost fulsome letter of praise from Ernest Bevin, the Minister of Labour.[34] The report's proposals were a matter of some satisfaction to Simon who recalled his own contribution to the field of social welfare, both as Solicitor-General before the First World War and as the Chancellor of the Exchequer who had devised and established supplementary pensions for the elderly.[35]

It was perhaps Simon's wide-ranging brief in the upper house which entitled him, at least in his own mind, to intervene on occasions in areas of policy which were clearly outside the normal scope of a wartime Lord Chancellor. One such matter was the rumour which circulated in May 1942 that Britain was about to sign a treaty with the Soviet Union which would give British recognition to the Soviet frontiers of 1941, including possession of the Baltic States. Molotov was pressing for such a step and found Eden sympathetic. Simon sent Churchill a long letter couched in high moral tones in which he protested against such a course of action. He was particularly concerned that it seemed that the United States would not be a party to any such agreement and warned that Stalin's aim might be to cause a rift in Anglo-American relations which would create problems when it came to a settlement of the post-war world. In what might well have been a blue-print for post-war British foreign policy the Lord Chancellor asked:

Is it too much to say that our guiding principle should be that we sign no agreements with anybody that either have not the approval of the United States or to which the United States cannot be a consenting party.

Simon went so far as to warn that if such an Anglo-Soviet transaction came to be debated in the House of Lords, he would not be able to defend it – 'and you know how willingly I do what I can to help your Government there.'[36] Churchill was not unmoved by these remarks, particularly as other ministers including Duff Cooper, the Chancellor of the Duchy of Lancaster, also expressed concern, and he warned Eden that he did not wish to face 'a bunch of resignations'.[37]

For the most part, however, Simon's war work was of a useful rather than dramatic character. In the autumn of 1942 he chaired a ministerial committee on war criminals and by December was able to tell the House of Lords that the leading Nazis would receive 'exemplary punishment'.[38] A year later he took on the chair of the Royal Commission on the Birth Rate. The war inevitably brought the problem of India's future back into sharp focus. The cabinet's India Committee saw the re-establishment of Simon's partnership with Attlee – both men had been on the Statutory Commission over a decade earlier. In conjunction with Anderson, Amery, Cripps and Grigg much progress was made towards Indian self-government at the end of the War. As Chairman, Attlee's main problems were not with Simon but with the Prime Minister whom Attlee found 'both obstinate and ignorant' about Indian problems.[39] Simon also served under Attlee on a cabinet committee on the reform of the Foreign Service, where Dalton found his presence somewhat ironic. 'Does he, I wonder, ever remember that others remember *his* record at the Foreign Office!'[40]

A minister more centrally involved in the direction of war policy than Simon would not perhaps have had the time to concern himself to the extent that the Lord Chancellor did in the question of whether or not the government should publish a selection of Foreign Office documents dealing with the origins of the war. This would follow the precedent of the earlier *British Documents on the Origins of the War* dealing with the period 1898–1914. Throughout his career Simon was intensely concerned to protect his own reputation in history and this was undoubtedly his primary concern when he heard from Halifax in the autumn of 1941 of the proposed publication. As he once put it, 'If you want to escape criticism the best thing is to say nothing, do nothing and be nothing.'[41] Simon judged, however, that his objections might carry more weight if voiced in terms of the need to protect the reputation of Neville Chamberlain, who had died a year earlier. After glancing through some of the papers which it was proposed to publish, Simon rather surprisingly asserted that it might be 'a good thing to take a decision on publication on the principle that it is half the battle to get your blow in first'.[42] But when asked for his opinion at the cabinet in December

Simon began to stall. Four months later Simon was said to be 'still reading' the documents, but it was becoming clear that he was going to do his best to prevent publication.[43]

A paper which the Lord Chancellor circulated to the cabinet in May 1942, purporting to put the arguments for and against publication in the manner in which Simon was so skilled, amounted in practice to a clear rejection of the idea. The arguments which Simon put forward were not particularly convincing and serve in retrospect to underline the personal factor which determined his objections. He suggested that the diplomatic documents could not recount the whole history of pre-war events, that few people would read them and that their publication could only engender undesirable controversy.[44] With Simon continuing to stall, the matter came to a head at a meeting of the cabinet on 7 September 1942. The Lord Chancellor had succeeded in gaining the support of a number of other ministers including Sir Kingsley Wood, the Chancellor of the Exchequer, and the compromise decision was reached that the documents should be prepared for publication but then await further authorisation from the cabinet.[45] Professor Llewelyn Woodward, who had been commissioned to edit the diplomatic documents, wryly suggested that Simon's opposition to publication had been misplaced. 'His stock cannot go lower but rise a little by the publication of some of his despatches.' Woodward even believed that Simon was so desperate to protect his reputation that he had tried to bribe him:

Last All Souls Day he asked me whether I had any ex-pupil I would care to support for a living in the gift of the Lord Chancellor.[46]

By the end of 1942 Simon was ready to view the international situation with greater optimism. With some considerable insight he noted:

I think the most important single event was the battle of Midway Island. If the Japanese had won this, Australia might have been open to them . . . We shall have plenty of troubles in the future, but I think the solid ground for confidence is growing.

He also took comfort that the national economy was withstanding the unprecedented strains of the war effort, even though there would certainly be stupendous economic problems to face after peace returned, and he believed that his own budget of September 1939 had played a useful part in laying the right foundations.[47]

At the end of 1943 there were rumours that Simon might vacate the Woolsack in a government reshuffle, possibly to become President of an International War Crimes Tribunal.[48] In the event, however, he remained in office throughout the war. Towards the end of his term of office a prospect of supreme irony confronted the Lord Chancellor. At the beginning of 1945 Lloyd George, fearful of his ability to hold on to his Caernarvon seat at the next general election, accepted an earldom so as to guarantee himself a parliamentary voice in the discussion of the peace settlement. Upon introduction to the Lords, Simon's old rival and sparring partner would be obliged in comformity with ancient ceremonial practice to bow to the Lord Chancellor. The humour of the situation was not lost on Simon who wrote wittily to Lloyd George:

Never in my wildest dreams did I think that you would have to bow the knee to *me*, but such is the protocol if a new Earl is admitted to the Lords when I am Chancellor. So, in addition to sending you congratulations and good wishes, I include a dispensation from the strict rule of the House and beg to assure you that a slight genuflection when you are introduced will be all that is required. . . .[49]

In the event this unlikely scene never materialised. Lloyd George was already a dying man when he accepted his earldom and he did not live to take his seat in the upper house.

As the end of hostilities approached, Simon began inevitably to contemplate the post-war political horizon. If, as he hoped, Churchill led his followers into a general election, he, Simon, intended to be one of them. The probability was that the independent Liberals under Archibald Sinclair would seek to go their own way again, but Simon was convinced that Liberal Nationals should continue to support Churchill. 'His services to the country throughout the war are absolutely unique and beyond all measure.'[50] Indeed when, at the defeat of Germany, Churchill gave his coalition partners the choice of remaining in partnership with him until the final defeat of Japan (anticipated at that time to require a further eighteen months of warfare) or breaking up immediately, both Labour and Liberal parties decided to go their separate ways. Churchill now formed a caretaker government to prepare for a general election, with Simon still Lord Chancellor and another Liberal National, Lord Rosebery, Secretary of State for Scotland. Yet, though Churchill restored the cabinet to its traditional peacetime dimensions, there was no seat for Simon within it – a unique exclusion for the Lord Chancellor in twentieth-century history. It was perhaps an indication that Churchill and Simon were never as reconciled to one another as Simon sometimes liked to claim.

In 1945 Simon was seventy-two years of age and had been in high office for fourteen continuous years. No one in the government could match his record, at least in length of service. He still got 'through a lot of work without feeling any older' and, presumably extrapolating from his own situation, attributed a general improvement in the public health during the war years to the fact that a great many people had had something more to think of than 'their personal ailments and the behaviour of their inscrutable insides.'[51] He approached the general election with enthusiasm. The Liberal Nationals fought the campaign in full co-operation with the Conservatives and Simon tried to persuade the Conservative Chief Whip to let him take one of the government's party political broadcasts.[52] Like many other government spokesmen Simon clashed bitterly with Harold Laski, the brilliant but erratic chairman of Labour's National Executive Committee, in the course of the campaign, when the latter seemed to want to use his office to restrict the prerogatives of any future Labour Prime Minister.

Most observers predicted a close contest between Conservative and Labour parties. The evidence of a strong move towards the left on the part of the British electorate during the war years could not be ignored. Few, however, anticipated the scale of Attlee's victory. With 393 members returned to the House of Commons, Labour had a parliamentary majority for the first time in its history. On 27 July 1945 Churchill's cabinet met for the last time. It was, noted Eden with little charity towards his former Foreign Office mentor, 'a pretty grim affair, with people like Simon present.'[53] On the following day Simon gave up the seals of office. His ministerial career, which had begun thirty-five years earlier, was at an end.

Notes

1 Simon to Cave 1924, cited Sir C. Mallet, *Lord Cave* (London, 1931) p. 270.
2 Simon to Lloyd George 18 May 1915, Lloyd George MSS C/8/3/8; see above pp. 33–4.
3 James (ed.), *Chips* p. 252.
4 B. Webb diary 20 May 1940.
5 Boothby to Lloyd George 15 June 1940, Lloyd George MSS G/3/13/23.
6 H. Pelling, *Britain and the Second World War* (pb. edn., London, 1970) p. 91.
7 M. Gilbert, *Horace Rumbold: Portrait of a Diplomat* (London, 1973) p. 451.
8 Dalton, *Fateful Years* p. 313.
9 Simon to R. D. Blumenfeld 16 May 1940, S P 86 fo. 87.
10 Lord Mersey, *Journal and Memories* (London, 1952) p. 22.
11 Simon to N. Chamberlain 2 Aug. 1940, S P 86 fo. 174.
12 Lord Mersey, *A Picture of Life 1872–1940* (London, 1941) p. 436.
13 Simon to Lord Templewood 27 Feb 1945, Templewood Papers XIV: 1.
14 Simon to N. Chamberlain 17 and 18 June 1940, S P 86 fos. 120, 123; Simon to Noel Buxton 1 Aug. 1940, ibid, fo. 165.
15 Simon to Judge William Clark 2 Sept. 1941, S P 89 fo. 40.
16 Heuston, *Lord Chancellors* ii, 3.
17 Simon to A. M. Langdon 30 April 1942, S P 90 fo. 200.
18 House of Lords Debates, 5th Series, vol. 185, cols. 267–8.
19 *The Times* 12 Jan. 1954.
20 See note 17.
21 E. T. Williams and H. M. Palmer (eds.), *The Dictionary of National Biography 1951–1960* (Oxford, 1971) pp. 892–4.
22 *Law Quarterly Review* April 1954, pp. 179–80.
23 Heuston, *Lord Chancellors* ii, 60–1. After Labour's victory in 1945, Walter Monckton assured Simon that he was 'unquestionably the best President of a Court before whom I ever appeared'. This was he asserted a judgement 'that the

profession as a whole agrees with'. Monckton to Simon 27 July 1945, S P 96 fo. 124.

24 Roskill, *Hankey* iii, 500.

25 Dilks (ed.), *Cadogan Diaries* p. 380.

26 W. R. Hess, *My Father Rudolf Hess* (London, 1986) p. 138.

27 Eden to Simon 27 May 1941, S P 88 fo. 41.

28 Transcript of interview, S P 88 fos. 75–152.

29 Ibid, fo. 118.

30 I. Kirkpatrick, *Inner Circle* p. 184.

31 Dilks (ed.), *Cadogan Diaries* p. 387.

32 House of Lords Debates, 5th Series, vol. 126, cols. 573–81.

33 Ibid, cols. 179–84; Taylor, *Beaverbrook* p. 542; M. Foot, *Aneurin Bevan* i, 388.

34 H. of L. Debs., 5th Series, vol. 126, col. 280; Bevin to Simon 26 Feb. 1943, S P 92 fo. 163.

35 Simon to Rowland Evans 26 Feb. 1943, ibid, fo. 164.

36 Simon to Churchill 8 May 1942, ibid, 91 fo. 20; J. Harvey (ed.), *The War Diaries of Oliver Harvey 1941–1945* (London, 1978) p. 124.

37 E. Barker, *Churchill and Eden at War* (London, 1978) pp. 239–40.

38 A. Tusa and J. Tusa, *The Nuremberg Trial* (London, 1983) p. 62.

39 Harris, *Attlee* p. 201.

40 Pimlott (ed.), *Dalton War Diary* p. 539. Simon's relations with the leading figures of the Labour party improved rapidly from their nadir of 1940. In an age when familiarity, even between colleagues in government, was not universal, Simon's correspondence contains many examples of apparently warm and cordial relations with such Labour leaders as Attlee ('My dear Clem'), Morrison and Bevin. Dalton, on the other hand, remained fundamentally hostile.

41 Simon to G. H. Cuming Butler 24 July 1942, S P 91 fo. 90.

42 U. Bialer, 'Telling the Truth to the People: Britain's Decision to Publish the Diplomatic Papers of the Inter-War Period', *Historical Journal* 26, 2 (1983) p. 357.

43 Ibid, p. 358; Harvey noted in November 1941: 'We've got Halifax and Hoare to agree, and now are only waiting for Simon.' *War Diary* p. 61.

44 Ibid, p. 359; Harvey considered Simon's arguments to be 'specious'. *War Diary* [28 Aug. 1942] p. 153.

45 Ibid, p. 360.

46 Ibid.

47 Simon to F. W. Hirst 21 Dec. 1942, S P 92 fo. 54.

48 H. M. Hyde, *Strong for Service: The Life of Lord Nathan of Churt* (London, 1968) p. 155; Pimlott (ed.), *Dalton War Diary* p. 669.

49 Simon to Lloyd George 2 Jan. 1945, S P 95 fo. 59; Simon diary 1 Jan. 1945, ibid, 13 fo. 16.

50 Simon to Alderman J. Wren 23 Oct. 1944, ibid, 95 fo. 7.

51 Simon to Miss Callender 21 March 1945, ibid, fo. 153.

52 Simon to J. Stuart 7 June 1945, ibid, 96 fo. 14.

53 Eden diary 27 July 1945, cited James, *Eden* p. 310.

CHAPTER TWELVE

OUT BUT NOT DOWN

As for me, I am made of leather.[1]

Simon was fond of quoting the words of Lord Rosebery on the fate of deposed Lord Chancellors. Whereas the Lord Chief Justice was not subject to the vagaries of electoral and political fortune, an ex-Lord Chancellor was 'nothing but a shabby old gentleman with £5,000 a year'.[2] Indeed, after almost forty years at Westminster, the last fourteen continuously occupying the highest offices of state, Simon might well have been expected to enjoy his retirement and pension. Yet for the remaining years of his life he continued intensely active in the political and legal affairs of the country, particularly in the House of Lords where he showed that he had 'lost none of the dazzling speed and power of his mental equipment, and [was still] ruthless in exploiting a weak point in the adversary's position'.[3]

Age in fact had been kind to Simon. An arthritic knee was one of the few visible signs of advancing years, though he could still play a reasonable game of golf.[4] In his last years he was able to read the London telephone directory without the aid of glasses and his memory remained prodigious. A barrister who interviewed Simon towards the end of his life later recorded:

Not long before he died he spoke to me for more than an hour, without a note, on some of his experiences in the courts and in Parliament. He paused only once in his discourse, and that was to check the exact wording of a statement he had made in the House of Commons forty years previously.[5]

So despite Labour's massive electoral victory in 1945 and the fact that, barring unforeseeable disaster, Attlee's government would remain in office for a full five years, Simon determined that he could still play a useful part in British public life.

A legal issue of the greatest complexity and significance awaited the new government and Simon was not slow to offer his services. Few, after all, could deny that he was now the country's most distinguished living lawyer. The trial of the leading Nazi war criminals would begin at Nuremberg in the autumn and Simon suggested to the Prime Minister that he might be included in the inter-Allied Tribunal. But for Attlee the vital factor remained Simon's past. Though his inclusion would 'have given great strength and reputation to the Tribunal' and have been 'in every other way . . . ideal':

There is, however, one objection. The fact that you were a member of the British

Government before the war might give an opportunity to war criminals . . . to raise all kinds of extraneous matters relating to past history.[6]

Simon's views on the trial of leading Nazis had undergone an interesting transformation. Churchill's original idea had been that the major war criminals should be declared world outlaws and that any Allied officer of the rank of major-general should be authorised to shoot them upon capture and establishment of identity. Simon had endorsed this view, adding that 'the treatment of the arch-war-criminals . . . is a political and not a juridical question. Judges, however eminent, could not try Hitler; still less could they sentence him.'[7] Yet by November 1945 Simon was writing an article for *The Sunday Times* in which he described the trial at Nuremberg as 'the greatest vindication of the force of moral justice in international relations that the world has ever seen'.[8] Later still he felt able to defend the Nuremberg proceedings against the doubts of Lord Hankey who felt that they were of questionable legal validity.[9]

Attlee's view ensured that Simon could have no direct role in the Nuremberg trials. But the ex-Lord Chancellor had plenty with which to occupy himself on the domestic front, particularly 'at the [new] Lord Chancellor's request in the judicial field'. Indeed it was pressure of work which compelled him in the spring of 1946 to withdraw from the Royal Commission on the Population which he had chaired for more than two years.[10] Yet if Simon still nurtured political ambitions it was scarcely likely that these could be pursued within the Liberal National movement. The political coalitions which in one form or another had governed the country for almost a decade and a half were at an end, and the electoral result of 1945, besides signalling the dominance of Labour, had marked the nation's return to a straightforward system of two-party politics, in which, for the foreseeable future, third forces would have no particular significance. Several Liberal National MPs had defected from the party's ranks during the course of the War and, though thirteen members were returned in 1945, the party had increasing difficulty in establishing an independent identity in the mind of the electorate, having fought the election in full alliance with the Conservatives. Some had seen salvation lying in reunion with the Liberal party but such hopes had come to an end when the Liberals, unlike the Liberal Nationals, had refused to remain inside Churchill's coalition after the defeat of Germany. In any case the election of 1945 showed that, even reunited, the two Liberal parties would not have represented a significant political force. The mainstream Liberal party had secured little more than two million votes. The parliamentary party was reduced from eighteen to eleven seats with all its former leaders, including Archibald Sinclair, going down to defeat.

Simon, judging that the election had created an entirely new political situation, drew the obvious conclusion and lost little time in sounding out Churchill as to how the latter would react to the suggestion of a merger between the Conservative and Liberal National parties.[11] Though Simon could no longer speak on behalf of his party, he was careful to imply that other Liberal Nationals were thinking along the same lines. His logic was compelling. The socialist programme of the new government posed a common threat – and one against which it was the duty of the opposition parties to unite to defend personal liberty and individual enterprise. 'No objects', noted Simon, 'could more naturally appeal to the innate liberalism of the country, using that word in the sense in which it has long inspired both professed Liberals and the best thought of the modern democratic Conservative.'[12] Churchill, however, was unenthusiastic particularly as his senior Conservative colleagues had scattered for the summer recess and could not be consulted easily.[13] For the time being, therefore, Simon was obliged to sit upon his thoughts. Not until May 1947 was an agreement finally reached between Lords Woolton and Teviot which regulated the electoral relationship between Conservatives and Liberal Nationals, allowing for the union of the two parties at constituency level and for the adoption of joint candidates. Still, however, Liberal Nationals maintained a theoretically independent existence.[14]

Though denied entry into the Conservative ranks Simon enjoyed a vigorous life inside the House of Lords. The Labour government's position there was nothing like as strong as in the lower house and Simon's debating skills made him a worthy adversary for the new Lord Chancellor, Jowitt. Over the Married Women (Restraint upon Anticipation) Bill of 1949, which Simon opposed on the grounds that it was retrospective and unequal as between men and women, Jowitt lost his normal composure and the two men exchanged heated remarks, with Jowitt taking exception to Simon's suggestion that he had glossed over the fact that the bill was retrospective.[15] Some of the government's legislation attracted Simon's particular attention – and scorn. Of a clause in the Criminal Justice Bill, thrown out by the Lords, he noted caustically in his diary:

It is said that this miserable clause was the concoction of the Cabinet itself, various of its members suggesting special instances of murder in which the death penalty must be retained. If this is an example of how the Socialist Government manages our affairs, it makes one shudder for its handling of more fundamental and dangerous problems.[16]

But not all Simon's contributions were negative. The Crown Proceedings Act of 1947, which increased the scope for the Crown to be sued, owed much to Simon, who presided over an informal scrutinising committee of Law Lords and others. Indeed the act grew out of a private member's bill which Simon introduced in February 1947, designed to enable the Crown to be sued as occupier in cases where an action for damages would lie if the occupier was a private person.[17] Similarly Simon took charge of the Adoption of Children Bill in late 1949 and secured significant amendments. The new act effected important reforms by providing that a mother could not sign a document expressing willingness to give up her child for adoption until at least six weeks after the birth.[18]

The future of India was a question in which Simon's past history compelled continued interest. Attlee regarded himself as morally committed to speeding up the process of independence, but with relationships between the government and the Viceroy, Lord Wavell, rapidly deteriorating, a situation of total deadlock appeared to have been reached by the beginning of 1947. Simon despaired that the whole Indian situation was 'rapidly passing beyond our grasp and nothing but wide-spread and bloody murder will be the result'. He feared that 'we shall come out of this with the maximum of discredit.'[19] But on 20 February the Prime Minister told the Commons that Wavell was being replaced by Lord Louis Mountbatten and that Britain would transfer power into Indian hands and remove her forces from the sub-continent no later than 1 June 1948. The decision left Simon 'very upset' and he played a major part in the debate in the House of Lords later in the month in what amounted to a motion of censure on the government put down by Lord Templewood, the former Samuel Hoare. Simon's concern focused on the government's determination to leave India by a fixed date, whether or not agreement had by then been reached between the Moslems and the Congress Party.[20] Only the intervention of Lord Halifax, with the authority he carried as an ex-Viceroy, saved the government from defeat.[21]

In line with his own inclinations and in the spirit of the Woolton-Teviot agreement Simon moved increasingly closer to the Conservative party. From the Liberal National ranks Simon became more and more remote. He did not attend the party's conferences nor mix with its Members of Parliament.[22] Simon's drift towards Conservatism made especially good sense in the House of Lords where Liberal National organisation was rudimentary to say the least.[23] Here Simon was regularly consulted by Lords Salisbury and Swinton and, by the late 1940s, he was sometimes being invited to attend meetings of Churchill's shadow cabinet, or 'consultative committee'. His legal skills were found to be of particular value when the Opposition was considering such constitutional matters as the Government of Ireland Act of 1949 and India's desire to assume republican status while remaining within the British Commonwealth. Over the question of Irish citizenship Simon was successful in forcing Jowitt to accept amendments to the government's bill to protect the rights of British citizens who had been born in what was to become the Republic of Ireland, but who had not lived there since the partition of 1922.[24] Simon regularly supported Conservative candidates at by-elections and provoked an angry exchange of letters with Isaac Foot, then the retiring president of the Liberal party, after his appearance on a Conservative platform in Epsom in December 1947. As Simon put it, it was:

the height of absurdity to imagine that the modern democratic Conservative is identical with the reactionary Tory of the past, whom we both used to criticise.[25]

A newspaper article which he wrote after this episode is indicative of Simon's thinking at this time:

Looking back over the forty years that have passed since I first entered the House of Commons, the two changes in the development of our internal politics that strike me most – apart from the growth of Labour – are the Liberalising of the old Tory Party and the ever decreasing authority and representation of the Liberal Party itself . . . The fact is that the country does not for a moment believe that this body can secure such representation in Parliament as will make it again a Governmental force.[26]

Despite such developments in his political ideas a further suggestion to Churchill that he should now join the Conservative party was rebuffed in November 1948. Churchill, perhaps hoping one day to catch a bigger fish and subsume the mainstream Liberal party and conscious that Simon's bargaining position was not strong, determined to keep his old adversary at arm's length.[27] Simon's reminders to Churchill of their common Liberal past cut little ice with the Leader of the Opposition. Notwithstanding their long political association the two men had 'never been intimate'.[28]

By the beginning of 1949 everyone's thoughts were beginning to turn to the next general election and Simon was ready to play an active role to defeat the government. 'I put the defeat of the Socialists at the next General Election far above attachment to any party label.'[29] After Simon had addressed a meeting in Sheffield, the local newspaper drew parallels with his platform performances of thirty years before:

Last night there were the same gestures with his long fingers, the same easy dissection of the difficulties of the day, the shattering scorn of incompetence, frank recognition of inescapable post-war handicaps.[30]

To the Conservative party chairman Simon appealed to be allowed to take a prominent role in the campaign, so that Clement Davies' Liberals would not be allowed to claim a monopoly of Liberal opinion in the public mind.[31] In an attempt to rally Liberal support behind Churchill Simon embarked on an extensive round of public speeches. Yet though the political pendulum swung strongly in the Conservatives' direction, it was not sufficient to deprive Attlee of the reins of government. A battered and in some cases exhausted Labour cabinet was given a renewed mandate by the electorate, although the overall Labour Commons majority was now down to five seats.

Still Simon at seventy-seven years of age was ready to look ahead. If Churchill could still hope to form another cabinet, Simon, a year his senior but in considerably better health, could still dream of being a member of it. His assessment of the situation was that as the Conservatives had probably polled to their full strength at the election, that party's task before the country was next called upon to deliver its verdict was to get all those who had voted Liberal to vote Conservative next time.[32] In view of Attlee's precarious parliamentary situation the time available to secure this aim might well not be long. By this stage in his career Simon's opposition to socialism was fundamental to his continued involvement in politics. Differences of emphasis between Conservatism and Liberalism were, by comparison, of little significance. To Richard Law he explained:

Where I agree with you is in thinking that Socialist philosophy and policy, if continuously pursued, leads to a slave state and that the losses, impalpable as they are, involved in this process are far greater than the gains . . . The loss of liberty is too high a price to pay in the vain struggle for equality.[33]

Simon clearly believed that he was uniquely qualified to bring about the anti-socialist alliance upon which a change of government was dependent. But his suggestion that he be now formally included in the shadow cabinet evoked no response from Churchill.[34]

With his cabinet breaking up around him and subjected to intolerable pressures in the Commons where Labour members had on occasions to be brought in on stretchers to record their votes, Attlee again went to the country in October 1951. Once more Simon campaigned vigorously for a Conservative victory. The *Evening Standard*, which described him as one of the three dominant personalities of the campaign, recorded that despite his seventy-eight years Simon was 'on the hustings almost every night. Lord Simon has spoken in many counties and always with great vigour.'[35] This time the political mood of the country shifted sufficiently to the right to ensure an overall majority for the Conservative party, even though in terms of the popular vote Labour remained the leading party and indeed secured its greatest ever endorsement. Simon's vision had been fulfilled to the extent that the Conservative victory was based on a collapse in the vote of the official Liberal party. The tattered remnant of the great party which Simon had once known – the party upon whose landslide victory he had first been returned to Westminster in 1906 – was now reduced to a mere 730,000 votes.

Winston Churchill had finally achieved his ambition of winning a general election and forming a peacetime administration. Though the identity of the new Lord Chancellor was not disclosed in the first batch of ministerial appointments, Simon's candidature does not seem to have been given much consideration by the new Prime Minister. Churchill's first thought was to nominate Lord Asquith, son of the former Liberal premier, on the rather dubious grounds that his last cabinet, like the first of which he had been a member in 1908, should contain an Asquith. But Asquith's health was poor and he declined Churchill's offer.[36] So the Prime Minister turned instead to Gavin Simonds, a Law Lord of no previous political experience and a man with whom he was not personally acquainted. From Simon's point of view the appointment was ironic, for in 1944 it had been he who had recommended Simonds' appointment as a Chancery Law Lord to

Churchill stressing that Simonds had 'an excellent reputation.'[37]

Simonds' appointment continued to rankle with Simon, especially in view of his lack of political experience. The new Lord Chancellor was 'as innocent of politics as a newly baptized babe', but he 'obviously enjoyed his immersion enormously'.[38] In 1952, during a debate on a motion 'to restore and preserve' the liberties of the subject, Simon slipped in a cutting comment about the Lord Chancellor's late start in politics. Simonds reacted angrily and called for the withdrawal of 'a singularly unpleasant observation', but Simon managed to avoid doing this.[39] As Simon explained to a correspondent, 'one of the reasons why a Lord Chancellor should usually have been a Law Officer in the House of Commons is that it is only in this way that a first-class lawyer learns to endure the "rough and tumble" of debate.' Simonds' speech at the end of a debate about commercial broadcasting 'was a fearful example of the way a fresh-water fish behaves when it first gets into salt water.'[40]

Despite the realisation that he would now never again hold office, Simon continued to play a vigorous and useful role in the House of Lords until a few weeks before his death. Though he was not a minister, the government did occasionally make use of Simon's services in parliamentary debates, as for example when he took charge of the Defamation Bill in 1952. He was particularly interested in the reform of the upper chamber. February 1952 saw him suggesting to Lord Salisbury that he would be willing to join a parliamentary committee on this question in the event that the pressure of governmental business precluded the setting up of a purely cabinet committee.[41] By the end of the year Simon had introduced a private member's bill to create life peerages for men and women. The cabinet considered the question in December but was reluctant to take Simon's bill on board while discussions with the Labour opposition were being suggested on the whole question of Lords' reform. Simon's bill was adjourned in 1953 in the hope of wider agreement between party leaders, but such hopes were not to be fulfilled. Life peerages were delayed until 1958.

As an ex-Lord Chancellor Simon continued to carry out judicial functions in both the House of Lords and the Privy Council. Wartime damage to the Palace of Westminster obliged the Law Lords to move from the chamber of the House to a committee room, thus translating into physical reality the constitutional split between the legislative and judicial functions of the upper house. It was not a development which Simon favoured and when in May 1948 Jowitt proposed a motion formally to establish an Appellate Committee of the Lords, Simon voiced serious misgivings. The change might be the thin end of the wedge, signalling a final departure from the ancient principle whereby the Lords, as the highest court in the land, was seen as the *alter ego* of parliament, the supreme legislative body. He was also worried that future Lord Chancellors would find themselves forced to concentrate increasingly upon their legislative at the expense of judicial functions, (since the two activities could now proceed simultaneously), thus increasingly removing them from close association with the legal world.[42] Despite Simon's warnings the Appellate Committee was duly set up, with some of the long-term consequences which he had predicted. In the period 1951–70 the functions of the Lord Chancellorship became less obviously judicial and on only thirty-nine occasions within these years did the incumbent preside over an appeal.[43] Simon himself registered his personal disquiet by almost ceasing his own participation in the Lords' judicial business.[44] Even so, at the time of his death Simon had just completed his draft speech in an Inland Revenue appeal from Scotland over which he had presided in November 1953. In the Privy Council his legal brain remained as penetrating as ever. In 1952 he presided over a complicated appeal concerning the ownership of a fleet of aeroplanes in Hongkong. Simon's personality dominated the proceedings and, even in his eightieth year, his mastery of the subject matter was impressive.[45]

At no time in his long life could Simon have been described as a popular figure. But in his last years his character did mellow somewhat and it has been truly said that on his eightieth birthday he had more friends than on his seventieth.[46] 'In old age he paid more attention to others.'[47] With increasing regularity and pleasure he returned to Oxford and in the Common Room of All Souls was at his happiest. There he could satisfy his life-long yearning for intellectual debate and stimulation, quoting his favourite poets and exercising his still considerable powers of persuasion upon all who were ready to listen to him. At Oxford he found some of the warmth and friendship which had largely escaped him in public life, but for which he had a real if not always appreciated need. Simon donated generously to All Souls and helped, as Senior Fellow, to supervise the election of a new warden.[48] After one All Souls Gaudy Simon recorded:

I was toasted as the 'Senior Fellow'. There was a large gathering of Fellows and Quondams, including Halifax, Amery and Professors galore. I replied to the toast, thanking the Sub-Warden for proposing it, but protesting at his directing attention to my antiquity.[49]

The death of Lord Sankey in 1948 brought a vacancy in the honorific post of High Steward of the University to which Simon was duly appointed. It meant, as he said, 'Nothing to do and £5 a year.'[50]

Simon's last years also allowed time for writing. Newspaper articles on such varied questions as the Nuremberg trials, the issue of capital punishment and the Oxford Union added a useful contribution to his earnings. In 1949 Simon's yearly income was estimated at £8,500 (£3,300 after tax), a not inconsiderable sum in those days but only a fraction of the figure he had commanded at the bar thirty years earlier. He also supervised the publication of *Simon's Income Tax* in 1948 which became a standard text, but other literary ventures were less successful. There had for some time been interest in the idea that Simon might write his memoirs,[51] but such a venture had not been possible so long as he continued to occupy high office. Yet if Simon delayed too long the opportunity might be lost altogether. As 1949 opened, therefore, Simon set himself an ambitious programme of literary New Year resolutions which included the completion of his autobiography, a small volume entitled 'Select Judgments' consisting of judicial pronouncements memorable for their style or humour, and a Christmas book to be called 'Nine Tales', of which, he noted, five had already been written.[52] Simon envisaged that his memoirs would form an important contribution to historical literature, particularly in relation to the twenties and thirties:

There is a great deal that I should like to put on record about the period between the wars and I should want to write frankly about policies and personalities, and not merely to pour out a stream of justifications. The years that the locusts have eaten are, as yet, rather a blind spot in modern political history and I hope I could contribute something which is authoritative and worth reading.[53]

But progress proved less easy than Simon had hoped, particularly in view of his continued involvement in political and judicial affairs. By November he noted that the task was proving to be 'an enormous grind' and 'though I have a number of shreds and patches there is nothing like what there ought to be at this stage.'[54] Simon approached the historian, Margaret Lambert, one of the editors of the *Documents on British Foreign Policy* to help him write those chapters of his book which related to foreign affairs, but she, though willing to offer advice, could not spare the time from her editorial duties to give more formal assistance. Thus, by the end of 1949 and with a general election in which he hoped to play a significant role pending, Simon had completed none of the three tasks he had set himself at the beginning of the year. Half of the autobiography was completed, but to fulfil his contract with Hutchinsons to produce a completed manuscript of about 120,000 words by the middle of March 1950 would be no easy matter. 'Select Judgments' remained only an idea in his head, while one of the 'Nine Tales' still remained to be written.[55] The March deadline came and went and by July 1950 Simon had set himself a new target for completion by the end of the year.[56] Illness in 1951 caused further delay – Simon felt 'a good deal knocked out' and soon after the election of that year took to his bed with 'threatened pneumonia' – and the decision was taken that he should not attempt to reach the original target of 120,000 words.[57] Finally *Retrospect* was published in June 1952.

Although there were some very favourable contemporary reviews, later assessments have been harsh. Few historians would depart very far from Norman Rose's view that these memoirs 'must be classified among the least revealing ever written'.[58] A number of factors explain this. Some of the practical difficulties which Simon encountered have already been alluded to. He was never able to devote himself wholeheartedly to the task and in many ways the completed work is careless and marred by unnecessary errors.[59] In addition Simon clearly felt bound by the guidelines laid down by Maurice Hankey regarding the memoirs of cabinet ministers which precluded the disclosure of detailed political and diplomatic information. The era of instant revelation was not even anticipated in the early 1950s.[60] A year after his own memoirs had appeared Simon was advised by Lord Winterton that Duff Cooper's memoirs when published would contain details of cabinet meetings including the quoted words of Neville Chamberlain. Simon took this matter up with Normanbrook, the cabinet secretary, and drafted a letter of protest to the *Sunday Times*. But Simon could only drop the matter when he found out that Cooper had received royal sanction for this departure from accepted constitutional practice.[61]

Yet there is a more important reason still why *Retrospect* is such a disappointing work. On reading the book Jowitt complained, 'I am afraid it is not very interesting. It suffers from the fact that he can never let himself go.'[62] A perceptive reviewer in the *Daily Telegraph* noted:

Even in this designedly personal passage, the judicial cloak remains seamless – no single shaft of emotion illuminates with its fire the steady, clear but almost dehumanised light which is the Simonian mind.[63]

This most intensely private of men could not bring himself in the writing of his memoirs to reveal the character which so few had penetrated during nearly half a century in the public light.

1953 saw no appreciable slackening in the tempo of Simon's activities. He celebrated his eightieth birthday in February by attending an England-France rugby match and in May delivered the Romanes lecture in Oxford on the theme of 'Crown and Commonwealth'. He also spoke at Hawarden on 'The Stature of Gladstone'. Short contributions were completed in two volumes on essays in Churchill's honour and Simon also began planning a further book on prominent legal personalities whom he had known. The Bench and Bar of England gave a dinner in his honour on 20 October attended by more than 200 guests. Just before parliament rose for Christmas he spoke in the Lords on the government's negotiations with Egypt and the day before he had initiated a debate on capital punishment. He was keen to leave the law as it was, with the death penalty for murder but with the Home Secretary having the right to administer clemency. But during the recess Simon suffered a stroke and he died peacefully in hospital on 11 January 1954. He was just seven weeks short of his eighty-first birthday. It was in every way characteristic of the man that during his last illness he struggled to complete a classical conundrum, the sort of intellectual challenge in which he had always delighted. Despite his upbringing as a 'son of the manse', Simon had no compelling religious faith, and in accordance with his own instructions, he was cremated in his Oxford robes without religious ceremony.

Notes

1 Simon to Lord Salisbury 13 Jan. 1953, SP 101 fos. 124–5.
2 SP 13 fo. 25; Simon, *Retrospect* p. 286.
3 Heuston, *Lord Chancellors* ii, 127.
4 Simon was still taking golf lessons in the last year of his life.
5 H. M. Hyde, *United in Crime* (London, 1955) p. 57.
6 Attlee to Simon 28 Aug. 1945, SP 96 fo. 157.
7 Simon to C. Grant Robertson 27 Oct. 1944, SP 95 fo. 13; Lord Elwyn Jones, *In My Time* (London, 1983) pp. 100–1. 'Fancy "trying" Hitler!' Simon to Eden May 1944, Tusa and Tusa, *Nuremberg Trial* p. 25.
8 *Sunday Times* 25 Nov. 1945.
9 Roskill, *Hankey* iii, 640–1.
10 Simon to Henderson 8 May 1946, SP 96 fo. 207.
11 This episode and the whole question of the post-war position of the Liberal National party are discussed in the present author's article, 'John Simon and the Post-War National Liberal Party: An Historical Postscript,' *Historical Journal* 32, 2 (1989) pp. 357–67.
12 Simon to Churchill 2 Aug. 1945, SP96 fos. 137–40.
13 Churchill to Simon 9 Aug. 1945, SP 96 fo. 145.
14 The party organisation was finally wound up in 1968.
15 Heuston, *Lord Chancellors* ii, 112–3; H. of L. Debs., 5th Series, vol. 163, cols. 916–17.
16 Simon diary July 1948, SP 13 fo. 38.
17 Ibid, 4 Feb. 1947, SP 13 fo. 26; Heuston, *Lord Chancellors* ii, 118.
18 Ibid, 16 Dec. 1949, SP 13 fo. 69.
19 Simon to Eden 7 Feb. 1947, SP 97 fo. 15.
20 C. Stuart, *The Reith Diaries* (London, 1975) p. 359; H. of L. Debs., 5th Series, vol. 145, cols. 994–1009.
21 K. Harris, *Attlee* p. 380.
22 Letter from Viscount Muirshiel (J. S. Maclay) to the author, 1 Aug. 1987.
23 The Liberal National whip was nominally sent to thirteen peers, but in practice the party's strength was much less than this in the upper house and there were, not infrequently, days when Simon and Lord Teviot were the party's only representatives.
24 Simon diary May 1949, SP 13 fo. 59.
25 Simon to Foot 1 Dec. 1947, SP 97 fo. 50.
26 *Sunday Times* 7 Dec. 1947.
27 Simon to Churchill n.d. (but Nov. 1948) and Churchill to Simon 13 Nov. 1948, SP 97 fos. 140–3.
28 W. S. Churchill, *The Second World War* iv (London, 1951) p. 66.

29 Simon to Teviot 26 July 1949, SP 98 fos. 3–5.
30 *Sheffield Telegraph* 1 Nov. 1949.
31 Simon to Woolton 6 Jan. 1950, SP 98 fo. 106.
32 Simon memorandum 27 Feb. 1950, SP 98 fos. 130–1.
33 Simon to Law 18 Dec. 1950, SP 99 fos. 28–9.
34 Woolton to Churchill 9 March 1950, Woolton MSS 21 fo. 103.
35 *Evening Standard* 17 Oct. 1951.
36 Churchill thus had to content himself with the inclusion of a Lloyd George in his cabinet. Gwilym Lloyd George now became Minister of Food, H. Macmillan, *Tides of Fortune* (London, 1969) p. 356.
37 Heuston, *Lord Chancellors* ii, 146.
38 Lord Kilmuir, *Political Adventure* (London, 1964) p. 194.
39 Heuston, *Lord Chancellors* ii, 151; H. of L. Debs, Fifth Series, vol. 177, col. 1200.
40 Simon to J. Sparrow 18 July 1952, SP 100 fos. 165–6.
41 Simon to Salisbury 2 Feb. 1952, SP 100 fo. 20.
42 P. Purpole, 'Comment', *New Law Journal* 5 Dec. 1968, p. 1160.
43 Heuston, *Lord Chancellors* ii, 27.
44 L. Blom Cooper & G. Drewry, *Final Appeal: A Study of the House of Lords in its Judicial Capacity* (Oxford, 1972) p. 113.
45 Hyde, *United in Crime* p. 57.
46 *Dictionary of National Biography 1951–1960* p. 894.
47 C. M. Bowra, *Memories 1898–1939* (London, 1966) p. 142.
48 Heuston, *Lord Chancellors* ii, 62; *Law Quarterly Review* April 1954 p. 180.
49 Simon diary 8 Nov. 1948, SP 13 fo. 41.
50 Ibid, fo. 31.
51 See, for example, Simon to W. P. Watt (literary agent) 29 Jan. 1943, SP 92 fo. 132.
52 Simon diary 1 Jan. 1949, SP 13 fo. 51.
53 Simon to Spencer Curtis Brown 28 Jan. 1949, Add. SP.
54 Ibid, 13 Oct. 1949.
55 Simon diary 31 Dec. 1949, SP 13 fo. 71.
56 Note by Simon 20 July 1950, Add. SP.
57 Simon to L. G. Curtis Brown 29 Nov. 1951, Add. SP.
58 N. Rose, *Vansittart* p. 104.
59 For example, Simon seems to be confused about his first recollection of F. E. Smith at the Oxford Union and he misspells the name of Ralph Wigram, the Foreign Office official with whom he must have worked closely in the early thirties.
60 J. F. Naylor, *A Man and an Institution* (Cambridge, 1984) p. 235.
61 Simon to Winterton 4 Nov. 1953, SP 103 fos. 56–8.
62 Quoted in Heuston, *Lord Chancellors* ii, 132.
63 *Daily Telegraph* 6 June 1952.

CHAPTER THIRTEEN
THE MAN

The longer I live the more I feel that great intelligence is not the most valuable of God's gifts.[1]

John Simon would probably have been horrified at the thought that anyone should attempt to draw a picture of his character and personality. Though always concerned, particularly in his later years, with the verdict of history, Simon took positive steps to deny to posterity any more revealing glimpses of the private man than he had reluctantly conceded during his own lifetime. Political memoirs often leave the feeling that the author has something to hide. In Simon's case the object to be concealed was clearly himself. His surviving private papers, carefully selected and preserved to convey an impression of which Simon himself would have approved, contain none of the entirely private and family correspondence which might have allowed penetration of the subject's public mask. It was said that Simon wrote two or three times a week to his mother, who lived into her nineties to to see her son reach the office of Foreign Secretary. Yet none of these letters appear to have survived. Even Simon's intermittently kept diary is a patently self-conscious document, a tract written with one eye to the historical legacy and containing none of the careless asides, the spontaneous indiscretions, the injudicious outbursts which so often characterise such records. Yet whatever Simon may have intended, the effort to peel away the shrouds which conceal the real man needs to be made. Character is an important factor in the make-up of any political figure. In Simon's case it is quite crucial to an understanding of both the achievements and limitations of his public career.

Boswell doubted whether anyone could write the life of a man who had not eaten, drunk and lived in social intercourse with him. Though the present author cannot claim to have fulfilled this precondition, he doubts whether anyone was really in a position to play Boswell to Simon's Johnson. 'He hasn't a friend even in his own party,' judged Neville Chamberlain in 1935.[2] Contemporaries not only failed to penetrate the inner depths of Simon's personality, but recognised their inability to do so. 'One never seems quite to get to the point with him of complete understanding,' noted Edward Wood perceptively.[3] And while Simon erected barriers to protect the privacy of his own soul, others found it difficult to relate to him with the intimacy of real friendship:

He seems to have given an impression . . . of keeping all his own personality within locked doors while inviting other people to disclose theirs. And this of course breeds a certain lack of confidence in the minds of the average man. . . .[4]

Challenged with the locked enigma of Simon's personality, Lloyd George dismissively suggested that 'there is no further to get', but this was unfair.[5] A tiny few did manage to penetrate the mask, or at least pierce holes through it, and found a very different character from that displayed to the public gaze. Inevitably this created a yawning chasm between the general view of Simon and that seen by a few perceptive observers.

Simon's family life does not intrude forcefully across the pages of his political career. Yet it was important nonetheless. The staggering impact of his early widowerhood has already been described. It intensified tendencies already present in his still young personality. The quest for solace drove him into a single-minded absorption in his work, which to the outside world gave him a somewhat dehumanised appearance. The three children of his marriage grew up in this atmosphere with a certain distance created between them and their father. For some time his name was linked romantically with the renowned socialite Mrs. Ronnie Greville. Cynics suggested that he would have married her had he not been afraid she would spoil his chances of becoming Prime Minister.[6] But Mrs. Greville once showed Robert Boothby the spot where 'Jack Simon fell on his knees to ask me to marry him. I refused.'[7] Leo Amery heard that Simon then wrote Mrs. Greville a letter in which he vowed that he would now marry the first woman he came across – and that Lady Simon was the result.[8] Be that as it may, Mrs. Greville was reputed to exercise great influence over Simon even after he had become Foreign Secretary. 'In those countries where she is not given a special train, the local British ambassador or minister is sacked,' quipped one observer.[9]

After many years of widowerhood Simon did remarry and to his second wife was hardly less devoted than to his first. Some of the more revealing and personal of his diary entries relate his anxiety over his wife's frail health.[10] Yet this marriage too had its problems. Lady Simon was a strong minded and good-humoured Irish woman, devoted to the cause of abolishing slavery across the world. She proved quite capable of intimidating her husband.[11] But she was socially rather gauche, suffered from prolonged periods of ill-health and became in later years increasingly embarrassing. When she joined her husband in India during the proceedings of the Statutory Commission, one of Simon's fellow commissioners described her as 'a good hearted creature . . . with a tousled Irish head and a great gift for saying the wrong thing . . . for the exterior can only be described as vulgar'.[12] Austen Chamberlain once invited himself to the home of Robert Bruce-Lockhart 'to escape, as he said, from Lady Simon'.[13] Drinking to excess, she nonetheless managed to survive her husband by one year. Though Simon's loyalty to her never wavered, the strains created by his second marriage were sometimes almost as hard to bear as those posed by his first wife's early death. Some of the most critical episodes in Simon's political career, including the crisis of

1939–40, were conducted against a background of serious anxiety about his wife's health. One of the main reasons why he decided in 1938 to end his long association with Spen Valley and seek another constituency nearer London – he was soon adopted for Great Yarmouth – was his desire to spare his wife the ordeal of unnecessary travel. Yet many contemporaries recorded their unfavourable impressions of Simon's second wife and their surprise at his choice of spouse. Amery found her 'an incredible woman', 'Chips' Channon described 'a simple haus frau', while Neville Chamberlain found her 'a sore trial'.[14] 'Why did Sir J.S. marry Lady S?' mused Richard Holt. 'She appears to be quite inferior.'[15]

One other woman exercised a profound influence upon John Simon and that was his mother, Mrs. Fanny Simon. Mother and son were extremely close during Simon's childhood and the relationship continued until her death in 1936. Surrounded by the cares of high office, Simon would seize any available opportunity to absent himself from London to make the long journey to Pembrokeshire to be with her, even when the affairs of state precluded a visit of more than a few hours. He even made an oblique and anonymous reference to her on her birthday during an election broadcast in 1931. On her death Simon wrote a short memoir about his mother in which he revealed flashes of a softer and warmer personality than he usually displayed in public.[16] For years afterwards it became almost a ritual for him that, when a friend or colleague was similarly bereaved, he should send a copy of this little book to the person concerned. It seems never to have struck him that others might find this an inappropriate gesture at a time of private grief. Some observers, indeed, came to see Simon's relationship with his mother in terms of an obsession. After visiting the Simon home in 1938, 'Chips' Channon recorded:

And the guests were then requested to file out through the study so that they might look at his mother's portrait by Gerald Kelly, a remarkable old lady. She looks like Simon's twin with a touch of Whistler's mother. Simon worshipped her. He is as mother-mad as Belisha.[17]

In his private life Simon led a fairly simple existence despite the wealth he earned at the bar. Though capable of acts of considerable generosity, he was throughout his life careful with money, cancelling his annual subscription of 10s. 6d. to the Oxfordshire Historical Society during the recession of 1932.[18] He drank very little and smoked only the occasional cigar or cigarette. In 1911 he purchased Fritwell Manor, a large house near Banbury, but he never adopted the style of a country squire. His repeated anxiety about money is difficult to comprehend. 'Truth to tell,' he wrote after giving up the bar to take on the Indian Statutory Commission, but with several years as the country's highest paid barrister behind him, 'the next two years are going to be very anxious for me, as I have substituted paying taxes for earning a living and I do not quite know how I am going to get through.'[19] His pleasures were essentially middle-class – golf, chess, dancing, theatre and, like Samuel Hoare, skating. Golf was his favourite pastime. His victory in the Parliamentary Golf Handicap in 1934 and captaincy of the Royal and Ancient in 1936–7 caused him great satisfaction and he was still taking lessons in the last year of his life. The sport perhaps reflected his character. Cynics joked that it was his habit to putt around bunkers.[20] A more charitable observer recorded:

His putting is as precise and deadly as his cross-examination . . . And he was quite definite in agreeing to play for the stake of one golf ball, not two, as had been suggested . . . by his hopeful opponent.[21]

Simon sold Fritwell in 1933, by which time his income had fallen considerably, and moved to a more modest house close to Walton Heath golf course.

★ ★ ★

Observers who all too easily found flaws in Simon's character were at least impressed by his physical appearance.[22] In a different age he might even have laid claims to the quality of 'charisma'. He certainly cut a fine figure, full of distinction. Tall, slim, athletically built with graceful limbs and sensitive hands, he had, thought one contemporary, 'the most remarkable head in London'.[23] He was bald from comparative youth and had something of the air of a cleric about him, with a smooth complexion, piercing blue eyes and a serene though not altogether spontaneous smile.[24] His face changed remarkably little over the second forty years of his life. Seeing Simon shortly before his death, one of his former legal pupils, J. W. Scobell Armstrong, 'caught a last glimpse of the confident, handsome, young face, little changed' from the one he had known in his early career at the bar more than half a century before.[25]

The distinguished head contained an equally distinguished brain. The most important element in Simon's make-up was undoubtedly his intellect. 'In sheer intellectual ability,' suggested Gwilym Lloyd George, 'which is a different thing to political ability, I would say no-one in the inter-war period surpassed Sir John Simon.'[26] It was the key to both the successes and, paradoxically, some of the failures of his public career. Without exceptional brainpower the humble son of a congregational minister – the latter's own parents were manual workers – could never have secured those academic qualifications which were the launching pad for his later rise to fame. It was this quality which propelled him via Fettes, Wadham and All Souls towards distinction in both his legal and political careers. Even when, as in 1935 and 1940, his political reputation stood at a low ebb, recognition above all else of Simon's intellectual powers ensured his continued presence inside the British government. His, noted Thomas Jones, was a 'Rolls Royce brain'.[27]

Simon was also endowed with a prodigious memory, a particular asset in a lawyer. Throughout his life he set himself formidable tests of memory and constantly surprised those who worked with him by his unfailing recollection of detail.[28]

Apart from the law Simon was erudite both as a classicist and as a mathematician. 'His idea of making himself socially agreeable,' remarked Sir John Colville, 'was to quote Homer at length and follow it up with an exposition of the Binomial Theorem.'[29] Even the war crisis of 1914 saw him, in a lull between cabinet meetings, discussing with Asquith the parallel between the guarantee of Belgian neutrality and that of the little town of Plataea in the second year of the Peloponnesian War.[30] His love of the classics and of Greek writers in particular remained with him throughout his life. 'Truly,' Simon once told the Greek ambassador, 'the Ancients of your race have said everything that is to be said, and what is more they have done it simply and quietly.'[31] The composition of fluent and witty Greek verse came to him with effortless facility. Even during his final illness he struggled to complete a Greek linguistic conundrum, his mind sparkling to the end.[32]

Inspiration and perspiration are more often linked than is sometimes conceded. This was certainly true in the person of John Simon. His successes owed much to a capacity for hard work which aptly complemented his intellectual power. His work practices were extremely methodical. Walter Monckton recorded:

I learnt how important it is to do well the mechanical job of managing and handling your books and papers. He liked to start with a large empty table and notebook which became not only a guide to the argument but also a key to the documents.[33]

Long hours were part and parcel of his life from his early days at the bar until the end of his ministerial career. It was characteristic of Simon to throw himself wholeheartedly into everything he did. His commitment to his work as chairman of the Indian Statutory Commission stands perhaps as the outstanding example of this characteristic. Only briefly at the Foreign Office did the strain of his enormous industry appear too much for him. He was physically strong and, as a young barrister, had got used to working all through the night when the occasion demanded it. His energy and sheer enthusiasm for work occasioned both respect and disbelief. Walter Monckton recalled the Labrador Boundary dispute of 1926:

Several times we scarcely had an hour in bed, but we often told each other that we really couldn't complain since Simon worked himself equally hard. . . . The case finished just before lunch and [we] decided to go off and celebrate in a joyful lunch. We were debating to ask Simon to join us when we heard him say to his clerk: 'What is the next thing, Ronald?' and we were deterred.[34]

Simon's power of analysis was his greatest asset. His logical mind could be almost frighteningly compelling. There was a razor-edged quality to his brain which sometimes gave the impression of an intellectual machine, perfectly functioning with a relentless and almost inhuman precision. Such attributes could evoke admiration; yet they were unlikely to breed affection. Indeed few things are as likely to alienate the average mortal as being shown remorselessly and unfailingly that he is in the wrong. One witness recorded a revealing episode:

At a dinner party a year or two ago I sat near him and heard him score off half a dozen other guests in a manner that made the rest of us want to applaud. It was quite astonishing. Quick as lightning he would take up a point from one quarter, deliver the rapier-like reply, parry and thrust, thrust and parry, now here, now there, without interval, while we sat around and gasped . . . After that he answered, almost without hesitation, a dozen difficult conundrums – an amazing feat when one considers that he was engaged at the time in a complicated case in the law courts.[35]

It is often men's failings which make them attractive. In respect of his intellect, at least, Simon appeared to be unblemished. Asquith's invention of the nickname 'the Impeccable' has its echo in Churchill's double-edged comment that the trouble with Simon was that he was always right.[36] 'He makes one understand,' noted the *Evening Standard*, 'why certain ancient Greeks blackballed the Sir John Simon of their own day because they were tired of hearing him called "the Just".'[37] 'There is something "uncanny" about him,' confirmed a fellow MP. 'One feels he is not human at all. For "to err is human." Simon never "errs".'[38] His perfectly ordered brain was easily irritated by mental flabbiness. Not suffering fools gladly, Simon could be an extremely difficult person to work for. Many found him 'too much inclined to draw the sword-edge of his logical precision across the infant necks of their ideas'.[39] The young civil servant, Burke Trend, destined to become Secretary to the cabinet, found the first memorandum he prepared for Simon as Chancellor of the Exchequer returned to him neatly torn into four pieces and without comment.[40]

Yet no man's mind is really perfect. Though Simon never failed to be accurate, exact and incisive, it was a weakness that he tried to reduce everything to a merely cerebral exercise. For all his intellectual capacity, there was a certain lack of originality in Simon's thinking.[41] Breadth of view was sometimes lacking.[42] He seemed to have no room for imagination and the emotions. His piercing intelligence could cut through the most twisted tangle of sophistries. Every problem, however complex, could be made to appear almost unbelievably simple. He once claimed to be able to explain the Covenant of the League of Nations to any man in half an hour.[43] Yet in the realm of human affairs where pure logic is not enough, Simon was found wanting. 'We see him pitifully seeking with his intellect,' noted a perceptive writer in the *New Statesman*, 'for the answer which his heart should supply.'[44] His report on India is perhaps the best example of what was both a strength and a failing in his intellectual make-up. He leaves you, noted

Harold Laski, 'with the impression that . . . all is calculated and deliberate from premisses to conclusion'.[45] Simon represented, at his *Times* obituary pointed out, an almost perfect example of the limitations as well as the uses of a great legal brain.[46]

It was the supreme irony of Simon's career that his talents best fitted him for the role he least wished to play. He never, until perhaps his final elevation to the Woolsack in 1940, regarded the law as other than the means by which a talented man of humble birth might secure the financial independence from which to launch into political life. He took an almost perverse delight in denigrating his achievements in a profession which many would have viewed as the summit of ambition. The label of lawyer-politician – 'my right honourable and learned friend' – was one from which he almost visibly recoiled. It always pleased him to recall Arthur Balfour's observation – 'the greatest compliment ever paid me in my early days in the House' – 'Why, I did not know that you were a lawyer.'[47] When a fellow barrister of a younger generation made his maiden parliamentary speech, Simon was quick to offer advice based on his own experience:

Remember this is the only legislative assembly in the world where lawyers as such are unpopular . . . Try and make your speeches on some political topic and not on a legal one. Get them to regard you as one of themselves and dispose of the idea that you could make just as effective a speech for the other side of the argument.[48]

It was sound advice. Yet Simon had never fully taken it himself. Throughout his life in politics he never entirely succeeded in shaking off the image of a lawyer who had simply transferred his skills from the courts to the House of Commons. The great advocate always remained the great advocate. A listener who heard a political broadcast Simon made in 1929 recorded his reaction:

Personally, I felt sure I saw that other equally characteristic little gesture, the careful adjustment of his silk gown on his shoulders as he paused to deliver the thrust.[49]

Those legal skills were, of course, formidable. Simon's generation produced a clutch of distinguished barristers including F. E. Smith, Edward Carson and Rufus Isaacs. Like Simon each made his mark in the political arena. Yet as a lawyer Simon was possibly the most distinguished of them all. His scope was more wide-ranging. There was scarcely a branch of the law in which he failed to prove himself a master. Not surprisingly, his fees reached astronomical proportions. Opposing clients jostled for his services. Yet his skill was primarily that required to convince a judge rather than to sway a jury. Carson, Smith and Isaacs were all more adept than Simon at using their emotions to charm and persuade, and to stir the emotions of others. Simon's appeal was predictably legal and intellectual. 'He was very persuasive, with his calm, intellectual and clear presentation,' remembers Lord Denning.[50] With immense learning and lucid argument, but without histrionics or excessive drama, he could lead a judge to the required conclusion.[51] It was this fact which perhaps explains why he never achieved genuine popularity at the bar.[52] No judge liked to feel that he was being led by the nose by counsel. 'His going,' noted the *New Statesman* when Simon left the bar, 'made less commotion than would a white-bait in the Bay of Biscay.'[53]

Simon's style of speaking inevitably made him a greater force in the courts of law than it did in parliament. His habitual attitude was one of untroubled calm, avoiding everything that savoured of declamation or dramatic gesture. His was a cumulative power, not of driving but of reasoning home his points. Without purple passages and stage effects Simon could still show his unrivalled gift of lucid exposition of even the most complicated subject.

Such mannerisms as he had were those of the law court. At reflective passages his right hand spanned his side; at moments of leaving his listeners with reasoned arguments he bowed slightly; and at times of emphasis his hands instinctively grasped his jacket lapels. Occasionally he would make use of a declamatory fore-finger or a sweep of the arm. His voice was pitched low, with a smooth insinuating tone. Scorn, sarcasm and admiration could all be introduced with the merest inflection of the voice. But his message was always directed to the intellect of his peers. The descent into demagogy to move a lesser mind held no appeal for him. Juries sometimes found him disdainful and condescending. The *Daily Telegraph* compared his qualities to waxen fruits in a glass case – 'not a blemish in the basket, but no appetite is stirred.'[54]

Lord Cranborne once complimented Simon on being the greatest master of exposition he had ever heard in the House of Commons.[55] In similar vein Lord Strauss recalls that his speeches were 'masterpieces of lucid, logical argument that carried rational but little emotional weight'.[56] But the great parliamentary orators have sought to raise passions as well as to win minds. As a parliamentary orator Simon seldom showed the self-confidence he felt in the courts of law. 'When I get up in the Law Courts I don't turn a hair,' he told Lord Moran. 'But I never rise to address the House of Commons without feeling that it is a mill-stream running away from me.'[57] Due to wind up a debate for the government, he once confessed that he felt 'just like a man sentenced to death, who is to be hanged shortly'.[58] In his early career contemporaries often drew a comparison with F. E. Smith. After their legal careers had marched forward in competing unison, their parliamentary paths also frequently crossed, with Simon being asked by his party to follow Smith in debate. One observer recorded:

High as were the style and standard of his speeches, when contrasted with F. E. Smith's full-blooded attack, they gave the impression of an impersonal frigidity . . . Usually there was a perceptible lessening of tension, emotion and interest in the Chamber after he had been speaking for a few minutes, though he was treated with the respect which is always shown to brilliant young men who are also good parliamentarians.[59]

Only occasionally did Simon let go of himself in public speeches. When it happened, it was worthy of comment. After one such performance in a debate on governmental economies the *Morning Post* recorded:

Parliament has never before been treated to the spectacle of its chief Liberal legal expert waving his arms like a tub-thumper, acknowledging his distaste for technicalities, allowing his voice to rise to passionate shouts and permitting his austere countenance first of all to redden and then to become almost purple with anger. He did all this tonight. . . .[60]

In one sense Simon may have been too able a lawyer ever to be fully successful as a politician, for he always gave the impression that he could speak to any brief. The game of logical argument sometimes seemed more important to him than questions of conviction and principle. It is, after all, no part of the lawyer's job to announce that he does not believe in his client's innocence. 'It sometimes needs quite an acute intelligence', noted the *Evening Standard*:

to tell at the end of certain Simonite speeches which side he had been supporting, and even then there is left the impression that his real opinion might possibly be quite different but that for great and good reasons he thought it necessary to support the other side.[61]

Simon could display his great cleverness with ease. But he found it altogether harder to convince an audience that what he said was deeply felt. Some members of his profession could shake off this legal trait when they entered the political arena. No one, for example, could doubt that Edward Carson felt passionately on the question of Ulster. With Simon there was often the impression that in slightly different circumstances he could have argued for the other side. Robert Vansittart claimed that Simon lacked the quality of being ready to go to the stake over an issue in which he believed.[62] In the courts he had a particular skill in persuading judges to accept as self-evident an argument in which he had carefully concealed a logical flaw.[63] What may have been necessary on a client's behalf in the courts of law gave Simon in the political sphere the reputation of lacking sincerity.

The charge was repeated throughout his career. Even the *Isis* of his undergraduate days had drawn attention to 'an affectation of intense earnestness which is (with or without cause) unanimously derided as insincere'.[64] In later years observers as diverse as Margot Asquith, Beatrice Webb, Aneurin Bevan – 'nobody believed he believed' – and Neville Chamberlain reiterated the complaint.[65] Only the last named believed that the charge might be unjustified, yet in politics the appearance of sincerity is even more important than sincerity itself. Not only as a politician, but even more as a person Simon found it difficult to convey sincerity. In the daily social round which is so much a part of the life of a public figure, he affected an excessively polite manner which failed to carry conviction. 'His manner is so formal and so insincerely polite and condescending that he completely baffled me,' commented Lady Ottoline Morrell in 1916.[66] One of those who met him during the work of the Indian Statutory Commission drew a parallel with an 'ingratiating family doctor', while for other observers the character of Uriah Heep came easily to mind.[67] 'Somehow', noted a perceptive writer in the *Daily Express*

he never has shaken off that insinuating court manner of his. You know the type of lawyer who washes his hands with invisible soap. Well, Sir John is so smooth that he looks as though he were rubbed down with vast cakes of soap every day.[68]

He did not in fact find communication with his fellow human beings at all easy. He lacked a sufficiency of automatic good manners to conceal his passing moods.[69] Contemporaries commented on his lack of a sense of humour.[70] 'I have never yet succeeded in feeling quite comfortable in his company,' confessed H. A. L. Fisher.[71] Perhaps the most repeated of all anecdotes about Simon relates to his unfortunate habit of feigning convivial familiarity by slapping someone on the back and then calling him by the wrong name.[72] On a different occasion the same person might have been completely ignored. 'He is not at his best when he wants to be friendly.'[73] The effect of this false bonhomie on others was often disastrous. With some sensitivity for Simon's feelings Kingsley Martin, as editor of the *New Statesman*, removed from a pen-portrait published in 1933 a sentence which began, 'Many of those who have shivered as he took their arm. . . .'[74] Harold Nicolson did not need to excise his true feelings from the private pages of his diary:

As I walked out I felt my arm gripped from behind. It was the Lord Chancellor . . . God, what a toad and a worm Simon is![75]

Simon seemed largely unaware of the effect his manner had on others, and he was certainly incapable of doing anything about it. Yet his unctuous attempts to ingratiate himself reflected above all else the efforts of a lonely man to compensate for an innate and deep-seated shyness, a characteristic which became especially pronounced after the crushing blow of his first wife's early death. Like many others of great intellectual prowess Simon did not thrive in the trivia of small talk. His attempts to do so could be painfully embarrassing. 'He smiles and smiles and bows his head and I murmur to myself, "Serpent",,' recorded one victim of Simon's attempted charm.[76] This was no isolated reaction. The effort at friendship was all too easily interpreted as a sign of condescension. He could never fully shake off a distinctly *de haut en bas* manner of address. It was one of the ironies of Simon's life that a man who wanted desperately to be liked succeeded only in alienating the majority of those who came into casual or professional contact with him. He who would be loved appeared unlovable. There is a story that during the 1930s Simon urged his cabinet colleagues to address him as Jack. Only Jimmy Thomas could bring himself to do so.[77]

Simon's personality could not glow, nor could it kindle a glow in others. For that reason he never attracted the sort of following which a successful politician needs, especially if he aspires to the highest office. A journalist described one of his election meetings:

No one, of course, would dream of shouting "Good old John" as they shouted "Good old Ramsay" at Seaham, and it is inconceivable that he should ever enter so completely into alliance with his constituents as to be, in the Henderson manner, "Uncle Jack." There is something about Sir John that does not permit these things.[78]

He did not command loyalty because his character repelled the affection upon which loyalty depends. An interview with Simon could be an intimidating experience. The journalist Ian Colvin remembered a meeting in 1939:

When I told him that we should be firm in support of Poland, he joined his fingertips and asked me dryly: 'How shall we be firm?' I said by a naval blockade of Germany. 'That means war?' 'Yes, sir'. He asked me whether I had been in the last, which was a disconcerting question. Finally he smiled a smooth smile and assured me that whatever decision was reached, it would be the product of complete agreement between himself, the Prime Minister and Lord Halifax.[79]

Probably no adjective was used more often in contemporary descriptions of Simon than 'cold'.[80] 'There blows about him a chilly wind that keeps his followers at a distance,' noted one journalist.[81] 'It is Simon's tragedy that he has no warmth,' agreed another.[82] Douglas Jerrold remembered him freezing an audience in five minutes.[83] Despite his eagerness to ingratiate himself he could only rarely break down the barriers which divided him from his fellow men. He could command assent, approval, even admiration; but seldom did he penetrate to the hearts of his listeners. Even his writing displayed the same failing. 'This is a cold book,' noted a reviewer of *Retrospect*:

The men and women who cross the stage are rarely, if ever, illumined with the warm glow of sympathy and understanding; rarely, if ever, do these figures flash to life in the intensity of heroic endeavour, or reveal their limitations by the frailties, even the trivialities, which humanise the great and make lovable the weak.[84]

Again, it came down to the difficulty experienced by a man of great intellectual capacity in descending from his Olympian heights to traffic with more ordinary mortals.

Simon's inability to convey sincerity and warmth both in his public speaking and in his personal relations had a major impact upon the development of his historical reputation. After 'cold' the word 'sly' perhaps appears most frequently in contemporary descriptions. 'I am always trying to like him,' stressed Neville Chamberlain

and believing I shall succeed when something crops up to put me off. He has a certain air of – what is it – *slyness* which is rather disconcerting in a man of the first rank.[85]

A fellow Liberal thought him 'shifty'.[86] Simon seemed always to be looking ahead and calculating his every move with a view to personal advantage. The result has been a tendency when interpreting the major episodes of Simon's career to attribute unattractive motives, even when the actual action taken appears to have been correct. As *The Times* put it at his death:

He had . . . a certain coldness of approach and a reserve which sometimes tended, however unjustly, to suggest that he had hidden motives.[87]

His decision to remain in office in 1914 has been seen as prompted by the promise of ministerial advancement. His resignation over conscription in 1916 emerges as a political miscalculation in which no point of principle was at stake. In 1931 he abandoned his party and his beliefs in a desperate bid for office in the National Government. Even his crucial role in persuading Chamberlain to declare war in September 1939 represented his one hope of securing the premiership for which he longed. In short, the only truly important motive force is seen as Simon's ambition. A. K. Chesterton summed up a common view:

John Simon . . . organised his entire life for victory – and that victory was to take the form of a long and glorious leadership of the British nation as a Cabinet Minister of the front rank, and one day, perhaps, of the first eminence. Every waking moment was dedicated to this ambition.[88]

Ambition was certainly an important factor in Simon's make-up. But he was never as personally grasping as many supposed. At least at some of the critical moments of his career his motivation deserves to be given the benefit of the doubt.

It did Simon's reputation no good at all that he failed to remain loyal to the parliamentary Liberal party. Few attributes are as valued in the British political system as loyalty to party. The motives of those who change allegiance are almost invariably regarded as suspect. Yet there was a greater consistency in Simon's political thinking than might at first appear to be the case. 'Liberalism was his creed,' asserted Lord Salisbury at the time of Simon's death, 'and he never swerved from it.'[89] Where Simon did change was in his perception of how best the cause of liberalism could be served. Throughout his life, but particularly from the early 1920s, and into his retirement after the Second World War, he displayed a steady opposition to socialism as the ultimate threat to liberal values. Never a pronounced constructive radical, the preservation of abstract freedoms was always more important to him than any common ground of reforming zeal which some Liberal politicians thought they shared with the Labour party. Many

Liberals in the 1920s failed to see that, denied electoral reform, their party faced a mortal challenge from the rise of Labour. After the experience of 1923–4 Simon saw this point very clearly. He told a Liberal rally in Liverpool in May 1929 that, if the forthcoming general election produced the same result as in 1923, the Liberal party would not repeat the experiment of putting Labour in office.[90] His subsequent alienation from the Lloyd Georgeite party is altogether understandable. Furthermore, he came to see that in the Conservative party of Baldwin and Neville Chamberlain a liberalising process had genuinely taken place which made political accommodation, unthinkable before 1914, an acceptable proposition. This was even more the case after World War Two when the Conservative party fell increasingly under the influence of men on its own liberal wing such as Macmillan, Eden and Butler. Thus Simon came to favour a broad Liberal-Conservative front as the best way to oppose socialism. By the last years of his life he was ready to become a Conservative himself.

★   ★   ★

Effectively though he concealed it from most of those with whom he came into contact in politics and at the bar, Simon did have a warmer and more human side. When his inherent shyness and reserve had been broken down a few intimates saw an altogether more attractive aspect to his character. 'From my own personal experience of him,' declared the Labour peer, Lord Alexander, 'behind all that apparent coldness was one of the most human and feeling personalities it would be possible to meet.'[91] Likewise Bechhofer Roberts found 'geniality and abundant humanity under the surface'.[92] It was an atmosphere such as that at All Souls that Simon found it possible to relax his guard. Here his reserved nature thawed to an extent that the outside world would have found it difficult to imagine. Though grudging to himself he could be extremely generous to others. It is said that he used his first savings to send his father on holiday to America.[93] Contemporaries sometimes found their sons' school fees being paid for them; colleagues in difficulties might receive interest-free loans; junior barristers in his chambers would be invited to golfing holidays at Gleneagles with all expenses met; to All Souls he made repeated benefactions.[94] Certainly there was a very considerate side to Simon's nature. Still in part this was the unpopular man, striving for favour, deeply concerned by what people might think of him. Robert Boothby, obliged to resign office in 1940 over his failure to declare an interest in Czech assets frozen in London, received a charming note in Simon's own hand, saying that he had had nothing whatever to do with the events leading to Boothby's fall and wishing him well 'in this unconscionable world'.[95] But many were moved by Simon's kindness. Douglas Hogg recalled a particularly thoughtful act:

I came back as a junior after five months illness expecting to find my practice vanished and myself nearly forgotten. You were on the doorstep to welcome me and to give me fresh courage.[96]

Simon's surviving papers contain the admittedly rather self-consciously preserved copies of dozens of letters of congratulation, commiseration, appreciation and condolence.[97] Nor were these gestures reserved for the great and famous:

One afternoon I had to see Sir John Simon, then Home Secretary . . . He looked tired out. His daughter was ill in the country and I believe that he spent every night at her side. When I went in he was writing letters – 'all to people who had done things for the Government and whom no one has yet troubled to thank.'[98]

Sadly for his historical reputation, this was not the John Simon known to the world at large.

The fact that, by and large, Simon was not a popular man goes a long way to explain the limitations of his political career. 'The fact that he creates such an [unfavourable] impression,' noted Lord Irwin in 1929, 'militates against his ever achieving the biggest success in parliamentary life.'[99] But it was certainly not the only factor. There were other important defects in his character. Chief perhaps was his notorious indecision. He was 'cautious to the verge of pessimism'.[100] Lloyd George's stinging words bear repetition:

Simon has sat on the fence so long that the iron has entered into his soul.[101]

Simon had an almost monumental capacity for seeing all aspects of a question. In one sense this was a virtue. His subtle brain appreciated complexities and complications where simpler minds saw none. Horace Wilson condemned him simply for being long-winded – 'took an hour over things that didn't need more than ten minutes'.[102] But politics – particularly political leadership – is ultimately about taking decisions and this Simon found extremely difficult. His brilliant intellect could always see the imperfections of any proposed policy. His solution was usually to hedge and leave it to others to cast the die. Despising decision-making he found in qualifications and nuances the reasons to avoid taking action. About very few matters was Simon ready to be unequivocal. Even on questions of little moment his conviction seemed fragile. Writing of his childhood, he described the countryside of Pembrokeshire from Tenby to Milford Haven, which 'in the enchantment of its varied and haunting beauty, has no rival in our island'. Then, almost as if he realised that there might be other points of view, he added, 'So at least it has always seemed to me.'[103]

Simon's desire to embrace as many alternatives of policy as possible proved most damaging during his years as Foreign Secretary, though, as has been suggested above, this was not a time when anyone charged with the direction of British diplomacy would have found easy answers to the country's problems. The cartoonist David Low explained his characteristic depiction of the Foreign Secretary: 'I sometimes draw him with a sinuous writhing body because that conveys more or less his disposition to subtle compromise.'[104] But the problem went back much earlier in Simon's career. His indecision had been commented on during the war crisis of 1914.[105] He was 'vacillating in the extreme,' noted William Wedgwood Benn in 1925.[106] To explain away this failing simply as a characteristic of Simon's profession is only partially satisfactory. 'A legal training,' it has been argued, 'does not encourage decisiveness.'[107] This may be so. Certainly a lawyer's instinct is to conduct a case so as to avoid questions which do not require an immediate answer and questions to which he does not himself know the answer. He will try if possible to skirt around a problem if the attempt to resolve it involves dangers for his case.[108] Yet not all lawyers have been beset in politics by the irritating trait of indecision. The fault must in part be seen as personal to Simon.

★   ★   ★

What then, finally, is one to make of the career of John Simon? The factual achievements of his life are beyond dispute. That these achievements were secured with no obvious advantages of birth makes them all the more remarkable. Few men in British history, and none of his own generation except for Winston Churchill, held a greater number and variety of the highest offices of state. To say that this immensely talented man would have been worthy of all his offices had he never held them is a cruel overstatement.[109] Yet there is about him an unmistakable air of failure, of promise unfulfilled. The question always to be asked is not why he got as far as he did, but rather why he did not go farther. The talents which inevitably brought him into the first rank never made him the first man in that rank. There is a sense in which the great barrister who won so many cases for others lost his own.

Political success is inevitably measured not by the mere occupancy of office, but by the constructive achievements secured therein. In this respect it is easy to understand the feeling of disappointment which characterises Simon's career and which he probably shared. Yet it was Simon's lot to occupy office when this sort of creativity was almost out of human reach. His political power was at its peak in the thirties, a decade which has been ruthless in its destruction of historical reputations, not least his own. Yet the deeper our appreciation of the problems confronting British statesmen in these years, the more clearly we sense the good fortune of those who were then excluded from power. The constraints within which politicians work are usually more narrow than contemporaries and many later historians are ready to admit. To have been Foreign Secretary during the worst years of economic depression, during the first major challenge to the authority of the League and during the rise of Adolf Hitler was not the environment within which a creative architect of British diplomacy would choose to display his talents. To have held the Exchequer when circumstances demanded both an effective response to national defence and a protection of the country's fragile economic recovery offered an equally uninviting prospect. Even to sit on the Woolsack for the duration of a world war was scarcely an ideal proposition. Simon, of course, made mistakes. He had palpable weaknesses. And it is no part of the historian's task, even his biographer's, to conceal these. But if the background of office is borne in mind and the deeply ingrained historiographical hostility towards him is stripped away, Simon's 'achievement' looks creditable if not spectacular.

Achievement was certainly important to Simon. His nonconformist background may well have instilled this attitude into him from an early age. 'Simon always remained the head boy of Fettes,' suggested A. L. Rowse, 'he *had* to get all the prizes.'[110] Many considered that Simon had a great opinion of himself.[111] But others were less sure. Harold Nicolson, no friend of Simon's, struck a different and perceptive note in his review of *Retrospect*:

The nectarines and peaches of office dropped one by one into Lord Simon's hands; he describes them as if they were a bag of prunes . . . A man who looks along the corridor of his career, who sees it adorned with such integrity and worth, has the right, even the duty, to show that he is pleased with himself. Lord Simon manifests no such pleasure.[112]

Thus the man who was always going to be great never quite was:

Often he could touch with his finger-tips the ivory gates and the golden – and he never got inside. Perhaps he annoyed the gate-keeper by slapping him on the shoulder and calling him by the wrong name.[113]

Notes

1 Irwin to Lane Fox 29 July 1928, Irwin MSS Eur C152/18.
2 N. Chamberlain to H. Chamberlain 22 May 1935, Chamberlain MSS NC 18/1/918.
3 Irwin to N. Chamberlain 15 April 1929, Irwin MSS Eur C152/18.
4 Irwin to Archbishop of Canterbury 15 April 1929, ibid.
5 Lord Swinton, *Sixty Years of Power* p. 49.
6 K. Young (ed.), *Bruce-Lockhart Diaries* i, 279.
7 Lord Boothby, *Recollections of a Rebel* (London, 1978) p. 68.
8 Barnes and Nicholson (eds.), *Amery Diaries* ii, 696.
9 Young (ed.), *Lockhart Diaries* i, 305.
10 See, for example, Simon diary 31 Jan. 1940, S P 11 fo. 63.
11 Lord Sherfield [Roger Makins] recalls Simon's anxiety as Foreign Secretary when he was obliged to receive his wife formally as a representative of the anti-slavery movement. Interview with the author, 19 May 1986.
12 Lane Fox to Baldwin 27 Nov. 1928, Baldwin MSS vol. 102 fos. 247–9.
13 Young (ed.), *Lockhart Diaries* i, 198.
14 Barnes and Nicholson (eds.), *Amery Diaries* ii, 696; R. R. James (ed.), *Chips* p.

224; N. Chamberlain to Ida Chamberlain 30 Oct. 1937, Chamberlain MSS NC 18/1/1026. On another occasion Chamberlain wrote: 'How he came to marry that wife I don't know. She doesn't seem to fit the part of a grande dame!' Chamberlain to Irwin 12 Aug. 1928, Irwin MSS Eur C 152/18.

15 Richard Holt diary 9 Feb. 1919, 920 DUR 1/11.

16 Sir J. Simon, *Portrait of my Mother* (London, 1936). See also the obituary written by Simon in *The Times* 2 Nov. 1936.

17 James (ed.), *Chips* pp. 224–5.

18 R. Heuston, *Lord Chancellors* ii, 18.

19 Simon to D. MacLean 8 May 1928, S P 61 fo. 188.

20 J. Gunther, *Inside Europe* (London, 1936) p. 269.

21 *The People* 25 Sept. 1927.

22 Lloyd George was an exception: 'I've always been interested in phrenology. Simon and Neville have big bumps of conceit.' T. Jones, *Diary with Letters* p. 470. The caricaturist Emery Kelen thought Simon's head was 'much too small for his body'. E. Kelen, *Peace in Their Time* (London, 1964) p. 278.

23 Leslie Hore-Belisha, 'Sir John Simon's Day', *Evening Standard* 27 Nov. 1924.

24 Churchill wrote of Simon's 'marble smile', *Sunday Pictorial* 8 Nov. 1931. Preparing an article on Simon for the *New Statesman*, Daniel O'Connell wrote: 'His smile illuminates his countenance as the nameplate does a coffin.' K. Martin, *Editor* (pb. edn., London, 1969) pp. 168–9.

25 J. Scobell Armstrong, *Yesterday* p. 122.

26 Notes for autobiography in possession of Viscount Tenby.

27 T. Jones, *Diary with Letters* p. 454. Significantly Jones added, 'but cannot steer'.

28 Interview with the Second Viscount Simon, 14 Nov. 1985; J. Colville, *Fringes of Power* pp. 103–4.

29 J. Colville, *Man of Valour* (London, 1972) p. 105.

30 *Retrospect* p. 96.

31 Simon to D. Caclamanos 1 Sept. 1942, S P 91 fo. 128.

32 Interview with the Second Viscount Simon, 14 Nov. 1985.

33 Lord Birkenhead, *Walter Monckton* (London, 1969) p. 78.

34 Ibid, pp. 77–8.

35 Hesketh Pearson, 'A Political Dark Horse', *John Bull* 7 Feb. 1925.

36 Interview with the Second Viscount Simon, 14 Nov. 1985.

37 *Evening Standard* 28 May 1930.

38 Ben Spoor, 'Sir John Simon', *British Weekly* 10 Sept. 1925.

39 *The World* 11 Dec. 1914.

40 Colville, *Fringes of Power* p. 35.

41 A. Rowse, *All Souls and Appeasement* p. 16; 'He can only work to a brief.' M. Asquith to Baldwin 1 Dec. 1931, Baldwin MSS vol. 45 fo. 222.

42 'Lloyd George says Balfour describes John Simon as a small man for a big job and a big man for a small job . . . He has no breadth of view.' J. McEwen (ed.), *Riddell Diaries* p. 84.

43 Thumbnail biography by W. Foss and A. B. Austin, S P 183 fo. 137.

44 'Sir John Simon', *New Statesman and Nation* 16 Dec. 1933.

45 *Daily Herald* 19 July 1930.

46 *The Times* 12 Jan. 1954.

47 Simon to D. Maxwell Fyfe 30 July 1935, S P 82 fo. 196.

48 Lord Kilmuir, *Political Adventure* (London, 1964) p. 34.
49 *The Star* 27 May 1929.
50 Lord Denning to the author 19 Jan. 1987.
51 Edward Marjoribanks drew a distinction between Simon as the greatest lawyer of his time and Carson as the greatest advocate. K. Young (ed.), *Lockhart Diaries* i, 198.
52 Young (ed.), *Lockhart Diaries* i, 279, 400; J. Colville, *Man of Valour* p. 105; Bishop Henson journal 13 March 1931.
53 'Sir John Simon', *New Statesman and Nation* 16 Dec. 1933.
54 *Daily Telegraph* 28 Feb. 1930.
55 Cranborne to Simon 26 Feb. 1942, S P 90 fo. 96.
56 Lord Strauss to the author 10 Dec. 1985.
57 Lord Moran, *Churchill: the Struggle for Survival* (London, 1966) p. 686.
58 G. Shakespeare, *Let Candles be Brought In* p. 41.
59 Lord Winterton, *Orders of the Day* p. 35.
60 *Morning Post* 15 April 1926.
61 *Evening Standard* 28 May 1930; 'One sometimes got the impression that in politics, as in law, he was willing to speak to almost any brief and would ruthlessly devote all his mental energies to the task so long as it lasted.' G. Lloyd George notes for autobiography.
62 A. J. P. Taylor (ed.), *Off the Record* p. 143.
63 *Law Quarterly Review* April 1954, pp. 177–8.
64 Quoted by 'Ephesian' [C. E. Bechhofer Roberts] in 'Simon: A Study in Silk', *The People* 25 Sept. 1927.
65 M. Asquith to H. Samuel 20 Sept. 1932, Samuel MSS A/89/56; B. Webb diary 18 Oct. 1931; M. Foot, *Aneurin Bevan* vol. 2 (London, 1973) p. 246; N. Chamberlain to H. Chamberlain 22 May 1935, Chamberlain MSS 18/1/918.
66 R. Gathorne-Hardy (ed.), *Ottoline at Garsington* (London, 1974) p. 98.
67 N. Chamberlain diary 26 July 1929, NC 2/22; C. Lysaght, *Brendan Bracken* p. 160; B. Liddell Hart, *Memoirs* i, 205.
68 G. Edinger, 'Simply Simon', *Daily Express* 20 Oct. 1933.
69 J. Scobell Armstrong, *Yesterday* pp. 120–1.
70 T. Clarke, *Lloyd George Diary* p. 36; R. Bernays, *Naked Fakir* (London, 1931) pp. 52–3.
71 Fisher to Irwin 9 May 1929, Irwin MSS Eur C 152/18.
72 J. Gunther, *Inside Europe* p. 269; D. Foot, *British Political Crises* p. 123; *Daily Express* 20 Oct. 1933; Kelen, *Peace in Their Time* p. 279; G. McDermott, *The Eden Legacy* (London, 1969) p. 51.
73 *Daily Express* 20 Oct. 1933. See also Ormsby-Gore to Baldwin 8 Oct. 1933, Baldwin MSS vol. 121 fos. 83–4: 'Personally I don't dislike or think ill of Simon except when he tries to be kind.'
74 K. Martin, *Editor* pp. 168–9.
75 H. Nicolson, *Diaries and Letters* ii, 407.
76 Gathorne-Hardy (ed.), *Ottoline* p. 98.
77 D. Foot, *British Political Crises* p. 123; Lord Egremont, 'Success', *The Spectator* 8 April 1966. The Spanish delegate to the League of Nations offered an interesting explanation: 'The fact that he had to stoop to talk to most people made it natural for him to be or seem to be condescending.' S. de Madariaga, *Morning*

Without Noon p. 210.

78 *Manchester Guardian* 15 Oct. 1931.

79 I. Colvin, *Vansittart in Office* (London, 1965) p. 303.

80 See, for example, Young (ed.), *Lockhart Diaries* i, 400; H. A. L. Fisher to Irwin 9 May 1929, Irwin MSS Eur C 152/18; Lord Williams of Barnburgh, *Digging for Britain* (London, 1965) p. 65.

81 Article by George Godwin, *Referee* 1 June 1930.

82 *New Statesman* 16 Dec. 1933.

83 D. Jerrold, *Georgian Adventure* (London, 1937) p. 328.

84 *Birmingham Post* 10 June 1952.

85 R. Chamberlain to Irwin 12 Aug. 1928, Irwin MSS Eur C 152/18.

86 Ernest Benn to W. Benn 29 April 1925, cited M. Bentley, *Liberal Mind* p. 97.

87 *The Times* 12 Jan. 1954.

88 *The Weekly Irish Times* 22 Nov. 1930.

89 H. of L. Debs, 5th Series, vol. 185, col. 262.

90 *Liverpool Post* 7 May 1929.

91 H. of L. Debs, 5th Series, vol. 185, col. 264. 'Simon is the warmest-hearted iceberg there ever was.' *Sunday Express* 24 March 1940.

92 'A Study in Silk', *The People* 25 Sept. 1927.

93 Ibid.

94 Heuston, *Lord Chancellors* ii, 41.

95 Lord Boothby to the author 9 Dec. 1985.

96 Heuston, *Lord Chancellors* i, 466.

97 See, for example, Simon to Clementine Churchill 1 June 1915, following Churchill's demotion from the Admiralty, M. Gilbert, *Churchill* iii, companion pt. 2 p. 984.

98 Lord Mersey, *Picture of Life* p. 266.

99 Irwin to Archbishop of Canterbury 15 April 1929, Irwin MSS Eur C 152/18.

100 Jerrold, *Georgian Adventure* p. 328.

101 Though attributed to Lloyd George, these words may not have originated with him. 'I told him the *bon mot* about Simon, and never in my life have I seen the phrase "exploded with laughter" more nearly realised in practice. He asked who had first spoken the judgement on Simon and when I suggested Ramsay Muir, he replied: "No, a dry old stick like that would be quite incapable of that sort of brilliance".' Sir R. Acland to the author 1 Sept. 1988.

102 C. Stuart (ed.), *The Reith Diaries* (London, 1975) p. 229.

103 *Retrospect* p. 14.

104 D. Low, *Ye Madde Designer* (New York, 1935) p. 55.

105 See above pp. 30–2.

106 Wedgwood Benn diary 7 May 1925, Stansgate MSS ST/66.

107 *New Statesman* 16 Dec. 1933.

108 *Law Quarterly Review* April 1954 p. 179.

109 C. Coote, *A Companion of Honour: the Story of Walter Elliot* (London, 1965) p. 91.

110 A. Rowse, *All Souls* p. 16; cf. Lord Vansittart, *Mist Procession* p. 428, 'the eternal prizeman boyishly eager for the good report which the grown world grudges'.

111 See, for example, Ramsay MacDonald diary 21 Oct. 1931, citing the opinion of

William Jowitt.

112 Quoted in H. Williamson, *The Walled Garden* (London, 1956) p. 23.
113 G. Edinger, 'Simply Simon', *Daily Express* 20 Oct. 1933; cf. Lord Egremont, 'Success', *The Spectator* 8 April 1966. Studying Simon's features during an interview in 1935, W. P. Crozier concluded: 'If I had never known anything at all about him I would have said that he was a bitter and disappointed man.' A. J. P. Taylor (ed.), *Off the Record* p. 34.

BIBLIOGRAPHY

A MANUSCRIPT COLLECTIONS
1 *Public Records*
Cabinet papers: CAB 23 (Cabinet conclusions)
                 CAB 65 (War Cabinet conclusions)

2 *Private Papers*
Altrincham papers (Bodleian Library, Oxford, microfilm)
Amulree papers (Bodleian Library, Oxford)
Asquith papers (Bodleian Library, Oxford)
Baldwin papers (Cambridge University Library)
Cadogan papers (Churchill College, Cambridge)
Cecil of Chelwood papers (British Library)
Austen Chamberlain papers (Birmingham University Library)
Neville Chamberlain papers (Birmingham University Library)
Dawson papers (Bodleian Library, Oxford)
H. A. L. Fisher papers (Bodleian Library, Oxford)
Gardiner papers (British Library of Political and Economic Science)
David Lloyd George papers (House of Lords Record Office)
Gwilym Lloyd George papers (in possession of Viscount Tenby)
Herbert Gladstone papers (British Library)
Bishop Henson papers (Dean and Chapter Library, Durham)
Hannon papers (House of Lords Record Office)
Holt papers (Liverpool City Library)
Irwin papers (India Office Library)
Kennet papers (Cambridge University Library)
Lane-Fox papers (in possession of family)
†MacDonald papers (Public Record Office)
Murray papers (Bodleian Library, Oxford)
Reading papers (India Office Library)
Rumbold papers (Bodleian Library, Oxford)
Runciman papers (Newcastle University Library)
Samuel papers (House of Lords Record Office)
Sankey papers (Bodleian Library, Oxford)
Selborne papers (Bodleian Library, Oxford)
Somervell papers (Bodleian Library, Oxford)
*Simon papers (Bodleian Library, Oxford, Public Record Office and India Office Library)
Stansgate papers (House of Lords Record Office)
Templewood papers (Cambridge University Library)
Trevelyan papers (Newcastle University Library)

Tweedsmuir papers (Queen's University, Kingston, Canada)
Wallace papers (Bodleian Library, Oxford)
Beatrice Webb diary (Harvester microfiche)
Woolton papers (Bodleian Library, Oxford)
†All users of MacDonald's diary are asked to state that 'The contents of these diaries were, in Ramsay MacDonald's words, "meant as notes to guide and revive memory as regards happenings and must on no account be published as they are".'
*The main collection of Simon papers in the Bodleian Library is referred to in the notes by abbreviation 'SP'; those in the Indian Office Library by 'Simon MSS'; the Public Record Office papers are in the series FO 800.

B OFFICIAL PAPERS

Hansard, *Parliamentary Debates*
Report of the Indian Statutory Commission (2 vols., London, 1930) Cmd. 3568–9
Documents on British Foreign Policy 1919–1939: Second Series (edited by W. N. Medlicott, D. Dakin and M. E. Lambert); Third Series (edited by E. L. Woodward and R. Butler)

C NEWSPAPERS AND PERIODICALS [largely consulted through the extensive collection of press cuttings in the Simon papers in the Bodleian Library]

The Birmingham Post	*The Northern Mail*
British Weekly	*The Observer*
The Cleckheaton Guardian	*The Pembrokeshire Telegraph*
The Congregational Quarterly	*The People*
The Daily Dispatch	*Punch*
The Daily Express	*Referee*
The Daily Herald	*The Sheffield Telegraph*
The Daily News	*The Spectator*
The Daily Telegraph	*The Spenborough Guardian*
The Derby Daily Telegraph	*The Star*
The Eastern Daily Press	*The Sunday Express*
The Economist	*The Sunday News*
The Evening Standard	*The Sunday Pictorial*
The Irish Weekly Times	*The Sunday Times*
John Bull	*The Times*
The Law Quarterly Review	*The Welsh Gazette*
The Leeds Mercury	*The Western Mail*
The Liverpool Post	*The Western Morning News*
The Manchester Guardian	*The Westminster Gazette*
The Morning Post	*The World*
The New Law Journal	*The Yorkshire Observer*
The New Statesman and Nation	*The Yorkshire Post*

D PUBLISHED DIARIES AND MEMOIRS [place of publication is London unless otherwise stated].

C. Addison, *Politics from Within 1911–1918* (2 vols., 1924)
C. Addison, *Four and a half Years* (2 vols., 1934)
L. S. Amery, *My Political Life* (3 vols., 1953–5)
C. Asquith, *Diaries 1915–1918* (1968)

C. R. Attlee, *As it Happened* (1954)

Lord Avon, *Facing the Dictators* (1962)

Lord Avon, *The Reckoning* (1965)

J. Barnes and D. Nicholson (eds.), *The Leo Amery Diaries* (2 vols., 1980–8)

E. C. Bentley, *Those Days* (1940)

R. Blake (ed.), *The Private Papers of Douglas Haig 1914–1919* (1952)

B. Bond (ed.), *Chief of Staff: the Diaries of Lieutenant-General Sir Henry Pownall* (1973)

Lord Boothby, *I Fight to Live* (1947)

Lord Boothby, *Recollections of a Rebel* (1978)

C. M. Bowra, *Memories 1898–1939* (1966)

M. V. Brett and O. Brett (eds.), *Journals and Letters of Reginald, Viscount Esher* (vols. 2–4, 1934–8)

M. Brock and E. Brock (eds.), *H. H. Asquith: Letters to Venetia Stanley* (Oxford, 1982)

Lord Butler, *The Art of the Possible* (1971)

Viscount Cecil, *A Great Experiment* (1941)

Viscount Cecil, *All the Way* (1949)

Sir A. Chamberlain, *Politics from Inside* (1936)

Lord Chatfield, *It Might Happen Again* (1947)

W. S. Churchill, *The Gathering Storm* (1949)

W. S. Churchill, *The Hinge of Fate* (1951)

T. Clarke, *My Lloyd George Diary* (1939)

Sir J. Colville, *Footprints in Time* (1976)

Sir J. Colville, *The Fringes of Power: Downing Street Diaries 1939–1955* (1985)

A. Duff Cooper, *Old Men Forget* (1953)

C. R. Coote, *Editorial* (1965)

C. Cross (ed.), *Life with Lloyd George: The Diary of A. J. Sylvester 1931–45* (1975)

H. Dalton, *The Fateful Years* (1957)

E. David (ed.), *Inside Asquith's Cabinet* (1977)

D. Dilks (ed.), *The Diaries of Sir Alexander Cadogan* (1971)

P. Einzig, *In the Centre of Things* (1960)

Lord Elwyn-Jones, *In My Time* (1983)

Sir A. Fitzroy, *Memoirs* (vol. 2, n.d.)

C. B. Fry, *Life worth Living* (1939)

R. Gathorne-Hardy (ed.), *Ottoline at Garsington: Memoirs of Lady Ottoline Morrell 1915–1918* (1974)

D. Lloyd George, *War Memoirs* (2 vols., 1936–8)

Lord Gladwyn, *Memoirs* (1972)

Lord Halifax, *Fullness of Days* (1957)

Lord Hankey, *The Supreme Command* (vol. 1, 1961)

B. H. Liddell Hart, *The Memoirs of Captain Liddell Hart* (2 vols., 1965)

J. Harvey (ed.), *The Diplomatic Diaries of Oliver Harvey* (1970)

J. Harvey (ed.), *The War Diaries of Oliver Harvey* (1978)

Lord Hemingford, *Back-Bencher and Chairman* (1946)

F. W. Hirst, *In the Golden Days* (1947)

Lord Home, *The Way the Wind Blows* (1976)

R. R. James (ed.), *Chips: the Diaries of Sir Henry Channon* (1967)

R. R. James (ed.), *Memoirs of a Conservative: J. C. C. Davidson's Memoirs and Papers, 1910–37* (1969)

D. Jay, *Change and Fortune* (1980)

D. Jerrold, *Georgian Adventure* (1937)

T. Jones, *A Diary with Letters 1931–50* (1954)

E. Kelen, *Peace in Their Time* (1964)

Lord Kilmuir, *Political Adventure* (1964)

Sir I. Kirkpatrick, *The Inner Circle* (1959)

Lord Lee of Fareham, *A Good Innings* (privately published 1939–40)

D. Low, *Ye Madde Designer* (New York, 1935)

J. M. McEwen (ed.), *The Riddell Diaries 1908–1923* (1986)

N. MacKenzie and J. MacKenzie (eds.), *The Diary of Beatrice Webb* (vols. 3 and 4, 1984–5)

R. Macleod and D. Kelly (eds.), *The Ironside Diaries 1937–40* (1962)

H. Macmillan, *The Winds of Change 1914–1939* (1966)

H. Macmillan, *Tides of Fortune 1945–1955* (1969)

S. de Madariaga, *Morning Without Noon* (Farnborough, 1974)

K. Martin, *Editor* (pb. edn. 1969)

V. Massey, *What's Past is Prologue* (1963)

Viscount Mersey, *A Picture of Life 1872–1940* (1941)

Viscount Mersey, *Journal and Memories* (1952)

K. Middlemas (ed.), *Thomas Jones: Whitehall Diaries* (vols. 1–2, 1969)

R. J. Minney (ed.), *The Private Papers of Hore-Belisha* (1960)

Lord Moran, *Churchill: The Struggle for Survival* (1966)

K. O. Morgan (ed.), *Lloyd George: Family Letters 1885–1936* (University of Wales, 1973)

Viscount Morley, *Memorandum on Resignation, August 1914* (1928)

Sir O. Mosley, *My Life* (1968)

N. Nicolson (ed.), *Harold Nicolson: Diaries and Letters 1930–39 and 1939–45* (1966–7)

Earl of Oxford and Asquith, *Memories and Reflections 1852–1927* (2 vols., 1928)

Sir C. Petrie, *A Historian Looks at His World* (1972)

V. Phillipps, *My Days and Ways* (privately published c. 1943)

B. Pimlott (ed.), *The Political Diary of Hugh Dalton 1918–40, 1945–60* (1986)

B. Pimlott (ed.), *The Second World War Diary of Hugh Dalton 1940–45* (1986)

E. Raczynski, *In Allied London* (n.d.)

J. A. Ramsden (ed.), *Real Old Tory Politics* (1984)

Lord Riddell, *More Pages from my Diary 1908–1914* (1934)

Lord Riddell, *War Diary 1914–1918* (1933)

Viscount Samuel, *Memoirs* (1945)

Sir G. Schuster, *Private Work and Public Causes* (Cowbridge, 1979)

J. W. Scobell Armstrong, *Yesterday* (1965)

Sir G. Shakespeare, *Let Candles be Brought In* (1949)

Sir J. Simon, *Three Speeches on The General Strike* (1926)

Sir J. Simon, *Comments and Criticisms* (1930)

Sir J. Simon, *Retrospect* (1952)

H. Slesser, *Judgment Reserved* (1941)

F. Stevenson, *The Years that are Past* (1967)

H. L. Stimson and M. Bundy, *On Active Service in Peace and War* (New York, 1948)

Lord Strang, *Home and Abroad* (1956)

C. Stuart (ed.), *The Reith Diaries* (1975)

Earl Swinton, *Sixty Years of Power* (1966)

A. J. P. Taylor (ed.), *My Darling Pussy* (1975)

A. J. P. Taylor (ed.), *Lloyd George: A Diary by Frances Stevenson* (1971)

Viscount Templewood, *Nine Troubled Years* (1954)

G. Thompson, *Front-Line Diplomat* (1959)

Lord Vansittart, *Lessons of My Life* (1943)

Lord Vansittart, *The Mist Procession* (1958)

J. Vincent (ed.), *The Crawford Papers* (Manchester, 1984)

Lord Williams of Barnburgh, *Digging for Britain* (1965)

H. R. Williamson, *The Walled Garden* (1956)

P. Williamson (ed.), *The Modernisation of Conservative Politics: The Diaries and Letters of William Bridgeman, 1904–1935* (1988)

T. Wilson (ed.), *The Political Diaries of C. P. Scott 1911–1928* (1970)

Earl Winterton, *Orders of the Day* (1953)

K. Young (ed.), *The Diaries of Sir Robert Bruce Lockhart* (2 vols., 1973–80)

E BIOGRAPHIES

S. Aster, *Anthony Eden* (1976)

A. W. Baldwin, *My Father: The True Story* (1955)

J. Barros, *Office without Power: Secretary General, Sir Eric Drummond* (Oxford, 1979)

D. Bennett, *Margot: A Life of the Countess of Oxford and Asquith* (1984)

R. Bernays, *Naked Fakir* (1931)

Lord Birkenhead, *Walter Monckton* (1969)

Lord Birkenhead, *Halifax* (1965)

Lord Birkenhead, *F. E.: The Life of F. E. Smith, First Earl of Birkenhead* (1959)

R. Blake, *The Unknown Prime Minister* (1955)

J. Bowle, *Viscount Samuel: a biography* (1957)

A. Boyle, *Trenchard: Man of Vision* (1962)

L. Broad, *Sir Anthony Eden: The Chronicles of a Career* (1955)

A. H. Brodrick, *Near to Greatness: A Life of the Sixth Earl Winterton* (1965)

T. Burridge, *Clement Attlee: A Political Biography* (1985)

J. R. M. Butler, *Lord Lothian* (1960)

J. Campbell, *Lloyd George: Goat in the Wilderness 1922–1931* (1977)

J. Campbell, *Nye Bevan and the Mirage of British Socialism* (1987)

J. Campbell, *F. E. Smith: First Earl of Birkenhead* (1983)

A. Campbell-Johnson, *Eden: The Making of a Statesman* (New York, 1955)

D. Carlton, *Eden* (1981)

J. Charmley, *Duff Cooper: The Authorized Biography* (1986)

R. S. Churchill, *The Rise and Fall of Sir Anthony Eden* (1959)

R. S. Churchill and M. Gilbert, *Winston S. Churchill* (vols. 2–6 and companion volumes, 1967–83)

J. R. Colville, *Man of Valour* (1972)

I. Colvin, *Vansittart in Office* (1965)

C. Coote, *A Companion of Honour: The Story of Walter Elliot* (1965)

J. A. Cross, *Lord Swinton* (Oxford, 1982)
J. A. Cross, *Sir Samuel Hoare* (1977)
D. Dilks, *Neville Chamberlain* (vol. 1, Cambridge, 1984)
F. Donaldson, *Edward VIII* (1974)
D. J. Dutton, *Austen Chamberlain: Gentleman in Politics* (Bolton, 1985)
A. Edwards, *Matriarch: Queen Mary and The House of Windsor* (1984)
K. Feiling, *The Life of Neville Chamberlain* (1946)
M. Foot, *Aneurin Bevan* (2 vols., 1962–73)
M. Gilbert, *Sir Horace Rumbold: Portrait of a Diplomat 1869–1941* (1973)
J. Grigg, *Lloyd George: From Peace to War* (1985)
K. Harris, *Attlee* (1982)
W. R. Hess, *My Father Rudolf Hess* (1986)
H. M. Hyde, *Lord Reading* (1967)
H. M. Hyde, *Sir Patrick Hastings: His Life and Cases* (1960)
H. M. Hyde, *Norman Birkett* (1964)
H. M. Hyde, *Baldwin: the Unexpected Prime Minister* (1973)
H. M. Hyde, *Strong for Service: the Life of Lord Nathan of Churt* (1968)
D. Irving, *Hess: the Missing Years 1941–45* (1987)
R. R. James, *Anthony Eden* (1986)
R. R. James, *Churchill: A Study in Failure 1900–1939* (1970)
R. R. James, *Victor Cazalet: a portrait* (1976)
R. Jenkins, *Asquith* (1964)
J. H. Jones, *Lord Stamp: Public Servant* (1964)
D. Judd, *Lord Reading* (1982)
S. Koss, *Asquith* (1976)
S. Koss, *Sir John Brunner: Radical Plutocrat* (Cambridge, 1970)
C. E. Lysaght, *Brendan Bracken* (1979)
J. W. Mackail and G. Wyndham, *Life and Letters of George Wyndham* (vol. 2, n.d.)
I. Macleod, *Neville Chamberlain* (1961)
Sir C. Mallet, *Lord Cave: a Memoir* (1931)
W. Manchester, *The Caged Lion: Winston Spencer Churchill 1932–1940* (1988)
E. Marjoribanks, *The Life of Lord Carson* (vol. 1, 1932)
D. Marquand, *Ramsay MacDonald* (1977)
L. Masterman, *C. F. G. Masterman: A Biography* (1939)
K. Middlemas and J. Barnes, *Baldwin: a Biography* (1969)
T. Morgan, *Churchill: The Rise to Failure 1874–1915* (pb. edn., 1984)
A. J. A. Morris, *C. P. Trevelyan 1870–1958: Portrait of a Radical* (Belfast, 1977)
H. Nicolson, *George V* (1952)
F. Owen, *Tempestuous Journey: Lloyd George, His Life and Times* (1954)
H. Pelling, *Winston Churchill* (1974)
Sir C. Petrie, *Walter Long and his Times* (1936)
J. Pope-Hennessy, *Lord Crewe 1858–1945: The Likeness of a Liberal* (1955)
R. Pound and G. Harmsworth, *Northcliffe* (1959)
Lord Reading, *Rufus Isaacs, First Marquess of Reading* (2 vols., 1942–5)
K. Robbins, *Sir Edward Grey* (1971)
C. E. B. Roberts, *Sir John Simon* (1938)
K. Rose, *King George V* (1983)
N. Rose, *Vansittart: Study of a Diplomat* (1978)

S. Roskill, *Hankey: Man of Secrets* (3 vols., 1970–4)

S. Salvidge, *Salvidge of Liverpool* (1934)

Sir J. Simon, *Portrait of my Mother* (1936)

J. A. Spender and C. Asquith, *Life of Herbert Henry Asquith, Lord Oxford and Asquith* (vol. 2, 1932)

M. D. Stocks, *Eleanor Rathbone* (1949)

A. J. P. Taylor, *Beaverbrook* (1972)

Sir J. Wheeler-Bennett, *John Anderson, Viscount Waverley* (1962)

F. Williams, *A Prime Minister Remembers* (1961)

D. Wilson, *Gilbert Murray, O.M.* (Oxford, 1987)

W. E. Wrench, *Geoffrey Dawson and our Times* (1955)

G. M. Young, *Stanley Baldwin* (1952)

F   OTHER BOOKS

R. J. Q. Adams and P. P. Poirier, *The Conscription Controversy in Great Britain 1900–18* (1987)

A. P. Adamthwaite, *The Making of the Second World War* (1977)

A. P. Adamthwaite, *France and the Coming of the Second World War* (1977)

P. Addison, *The Road to 1945* (1975)

C. Andrew, *Secret Service* (1985)

C. Andrew and D. Dilks (eds.), *The Missing Dimension* (1984)

E. M. Andrews, *The Writing on the Wall* (1987)

S. Aster, *1939: The Making of the Second World War* (1973)

G. Baer, *The Coming of the Ethiopian War* (Harvard, 1967)

M. Balfour, *Propaganda in War, 1939–1945* (1979)

S. Ball, *Baldwin and the Conservative Party: The Crisis of 1929–1931* (1988)

E. Barker, *Churchill and Eden at War* (1978)

C. Barnett, *The Collapse of British Power* (1972)

R. Bassett, *Democracy and Foreign Policy* (2nd edn., 1968)

R. Bassett, *1931: Political Crisis* (1958)

M. Beaumont, *The Origins of the Second World War* (1978)

Lord Beaverbrook, *The Abdication of King Edward VIII* (1966)

M. Beloff, *Britain's Liberal Empire 1897–1921* (1969)

M. Bentley, *The Liberal Mind 1914–1929* (Cambridge, 1977)

U. Bialer, *The Shadow of the Bomber: the Fear of Air Attack and British Politics 1932–1939* (1980)

Lord Birkenhead, *Last Essays* (1930)

D. S. Birn, *The League of Nations Union 1918–1945* (Oxford, 1981)

R. Blake, *The Decline of Power 1915–1964* (1985)

L. Blom-Cooper and G. Drewry, *Final Appeal: A Study of the House of Lords in its Judicial Capacity* (Oxford, 1972)

R. Blythe, *The Age of Illusion* (pb. edn., 1964)

B. Bond, *British Military Policy between the Two World Wars* (Oxford, 1980)

D. Boulton, *Objection Overruled* (1967)

K. D. Brown (ed.), *Essays in Anti-Labour History: Responses to the Rise of Labour in Britain* (1974)

J. Bryan and C. J. V. Murphy, *The Windsor Story* (1979)

D. Butler (ed.), *Coalitions in British Politics* (1978)

Lord Butler (ed.), *The Conservatives* (1977)
E. H. Carr, *International Relations between the Two World Wars, 1919–1939* (1947)
'Cato', *Guilty Men* (1940)
P. F. Clarke, *Liberals and Social Democrats* (Cambridge, 1978)
P. F. Clarke, *Lancashire and the New Liberalism* (Cambridge, 1971)
I. Colvin, *The Chamberlain Cabinet* (1971)
C. Cook, *Short History of the Liberal Party* (1976)
C. Cook, *The Age of Alignment* (1975)
C. Cook and J. Ramsden (eds.), *By-Elections in British Politics* (1973)
P. Cosgrave, *Churchill at War: Alone 1939–40* (1974)
M. Cowling, *The Impact of Hitler* (Cambridge, 1975)
M. Cowling, *The Impact of Labour 1920–1924* (Cambridge, 1971)
A. J. Crozier, *Appeasement and Germany's Last Bid for Colonies* (1988)
Sir M. Dean, *The Royal Air Force and Two World Wars* (1979)
D. Dilks (ed.), *Retreat from Power* (2 vols., 1981)
R. Douglas, *History of the Liberal Party 1895–1970* (1971)
R. Douglas, *In the Year of Munich* (1977)
J. Douglas-Hamilton, *Motive for a Mission: The Story Behind Hess's Flight to Britain* (1971)
S. L. Endicott, *Diplomacy and Enterprise* (Manchester, 1975)
Sir D. Foot, *British Political Crises* (1976)
M. Foot, *Armistice 1918–39* (1940)
D. French, *British Economic and Strategic Planning 1905–1915* (1982)
D. French, *British Strategy and War Aims 1914–1916* (1986)
M. G. Fry, *Lloyd George and Foreign Policy, 1890–1916* (1977)
L. W. Fuchser, *Neville Chamberlain and Appeasement: A Study in the Politics of History* (New York, 1982)
F. R. Gannon, *The British Press and Nazi Germany, 1936–1939* (Oxford, 1971).
A. G. Gardiner, *Pillars of Society* (1916)
M. George, *The Hollow Men* (1965)
N. H. Gibbs, *Grand Strategy* (vol. 1, 1976)
B. B. Gilbert, *Britain since 1918* (1980)
M. Gilbert, *The Roots of Appeasement* (1966)
M. Gilbert and R. Gott, *The Appeasers* (pb. edn., 1967)
G. A. H. Gordon, *British Seapower and Procurement between the Wars* (1988)
R. Griffiths, *Fellow Travellers of the Right* (Oxford, pb. edn., 1983)
J. Gunther, *Inside Europe* (1936)
P. Haggie, *Britannia at Bay* (Oxford, 1981)
D. A. Hamer, *Liberal Politics in the Age of Gladstone and Rosebery* (Oxford, 1972)
F. Hardie, *The Abyssinian Crisis* (1974)
C. Hazlehurst, *Politicians at War, July 1914 to May 1915* (1971).
P. Hayes, *The Twentieth Century 1880–1939* (1978)
R. F. V. Heuston, *Lives of the Lord Chancellors* (2 vols., Oxford, 1964–87).
F. H. Hinsley et al., *British Intelligence in the Second World War* (vol. 1, 1979).
Q. Hogg, *The Left was Never Right* (1945).
H. M. Hyde, *British Air Policy Between the Wars 1918–1939* (1976).
H. M. Hyde, *United in Crime* (1955).
B. Inglis, *Abdication* (1966).

L. S. Jaffe, *The Decision to Disarm Germany* (1985).

P. Jalland, *The Liberals and Ireland* (Brighton, 1980).

R. R. James, *The British Revolution* (2 Vols., 1976–7).

D. E. Kaiser, *Economic Diplomacy and the Origins of the Second World War* (Princeton, 1980).

R. Kee, *The World We Left Behind* (1984).

M. Kinnear, *The Fall of Lloyd George* (1973).

S. E. Koss, *Nonconformity in Modern British Politics* (1975).

W. R. Louis, *British Strategy in the Far East 1919–1939* (Oxford, 1971).

G. McDermott, *The Eden Legacy and the Decline of British Diplomacy* (1969).

C. A. Macdonald, *The United States, Britain and Appeasement 1936–1939* (1981).

B. J. C. McKercher and D. J. Moss (eds.), *Shadow and Substance in British Foreign Policy 1895–1939* (Edmonton, 1984).

H. Macmillan, *The Past Masters* (1975)

N. Mansergh, *The Commonwealth Experience* (vol. 2, 1982)

A. J. Marder, *From the Dreadnought to Scapa Flow* (vol. 1, 1961).

W. N. Medlicott, *British Foreign Policy since Versailles 1919–1963* (pb. edn., 1968).

K. Middlemas, *Diplomacy of Illusion* (1972).

W. J. Mommsen and L. Kettenacker (eds.), *The Fascist Challenge and the Policy of Appeasement* (1983).

R. J. Moore, *The Crisis of Indian Unity 1917–1940* (Oxford, 1974).

A. J. A. Morris, *Radicalism Against War* (1972).

C. L. Mowat, *Britain between the Wars 1918–1940* (1955).

M. Muggeridge, *The Thirties: 1930–1940 in Great Britain* (1967).

J. F. Naylor, *Labour's International Policy* (1969)

J. F. Naylor, *A Man and An Institution: Sir Maurice Hankey, the Cabinet Secretariat and the Custody of Cabinet Secrecy* (Cambridge, 1984).

S. Newman, *March 1939: The British Guarantee to Poland* (Oxford, 1976).

I. Nish (ed.), *Anglo-Japanese Alienation, 1919–1952* (Cambridge, 1982).

F. S. Northedge, *The League of Nations: its Life and Times 1920–46* (Leicester, 1986).

F. S. Northedge, *The Troubled Giant: Britain Among the Great Powers 1916–1939* (1966).

R. Ovendale, *Appeasement and the English Speaking World* (Cardiff, 1975).

R. Parkinson, *Peace for our Time* (1971).

G. C. Peden, *British Rearmament and the Treasury 1932–1939* (Edinburgh, 1979).

G. Peele and C. Cook (eds.), *The Politics of Reappraisal 1918–1939* (1975).

H. Pelling, *Britain and the Second World War* (pb. edn., 1970).

A. R. Peters, *Anthony Eden at the Foreign Office 1931–38* (1986).

Sir J. Pratt, *War and Politics in China* (1943).

A. Preston (ed.), *General Staffs and Diplomacy before the Second World War* (1978).

M. Pugh, *Electoral Reform in War and Peace 1906–18* (1978).

M. Pugh, *The Making of Modern British Politics 1867–1939* (Oxford, 1982).

J. Rae, *Conscience and Politics* (Oxford, 1970).

C. à C. Repington, *The First World War 1914–1918* (vol. 1, 1920).

K. Robbins, *The Abolition of War* (Cardiff, 1976).

K. Robbins, *Munich, 1938* (1968).

W. R. Rock, *British Appeasement in the 1930s* (1977).

W. R. Rock, *Appeasement on Trial* (Hamden, 1966).

S. Roskill, *Naval Policy between the Wars* (vol. 2, 1976).

N. Rostow, *Anglo-French Relations 1934–36* (1984).

P. Rowland, *The Last Liberal Governments: Unfinished Business, 1911–1914* (1971).

A. L. Rowse, *All Souls and Appeasement* (1961).

B. E. V. Sabine, *British Budgets in Peace and War 1932–1945* (1970).

G. Scott, *The Rise and Fall of the League of Nations* (1973).

A. Seldon, *Churchill's Indian Summer* (1981).

J. A. Simon and others, *Essays in Liberalism* (1897).

R. Skidelsky, *Politicians and the Slump* (pb. edn., 1970).

M. Smith, *British Air Strategy Between the Wars* (Oxford, 1984).

T. Stannage, *Baldwin Thwarts the Opposition* (1980).

R. Stevens, *Law and Politics: The House of Lords as a Judicial Body, 1800–1976* (1979).

H. L. Stimson, *The Far-Eastern Crisis* (New York, 1936).

M. Swartz, *The Union of Democratic Control in British Politics during the First World War* (Oxford, 1971).

J. Symons, *The General Strike* (1957).

A. J. P. Taylor, *English History 1914–1945* (Oxford, 1965).

A. J. P. Taylor, *The Origins of the Second World War* (1961).

A. J. P. Taylor (ed.), *Lloyd George: Twelve Essays* (1971).

A. J. P. Taylor (ed.), *Off the Record: Political Interviews 1933–1943* (1973).

T. Taylor, *Munich: the Price of Peace* (1979).

H. Thomas, *The Murder of Rudolf Hess* (1979).

N. Thompson, *The Anti-Appeasers: Conservative Opposition to Appeasement in the 1930s* (Oxford, 1971).

C. Thorne, *The Limits of Foreign Policy: The West, the League and the Far Eastern Crisis of 1931–1933* (1972).

A. J. Toynbee, *Survey of International Affairs, 1932* (1933).

E. S. Turner, *The Phoney War on the Home Front* (1961).

A. Tusa and J. Tusa, *The Nuremberg Trial* (1983).

N. Waites (ed.), *Troubled Neighbours* (1971).

W. Wark, *The Ultimate Enemy* (Oxford, pb. edn., 1986).

D. C. Watt, *Personalities and Policies* (1965).

Sir J. Wheeler-Bennett, *Munich: Prologue to Tragedy* (1948).

F. Williams, *A Pattern of Rulers* (1965).

C. Wilmot, *The Struggle for Europe* (1952).

K. M. Wilson, *The Policy of the Entente* (Cambridge, 1985).

T. Wilson, *The Downfall of the Liberal Party 1914–1935* (pb. edn., 1968).

G ARTICLES

P. M. H. Bell, 'Great Britain and the Rise of Germany, 1932–34', *International Relations* 2 (1964).

U. Bialer, 'Telling the Truth to the People: Britain's Decision to Publish the Diplomatic Papers of the Inter-War Period', *Historical Journal* 26, 2 (1983).

A. Booth, 'Economic Advice at the Centre of British Government, 1939–41', *Historical Journal* 29, 3 (1986).

E. David, 'The Liberal Party Divided 1916–18', *Historical Journal* 13, 3 (1970).

D. J. Dutton, 'John Simon and the Post-War National Liberal Party: an Historical Postscript', *Historical Journal* 32, 2 (1989).

A. L. Goldman, 'Sir Robert Vansittart's Search for Italian Cooperation against Hitler, 1933–36', *Journal of Contemporary History* 9, 3 (1974).

H. H. Hall, 'The Foreign Policy-Making Process in Britain, 1934–1935, and the Origins of the Anglo-German Naval Agreement', *Historical Journal* 19, 2 (1976).

C. J. Hill, 'Great Britain and the Saar Plebiscite of 13 January 1935', *Journal of Contemporary History* 9, 2 (1974).

B. Kovrig, 'Mediation by Obfuscation: The Resolution of the Marseille Crisis, October 1934 to May 1935', *Historical Journal* 19, 1 (1976).

P. Lockwood, 'Milner's entry into the War Cabinet in 1916', *Historical Journal* 7, 1 (1964).

R. Manne, 'The British Decision for Alliance with Russia, May 1939', *Journal of Contemporary History* 9, 3 (1974).

R. A. C. Parker, 'The British Government and the Coming of War with Germany, 1939' in M. R. D. Foot (ed.), *War and Society* (1973).

J. C. Robertson, 'The British General Election of 1935', *Journal of Contemporary History* 9, 1 (1974).

J. C. Robertson, 'The Origins of British Opposition to Mussolini over Ethiopia', *Journal of British Studies* 9, 1 (1969).

C. Thorne, 'Viscount Cecil, the Government and the Far Eastern Crisis of 1931', *Historical Journal* 14, 4 (1971).

D. C. Watt, 'The Anglo-German Naval Agreement of 1935', *Journal of Modern History* 23, 2 (1956).

K. M. Wilson, 'The Cabinet Diary of J. A. Pease 24 July to 5 August 1914', *Proceedings of the Leeds Philosophical and Literary Society* 19, 3 (1983).

D. J. Wrench, ' "Cashing In." The Parties and the National Government, August 1931–September 1932', *Journal of British Studies* 23, 2 (1984).

H UNPUBLISHED THESIS

E. B. Segal, 'Sir John Simon and British Foreign Policy: the Diplomacy of Disarmament in the Early 1930s', *University of California, Berkeley, Ph.D. thesis* 1969.

INDEX